INTRODUCTION TO

BIBLICAL COUNSELING

INTRODUCTION TO

BIBLICAL COUNSELING

A BASIC GUIDE TO THE PRINCIPLES
AND PRACTICE OF COUNSELING

JOHN F. MacARTHUR, JR.
WAYNE A. MACK
AND THE MASTER'S COLLEGE FACULTY

WORD PUBLISHING
Dallas•London•Vancouver•Melbourne

INTRODUCTION TO BIBLICAL COUNSELING

Library of Congress Cataloging-in-Publication Data

    MacArthur, John 1939–
    Introduction to biblical counseling / John MacArthur, Jr. and Wayne Mack with The Master's College Faculty.
      p. cm.
    Includes bibliographical references and index.
    ISBN 0-8499-1093-5
    1. Pastoral counseling   2. Discipling (Christianity)   3. Pastoral psychology—Controversial literature.   I. Mack, Wayne, A.   II. Master's College   III. Title.
    BV4012.M32   1994
    253.5—dc20   94-10306
                                            CIP

Printed in the United States of America

456789 BVG 987654321

Dedicated to Biblical Counselors-in-Training
at The Master's College and Seminary.

Contents

PART IV. THE PRACTICE OF BIBLICAL COUNSELING

Preface

This book is written to present a system of biblical truth that brings together people, their problems, and the living God. *Introduction to Biblical Counseling* is based on the convictions that (1) God's Word should be our counseling authority, (2) counseling is a part of the basic discipling ministry of the local church, and (3) God's people can and should be trained to counsel effectively.

Introduction to Biblical Counseling is written for all of God's people: pastors, elders, and lay people. We foresee the book as a potential textbook in biblical counseling or pastoral theology at the Christian college and seminary levels. Veteran pastors with a great deal of training and experience and pastors without seminary training or much practical experience can all profit from this volume. Sincere lay people who want to improve their skills in serving Christ and His people will also find many useful, practical, and stimulating insights in this publication.

In preparing this book, we have labored to present material that is accurately biblical rather than humanistic or secular, basically proactive rather than reactive or polemic, practical rather than theoretical and abstract, and easily understood rather than technical or complicated. We have written to inform, to excite, to instruct, to confirm, to enlarge, and to promote spiritual and ministerial growth in the readers.

This book has been written with eleven objectives in mind:

1. To enlarge and reinforce the confidence of God's people in the sufficiency, superiority, and practicality of Scripture for dealing with all of the issues of life, and to convince Christians that the resources we have in Christ and His Word are not only sufficient for handling and solving all of the personal and interpersonal problems of life but are superior to the resources that are found in the world, i.e., to answer the questions, "Do we need more than what the Scriptures offer to be effective in our counseling ministries? What do the Scriptures say about counseling? What is the biblical basis for using Scriptures in counseling?"

2. To encourage Christians to think biblically about all counseling-related issues, i.e., to answer the question, "What does it mean to think biblically, and how can we develop a biblical mind-set or consistently biblical worldview?"

3. To help Christians understand people and their problems through the lens of Scripture, i.e., to answer the question, "What do the Scriptures say about who and what people are and why they have the problems they have?"

4. To demonstrate how our counseling methods must be consistent with our theological convictions, i.e., to answer the question, "How should what we believe interface with and relate to our counseling ministry?"

5. To provide biblical guidelines to effectively counsel people who are struggling with problems, i.e., to answer the question, "How does one do biblical counseling?"

6. To motivate Christians to be more involved in the ministry of counseling and to equip them to be more competent in this work, i.e., to answer the questions, "Why should I be concerned about biblical counseling, and how can I become a more effective counselor?"

7. To give Christians specific biblical principles for discerning the difference between counseling that purports to be biblical and counseling that actually is, i.e., to answer the question, "What are the distinctives of biblical counseling?"

8. To foster an approach to Scripture that is both exegetically correct and extremely practical, i.e., to answer the questions, "What should our attitude be as we study and interact with the Bible? How should we study and apply the Scriptures?"

9. To present a brief historical perspective on the ministry of counseling; to discuss how secular psychology filtered into and influenced the Church during the twentieth century; and to relate how the biblical counseling movement is progressing, i.e., to answer the questions, "Who have been some of the promoters and practitioners of biblical counseling? How did the Church became enamored with the insights of secular psychology in the twentieth century? How was the emphasis on and concern for true biblical counseling recovered? What progress is being made in the movement?"

10. To encourage the Church to accept its God-given responsibility to do counseling and to present a method for developing a counseling ministry, i.e., to answer the questions, "Where does counseling fit in the Church's ministry? Who should be involved in counseling? How does a church develop a biblical counseling ministry?"

11. To respond to some of the objections that are raised against biblical counseling and to clarify what is meant by biblical counseling, i.e., to answer questions such as, "Isn't it simplistic to insist that the Bible gives us all that we need to deal with the problems of people? Can the Bible provide everything that is necessary to counsel people with serious problems? Don't some people need an expert—someone with a lot of psychological training—to understand and help them?"

The book is arranged in three parts. The first part, devoted to the historical perspectives on biblical counseling, sets the tone and provides some of the rationale for the book. The second part presents the crucial theological issues that function as underpinnings for biblical counseling. The third part of the book focuses on the practical implementation of biblical counseling. Indexes of authors, Scripture, and subjects are provided at the end of the volume.

We gratefully acknowledge the help of many in the preparation of this volume. To David Swavely, John Hotchkiss, Phil Johnson, and Jay Flowers we extend appreciation for their editorial work. Their invaluable skills have made this book more readable and helpful. Dennis Swanson supervised and coordinated the material on resources for biblical counselors as well as the chapter on frequently asked questions and the indexes. We extend our thanks also to David Powlison of the Christian Counseling and Educational Foundation, Pastor Bill Goode of the Faith Baptist Church, Ken Sarles of the Master's Seminary, and Lance Quinn and Carey Hardy of the Grace Community Church for joining with The Master's College faculty in making valuable contributions on topics of special interest to them. Recognition must also be given to Dr. Robert Smith who wrote one of the chapters in the book and was instrumental in the initial development of the Biblical Counseling Program at The Master's College. We also want to acknowledge our appreciation to Dr. John Stead, Vice President for Academic Affairs, for his encouragement and support during the development of this publication. And most of all, we want to give praise to our great triune God for giving us the privilege of knowing and serving Him and His people in many ways—especially in writing this volume.

We who serve Christ at The Master's College and have had a part in producing this book, dedicate *Introduction to Biblical Counseling* to the honor and glory of Christ and pray that our God will use it for the good of His people, whom He loved and for whom He gave Himself. Our prayer is that He will use this material to equip pastors and lay people for the work of the ministry in building up the body of Christ. May He be pleased to utilize the concepts and information presented in this book in making us more skillful in preparing and repairing the saints so that He might receive the praise and glory He so richly deserves.

Wayne A. Mack

Introduction

The November 29, 1993 issue of *Time* featured a series of articles on the turmoil in modern psychology. The magazine's cover featured a retouched photograph of Sigmund Freud—his head a hollow, incomplete, three-dimensional jigsaw puzzle—and the caption, "IS FREUD DEAD?"

One of the articles inside raised the question, "What if Freud was wrong?" Noting that this century has already seen the sudden collapse of Marxism, the article suggested that we might be about to witness a similarly dramatic toppling of "the complex Freudian monument."[1]

Evangelicals not so long ago would have roundly cheered such news. But, alas, we live in strange times. Ironically, while the secular world has grown increasingly disaffected with the professional psychotherapy industry, the evangelical world has been frantically trying to marry secular psychology and biblical truth. While the world becomes more and more suspicious of psychology, Christians seem to be growing more and more committed to it. Perhaps it is fair to say that many in the Church are addicted to psychotherapy.

The rush to embrace psychology within the Church is frankly mystifying. Psychology and Christianity have been enemies from the beginning. Freud's presuppositions were atheistic and cynical. He called religion a "universal, obsessional neurosis."[2] To him, religion was an illusion that derived its strength from irrational, wishful thinking rooted in human instinct.[3] Those who followed Freud at first were uniformly hostile to biblical belief. The foundational doctrines of the movement were therefore based on blatantly anti-Christian presuppositions. To Freud and his followers the human being was nothing but an animal motivated by the sex drive and other ego needs.

---

1. Paul Gray, "The Assault on Freud," *Time* 29 November 1993: 47.

2. Cited in Frank B. Minirth, *Christian Psychiatry* (Old Tappan, N.J.: Revell, 1977), 27.

3. Sigmund Freud, *New Introductory Lectures on Psychoanalysis*, lecture 35 (New York: Norton, 1977).

The Church was naturally wary of these ideas—and justifiably so. Freudianism was one of several atheistic hypotheses—along with Darwinism and Marxism—that were gaining popularity at the turn of the century. The Church's greatest battlefield at that time, however, was against another insidious enemy: theological liberalism, a pseudo-Christianity that denied the authority of Scripture and questioned the supernatural. This was yet another doctrine that was contributing to the rapid secularization of society.

Among professing Christians, only theological liberals found allies among the atheistic psychologists. Carl Jung wrote much about religion. In his system, however, the human unconscious was divine. William James, father of modern pragmatism, also blended behavioral theory and religion into a humanistic creed that made lavish use of theological terminology. But these men were by no means Christians. They utterly rejected supernaturalism, repudiated the authority of Scripture, and discarded most of the central tenets of historic Christian belief.

Psychology was thus ideally suited for an increasingly secular age. By the middle of this century, the new discipline was accepted by the popular mind as a full-fledged science, even though the movement was already beginning to fragment into dozens of competing schools and philosophies, and even though its hypotheses could not be tested or its results verified through any of the traditional means of true science. None of that could slow psychology's acceptance in an age that had grown hostile to the notion of absolute truth.

Within a few short decades, the psychotherapy industry and evangelicals settled into a more or less guarded coexistence. Christians seemed intimidated by the world's overwhelming acceptance of psychotherapy as a true science. The psychotherapists believed they were privy to a higher knowledge and more effective therapies than traditional spiritual counsel could ever offer. They stated in no uncertain terms that spiritual counselors and the clergy should stay off their turf.

One textbook on pastoral psychology written in the 1950s summed up the professional therapists' attitude to pastoral counsel:

> It is [the pastor's] duty not to try to enact the role of the psychiatrist, but *as quickly as possible, he must refer the sick person to the professional man.* Oftentimes he must secure the judgment of the psychiatrist regarding the symptoms which a petitioner displays. Moreover, *the clergyman, in such instances, must place himself under the direction of the psychiatrist*, in the event that the latter believes his assistance as a religionist is helpful. Psychotherapy and religio-therapy demand consistent, patient treatment, over long periods of time, and

the clergyman rarely finds the hours to furnish this. Therefore he must have a specialist as a member of the staff of his church or synagogue, to whom he can refer cases. Or if such a professional is not a member of the institution's staff, he may be a friend and advisor of the clergyman when required. All this entails the expenditure of time and money, and it must not be forgotten that while the clergyman is willing to give his time freely, the professional psychiatrist must make his hours count in monetary terms. *Too often distressed persons come to the clergyman when they have been unsuccessful in their consultations with the psychiatrist, but it is an astute pastor who immediately turns them back to their psychiatrist.*

Frequently the clergyman and the psychiatrist can work hand in hand, especially in the case of parishioners who, at one time, will accept guidance from the clergyman, and, at another moment, from the psychiatrist. Husbands and wives have been brought together as a consequence of this technique. Sometimes the psychiatrist will recommend to the clergyman that he accept a convalescent youth as a member of the religious institution's young people's organization, in the hope that social opportunities will accelerate the cure. Sometimes the psychiatrist will appreciate the value of attendance at divine worship, the reading of religious literature, and the performance of traditional rites and ceremonies. *In every such instance, the psychiatrist must be the mentor and the director of the treatment.*[4]

Too many pastors capitulated to such thinking, and over the past forty years or so, counseling has steadily moved out of the Church and into the clinics. Now "Christian" psychology is a billion-dollar business. Yet has the spiritual and emotional state of believers been improved by this trend? Surely no one would argue seriously that it has.

One of the promising trends in the evangelical world today is the emergence of a renewed emphasis on counseling that is *biblical*—not mere psychology colored with biblical words and phrases but an earnest effort to help people solve their problems by turning them to the objective, life-changing truth of Scripture.

Scripture does, after all, claim to be the only reliable resource to which we can turn to solve our spiritual problems:

- How can a young man keep his way pure? By keeping it according to Thy word (Ps. 119:9).

---

4. Vergilius Ferm, *A Dictionary of Pastoral Psychology* (New York: Philosophical Library, 1955), 208 (emphasis added).

- Thy testimonies also are my delight; They are my counselors (Ps. 119:24).

- Thy commandments make me wiser than my enemies, for they are ever mine. I have more insight than all my teachers, for Thy testimonies are my meditation. I understand more than the aged, because I have observed Thy precepts (Ps. 119:98–100).

- All Scripture is inspired by God and profitable for teaching, for reproof, for correction, for training in righteousness; that the man of God may be adequate, equipped for every good work (2 Tim. 3:16–17).

Dozens of similar passages could be quoted to demonstrate the utter superiority and absolute sufficiency Scripture claims for itself. Either we believe what God's Word teaches in this regard, or we open ourselves to all kinds of corrupt influences from worldly thinking. The choice is as simple as that.

I am encouraged to see a large movement of Christians returning to Scripture as the sole source of wisdom and correction for the human soul. I am grateful to God for the men and women He is using to awaken the Church to this need.

Wayne Mack is one of those who has been at the forefront of this issue for many years. Under his wise leadership, The Master's College is building a biblical counseling program that is unequalled anywhere. While carrying out that task, Dr. Mack has also found time to compile and edit this book. It is the realization of a longtime desire of mine to have a comprehensive textbook on the issues that Christian counselors struggle with—a guidebook for those who want to offer truly *biblical* counsel, not just warmed-over concepts from the scrap heap of secular psychology. I believe this book will effectively equip and embolden Christian counselors who have been intimidated or confused by the claims of modern psychology. It will also instruct and assist those who are already committed to biblical counseling, so that they can be more effective.

Whether you are a seasoned biblical counselor or someone just starting out, I know you will find much to help and encourage you in this volume. My prayer is that it will be a major catalyst in moving the Church away from the toxic, false counsel of worldly wisdom and back to the pure milk of the Word.

John MacArthur, Jr.

Part I

The Historical Background of Biblical Counseling

1

Rediscovering Biblical Counseling

John MacArthur, Jr.[1]

Ever since apostolic times, counseling has occurred in the Church as a natural function of corporate spiritual life. After all, the New Testament itself *commands* believers to "admonish one another" (Rom. 15:14); "encourage one another" (Heb. 3:13, KJV); "comfort one another with these words" (1 Thess. 4:18); "encourage one another, and build up one another" (1 Thess. 5:11); "confess your sins to one another, and pray for one another, so that you may be healed" (James 5:16).

The apostle Paul wrote, "We who are strong ought to bear the weaknesses of those without strength and not just please ourselves" (Rom. 15:1). And, "Even if a man is caught in any trespass, you who are spiritual, restore such a one in a spirit of gentleness; each one looking to yourself, lest you too be tempted. Bear one another's burdens, and thus fulfill the law of Christ" (Gal. 6:1–2).

All those instructions apply to rank-and-file church members—not only to some priestly caste of experts. Counseling—particularly counseling that skillfully employs and applies God's Word—is a necessary duty of Christian life and fellowship. It is also the expected result of true spiritual maturity: "Let the word of Christ richly dwell within you, with all wisdom teaching and admonishing one another with psalms and hymns and spiritual songs, singing with thankfulness in your hearts to God" (Col. 3:16).

---

1. Much of this chapter has been adapted and expanded from John MacArthur, Jr., *Our Sufficiency in Christ* (Dallas: Word, 1991), 55–72.

In recent years, however, there has been a strong and very influential movement within the Church attempting to replace biblical counseling in the church body with "Christian psychology"—techniques and wisdom gleaned from secular therapies and dispensed primarily by paid professionals. Those who have championed this movement often *sound* vaguely biblical. That is, they quote Scripture and often blend theological ideas with the teachings of Freud, Rogers, Jung, or whatever school of secular psychology they follow. But the movement itself is certainly *not* taking the Church in a biblical direction. It has conditioned Christians to think of counseling as something best left to trained experts. It has opened the door to a whole range of extrabiblical theories and therapies. Indeed, it has left many with the feeling that God's Word is incomplete, insufficient, unsophisticated, and unable to offer help for people's deepest emotional and spiritual problems. It has directed millions of Christians seeking spiritual help away from their pastors and fellow believers and into psychological clinics. It has given many the impression that adapting secular methods such as twelve-step recovery plans can be more helpful than spiritual means in weaning people from their sins. In short, it has diminished the Church's confidence in Scripture, prayer, fellowship, and preaching as means through which the Spirit of God works to change lives.

If the presuppositions behind this movement were sound, we might expect that Christians today would be the most well-adjusted and mentally healthy generation who ever lived. After all, they have the benefit of several generations of psychological expertise, applied by men and women who claim to be able to synthesize such knowledge with Scripture and make it "Christian."

But, clearly, that is not the case. Record numbers of people are seeking psychological treatment. More Christians than ever before are lining up at the doors of clinics and professional counselors. Christian psychologists offering live counsel are now heard daily on thousands of Christian radio stations around the country. In the past decade and a half, Christian psychology has become a billion-dollar industry. Millions of evangelical Christians, it seems, are addicted to therapy.

In contrast to those trends, however, another movement has been gaining strength among evangelicals. Clear voices are beginning to call the Church back to the Scriptures as a sufficient help for people's spiritual problems. A ground swell of support has been building for a return to biblical counseling in the Church. Every week I hear from pastors and church leaders who are rediscovering the importance of biblical counseling. They are realizing what they have actually always believed: that Scripture is superior to human wisdom (1 Cor. 3:19); that the Word of God is a more effective discerner of the human heart than any earthly means (Heb. 4:12); that the Spirit of God is the only effective agent of recovery and regeneration (Eph. 5:18–19); and that all the treasures of wisdom and knowledge are found in Christ Himself (Col. 2:3).

Those truths are so basic to Christian belief that it is astonishing to think they would ever come under fire from within the Church itself. But of course that is precisely what has happened over and over in church history. And it is happening even now as psychology is being peddled in the Church as a necessary—and even superior—solution to spiritual problems.

I was first thrust into the forefront of the battle between psychology and biblical counseling in 1980, when our church was hit with the first ever "clergy malpractice" lawsuit. The suit charged that the pastors on our staff were negligent because we tried to help a suicidal young member of our church by giving him biblical truth. It was the first such case ever heard in the American court system. The secular media had a field day as the case dragged on for years. Some national news sources even alleged that our church had encouraged the young man to kill himself, teaching him that suicide was a sure way to heaven. Of course, that was not true. We showed him from Scripture that suicide is wrong. We urged him to let the Word of God lead him to intimate knowledge and appropriation of the resources available in the One who wanted to heal his troubled mind. Tragically, he refused our counsel and took his own life.

The case raised the question of whether churches should have the legal right to counsel troubled people using only the Bible. The plaintiffs argued that giving a depressed or suicidal person advice from Scripture is a simplistic and irresponsible approach to counseling. They brought forward several "experts" who testified that spiritual counsel is not appropriate for people who have *real* problems. Victims of chronic depression, suicidal tendencies, and similar emotional and mental problems should be referred to a psychological expert, they claimed. Pastors and church counselors should be *required* to refer such people to mental-health professionals, the lawsuit contended. Their basic charge was that attempting to counsel troubled people from the Bible amounts to recklessness and negligence for which church counselors must be held morally and legally culpable. Had they won the case, *any* church that practiced biblical counseling would be taking a huge liability risk.

The facts of the case that came out in court received little or no coverage on the network news. Testimony showed that this young man *was* under the care of professional psychiatrists. In addition to the biblical direction he received from our pastoral staff, he had sought psychiatric treatment. Moreover, our staff had seen to it that he was examined by several medical doctors, to rule out organic or chemical causes for his depression. He was receiving every kind of therapy available, but he chose to end his life anyway. We did all we could to help him; he rejected our counsel and turned his back on his spiritual sufficiency in Christ.

Three different courts actually heard evidence in the case—and all three ruled in favor of the church. Twice those rulings were overturned on appeal because of technicalities, but every court that actually tried the case agreed in the verdict absolving the church from any blame. Eventually, the case was appealed to the United States Supreme Court. The High Court refused to hear the case, thereby letting stand the California State Supreme Court's ruling that finally vindicated the church.

All three times the case was heard and a ruling was given, the judges also expressed the opinion that the church had *not* failed in its responsibility to give proper care. Their judgment was that our staff had more than fulfilled their legal and moral obligations in how we had attempted to help this young man who had sought our counsel. But even more important, the courts affirmed every church's constitutional right to counsel from the Bible. The case established a legal precedent upholding an important First-Amendment right of freedom of religion. The court's ruling means that secular courts have no right to encroach on the area of counseling in the church.

Psychologizing the Church

That clergy malpractice trial thrust me into the midst of the debate about psychology and biblical counseling. Before that, I had noticed that Christian psychologists, once unheard of, were becoming more and more common, more and more outspoken. Unfortunately, I had paid little attention to the trend and was not listening closely to how they were marketing psychology in the Church.

But during the trial itself, a surprising number of the "experts" who were called to argue against biblical counseling were professional Christian counselors. I was startled and dismayed during the trial to hear men who identified themselves as evangelicals testifying that the Bible alone does not contain sufficient help to meet people's deepest personal and emotional needs. These people were actually arguing before a secular court that God's Word is not an adequate resource for dealing with people's spiritual problems! What is truly appalling is the number of evangelicals who are willing to accept the word of such professionals.

There is no denying that psychology has made incredible inroads into evangelical culture over the past twenty-five years. The influence of psychology is reflected in the kind of sermons that are preached from evangelical pulpits, in the kind of counseling that is being offered over the radio airwaves, in the proliferation of psychologists who cater primarily to evangelical Christians, and in the books that are being offered by many evangelical publishers.[2]

Over the past decade a host of evangelical psychological clinics have sprung up. Though almost all of them claim to offer biblical counsel, most merely dispense secular psychology disguised in spiritual terminology. This can be seen clearly in the literature spawned by the movement. As Jay Adams observed, "Nearly all recent counseling books for ministers, even conservative ones, are written from the Freudian perspective in the sense that they rest largely upon the presuppositions of the Freudian ethic of non-responsibility."[3]

The rise of counseling clinics poses another problem for the Church: the trend has removed the counseling ministry from its proper arena in the church body and conditioned most Christians to think of themselves as incompetent to counsel. Many pastors, feeling inadequate and perhaps afraid of possible malpractice litigation, are perfectly willing to let "professionals" take over what used to be seen as a vital pastoral responsibility.[4] Too many have bought the lie that a crucial realm of spiritual wisdom exists outside Scripture, and that some idea or technique from that extrabiblical realm holds the real key to helping people with their deep problems.

---

2. Cf. Martin and Deidre Bobgan, *PsychoHeresy* (Santa Barbara: EastGate, 1987), 53–54. The Bobgans list eight evidences of the "psychologizing of the church."

3. Jay Adams, *Competent to Counsel* (Grand Rapids: Baker, 1970), 17–18. Adams's extraordinarily accurate analysis of the state of counseling in evangelicalism is now more than a quarter of a century old but is more apropos than ever. He has given the Church an indispensable corrective to several trends that are eating away at the Church's spiritual vitality. Christian leaders would do well to heed his still-timely admonition.

4. Jay Adams, *More Than Redemption* (Phillipsburg, N. J.: Presbyterian and Reformed, 1979), x–xi.

What Is Wrong with Psychology?

The word *psychology* literally means "the study of the soul." True soul-study cannot be done by unbelievers. After all, only Christians have the resources for comprehending the nature of the human soul and understanding how it can be transformed. The secular discipline of psychology is based on godless assumptions and evolutionary foundations and is capable of dealing with people only superficially and only on the temporal level. Sigmund Freud, the father of modern psychology, was an unbelieving humanist who devised psychology as a substitute for religion.

Before Freud, the study of the soul was thought of as a spiritual discipline. In other words, it was inherently associated with religion. Freud's chief contribution was to define the human soul and the study of human behavior in wholly secular terms. He utterly divorced anthropology (the study of human beings) from the spiritual realm and thus made way for atheistic, humanistic, and rationalistic theories about human behavior.

Those fundamentally antibiblical theories became the basis of all modern psychology. Of course, today's psychologists use hundreds of counseling models and techniques based on a myriad of conflicting theories, so it is impossible to speak of psychotherapy as if it were a unified and consistent science.[5] But the basis of modern psychology can be summarized in several commonly-held ideas that have their roots in early Freudian humanism. These are the very same ideas many Christians are zealously attempting to synthesize with biblical truth:

- Human nature is basically good.

- People have the answers to their problems inside them.

- The key to understanding and correcting a person's attitudes and actions lies somewhere in that person's past.

- Individuals' problems are the result of what someone else has done to them.

- Human problems can be purely psychological in nature— unrelated to any spiritual or physical condition.

- Deep-seated problems can be solved only by professional counselors using therapy.

---

5. Sigmund Koch, "Psychology Cannot Be a Coherent Science," *Psychology Today* September, 1969: 66.

- Scripture, prayer, and the Holy Spirit are inadequate and simplistic resources for solving certain types of problems.

Those and other similar godless theories have filtered down into the
Church from the assorted stuff in the psychological tank and are having a
profound and disturbing effect on its approach to helping people. Many
sincere Christians are seriously off track in their understanding of what
counseling is and what it is supposed to accomplish.

Some basic reminders might be helpful. For example, Scripture is
the only reliable manual for true soul-study. It is so comprehensive in the
diagnosis and treatment of every spiritual matter that, energized by the
Holy Spirit in the believer, it leads to making one like Jesus Christ. This is
the process of biblical sanctification. It is the goal of biblical counseling.

The Puritans, by the way, referred to the counseling ministry as "soul
work." They spoke of the minister's responsibility as "the cure of souls."
They understood that the only reliable help for the human soul is the infallible truth of Scripture applied by the Spirit of God. They knew that the
only genuine, effective, or permanent cure for the soul's maladies is the
transformation wrought by God's grace in the heart of a believer.

ARE PSYCHOLOGICAL TECHNIQUES EVER ADVISABLE?

Does that mean the modern behavioral sciences offer nothing of value
in treating emotional or behavioral problems? Don't medication, shock
therapy, group therapy, and other techniques help in some cases? Aren't
some soul-sicknesses actually medical problems that should be treated by
skilled psychiatrists?

Certainly, it is reasonable for people to seek medical help for medical
problems. We would send someone to the doctor for a broken leg, dysfunctional kidney, tooth cavity, or other physical malady. And it is true that certain
kinds of depression actually have physical causes requiring medical treatment. D. Martyn Lloyd-Jones, best known for his powerful expository
preaching ministry, was actually trained as a physician. He pointed out that
depression and certain mental illnesses often have causes that are physical
rather than spiritual. Pernicious anemia, arteriosclerosis, porphyria, and even
gout are all examples Lloyd-Jones suggests of physical diseases that can cause
dementia or produce depression.[6] It is entirely appropriate—even advisable—

---

6. D. Martyn Lloyd-Jones, *Healing and Medicine* (Eastbourne: Kingsway, 1987),
144–145.

for the counselor to advise the counselee suffering from such symptoms to seek medical advice or get a thorough physical examination to rule out such causes.

It is also sensible for someone who is alcoholic, drug addicted, learning disabled, traumatized by rape, incest, or severe battering, to seek help in trying to cope with their trauma. Some kinds of therapy or medical treatment can serve to lessen trauma or dependency. In extreme situations medication might be needed to stabilize an otherwise dangerous person.

It must be noted that these are relatively rare problems, however, and should not be used as examples to justify the indiscriminate use of secular psychological techniques for essentially spiritual problems. Dealing with the psychological and emotional issues of life in such ways is *not* sanctification. That is why such techniques are equally effective in modifying behavior in both Christians and non-Christians.

WHAT ABOUT "CHRISTIAN PSYCHOLOGY"?

"Christian psychology" as the term is used today is an oxymoron. The word *psychology* employed in that expression no longer speaks of studying the soul; instead, it describes a diverse menagerie of therapies and theories that are fundamentally humanistic. The presuppositions and most of the doctrine of psychology cannot be successfully integrated with Christian truth.[7] Moreover, the infusion of psychology into the teaching of the Church has blurred the line between behavior modification and sanctification.

The path to wholeness is the path of spiritual sanctification. Would we foolishly turn our backs on the Wonderful Counselor, the spring of living water, for the sensual wisdom of earth and the stagnant water of behaviorism?

Our Lord Jesus reacted in a perfect and holy way to every temptation, trial, and trauma in life—and they were more severe than any human could ever suffer. Therefore, it should be clear that perfect victory over all life's troubles must be the result of being like Christ. No "soul worker" can lift another above the level of spiritual maturity he is on. So the supreme qualification for all soul-work is Christlikeness.

The truly Christian counselor must be doing soul work in the realm of the deep things of the Word and the Spirit—not fooling around in the shallows of behavior modification. Why should believers choose to

---

7. Bobgan, *PsychoHeresy*, 5–6.

do behavior modification when we have the tools for spiritual transformation (like a surgeon wreaking havoc with a butter knife instead of using a scalpel)? The most skilled counselor is the one who most carefully, prayerfully, and faithfully applies the divine spiritual resources to the process of sanctification—shaping another into the image of Jesus Christ.

There may be no more serious threat to the life of the Church today than the stampede to embrace the doctrines of secular psychology. They are a mass of human ideas that Satan has placed in the Church as if they were powerful, life-changing truths from God. Most psychologists epitomize neo-gnosticism, claiming to have secret knowledge for solving people's real problems. Though many psychologists call their techniques "Christian counseling," most of them are merely using secular theory to treat spiritual problems with biblical references tacked on.[8]

Unfortunately, such thinking dominates most of the counseling theories that have pervaded contemporary evangelicalism. The distressing result is that pastors, biblical scholars, teachers of Scripture, and caring believers using the Word of God have been made to feel they are not qualified to counsel people.

That very opinion is often at the heart of the message conveyed in some of the most widely read textbooks on Christian counseling. One bestseller claims that Christian counselors who believe the Bible is a sufficient guide for counseling are frequently guilty of "a nonthinking and simplistic understanding of life and its problems."[9] Thus those who attempt to limit their counsel to the questions Scripture answers are disdained as naive, superficial, and altogether inadequate counselors.

The literature of Christian psychology commonly belittles Bible reading and prayer as pat answers or incomplete solutions for someone struggling with depression or anxiety. Scripture, the Holy Spirit, Christ, prayer, and grace—these are the traditional solutions Christian counselors have pointed people to. But Christian psychology now tells us that none of them *really* offers the cure for people's woes.

In fact, many would have us believe that secular psychology can help people *more* effectively than the counselor armed only with spiritual weapons. The same popular Christian bestseller I quoted above claims the Church

---

8. Cf. the comments of a psychological counselor cited in Bobgan, *PsychoHeresy*, 5–6: "At the present time there is no acceptable Christian psychology that is markedly different from non-Christian psychology. It is difficult to imply that we function in a manner that is fundamentally distinct from our non-Christian colleagues."

9. Larry Crabb, *Understanding People* (Grand Rapids: Zondervan, 1987), 54–58.

"promote[s] superficial adjustments while psychotherapists, with or without biblical foundations, . . . do a better job than the church of restoring troubled people to more effective functioning."[10] Later, that same author adds, "Secularists sometimes seem to have a corner on honestly facing the disturbing complexity of life while Christians recite clichés that push away real questions of the heart. As a result, nonbelievers often help people with emotional problems more effectively than Christians [do]."[11]

How Scientific Are the Behavioral Sciences?

As we noted earlier, psychology is not a uniform body of scientific knowledge like thermodynamics or organic chemistry. When we speak of psychology, we refer to a complex menagerie of ideas and theories, many of which are contradictory. Psychology has not even proved capable of dealing effectively with the human mind and with mental and emotional processes. Thus it can hardly be regarded as a science. Karl Kraus, a Viennese journalist, made this perceptive comment: "Despite its deceptive terminology, psychoanalysis is not a science but a religion—the faith of a generation incapable of any other."[12]

Most advocates of psychology simply assume that psychology is a true science.[13] But it is not. It is a pseudo-science—the most recent of several human inventions designed to explain, diagnose, and treat behavioral problems without dealing with moral and spiritual issues. Little more than a century ago debate was raging over a different kind of behavioral science called phrenology. Phrenology held that personality characteristics were determined by the shape of someone's skull. You have probably seen old phrenologists' diagrams; they were maps of the head with specific areas labeled, showing which zone of the brain determined a particular emotion or characteristic. A phrenologist would feel people's skulls, diagnosing their problems by the location of bumps on their head.

If you think behavioral science has advanced greatly since then, ask yourself how reasonable it is to surround an adult in the fetal position with pillows so he can get back in touch with his prenatal anxieties. Or consider

---

10. Crabb, *Understanding People*, 129.

11. Ibid., 211.

12. Quoted in Bobgan, *PsychoHeresy*, 23.

13. Cf. Gary R. Collins, *Christian Counseling: A Comprehensive Guide* (Dallas: Word, 1980), 19.

the type of treatment suggested by those who advocate primal scream therapy, a methodology that teaches people to let out their frustrations by screaming mindlessly at the top of their lungs.[14] Combine that idea with group therapy and imagine the result! Group members hold hands and shriek at each other to work out their problems. Believe it or not, some psychologists are already using precisely that form of therapy—and arguing that it is the most dramatically effective treatment psychology has yet discovered![15] Given the choice, I believe I would opt for a phrenologist poking around on my head!

Jay Adams quoted a paper written for a Harvard symposium more than twenty-five years ago. The author of the paper raised the question, "Where will psychoanalysis be even 25 years from now?" His bold prediction was: "It will take its place along with phrenology and mesmerism."[16] Unfortunately, the prediction proved overly optimistic. And strangely enough, psychology seems to owe its survival to an unholy alliance between the Church and popular culture.

At about the same time the Church was becoming infatuated with behavioral science, those who knew psychology best were beginning to voice aloud the question of whether it was a science at all. Eleven years ago, *Time* magazine ran a cover story called "Psychiatry on the Couch." It said this:

> On every front, psychiatry seems to be on the defensive. . . . Many psychiatrists want to abandon treatment of ordinary, everyday neurotics ("the worried well") to psychologists and the amateur Pop therapists. After all, does it take a hard-won M.D. degree . . . to chat sympathetically and tell a patient you're-much-too-hard-on-yourself? And if psychiatry is a medical treatment, why can its practitioners not provide measurable scientific results like those obtained by other doctors?
>
> Psychiatrists themselves acknowledge that their profession often smacks of modern alchemy full of jargon, obfuscation and mystification, but precious little real knowledge. . . .
>
> As always, psychiatrists are their own severest critics. Thomas Szasz, long the most outspoken gadfly of his profession, insists that there is

14. Arthur Janov, *The Primal Scream* (New York: Dell, 1970).

15. Daniel Casriel, *A Scream Away from Happiness* (New York: Grosset and Dunlap, 1972).

16. Leo Steiner, "Are Psychoanalysis and Religious Counseling Compatible?" Paper read to Society for the Scientific Study of Religion, Harvard, November 1958. Cited in Adams, *Competent to Counsel*, 18–19.

really no such thing as mental illness, only normal problems of living. E. Fuller Torrey, another antipsychiatry psychiatrist, is willing to concede that there are a few brain diseases, like schizophrenia, but says they can be treated with only a handful of drugs that could be administered by general practitioners or internists. . . . By contrast, the Scottish psychiatrist and poet R. D. Laing is sure that schizophrenia is real and that it is good for you. Explains Laing: it is a kind of psychedelic epiphany, far superior to normal experience.

Even mainline practitioners are uncertain that psychiatry can tell the insane from the sane.[17]

The article went on to chronicle the failures of psychiatry, noting that "of all patients, one-third are eventually 'cured,' one-third are helped somewhat, and one-third are not helped at all."[18] But as the article further stated,

The trouble is that most therapies, including some outlandish ones, also claim some improvement for two-thirds of their patients. Critics argue that many patients go into analysis after a traumatic experience, such as divorce or a loved one's death, and are bound to do better anyway when the shock wears off. One study shows improvement for people merely on a waiting list for psychoanalytic treatment; presumably the simple decision to seek treatment is helpful.[19]

The article concludes with a pessimistic forecast by Ross Baldessarini, a psychiatrist and biochemist at the Mailman Research Center. He told *Time*, "We are not going to find the causes and cures of mental illness in the foreseeable future."[20]

Several years later, a conference in Phoenix, Arizona brought together the world's leading experts on psychotherapy for what was billed as the largest meeting ever on the subject. The conference, called "The Evolution of Psychotherapy," drew seven thousand mental-health experts from all over the world. It was the largest such gathering in history, billed by its organizer as the Woodstock of psychotherapy. Out of it came several stunning revelations.

The Los Angeles Times, for example, quoted Laing, who "said that he couldn't think of any fundamental insight into human relations that has

---

17. "Psychiatry on the Couch," *Time* 2 April 1979: 74.

18. Ibid., 79.

19. Ibid.

20. Ibid., 82.

resulted from a century of psychotherapy. 'I don't think we've gone beyond Socrates, Shakespeare, Tolstoy, or even Flaubert by the age of 15.'"[21] Laing added,

> "I don't think psychiatry is a science at all. It's not like chemistry or physics where we build up a body of knowledge and progress."
>
> He said that in his current personal struggle with depression, humming a favorite tune to himself (he favors one called "Keep Right On to the End of the Road") sometimes is of greater help than anything psychotherapy offers.[22]

Time magazine, reporting on the conference, noted that in a panel discussion on schizophrenia, three out of four experts said there is no such disease.[23]

> R. D. Laing, the favorite shrink of student rebels in the '60s, retains his romantic opinion of schizophrenics as brave victims who are defying a cruel culture. He suggested that many people are diagnosed as schizophrenic simply because they sleep during the day and stay awake at night. Schizophrenia did not exist until the word was invented, he said. . . . At a later panel, a woman in the audience asked Laing how he would deal with schizophrenics. Laing bobbed and weaved for 27 minutes and finally offered the only treatment possible for people he does not view as sick: "I treat them exactly the same way I treat anybody else. I conduct myself by the ordinary rules of courtesy and politeness."[24]

One truth came out clearly in the conference: among therapists there is little agreement. There is no unified science of psychotherapy; only a cacophony of clashing theories and therapies. Dr. Joseph Wolpe, a leading pioneer of behavioral therapy, characterized the Phoenix conference as "a babel of conflicting voices."[25]

And indeed it was. One specialist, Jay Haley, described what he called his "shaggy dog" technique. Evidently he means it is like a fluffy animal

---

21. Ann Japenga, "Great Minds on the Mind Assemble for Conference," *The Los Angeles Times* 18 December 1985.

22. Ibid., 17.

23. "A Therapist in Every Corner," *Time* 23 December 1985: 59.

24. Ibid.

25. Japenga, "Great Minds."

that appears to be fat until it gets wet—there seems to be more substance than really exists. This is his approach to therapy:

> Get the patient to make an absolute commitment to change, then guarantee a cure but do not tell the patient what it is for several weeks. "Once you postpone, you never lose them as patients," he said. "They have to find out what the cure is." One bulimic who ate in binges and threw up five to 25 times a day was told she would be cured if she gave the therapist a penny the first time she vomited and doubled the sum each time she threw up. Says Haley: "They quickly figure out that it doubles so fast that they can owe the therapist hundreds of thousands of dollars in a few days, so they stop."[26]

Jeffrey Zeig, organizer of the conference, said there may be as many as a hundred different theories in the United States alone. Most of them, he said, are "doomed to fizzle."[27]

Not only do psychologists sell supposed cures for a high price, but they also invent diseases for which the cures are needed. Their marketing strategy has been effective. Invent problems or difficulties, harp on them until people think they are hopelessly afflicted, then peddle a remedy. Some of the supposed problems of our culture are pathetically trite. Self-image, looks, codependency, emotional abuse, mid-life crisis, unfulfilled expectations—today's "infirmities" were once seen more accurately as the pains of selfishness. Egocentricity has become a major market strategy for psychotherapists. By fostering people's natural tendency toward self-indulgence, psychology has sold itself to an eager public. And the Church has witlessly jumped on the bandwagon.

Psychology is no more a science than the atheistic evolutionary theory upon which it is based. Like theistic evolution, "Christian psychology" is an attempt to harmonize two inherently contradictory systems of thought. Modern psychology and the Bible cannot be blended without serious compromise to or utter abandonment of the principle of Scripture's sufficiency.

Though it has become a lucrative business, psychotherapy cannot solve anyone's spiritual problems. At best it can occasionally use human insight to superficially modify behavior. It succeeds or fails for Christians and non-Christians equally because it is only a temporal adjustment—a sort of mental

---

26. "Therapist," 59.
27. Japenga, "Great Minds."

chiropractic. It cannot change the human heart, and even the experts admit that.

THE FAILURE OF CHRISTIAN PSYCHOLOGY

Meanwhile, however, the attitude within the Church is more accepting of psychotherapy than ever. If the Christian media serve as a barometer of the whole Church, a dramatic shift is taking place. Christian radio, for example, once a bastion of Bible teaching and Christian music, is overrun with talk shows, pop psychology, and phone-in psychotherapy. Preaching the Bible is passé. Psychologists and radio counselors are the new heroes of evangelicalism. And Christian radio is the major advertising tool for the selling of psychology—which is pulling in money by the billions.

The Church is thereby ingesting heavy doses of dogma from psychology, adopting secular wisdom, and attempting to sanctify it by calling it Christian. Evangelicalism's most fundamental values are thus being redefined. "Mental and emotional health" is the new buzzword. It is not a biblical concept, though many seem to equate it with spiritual wholeness. Sin is called sickness, so people think it requires therapy, not repentance. Habitual sin is called addictive or compulsive behavior, and many surmise its solution is medical care rather than moral correction.[28]

Human therapies are embraced most eagerly by the spiritually weak—those who are shallow or ignorant of biblical truth and who are unwilling to accept the path of suffering that leads to spiritual maturity and deeper communion with God. The unfortunate effect is that these people remain immature, held back by a self-imposed dependence on some pseudo-Christian method or psycho-quackery that actually stifles real growth.

The more secular psychology influences the Church, the further people move from a biblical perspective on problems and solutions. One-on-one therapists are replacing the Bible, God's chief means of sanctifying grace (John 15:3; 1 Cor. 1:21; Heb. 4:12). The counsel these professionals dispense is often spiritually disastrous. Not long ago, I listened aghast as a Christian psychologist on live radio counseled a caller to express anger at his therapist by making an obscene gesture at him. "Go ahead!" he told the caller. "It's an honest expression of your feelings. Don't try to keep your anger inside."

---

28. Adams responds skillfully to this kind of thinking, citing O. Hobart Mowrer's *The Crisis in Psychiatry and Religion*. Adams, *Competent to Counsel*, xvi–xvii.

"What about my friends?" the caller asked. "Should I react that way to all of them when I'm angry?"

"Why, sure!" this counselor said. "You can do it to anyone, whenever you feel like it. Except those who you think won't understand—they won't be good therapists for you." That is a paraphrase. I have a tape of the entire broadcast, and what the counselor actually suggested was much more explicit, even to the point of being inappropriate to print.

That same week, I heard another popular Christian broadcast that offers live counseling to callers nationwide. A woman called and said she had had a problem with compulsive fornication for years. She said she goes to bed with "anyone and everyone" and feels powerless to change her behavior.

The counselor suggested that her conduct is her way of striking back, a result of wounds inflicted by her passive father and overbearing mother. "There's no simple road to recovery," this radio therapist told her. "Your problem won't go away immediately—it's an addiction, and these things require extended counseling. You will need years of therapy to overcome your need for illicit sex." The suggestion was then made for the caller to find a church that would be tolerant while she worked her way out of the "painful wounds" that were "making" her fornicate.

What kind of advice is that? First, the counselor in effect gave that woman permission to defer obedience to a clear command of Scripture: "Flee immorality" (1 Cor. 6:18; see also 1 Thess. 4:3). Second, he blamed her parents and justified her vengeance toward them. Third, he seemed to be suggesting she could taper off gradually from her sin—under therapy, of course.

Furthermore, he gave his nationwide audience the clear message that he has no real confidence in the Holy Spirit's power to immediately transform a person's heart and behavior. Worse, he encouraged churches to tolerate a person's sexual sin until therapy begins to work.

Contrast both of those radio counselors' advice with the profound simplicity of Galatians 5:16: "Walk by the Spirit, and you will not carry out the desire of the flesh." Do we really think years of therapy can bring people to the point where they walk by the Spirit? Certainly not if the therapist is someone who recommends obscene gestures, delayed repentance, and churches tolerant of chronic immorality! There is no biblical justification for such counsel—in fact, it flatly contradicts God's Word. The apostle Paul told the Corinthian church to turn an adulterer over to Satan, putting him out of the church (1 Cor. 5).

I thank God for men and women in the Church who depend on the Bible when counseling others. I am grateful for godly counselors who urge troubled people to pray and who point them to Scripture, to God, and to the fullness of His resources for every need.

I have no quarrel with those who use either common sense or social sciences as a helpful observer's platform to look on human conduct and develop tools to assist people in getting some external controls in their behavior. That may be useful as a first step for getting to the real spiritual cure. But a wise counselor realizes that all behavioral therapy stops on the surface—far short of actual solutions to the real needs of the soul, which are resolved only in Christ.

On the other hand, I have no tolerance for those who exalt psychology above Scripture, intercession, and the perfect sufficiency of our God. And I have no encouragement for people who wish to mix psychology with the divine resources and sell the mixture as a spiritual elixir. Their methodology amounts to a tacit admission that what God has given us in Christ is not really adequate to meet our deepest needs and salve our troubled lives.

God Himself does not think very highly of counselors who claim to represent Him but rely instead on human wisdom. Job 12:17–20 says:

> He makes counselors walk barefoot [a sign of humiliation],
> And makes fools of judges.
> He loosens the bond of kings,
> And binds their loins with a girdle.
> He makes priests walk barefoot,
> And overthrows the secure ones.
> He deprives the trusted ones of speech,
> And takes away the discernment of the elders.

God's wisdom is so vastly superior to man's that the greatest human counselors are made into a spectacle. Verses 24–25 add,

> He deprives of intelligence the chiefs of the earth's people,
> And makes them wander in a pathless waste.
> They grope in darkness with no light,
> And He makes them stagger like a drunken man.

If anyone had to endure the folly of well-intentioned human counselors it was Job. Their irrelevant, useless advice was as much a grief to him as the satanic afflictions he suffered.

The depth to which sanctified psychotherapy can sink is really quite profound. A local newspaper recently featured an article about a thirty-four-bed clinic that has opened up in Southern California to treat "Christian sex addicts."[29] (The reason for beds in this kind of clinic escapes me.) According to the article, the clinic is affiliated with a large and well-known Protestant church in the area. Its staff comprises specialists described as "real pioneers in the area [of sexual addictions]. These are all legitimate, licensed psychotherapists who happen to have a strong Christian orientation to therapy," according to the center's director.[30]

Does their "Christian" orientation happen to be solid enough to allow these psychotherapists to admit that lasciviousness is sin? Evidently not. Several were interviewed for the article. They consistently used the terms *illness, problem, conflict,* and *compulsive behavior, treatment,* and *therapy.* Words with moral overtones were carefully avoided. Sin and repentance were never mentioned.

Worse, these so-called experts scoffed at the power of God's Word to transform a heart and break the bondage of sexual sin. The article quoted the center's program director, who explained why he believes his treatment center specifically for Christians is so crucial: "There are some groups of Christians who believe the Bible is all you need."[31]

That statement is the echo of neo-gnosticism. Belittling those who believe the Bible is sufficient, these latter-day "clouds without water" (Jude 12) insist that they are privy to a higher, more sophisticated secret knowledge that holds the real answer to what troubles the human soul. Don't be intimidated by their false claims. No higher knowledge, no hidden truth, nothing besides the all-sufficient resources that we find in Christ exists that can change the human heart.

The Church must recover her confidence in the spiritual resources God provides. We must return to the conviction that Scripture alone is "inspired by God and profitable for teaching, for reproof, for correction, for training in righteousness" (2 Tim. 3:16). I am convinced that far more is at stake than the average Christian realizes. If evangelicals do not rediscover biblical counseling and reinstate God's Word to its rightful place as the supreme discerner and mender of the thoughts and intents of the heart (cf. Heb. 4:12), we will lose our testimony to the world, and the Church itself will die. These matters are that critical.

---

29. Nicole Brodeur, "Center Aids Christian Sex Addicts," *Orange County Register* 13 February 1989.

30. Ibid.

31. Ibid.

2

The English Puritans: A Historical Paradigm of Biblical Counseling

Ken L. Sarles

Puritan farmers were well-known for plowing straight furrows, a feat they accomplished by lining up two trees in their field of vision. In a similar way, we can line ourselves up with the Puritan practice of counseling to help us adopt contemporary methods of counseling that are biblically accurate. Puritan pastors, known as physicians of the soul, represent in the history of the Church "the first Protestant school of Biblical Counseling."[1] Thus, an important first step in recovering a biblical approach to counseling is to understand the essence of Puritan principles and doctrine.

WHO WERE THE PURITANS?

In the popular mind, the term *Puritan* conjures up the image of an austere, priggish, self-righteous, witch-hunting killjoy. But nothing could be further from historical reality. Though originally used as a derogatory label, the term *Puritan* simply connoted one who wanted to purify the worship of the Church and the lives of the saints. English Puritanism emerged in the 1560s. It appeared first as a liturgical reform movement but quickly expanded into a distinct attitude toward the Christian life.[2] The

---

1. Timothy Keller, "Puritan Resources for Biblical Counseling," *Journal of Pastoral Practice* 9 (1988): 11.

2. Horton Davies, *The Worship of the English Puritans* (Westminster: Dacre, 1948), 9. See also Allen Carden, *Puritan Christianity in America: Religion and Life in Seventeenth-Century Massachusetts* (Grand Rapids: Baker, 1990), 11-13.

Puritan phenomena could be defined as a movement in the English Church from the mid-sixteenth to the early eighteenth centuries that sought for a reformation in the life of the Church and a purification in the life of the individual believer. It was Calvinistic in theology and pietistic in orientation.

There have been, of course, numerous reform movements in the history of the Church, but what makes the Puritans stand out among the rest is their radical commitment to live to the glory of God. In this connection, no one has profiled the Puritan character more eloquently than J. I. Packer:

> The Puritans were great souls serving a great God. In them clearheaded passion and warm-hearted compassion combined. Visionary and practical, idealistic and realistic too, goal-oriented and methodical, they were great believers, great hopers, great doers, and great sufferers. But their sufferings, both sides of the ocean (in old England from the authorities and in New England from the elements), seasoned and ripened them till they gained a stature that was nothing short of heroic. . . .
> The Puritans' battles against the spiritual and climatic wildernesses in which God set them produced a virility of character, undaunted and unsinkable, rising above discouragement and fears.[3]

Puritans occupy a place of high honor among God's people, Packer concludes, because they remained "sweet, peaceful, patient, obedient, and hopeful under sustained and seemingly intolerable pressures and frustrations."[4] The God-honoring stability and fortitude that characterized the Puritans is certainly worth emulating today in our fast-paced, upwardly mobile, hi-tech, self-indulgent society. These same characteristics also pervaded their biblical approach to counseling. In order to comprehend Puritan counseling, and

---

3. J. I. Packer, *A Quest for Godliness: The Puritan Vision of the Christian Life* (Wheaton: Crossway Books, 1990), 22.

4. Ibid., 23. In addition, a number of secular scholars in the twentieth century have come to appreciate what the Puritans have to offer. As Samuel Eliot Morison remarked:

It is not easy to describe these people truthfully, yet with meaning to moderns. For the men of learning and women of gentle nurture who led a few thousand plain folk to plant a new England on ungrateful soil were moved by purposes utterly foreign to the present America. Their object was not to establish prosperity or prohibition, liberty or democracy, or indeed anything of currently recognized value. Their ideals were comprehended vaguely in the term puritanism, which nowadays has acquired various secondary and degenerate meanings. . . . My attitude toward seventeenth-century puritanism has passed through scorn and boredom to a warm interest and respect. The ways thus to emulate their approach, we need to distinguish certain elements of their thought, including their view of Scripture, God, man, and sin.

COMMITMENT TO SCRIPTURE

The Scriptures were the centerpiece of Puritan thought and life.

> Puritanism was, above all else, a Bible movement. To the Puritan the Bible was in truth the most precious possession that this world affords. His deepest conviction was that reverence for God means reverence for Scripture, and serving God means obeying Scripture. To his mind, therefore, no greater insult could be offered to the Creator than to neglect his written word: and, conversely, there could be no truer act of homage to him than to prize it and pore over it, and then to live out and give out its teaching. Intense veneration for Scripture, as the living word of the living God and a devoted concern to know and do all that it prescribes, was Puritanism's hallmark.[5]

For the Puritans the Bible was supreme in everything, including the practice of counseling.

The biblical foundation for Puritan counseling rested upon the doctrine of divine inspiration. The method of inspiration, as the Puritans saw it, was by the divine superintendence of the Holy Spirit in the choice of words without doing violence to the knowledge or personality of the human author.[6] The result was an inspiration of the text understood to be verbal, plenary, infallible, and inerrant.[7]

---

of the puritans are not my ways, and their faith is not my faith; nevertheless they appear to me a courageous, humane, brave, and significant people.

Quoted in *Eerdman's Handbook to Christianity in America*, ed. M. Noll, N. Hatch, and G. Marsden (Grand Rapid: Eerdmans, 1983), 31. Perry Miller concurred: "I assume that Puritanism was one of the major expressions of the Western intellect, that it achieved an organized synthesis of concepts which are fundamental to our culture, and that therefore it calls for the most serious examination." In Perry Miller, *The New England Mind: The Seventeenth Century* (New York: MacMillan, 1939), viii.

5. Packer, *A Quest for Godliness*, 98. Cf. Carden, *Puritan Christianity*, 45–46.

6. See John Owen, *Works*, ed. William Goold, 16 vols. (1850–53; reprint, Carlisle, Penn.: Banner of Truth Trust, 1965), 3:144–45; and William Ames, *The Marrow of Theology*, trans. John D. Eusden (1629; reprint, Durham, N.C.: Labyrinth Press, 1983), 187.

7. As Ames noted: "Only those who could set down the rule of faith and conduct in writing who in that matter were free from all error because of the direct and infallible direction they had from God" (*Marrow of Theology*, 185–86). Cf. Leland Ryken, *Worldly Saints: The Puritans As They Really Were* (Grand Rapids: Zondervan, Academic Books, 1986), 141–42.

Though many contemporary evangelicals would agree with this view of inspiration, the Puritans did more than give mere lip service to the doctrine. Puritan theologians emphasized both the perspicuity and profitableness of Scripture. Even the literary form of the inspired text made the Scriptures particularly adapted to the human condition.

> In form of expression, Scripture does not explain the will of God by universal and scientific rules, but rather by stories, examples, precepts, exhortations, admonitions, and promises. This style best fits the common usage of all sorts of men and also greatly affects the will by stirring up pious motives, which is the chief end of theology.[8]

By their very design, the Scriptures are intended to impart truth in such a way that the reader is moved in a godward direction. Not only is the Bible clear in what it affirms, but it is also self-authenticating in nature. In this connection, William Ames asserted: "The Scriptures need no explanation through light brought from outside, especially in the necessary things. They give light to themselves, which should be uncovered diligently by men."[9] This significant statement reveals the Puritan refusal to introduce foreign psychological theories into their interpretation of the text. The Bible was seen as the source of all divine direction, instruction, comfort, encouragement, and exhortation.[10] The result was a counseling method that was biblically centered rather than theory laden.

A direct corollary to the inspiration of Scripture is its implicit authority. Bearing the imprint of the divine, the authority of the Bible was considered to be final and absolute. Whatever Scripture said, God said. As Thomas Watson put it, "Think in every line you read that God is speaking to you."[11] This meant that the Bible sat in judgment on the individual's

---

8. Ames, *Marrow of Theology*, 187–88. Cf. John Jewel, in *Introduction to Puritan Theology*, ed. Edward Hindson (Grand Rapids: Baker, 1976), 61.

9. Ames, *Marrow of Theology*, 188. Cf. Owen, *Works*, 8:537; 16:318.

10. Ames, *Marrow of Theology*, 187. Keller observed that the Puritans "considered the Scripture more than comprehensive enough to deal with every basic human condition or problem" ("Puritan Resources," 12).

11. Thomas Watson, *A Body of Divinity* (1692; reprint, Carlisle, Penn.: Banner of Truth Trust, 1965), 35. In the same context, Watson waxes eloquent on the supremacy of Scripture:

> How sweetly does this harp of Scripture sound, what heavenly music does it make in the ears of a distressed sinner, especially when the finger of God's

conscience in all its commands and promises. In all that it said, it was as though God Himself were exhorting, encouraging, directing, comforting, urging, convicting, and instructing.[12]

Since the Word of God consisted in the very words of God, its authority was comprehensive, extending to every area of faith and practice, including everything necessary to life and godliness. As Richard Sibbes declared: "There is not anything or any condition that befalls a Christian in this life but there is a general rule in the Scriptures for it, and this rule is quickened by example."[13] In other words, the Puritans had a holistic theological perspective rooted in Scripture, leading William Ames to conclude: "There is no precept of universal truth relevant to living well in domestic economy, morality, political life, or lawmaking which does not rightly pertain to theology."[14] As far as the English Puritans were concerned, *every conceivable psychological need could be met and every imaginable psychological problem could be solved through a direct application of biblical truth.*

Application of the Scriptures was done most consistently through expository preaching. As Ames explained, "The duty of an ordinary preacher is to set forth the will of God out of the Word for the edification of the hearers."[15] The sermon served as a means of corporate counseling, edifying the body of believers gathered together. From the Puritan perspective, if the saints have not been edified, then the Word has not been preached. Speaking to the ministers of his day, Ames warned: "They sin, therefore, who stick to the naked finding and explanation of the truth, neglecting

---

Spirit touches this instrument! There is divinity in Scripture. It contains the marrow and quintessence of religion. It is a rock of diamonds, a mystery of piety. The lips of Scripture have grace poured into them. The Scripture speaks of faith, self-denial, and all the graces which, as a chain of pearls, adorns a Christian. It excites to holiness; it treats of another world, it gives a prospect of eternity! Oh, then search the Scripture! make the Word familiar to you. Had I the tongue of angels, I could not sufficiently set forth the excellency of Scripture. It is a spiritual optic-glass, in which we behold God's glory; it is the tree of life, the oracle of wisdom, the rule of manners, the heavenly seed of which the new creature is formed (34–35).

12. Notice the words of William Adams, who held that the purpose of the Bible was to "move and work kindly and sweetly upon the heart to persuade, to draw, to instruct, to correct, to awe, to unite the heart to God" (quoted in Carden, *Puritan Christianity*, 41).

13. Richard Sibbes, quoted in Ryken, *Worldly Saints*, 143.

14. Ames, *Marrow of Theology*, 78. Cf. William Ames, *Technometry*, trans., with introduction and commentary by W. Gibbs (1633; reprint, Pennsylvania: University of Pennsylvania Press, 1979), 113.

15. Ames, *Marrow of Theology*, 191.

the use and practice in which religion and blessedness consist. Such preachers edify the conscience little or not at all."[16] Puritan preaching, then,
constituted a form of preventative counseling, as the truths of Scripture
were applied to the conscience. To accomplish this purpose, every sermon
was divided into two major parts: doctrine and use. The result was preaching that was both deeply theological and intensely practical.

The passage of Scripture to be preached was analyzed grammatically,
logically, and contextually, and then related to other texts in order to ascertain its doctrinal import. Then "each doctrine when sufficiently explained
should immediately be applied to its use."[17] The use of the doctrine was
related either to discernment or direction. Discernment includes either information given to the mind or reformation made of the understanding.
(Information is the revelation of some truth while reformation is the refu-
tation of some error.) Direction consists of instruction and correction:
instruction is setting forth the life that ought to be followed, while correction is a condemnation of the life that ought to be shunned.[18] The manner
in which biblical truth was to be applied to the congregation by the pastor
was delineated by Ames: "To apply a doctrine to its use is to sharpen and
make specially relevant some general truth with such effect that it may
pierce the minds of those present with the stirring up of godly affections."[19]
Puritan laypeople were thoroughly equipped with proper motives in living
for God through practical instruction given from the Word of God. The
foundation upon which they built their lives was the Bible.

------

16. Ames, *Marrow of Theology*, 192. Ames also criticized pastors for focusing on eru-
dition rather than exposition:

> They sin who do care little about what they say provided it may appear that
> they may have thought about and spoken many things. They do this frequently,
> forcing many things out of the text which are not in it and often borrowing
> for it from other places, bringing anything out of everything. The result is the
> ruin rather than the edification of the hearers, especially among the untu-
> tored (193).

17. Ibid., 192. Ames continued: "Upon this part, unless there is some special reason
against it, great insistence must be made, since this contains the conclusion and the good
of the first part, and is closer to the chief purpose of the sermon, which is the edification of
the hearers" (192).

18. Ibid., 193.

19. Ibid. For further study of Puritan preaching see Harry S. Stout, *The New En-
gland Soul: Preaching and Religious Culture in Colonial New England* (New York: Oxford
University Press, 1986); and Sacvan Bercovitch, *The American Jeremiad* (Madison, Wis.:
University of Wisconsin Press, 1978).

CONFIDENCE IN GOD

Puritan commitment to the Word of God stemmed from devotion to the person of God as its author. In our own century, A. W. Tozer has best expressed the need for a high view of God:

> The gravest question before the Church is always God Himself, and the most portentous fact about any man is not what he at a given time may say or do, but what he in his deep heart conceives God to be like. We tend by a secret law of the soul to move toward our mental image of God. This is true not only of the individual Christian, but of the company of Christians that composes the Church. Always the most revealing thing about the Church is her idea of God, just as her most significant message is what she says about Him or leaves unsaid, for her silence is often more eloquent than her speech. She can never escape the self-disclosure of her witness concerning God.[20]

According to Tozer, a right concept of God is as basic to everyday life as it is to theology, "It is to worship what the foundation is to the Temple: where it is inadequate or out of plumb the whole structure must sooner or later collapse."[21] Virtually all doctrinal and moral errors can ultimately be traced back to a low view of God. Speaking of his own day, Tozer declared: "It is my opinion that the Christian conception of God current in these middle years of the twentieth century is so decadent as to be utterly beneath the dignity of the Most High God and actually to constitute for professed believers something amounting to a moral calamity."[22] Today, as we approach the end of the twentieth century, Tozer's comment is more accurate than ever before.

By contrast, the Puritans were known as a God-intoxicated people. Even theology itself was defined by one Puritan divine as the doctrine of living to God.[23] He elaborated on what he meant:

> Every art has its rules to which the work of the person practicing it corresponds. Since living is the noblest work of all, there cannot be any more proper study than the art of living.

---

20. A. W. Tozer, *The Knowledge of the Holy* (New York: Harper and Row, 1961), 9.

21. Ibid., 10.

22. Ibid.

23. Ames, *Marrow of Theology*, 77.

Since the highest kind of life for a human being is that which approaches most closely the living and life-giving God, the nature of theological life is living to God.

Men live to God when they live in accord with the will of God, to the glory of God, and with God working in them.[24]

This is expressive of a theocentric worldview—relating everything in one's life, including all personal problems, to the nature, character, and purpose of God. Accordingly, psychology, as the knowledge of man, was rooted in theology, constituting the knowledge of God. For Puritans, theology was not an esoteric, arcane science to be studied by the academic elite but, rather, an eminently relevant subject for all believers.

Now since this life so willed is truly and properly our most important practice, it is self-evident that theology is not a speculative discipline but a practical one—not only in the common respect that all disciplines have . . . good practice as their end, but in a special and peculiar manner compared with all others. . . . Theology, therefore, is to us the ultimate and the noblest of all exact teaching arts. It is a guide and master plan for our highest end, sent in a special manner from God, treating of divine things, tending towards God, and leading man to God.[25]

This Puritan God-centeredness resulted from a deep, heartfelt devotion to God. The seventeenth-century English divine, Thomas Watson, best captures the Puritan emphasis on love for God in his explanation of the nature, degree, and fruit of love. By its nature, love for God is to be entire, sincere, fervent, active, exclusive, and permanent.[26] According to Watson: "True love boils over but does not give over. Love to God, as it is sincere without hypocrisy, so it is constant without apostasy."[27] The degree of love for God is to be beyond measure, since He is the quintessence of all that is good. Since God is chief in our perception, He is to have the chief of our affections.[28]

---

24. Ames, *Marrow of Theology*, 77.

25. Ibid., 78.

26. Thomas Watson, *All Things for Good* (1663; reprint, Carlisle, Penn.: Banner of Truth Trust, 1986), 67–70.

27. Ibid., 70.

28. Ibid., 71. Watson added: "But if you love God, you place your love on the most noble and sublime object; you love that which is better than yourselves. God is better than the soul, better than angels, better than heaven" (94).

What Watson concluded from this is what differentiates the English Puritan view of God from the contemporary American evangelical attitude toward Him: "You may over-love the creature. You may love wine too much, and silver too much; but you cannot love God too much. If it were possible to exceed, excess here were a virtue; but it is our sin that we cannot love God enough."[29] Because God is infinite, He always transcends our love for Him and exceeds our knowledge of Him. Therefore, we are never to cease pursuing a greater understanding of His purposes and a greater devotion to His person. An all-consuming passion for Christ leaves little time for distractions such as seeking self-fulfillment. Consequently, God-loving Puritans were not as occupied with the needs of the self as those of us living in the "Me Generation." They understood the truth that an accurate knowledge of self comes only from a prior knowledge of God. Consequently, their theocentric vantage point gave them a different perspective on the nature of man, particularly as it relates to the functioning of the human faculties.

COMPREHENSION OF MAN

Puritan faculty psychology appears quaint by today's standards but proved quite useful in elucidating the interior life of the individual. The brain was thought to comprise six or seven compartments, each representing a different faculty of the soul. Sensory images of various objects, known as phantasms, are mediated through the five senses and enter the compartment of the brain known as common sense. This faculty identifies the phantasms, distinguishes them from one another, and relays them to the imagination. The imagination compares the phantasms with one another, assigns meaning and intelligibility to them, and is able to retain them when the object is no longer in view. The phantasms are then stored in the memory for future reference and recall.

The understanding summons phantasms from either the memory or the imagination; renders judgment as to whether they are right or wrong, true or false; and then makes a decision concerning a course of action to take. The will receives instructions from the understanding via the agency of the nervous system and directs the body accordingly. The affections then prompt the muscles of the body in accordance with the

---

29. Watson, *All Things*, 71.

direction of the will.[30] The following illustration demonstrates how the faculties functioned together:

> So the bear, encountered in the wilderness, causes in the eye a phantasm of the bear, which is identified as belonging to the species bear in common sense, recognized as dangerous in imagination, associated with remembered dangers in memory, declared an object to be fled in reason, made the signal of command to the will, which then excites the affection of fear, which finally prompts the muscles of the legs to run.
>
> Remembering that this description is shamelessly simplified, and that for every point there was a long background of dispute, we can nevertheless regard it as substantially the conception underlying all Puritan discourse about human behavior, about the sin of man, and regeneration.[31]

The one faculty left out of the illustration, which played a key role in Puritan counseling, is the conscience.

The conscience is that faculty of the soul, engaged in moral judgment, that deals with issues of right and wrong, good and bad. The English word is derived from the Latin *conscientiae*, meaning a knowledge (*scientia*) held jointly with (*con*) another, namely, God. The conscience speaks with the voice of God, representing a shared knowledge that is really the most accurate knowledge a man has of himself.[32] Ames defined the conscience as "a man's judgment of himself according to God's judgment of him."[33] David Dickson elaborated as follows: "Conscience, as it doth respect ourselves is . . . the understanding power of our souls examining how matters do stand betwixt God and us, comparing his will revealed, with our state, condition and carriage, in thoughts, words or deeds, done or omitted, and passing judgment thereupon as the case requires."[34]

---

30. The affections are of two types in Puritan thought. The sensual affections are instinctual, uncontrollable passions that bypass the understanding and are related to nourishment, preservation, and propagation. The rational affections follow knowledge and are subordinate to the understanding; therefore, they are capable of being controlled. See Miller, *New England Mind*, 252.

31. Miller, *New England Mind*, 241.

32. Packer, *A Quest for Godliness*, 109.

33. John Dykstra Eusden, introduction to *Marrow of Theology*, by William Ames, 43.

34. David Dickson, *Theraputica Sacra* (1664): 3, quoted in Packer, *A Quest for Godliness*, 109. According to Eusden: "The fundamental task of conscience in the Christian faith is to examine the relationship between man and God and therein to find answers to genuine questions and to produce grounds for decision and action" (Eusden, introduction to *Marrow of Theology*, 43).

Ames considered the conscience to be a practical judgment whereby people applied what they knew in evaluating themselves so that it became a rule to direct the will.[35] In Puritan thought, the conscience operated according to a syllogistic format. At this point, the Puritans borrowed from Catholic casuistry and utilized Aristotelian thought in the form of the *practical syllogism*. Though they used aspects of Catholic methodology, they denied Catholic results, particularly the concept of probability and the Jesuit emphasis on the ends justifying the means. The syllogistic structure was comprised of three parts: (1) the proposition, (2) the assumption, and (3) the conclusion. The proposition, or *syntersis*, was the standard to be used, arising out of the revealed will of God. The assumption, or *syneidesis*, was the individual's measure of himself against the declared standards. The assumption phase involved two steps: first, a comparison of the action in question with the proposition, and second, the judgment of the action based on the comparison. The conclusion, or *krisis*, passed sentence on one's action based on the judgment made in the *syneidesis*. The sentence would produce either joy and hope, or gloom and despair.[36]

A couple of examples will demonstrate how the practical syllogism works. The conscience of the unbeliever, when based on the testimony of Scripture, would reason thus:

> *Syntersis*: The person that lives in sin will die.
>
> *Syneidesis*: I live in sin.
>
> *Krisis*: Therefore, I will die.

If the gospel message is embraced by the unbeliever, that person's conscience will function as follows:

> *Syntersis*: Whoever believes in Christ will not die but live.
>
> *Syneidesis*: I believe in Christ.
>
> *Krisis*: Therefore, I will not die, but live.[37]

---

35. Eusden, introduction to *Marrow of Theology*, 42. Thomas Goodwin stated that conscience was a function of the practical reason in *Works*, 8 vols., ed. Alexander Grosart (1863; reprint, Carlisle, Penn.: Banner of Truth Trust, 1979), 6:272.

36. See Eusden, introduction to *Marrow of Theology*, 44–45.

37. Ibid.

Operating in this syllogistic fashion, the conscience judges independently of the will. "It stands over us, addressing us with an absoluteness of authority which we did not give it and which we cannot take from it."[38] The conscience functions as a spiritual nervous system—the pain of guilt informs the understanding that something is wrong and needs correction. For the Puritans, guilt neglected meant eventual destruction. Richard Sibbes compared the authority of the conscience to a divine court within the human soul, where it served as witness, accuser, judge, and executioner.[39] In *The Holy War*, which describes the takeover of the town of Mansoul by Diabolus, John Bunyan explained the effect of the conscience, which he named Mr. Recorder, upon the unbeliever:

> He was much degenerated from his former king, and also much pleased with many of the giant's laws and service; but all this would not do, forasmuch as he was not wholly his. He would now and then think upon Shaddai, and have dread of his law upon him, and then he would speak against Diabolus with a voice as great as when a lion roareth. Yea, and would also at certain times, when his fits were upon him, (for you must know that sometimes he had terrible fits,) make the whole town of Mansoul shake with his voice.[40]

In other words, the authority of the conscience could not be completely ignored, even in the unregenerate.

The basis for the functioning of the conscience is the law of God revealed in Scripture. The conscience is not itself the lawgiver, but, rather, it discerns and demands compliance with God's law. An erring conscience operates on standards other than the Word of God, and instead of being obeyed, it should be better instructed.[41] A healthy Christian conscience on the other hand,

> is constantly in operation, listening for God's voice in his word, seeking to discern his will in everything, active in self-watch and self-judgment. The healthy Christian knows his frailty and always suspects and distrusts himself lest sin and Satan should be ensnaring him unawares; therefore he regularly grills himself before God, scrutinising

---

38. Packer, *A Quest for Godliness*, 110.

39. Richard Sibbes, *Works*, ed. Grosart, 3:210–11.

40. John Bunyan, *The Holy War* (reprint; Grand Rapids: Baker, 1977), 16.

41. Packer, *A Quest for Godliness*, 113.

his deeds and motives and ruthlessly condemning himself when he finds within himself moral deficiency and dishonesty.[42]

The Puritan believer sought to sensitize his conscience toward sin. Accordingly, the degree of his self-condemnation became a measure of his Christ-likeness.[43]

For Puritans, godliness consisted primarily in obtaining and maintaining a clear conscience before God through a careful, informed response to biblical truth. This emphasis led to the rise of Puritan casuistry or cases of conscience, in which every conceivable circumstance or eventuality of daily life was considered in order to delineate the proper, God-honoring response. There were two ruling axioms of Puritan casuistry: "(1) that no known truth must be compromised or denied in practice and (2) that no avoidable sin must be committed, however great the good to which such compromise and sin might lead."[44] Conviction was never sacrificed for the sake of expediency, principle never succumbed to pragmatism. Hence, Puritan men and women were known as precisionists. They sought to live their lives in a precise way, as a living work of art dedicated to the Master Artist Himself. But just as works of art suffer from deformities and imperfections of various kinds, so Puritans took sin seriously as defacing what God had created.

THE PURITAN CONCEPT OF SIN

It is in the attitude toward sin that Puritanism stands in such stark contrast to our own age. In the Puritan view, human nature was radically defective, characterized constitutionally by an inclination to evil and an aversion to good. Many modern evangelicals have replaced the biblical realism of the Puritans with a shallow, superficial view of sin. Today, sin has been redefined as the result of either demonic affliction or addictive behavior. In either case, the sinner has been reclassified as a victim, and, therefore, not personally responsible for his or her actions. On the other hand, Puritans considered sin to be criminal and devoted much attention

---

42. Packer, *A Quest for Godliness.*, 116.

43. However, excessive introspection was discouraged. As Packer put it: "The gloomy self-absorption of the man who can never look away from himself, is bad Puritanism; the Puritans condemned it repeatedly" (ibid., 118).

44. Ibid., 121.

to it. As one historian observed, "Sin was the recipient of the greatest loathings the faithful Puritan could muster because it threatened the social order, violated reason, and most of all epitomized the antithesis of that which he professed to love most dearly—the Lord."[45]

Stephen Charnock expounded on sin as an affront to God: "All sin is found in secret atheism. . . . Every sin is a kind of cursing God in the heart, an aim at the destruction of the being of God, not actually, but virtually. . . . A man in every sin aims to set up his own will as his rule, and his own glory at the end of his actions."[46] Sin is a turning from the worship of God to the worship of self. The most important aspect about humanity is that we are worshipping creatures. Self-worship, then, is at the core of the sin problem.[47]

In light of the current infatuation with self-esteem, it is worth examining the Puritan teaching on self-love. In typically Puritan fashion, Charnock elucidated three types of self-love. The first type of love he styled "natural self-love," which he regarded as both necessary and commendable since it is the rule measuring our duty to our neighbor. This type of love is innate and constitutional, therefore it does not require inculcating.[48] Carnal self-love is "when a man loves himself above God, in opposition to God, with a contempt of God." This type of love "becomes criminal by the excess."[49] It is an inordinate self-love, and as such, it is the fundamental passion of the human heart and the gateway to all iniquity. Sinful self-love is "a shrinking from God into the mire of a carnal selfishness" from which there is no escape apart from divine grace.[50] This leads to the third type mentioned by Charnock, which is a gracious self-love, imparted to believers in regeneration. It is "when we love ourselves for higher ends than the nature of a creature, . . . in subserviency to the glory of God.

---

45. Carden, *Puritan Christianity in America*, 49. Carden quoted Thomas Shepherd, the Puritan pastor of Newton, as declaring: "In everie sin thou dost strike God, and sting a dagger at the heart of God." Shepherd added further, "The real greatness of sin is seen by beholding the greatness of God who is smitten by sin" (50).

46. Stephen Charnock, *Discourses Upon the Existence and Attributes of God*, 2 vols., (reprint; Grand Rapids: Baker, 1979), 1:93–94. In a similar vein, John Owen described the basic patterns of sinful imaginations as self-centeredness, self-gratification, and self-will (*Works*, ed. Goold, 7:164).

47. Keller, "Puritan Resources," 28.

48. Here Puritanism speaks loud and clear to our narcissistic culture. Advocating natural self-love, which is as instinctive as self-preservation, leads to inordinate self-love. The latter is sin while the former is not.

49. Charnock, *Attributes of God*, 136.

50. Ibid.

This is a reduction of the revolted creature to his true and happy order; a Christian is therefore said to be created in Christ to good works."[51] However, apart from a radical transformation of nature, the individual is left with his idolatry,

> when he acts so as if something below God could make him happy without God, or that God could not make him happy without the addition of something else. Thus the glutton makes a god of his dainties; the ambitious man of his honor; the incontinent man of his lust; and the covetous man of his wealth; and consequently esteems them as his chiefest good, and the most noble end, to which he directs his thoughts: thus he vilifies and lessens the true God, which can make him happy, in a multitude of false gods, that can only render him miserable. He that loves pleasure more than God, says in his heart there is no God but his pleasure. He that loves his belly more than God, says in his heart there is no God but his belly: their happiness is not accounted to lie in that God that made the world, but in the pleasure or profit they make their god.[52]

The fact that appetites and affections can create their own idols demonstrates the pervasiveness of the sin principle in its effect upon the human faculties.

The imagination and the will are particularly susceptible to sinful motions. Since the imagination is not bound by the senses, it can form phantasms beyond or in excess of nature. In its depraved state it is utterly lawless and creates unnatural phantasms to seduce both the understanding and the will. In a vain and mischievous way, it forges unreal images without any external sensation. In *The Soul's Conflict*, Richard Sibbes declared:

> The life of many men . . . is almost nothing else but a fancy; that which chiefly sets their own imagination, which setteth up an excellency, within itself, in comparison of which it despiseth all true excellency and those things that are of most necessary consequence indeed.[53]

The ungoverned imagination, Sibbes continued, "is a wild and ranging thing; it wrongs not only the frame of God's work in us, setting the baser

---

51. Charnock, *Attributes of God*, 136.

52. Ibid., 143.

53. Richard Sibbes, quoted in Miller, *The New England Mind*, 258.

part of a man above the higher, but it wrongs likewise the work of God in the creatures, and everything else, for it shapes things as itself pleaseth."[54] Because the imagination can so easily transgress, it is to be rigorously controlled by a Spirit-illumined reason grounded in the Scripture.

Likewise, the will can act independently, rebelling against the understanding. One notable Puritan conviction, which speaks volumes to our culture today, is that the supremacy of reason over will must be achieved by divine grace, not human education. Education, by itself, will only render a sinner more wicked. Only grace can tame a riotous will. People are depraved, not because they have a will, but because they have a will that prefers evil.

Because of the proneness to evil in human nature, the Puritans were well aware of the deceitfulness of sin. John Owen saw three stages in the deceit of sin. First of all, perspective is lost on the vileness of sin and the wonder of God's grace.[55] Sin's tendency is always to lessen sin's seriousness. Biblical truth loses its grip on the imagination and is reduced to mere cognitive content. As spiritual sensitivities are dulled, the saint loses that "holy relish" that had been the primary motive of his or her life.

Second, when the affections are not firmly set on the things of God, sin's attractiveness makes its appearance in the imagination. As sin is contemplated without a corresponding sense of disgust, it captures the imagination and becomes positively desirable. The imagination "rolls" the pleasure of sin, "like the rolling of food on the tongue for tasting."[56]

Third, the will consents to what appears to be good in the mind and develops rationalizations to justify the sin being contemplated. The affections are stirred and inflamed by the vivid representations of the pleasure of sin, while the convictions of conscience are silenced.[57] If this "chain of deceit" is not broken, it leads to sinful attitudes and actions. "Later, after indwelling sin has developed a habit pattern, the cycle can occur so quickly that there is no longer any consciousness of 'stages,' of 'parleying and enticing.' Instead, the behavior erupts swiftly and with little warning."[58]

In this connection, Thomas Brooks warns against the deception of sin when it appears in virtue's colors. In his description of the effect

---

54. Richard Sibbes, quoted in Miller, *The New England Mind*, 258.

55. Keller, "Puritan Resources," 33. See John Owen, *Works*, 6:218–23.

56. Keller, "Puritan Resources," 33. Cf. Owen, *Works*, 6:246.

57. Keller, "Puritan Resources," 33.

58. Ibid.

produced by the unmasking of sin, his eloquence matches the significance of the event and captures the intensity that is the hallmark of Puritanism:

> Ah, souls! when you shall lie upon a dying bed, and stand before a judgment seat, sin shall be unmasked, and its dress and robes shall then be taken off, then it shall appear more vile, filthy, and terrible than hell itself; then, that which formerly appeared most sweet will appear most bitter, and that which appeared most beautiful will appear most ugly, and that which appeared most delightful will then appear most dreadful to the soul. Ah, the shame, the pain, the gall, the bitterness, the horror, the hell that the sight of sin, when its dress is taken off, will raise in poor souls! Sin will surely prove evil and bitter to the soul when its robes are taken off. . . . Till we have sinned, Satan is a parasite: when we have sinned, he is a tyrant.[59]

Brooks further warns that yielding to a lesser sin moves the devil to tempt us to commit the greater sin. "Sin is of an encroaching nature; it creeps on the soul by degrees, step by step."[60] With this Owen concurred, presenting sin as a force within the human heart:

> First, it lusts, stirring and moving inordinate figments in the mind, desires in the appetite and the affections, proposing them to the will. But it rests not there, it cannot rest; it urgeth, presseth, and pursueth its proposals with earnestness, strength, and vigour, fighting, and contending, and warring to obtain its end and purpose. [61]

Thus, the bulk of Puritan counseling focused on the sin problem because of its pervasive extent, its deceitful character, and its perverted nature. Recognizing the deception resident within every human heart, Puritan counselors knew that what people wanted to hear the least was what they needed to hear the most. Hence, the solution Puritan pastors offered to the dilemmas created by the dominance of sin was the principle of *mortification*.

Mortification is putting to death the deeds of the body (Rom. 8:13). To mortify means to take away all the strength, vigor, and power of sin so

---

59. Thomas Brooks, *Precious Remedies Against Satan's Devices* (1652: reprint, Carlisle, Penn.: Banner of Truth Trust, 1984), 35–36.

60. Ibid., 39.

61. Owen, *Works*, 6:195.

that it cannot act on its own or exert itself in the life of the believer.[62] This entails not only the fruit of sin in external behavior patterns but also the root of sin in internal motives and desires.

In his development of the concept of mortification, Owen explains first what it is not before describing what it is. Mortification does not mean to so eliminate sin in this life that it is no longer a problem. Though this is the goal of sanctification, it cannot be reached this side of glory due to the presence of indwelling sin (Rom. 7:14–25). Second, mortification does not mean achieving a degree of civility or conformity to outward morality, for such "may seem to themselves and others very mortified men, when perhaps, their hearts are a standing sink of all abominations." Third, mortification is not the replacing of one sin for another, for all sin is worthy of death. Finally, occasional victories over sin do not constitute mortification of the sin principle.[63]

Owen's delineation of what mortification does involve has been summarized well by Ferguson:

> Rather, mortification involves the habitual weakening of sin, and constant fighting against it with a measure of success. The battle needs to be perpetual because each manifestation of sin contains the seeds of sin's evil dominion, and inclines to the same end. There is a necessary universal crucifying of the flesh by which sin is weakened.[64]

The secret of the Puritan character can be found in an attitude toward the Christian life of constant spiritual warfare against sin. This is quite different from the spate of spiritual-warfare seminars that are being offered today where Christians are taught to battle the demonic forces all around them. The Puritans did not battle demons but themselves, and, consequently, gained a degree of mastery over themselves, producing godliness of life.

In order to understand mortification we must answer the following question as framed by Owen:

> Suppose a man to be a true believer, and yet finds in himself a powerful indwelling sin, leading him captive to the law of it, consuming his heart with trouble, perplexing his thoughts, weakening his soul as to duties of communion with God, disquieting him as to peace,

---

62. Owen, *Works*, 6:8.

63. Ibid., 6:25–26.

64. Sinclair B. Ferguson, *John Owen on the Christian Life* (Carlisle, Penn.: Banner of Truth Trust, 1987), 149. See Owen, *Works*, 6:28.

and perhaps defiling his conscience, and exposing him to hardening through the deceitfulness of sin,—what shall he do?[65]

The question is significant because it reveals a sensitivity to sin not often found in contemporary evangelicalism. To ask the question is to begin moving in the direction of mortification.

To answer the question, one must consider the consequences of the sin that disquiets the soul when it is allowed to go unchecked. These consequences include hardness of heart, searing of the conscience, loss of peace and assurance, and corrective discipline from God.[66] After due consideration is given, the conscience in particular should be loaded with the guilt of sin.[67] "Sin should be brought into the light of the law and the gospel respectively, in the prayer that sin may be seen in the true light of God's holiness, grace and love, and the sacrifice of Christ for it."[68] The sinning saint ought to tremble before God for having offended His patience, sinned against His mercy, and taken His grace for granted.[69]

Conviction, if it takes hold in the heart, will be followed by a thoroughgoing repentance. Genuine repentance is far more than a mere acknowledgement of the sin.[70] As Keller points out: "It is natural for a person to briefly express sorrow over a sin and then to reassure himself quickly with a verse of forgiveness (e.g. 1 John 1:8–9.) But this can produce a tremendous hardness of heart, especially in people who are falling repeatedly into besetting sin."[71] It is also not sufficient to turn from the sin if the only reason for turning is a fear of the consequences. Real repentance, as Richard Sibbes expressed it, is "a working our hearts to such grief as will

---

65. Owen, *Works*, 6:24.

66. Keller, "Puritan Resources," 25.

67. Ferguson, *John Owen on the Christian Life*, 151. See Owen, *Works*, 6:56.

68. Ferguson, *John Owen on the Christian Life*, 151.

69. Owen demonstrates a healthy conviction of sin through rhetorical self-converse:

Say to thy soul, "What have I done? What love, what mercy, what blood, what grace have I despised and trampled on! Is this the return I make to the Father for his love, to the son for his blood, to the Holy Ghost for his grace? . . . Have I defiled the heart that Christ died to wash. . . . Do I account communion with him of so little value, that for this vile lust's sake I have scarce left him any room in my heart? . . . Entertain thy conscience daily with this treaty" (*Works*, 6:58).

70. Owen warns that "to apply mercy then to a sin that is not vigorously mortified is to fulfill the end of the flesh upon the gospel" (*Works*, 6:46).

71. Keller, "Puritan Resources," 26.

make sin more odious unto us than punishment, until we offer an holy violence against it."[72]

To those who have experienced conviction and repentance, Owen offers the following encouragement: "Set faith at work on Christ for the *killing* of thy sin. His blood is the great sovereign remedy for sin-sick souls. Live in this, and thou wilt die a conqueror; yea, thou wilt, through the good providence of God, live to see thy lust dead at thy feet."[73] Following repentance of sin, God will speak peace to the conscience. "It is his sovereign pleasure to do so, and Christ's prerogative to voice it to us by his word and Spirit."[74]

Before peace can be experienced, however, the source of that peace must be ascertained. Ferguson has captured the essence of Owen's instruction on this point:

> *How may the voice of Christ be distinguished from our personal inclinations?* The voice is that of our personal inclinations if it is not accompanied by a genuine hatred of sin, and not evidenced by a waiting patiently upon God. . . . It is man's voice and not Christ's, if peace is spoken easily, or spoken to a heart that harbors sin contentedly, or when the humiliation which attends a normal work of grace in such instances is absent.[75]

Correspondingly, Christ's voice speaks peace to the humbled soul who truly hates sin and is not content with its presence. This is the reflexive ministry of the Holy Spirit. In other words, the Holy Spirit ministers to saints contrary to the way saints judge themselves. If believers, in a state of carnal security, comfort themselves in their sin by nonchalantly discounting its impact on their lives, then the Holy Spirit will convict them, opposing their comfort with grief, misery, and the pangs of a tormented conscience. On the other hand, if believers judge themselves for their sin and deeply grieve over how they have offended the Savior, then the Holy Spirit will encourage and comfort them, and soothe their afflicted conscience. Thus, mortification is achieved. As the saint is crushed over sin and consoled by the Spirit, the power of sin in daily living is weakened. If the goal of the Church today is to develop

---

72. Sibbes, *Works*, 1:47.

73. Owen, *Works*, 6:79.

74. Ferguson, *John Owen on the Christian Life*, 152.

75. Ibid. See Owen, *Works*, 6:71–77.

spiritually and psychologically healthy Christians, then the Puritans have marked out the path to that goal in their emphasis on the mortification of sin. Owen said it best:

> *Constant self-abasement*, condemnation, and abhorrency, is another duty that is directly opposed unto the . . . rule of sin in the soul. No frame of mind is a better antidote against the poison of sin. . . . It is the soil wherein all grace will thrive and flourish. A constant due sense of sin as sin, of our interest therein by nature, and in the course of our lives, with a continual afflictive remembrance of . . . instances of it . . . is the soul's best posture. . . . To keep our souls in a constant state of mourning and self-abasement is the most necessary part of our wisdom . . . and it is so far from having any inconsistency with those consolations and joy, which the gospel tenders unto us in believing, as that it is the only way to let them into the soul in a due manner.[76]

CONCLUSION

Perhaps at this point, in accordance with Puritan practice, it would be best to ask of what *use* is the Puritan approach to the cure of souls for contemporary counseling ministry. Actually, the question is twofold: *why* and *how?*

Why should we use the Puritan approach? Because the spiritual devotion, theocentric commitment, and personal integrity of the Puritans reflects biblical reality and is worthy of present-day evangelical emulation. Puritan Christianity at its best "had a vigour, a manliness, and a depth which modern evangelical piety largely lacks. This is because Puritanism was . . . a sustained practice of seeking the face of God. . . . The Puritans were manlier Christians just because they were godlier Christians."[77] Packer has noted three points of contrast between seventeenth-century Puritans and contemporary evangelicals that is worth repeating:

> First, we cannot but conclude that whereas to the Puritans communion with God was a *great* thing, to evangelicals today it is a

---

76. Owen, *Works*, 7:532–33.

77. Packer, *Quest for Godliness*, 235.

comparatively *small* thing. The Puritans were concerned about communion with God in a way that we are not. . . .

Then, second, we observe that whereas the experiential piety of
the Puritans was *natural and unselfconscious*, because it was so utterly
God-centered, our own (such as it is) is too often *artificial and boast-
ful*, because it is so largely concerned with ourselves. . . .

Third, it seems undeniable that the Puritans' passion for spiritual
integrity and moral honesty before God, their fear of hypocrisy in
themselves as well as in others, and the humble self-distrust that led
them constantly to check whether they had not lapsed into religious
play-acting . . . *has no counterpart in the modern-day evangelical ethos.*
They were characteristically cautious, serious, realistic, steady, patient,
persistent in well-doing and avid for holiness of heart; we, by contrast, too often show ourselves to be characteristically brash, euphoric,
frivolous, superficial, naive, hollow and shallow.[78]

How should we use the Puritan approach? By applying the theological
truths they employed to the psychological presuppositions of our own day.
Their view of how sin dominates the life provides the key to understanding addictive behavior. Their god-centeredness establishes the framework
for a proper approach to self-image. As Keller elaborates: "By modern standards any person struggling with deep patterns of self-gratification or
self-will might be told, 'You aren't responsible' or 'A real Christian wouldn't
feel like that' or 'you must have a demon.'"[79] By contrast, the Puritan counselor first exhorted the person to mortify the sin through contrition,
confession, and repentance. Then the counselor encouraged the individual
that the struggle with sin was a good sign, indicating there was not yet a
complete dominance of sin. On this basis there was reason to hope that
the pattern of sin would be broken through the truth of the gospel. The
English Puritans would be appalled at the emphasis today on self-esteem;
they would regard it as nothing other than a form of self-worship. They
would eschew talk of "unmet needs," because in their view the only real
need to be met was the need to worship.[80] That is why Puritans practiced
sanctification by theology rather than by psychology. As Owen explained:

> Sanctification is an immediate work of the Spirit of God on the
> souls of believers, purifying and cleansing of their natures from the
> pollution and uncleanness of sin, renewing in them the image of God,

---

78. Packer, *Quest for Godliness*, 215–17.

79. Keller, "Puritan Resources," 28.

80. Ibid., 40.

and thereby enabling them from a spiritual and habitual principle of grace, to yield obedience unto God. . . . Or more briefly; it is the universal renovation of our natures by the Holy Spirit into the image of God, through Jesus Christ. Hence it follows, that our *holiness*, which is the fruit and effect of this work . . . as it compriseth the re-newed . . . image of God wrought in us, so it consists in a holy obedience unto God, by Jesus Christ, according to the terms of the covenant of grace.[81]

The defining characteristic of Puritanism was the stress on the sanc-tified life. Whether in the area of counseling, or any other area of Christian life and ministry, the Puritans challenge us today, more than any other generation in the history of the Church, by their absolute commitment to integrity between action and belief.

Let us, then, not think that we are any thing the better for our conviction of the truths of the great doctrines of the gospel . . . unless we find the power of the truths abiding in our own hearts and have a continual experience of their necessity and excellence in our standing before God and our communion with him.[82]

---

81. Owen, *Works*, 3:386.
82. Ibid., 12:52.

3

Biblical Counseling in the Twentieth Century

David Powlison

Happily, in the past twenty-five years the Church of Jesus Christ has rediscovered biblical counseling. Now in order to rediscover something, it must have been lost. How was biblical counseling lost in the Church? In order to understand how this happened we need to turn back the pages of history.

English-speaking believers have a long history of case-wise pastoral care. Many of the greatest Protestant writings are marked by an ability to bring Scripture to bear sensitively on varied "cases"; Thomas Brooks's *Precious Remedies Against Satan's Devices,* Richard Baxter's *A Christian Directory,* John Bunyan's *The Pilgrim's Progress,* and Jonathan Edwards's *A Treatise Concerning Religious Affections* all stand out. Each of these pastoral writers had God's burning concern for doctrinal correctness, moral uprightness, a disciplined devotional life, and Christian service. But these pastors also possessed a rich measure of the Shepherd's discerning love: not only did they know people intimately, but they had a feel for the road of progressive sanctification.[1]

Edwards's classic is almost 250 years old, the others more than 300 years old, and, identifiable biblical counseling could be found well into the 1800s. Jay Adams cites Ichabod Spencer as "a sample of one sort of pastoral

---

1. For a useful introduction to this heritage, see Timothy Keller, "Puritan Resources for Biblical Counseling," *The Journal of Pastoral Practice* 9, no. 3 (1988): 11–44, and chapter 2 of this book.

counseling that was done by a Presbyterian preacher prior to the near capitulation of the Christian ministry to psychiatry. In his *Sketches*, Spencer discussed a large variety of problems and how he handled them."[2] Spencer wrote in the 1850s, but the well of biblical counseling wisdom that had been trickling for years gradually went dry in subsequent decades.

In the nineteenth and twentieth centuries, American Christians basically lost the use of truths and skills they formerly possessed. That is, practical wisdom in the cure of souls waned, even while the conservative Church, by definition, retained its grasp upon orthodox doctrine, biblical moral absolutes, the spiritual disciplines, and the missionary calling. The Church lost that crucial component of pastoral skill that can be called *case-wisdom*—wisdom that knows people, knows how people change, and knows how to help people change. A shepherd's skill is an *applied* art and science, it is a form of love that abounds in knowledge and discernment in working with people. Yet this ability to apply truth to specific "cases" atrophied. In fact, by the early twentieth century liberal theology and secular psychology were ascendant in the counseling domain.[3] Only dim echoes and shadows of former wisdom could be heard and seen among conservative Christians.[4]

Instead, secular psychologies claimed the turf of counseling expertise and of insight into human nature. Conservative Christians may have retained parts of Jonathan Edwards's formal theology, but psychologist William James

---

2. Jay L. Adams, *The Christian Counselor's Manual* (Phillipsburg, N. J.: Presbyterian and Reformed, 1973), 130. The first volume of Ichabod Spencer's *A Pastor's Sketches* was published in 1850, the second in 1853. *Sketch* was Spencer's word for a case study. For a more detailed historian's look at Spencer, refer to chapter 4 in E. Brooks Holifield, *A History of Pastoral Care in America From Salvation to Self-Realization* (Nashville: Abingdon, 1983).

3. Readers interested in the history of the eclipse of the pastorate by the mental health professions can find a provocative analysis by Andrew Abbott, *The System of Professions: An Essay on the Division of Expert Labor*, (Chicago: University of Chicago Press, 1988). Read chapter 10, "The Construction of the Personal Problems Jurisdiction," 280–314, especially 294–314. Abbott speaks of how pastors had the inside track to address people's personal problems in the late nineteenth century. "But clergy analysis remained primitive. The gradual recognition of personal problems as legitimate categories of professional work did not bring a serious clergy effort to conceptualize them. The clergy's failure to provide any academic foundation for their practice with personal problems ultimately proved their undoing" (286). The newborn mental health professions seized the field. Abbott goes on to speak of the subsequent "drift of pastoral counseling towards secular psychotherapy" and "the clergy's willful desertion of its traditional work" (310, 313).

4. For example, compare R. A. Torrey's turn-of-the-century *Personal Work: A Book of Effective Methods* (New York: Fleming H. Revell, n.d.) with the earlier writers cited above. Though it has some redeeming qualities, Torrey's book is impoverished in its understanding of people, of Scripture, of pastoral ministry, and of the change process.

was heir to Edwards's style of careful observation and reflection.[5] The Christians took the Bible, and the psychologists took people—not a happy situation for needy people in either camp! The growing edge of pastoral care occurred not among ministers of the gospel of Jesus but among ministers of a secular or liberal gospel. Freud's psychoanalysis and other nascent psychotherapies were adapted to shepherd a people without the Shepherd: the mental hygiene movement, Harry Emerson Fosdick's pulpit, and Carl Rogers' therapeutic gospel of self are landmarks in the first half of the twentieth century.

The psychologies not only claimed the turf of counseling; they made good their claim. Sociologist Philip Rieff accurately titled his book on twentieth-century America *The Triumph of the Therapeutic* and noted astutely, "Religious man was born to be saved; psychological man is born to be pleased. . . . If the therapeutic is to win out, then surely the psychotherapist will be his secular spiritual guide."[6] Rieff nostalgically mourned the death of Christian culture, but he was a modern man making do, not a prophet calling people back to the living God.[7] The goals, the truths, the methods, even the possibility of biblical counseling vanished in the psychological revolution. In fact, biblical counseling not only disappeared; it became unthinkable.

By the mid-1960s when biblical counseling was rediscovered, it emerged as an alien in the midst of three psychologized communities. The cultural setting of the activity called counseling or psychotherapy could be likened to three nested circles whose differences—even sharp differences—occurred within a fundamental consensus. The huge and dominating outer circle was secular psychology. Within this circle the pioneering theory-builders, the university graduate and undergraduate programs, the credentials, the mental health system, the journals, and the books set the intellectual and methodological pace. The middle circle consisted of liberal pastoral theology, which defined the field of pastoral counseling, even in conservative seminaries. The smallest circle contained professing believers who were psychologists and therapists.

The larger circle dominated the intellectual agenda and therapeutic methods of the two lesser circles. Thus religious counselors joined clinical

---

5. Jonathan Edwards's method (and subject matter) in *A Treatise on Religious Affections* was taken over by William James in *The Varieties of Religious Experience* (n.p., 1902), one of the foundational monographs in modern psychology.

6. Philip Rieff, *The Triumph of the Therapeutic: Uses of Faith After Freud* (Chicago: University of Chicago Press, 1987), 24f.

7. Sociologist and apologist Os Guinness turns Rieff's insight into a multileveled call to repentance. See "America's Last Men and Their Magnificent Talking Cure," in *No God But God*, ed. Os Guinness and John Seel (Chicago: Moody Press, 1992), 111–132.

psychologists, social workers, guidance counselors, and psychiatric nurses in a vast army of practitioners within "enlisted" ranks of the cure-of-souls professions. The "officers" were the psychiatrists and personality theorists who provided cognitive content and philosophical rationale for the mental health endeavor. Anyone who wanted to talk about counseling, or read counseling, or join an association of counselors, or go to school in counseling, or do counseling, did it somewhere within the big circle. Biblical counseling emerged as a stranger in a strange land.

Secular psychology dominated counseling, defining discourse about people and their problems. The social, behavioral, and medical sciences attained enormous social power, intellectual prestige, and self-confidence. As a result, the entire practice of counseling in the twentieth century became encircled by and permeated with secular versions of how to understand and help people. Various forms of psychotherapy—secular pastoral work—overwhelmed the biblical cure of souls; various theoretical psychologies—secular theologies—overwhelmed biblical understandings of human nature and functioning; various therapeutic institutions—secular church communities—overwhelmed the Church as the primary location for helping people with their troubles.

The most perceptive psychologists recognized and frankly stated what they were doing. Even Freud, contrary to most of his disciples, denied that the psychoanalyst's role was a distinctly medical role. He stated that the psychoanalyst was a "secular pastoral worker" and need not be a doctor.[8] For example, Freud's noted disciple Erik Erikson had his professional training in art! Carl Jung commented in similar fashion, "Patients force the psychotherapist into the role of a priest, and expect and demand of him that he shall free them from their distress. That is why we psychotherapists must occupy ourselves with problems which, strictly speaking, belong to the theologian."[9] B. F. Skinner's *Walden Two* consciously and specifically offers substitutes for the truths, techniques, and institutions

---

8. "The words 'secular pastoral worker' might well serve as a general formula for describing the function which the analyst, whether he is a doctor or a layman, has to perform in his relation to the public." Sigmund Freud, "The Question of Lay Analysis, Postscript," in *The Freud Reader,* ed. Peter Gay (New York: W. W. Norton, 1989), 682f.

9. Carl Jung, *Modern Man in Search of a Soul* (New York: Harcourt Brace Jovanovich, 1933), 241. The last two chapters of this book, "The Modern Spiritual Problem" and "Psychotherapists or Clergy," are telling. Jung views "neurosis" as a crisis in spiritual meaning, not a medical issue. Psychotherapy seeks to give meaning to life. Jung exhorts therapists: what will they do when they see that the patient's problems arise "from his having no love, but only sexuality; no faith, because he is afraid to grope in the dark; no hope, because he is disillusioned by the world and by life; and no understanding, because he has failed to read the meaning of his own existence?" (225f). The psychotherapist must embrace the task of providing love, faith, hope, and understanding to a secular people.

of the Christian faith. In fact, behavioral psychologists are the priest-equivalents in Skinner's heaven on earth.[10] The big circle of secular psychology posited a secular universe. The leading psychologists and psychiatrists were secular people who wanted to help secular people. It is no surprise that they offered a substitute religion, because the problems they dealt with were fundamentally religious.[11]

Unfortunately, the liberal churches were wedded to this psychotherapeutic revolution from its beginning—thus the development of the second circle: liberal pastoral theology. In their abandonment of biblical truth and authority, leaders within these churches looked to the social sciences to provide authority and efficacy. Harry Emerson Fosdick, whose theological liberalism was one trip wire for the fundamentalist-modernist splits of the 1920s, was—not by coincidence—simultaneously, a leader in the mental hygiene movement. Using his pulpit to expound a new psychotherapeutic version of Christianity, his psychologism was the flip side of his unbelief in the "fundamentals." The very idea of pastoral counseling was defined by liberal theology's integration of secular psychologists—especially Carl Rogers and Alfred Adler—from World War I into the 1960s.

In general, conservative Christians simply did not talk or write about counseling.[12] And when they did begin to think about and practice

---

10. B. F. Skinner, *Walden Two* (New York: MacMillan, 1948), 199.

11. Charles Rosenberg's seminal article in the history of psychiatry, "The Crisis in Psychiatric Legitimacy," deserves wider readership (in *American Psychiatry Past, Present, and Future*, ed. George Kriegman et al. [Charlottesville: University Press of Virginia, 1975], 135–148; reprinted in Charles Rosenberg, *Explaining Epidemics and Other Studies in the History of Medicine* [New York: Cambridge University Press, 1992]). Rosenberg notes, first, that psychiatry has been assigned and has assumed a huge social role—the varied ills of the human soul—but it has little real knowledge or efficacy to offer. Second, psychiatry depends on its medical identity for legitimacy, yet it is unable to provide either understanding or relief consistent with its pretensions to be a truly medical specialty. Third, psychiatry's most clearly medical activity—caring for patients with chronic organic syndromes in hospitals—is low status; high status psychiatry is precisely where it becomes the most philosophical, pastoral, and quasi-theological. "Much of our century's most influential psychiatric writing has consisted of general statements about the human condition" (142). Rosenberg accepts psychiatry's legitimacy almost by default; by and large there is no other framework of meaning because older religious values "seem no longer compelling to most Americans" (147). But for those who still find the older religious values compelling, who believe in the God and Father of Jesus Christ, the alternative to psychiatry is delightful!

12. See Holifield, *A History of Pastoral Care*. The book, as the subtitle reveals, is essentially the story of how a psychologized liberalism replaced orthodoxy. Holfield does not tip his own hand, but does make some provocative statements. For example, "When Harry Emerson Fosdick referred to the sermon as counseling on a large scale, he forgot that Protestant sermons, at their best, have interpreted an ancient text that resists reduction to the psychological" (356).

counseling, they adopted the powerful paradigms of the encircling secular psychologies and liberal pastoral theologies. The presuppositions for both practice and thought were neither exposed by nor subjected to biblical analysis. There was no attempt to build a biblical practical theology of counseling from the ground up. The big circle of secular psychology and psychotherapy was always the dominant partner in the discussions. Meanwhile, the middle-sized circle, an implicitly or explicitly liberal theology, was always tugging at evangelical thought and practice. Fuller Theological Seminary's Graduate School of Psychology (founded in 1965) exemplified the hold secular and liberalizing paradigms had on professing Bible-believers.[13]

THE REDISCOVERY OF BIBLICAL COUNSELING

Godly people, wise and experienced in living the Word, have applied God's Word to the problems of life in all times and places. In this sense, wherever wise Christians have sought to encourage and admonish one another, biblical counseling has occurred. Although truths that are not systematized are jeopardized, it is to God's praise that informal wisdom has always operated. God has always enabled wise pastors to approach their people with love and patience, and to open their Bibles to the right places to "comfort the disturbed and disturb the comfortable." In spite of the fact that the systematic approaches to counseling recorded in books and taught in classrooms during the twentieth century have not been biblically-based, there has been a rediscovery of biblical counseling. From the human point of view, that rediscovery is linked primarily to the life and efforts of one man: Jay E. Adams. He began to see, discuss, and do counseling in ways that he and others had not been seeing, discussing, or doing previously.

Jay Adams (b. 1929) grew up in Baltimore, the only child of a policeman and a secretary. Converted to Christ in high school, he obtained a Bachelor of Divinity from Reformed Episcopal Seminary (Philadelphia) and a Bachelor of Arts in classics from Johns Hopkins University (Baltimore) in 1952. Adams served as an area director of Youth for Christ in the early 1950s, was ordained in 1952, and over the next thirteen years pastored several Presbyterian congregations. He also received a Masters in Sacred Theology from Temple University (Philadelphia) in 1958 and a Ph.D. in speech from the University of Missouri in 1969. Bible, theology, Greek, and preaching formed the heart of his education. But as a

---

13. I have written at greater length elsewhere on the relationship between modern psychology and conservative Christianity. See David Powlison, "Integration or Inundation?" in *Power Religion*, ed. Michael Horton (Chicago: Moody, 1992), 191–218.

pastor, the problems of people's lives continually troubled and weighed on him. "It bothered Jay so much during those years that he never could help people with their problems. He'd say, 'Psychology is just as bad as the liberals. It isn't right and doesn't work. But how do you really help people?'"[14]

Adams continually sought to upgrade his counseling skills. He read voraciously from all three circles of counseling: the leading twentieth-century psychologists, the standard works in pastoral counseling (which mediated Carl Rogers through liberal or neo-orthodox theology), and Clyde Narramore and other evangelicals who had begun to publish from either a Freudian or an eclectic point of view. While at Temple, he took two courses in counseling with a psychiatrist of Freudian bent.[15] Adams was disappointed and frustrated with this training. Indeed, he felt it was full of theory-driven speculations, was ineffective in practice, and was contrary to basic biblical truths. The approaches offered did not make sense of people, they did not help people, and they were overtly unbiblical. He had no coherent alternative, but muddled along doing what little he could in pastoral counseling situations. Workshops for pastors, which were regularly sponsored by mental health agencies, reiterated the litany that the pastor should not attempt much but should "defer and refer" to secular mental health experts. The bottom line message to pastors was, "Leave things to the professionals. There is little you can do besides provide an accepting atmosphere for people. Troubled people are not violators of conscience but morally neutral victims of an accusing conscience. They need professional help. Pastors shouldn't do more than refer."[16] Such propaganda was intimidating to thousands of conservative pastors.

In 1963, Adams was invited to teach practical theology at Westminster Theological Seminary. His responsibilities focused on preaching but included a course in pastoral theology that contained a segment on pastoral counseling. This course raised the stakes. What should he teach? Adams happened to hear of psychologist O. Hobart Mowrer and went to hear him speak. That speech, Mowrer's book *The Crisis in Psychiatry and Religion,* (Princeton: Van Nostrand, 1961), and a six-week intensive course with Mowrer that summer had a catalytic effect on Adams. Mowrer "cleared the field of rubble for me. He destroyed Freud, which was the reigning system, and he shook

14. Betty Jane Adams, interview by author, 4 December 1990.

15. Jay Adams writes about this experience in *The Power of Error,* (Phillipsburg, N. J.: Presbyterian and Reformed, 1978).

16. Jay E. Adams's notes from a talk given by the chaplain at Marlboro State Hospital (New Jersey) in the mid-1960s.

up faith in mental health professionals. His positive system was completely unbiblical, but he gave me the confidence to go forward."[17] Mowrer shook loose the death grip of secular propaganda. This freed Adams to challenge the reigning psychological orthodoxy and to follow his nose biblically. As a result, Adams did intensive Bible study about the conscience, guilt, anthropology, and change. He describes the next two years as "night and day, counseling and studying: studying people, studying counseling books, studying the Bible."[18]

Adam's first rough outline of biblical counseling began to emerge during that small segment of the pastoral theology course. At first it was little more than "sin is the problem, the Bible has the answers," incorporating a few case studies. Problems were addressed on an *ad hoc* basis as they arose in counseling or from a study of Scripture. But by 1967 Adams's thinking about counseling had jelled into a system, and he expanded the counseling segment of the theology course into a counseling course. Then when he published his first book in 1970, Adams's personal rediscovery of biblical counseling initiated a widespread rediscovery for the entire Church.

Adams has written prolifically to create and develop a system of biblical counseling. He considers four of his books to be basic texts. *Competent to Counsel,* his first book, dropped a bombshell on the conservative Christian world. It was both polemical and positive. The polemics attacked the preeminence of pagan psychology and psychiatry in the field of counseling, and the positive methods set forth an ideal of "nouthetic confrontation."[19] Adams saw the Bible's way of counseling as radically dependent on the work of the Holy Spirit to apply the Word of God to people's lives: the promises

17. Jay E. Adams, interview by author, 4 December 1990.

18. Jay E. Adams, interview.

19. From the Greek word *nŏuthĕtéō*, literally "place in mind," which means reproof or admonishment or pointedly personal teaching. It is a word linked with bringing specific truth to bear on the details of an individual's life. It is associated with intense love: for example, Paul's "admonishing with tears" in Acts 20:31 and his "as my beloved sons I admonish you" in 1 Corinthians 4:14. It serves as a summary word for verbal edification: whether to one another ("competent to counsel one another," Rom. 15:14), or under pastoral authority (1 Thess. 5:12). It also summarizes the verbal aspects of a parent raising children (e.g., "bring them up in the admonition of the Lord," Eph. 6:4). *Nŏuthĕtéō* "holds hands" with both teaching and worship in Colossians 3:16, reinforcing the sense of the word as involving a *personal* application of God's truth, expressed in humility and tenderness and submission to God. Adams has been criticized for not picking *parakaléō*, which is more frequently used in the New Testament and is also a summary word for verbal edification (e.g., Heb. 3:13; 10:25). But as Adams has noted, the choice of words is indifferent—they can cover the same semantic field. Both words involve God's truth applied to lives, both words communicate love and concern, and both words communicate an appropriate directness and toughness.

encourage and empower, the commands convict and guide, and the stories make application. The Bible calls for human counselors to be frank, loving, humble about their own failings, and change-oriented. They are to be servants of the Holy Spirit's agenda, not autonomous professionals or gurus. In Adams's shorthand, nouthetic counseling is confrontation that is done out of concern for the purposes of changing something God wants to change.[20] That something can involve attitudes, beliefs, behavior, motives, decisions, and so forth.

Adams's second book, *The Christian Counselor's Manual,* fine-tunes the philosophy of biblical counseling and provides counseling methods, including a discussion on how to understand and solve particular problems. A third book, *Lectures on Counseling,* brings together a number of essays on foundational topics, and a fourth book, *More Than Redemption* (republished as *A Theology of Christian Counseling*), expands the systematic base of biblical counseling.

Throughout his prolific written works, Adams challenges biblical counselors not to fall prey to rigid ways of thinking or to mechanical techniques. He insists that counselors must do justice both to the fundamental commonalities and to the diverse particulars of counseling situations and life situations.

> "*Insight* into the inner workings of sinful human beings, into their outer circumstances and problems, and into the correct meaning and applicability of appropriate Bible passages is absolutely essential to counseling. Likewise, the importance of *creativity* cannot be minimized. It is creativity that particularizes the common, fitting together the usual and the unusual in each situation. Without it, people are crammed into molds they don't fit; rather, the truth must be adapted and applied (but not accommodated) to each person as he is."[21]

Not only did Adams write abundant resources for the development of biblical counseling, but he also pioneered settings where biblical counseling was the *modus operandi* and agenda. As noted above, his first rudimentary courses in biblical counseling took place at Westminster Theological Seminary in the mid-1960s. Though Adams left Westminster in 1976 to devote himself to research and writing, the program continued to develop under the leadership of Adams's colleague, John Bettler. A

---

20. Jay E. Adams, *Ready to Restore* (Phillipsburg, N. J.: Presbyterian and Reformed, 1981), 9–12.

21. Jay E. Adams, *Insight and Creativity in Christian Counseling: An Antidote to Rigid and Mechanical Approaches* (Grand Rapids: Zondervan, 1982).

residential Doctor of Ministry in Counseling was begun in 1980 with a dozen courses offered in biblical counseling. When the residential program was replaced by a modular program, most of the courses migrated into the regular Westminster curriculum as electives. A Master of Arts and Religion with a counseling major was begun in 1984.[22]

Adams was concerned for pastors, even more than for students who might one day become pastors. He felt pastors needed a site where counseling was taking place, where they could learn to counsel and then return to their congregations and communities. Thus in 1967, Adams and several associates made plans to develop a counseling center that would offer both counseling and a place for pastors to observe and train. These plans crystallized in 1968 when Adams and John Bettler began the Christian Counseling and Educational Foundation (CCEF) in Hatboro, Pennsylvania. Counseling was offered to needy people, and education was offered to would-be helpers of needy people. During the first course, trainees sat in on counseling sessions during the day and evening and then discussed cases over supper. In 1974, John Bettler became CCEF's director and first full-time employee. As CCEF continued to grow, counseling sites were opened in San Diego, California, and at several places in Pennsylvania and New Jersey. The CCEF faculty currently teaches courses at Westminster Theological Seminary and Biblical Theological Seminary.[23]

As biblical-nouthetic counseling gained adherents, the need for a professional association became evident. Concerns for the growing group of practitioners included certification for biblical counselors, accountability for standards of biblical commitment and ethics, fellowship and interaction among biblical counselors, ongoing in-service training, and protection from lawsuits. To meet these and other needs, Adams joined with several men to found the National Association of Nouthetic Counselors (NANC) in 1976. Today, NANC publishes a quarterly newsletter, *The Biblical Counselor,* and coordinates a large annual conference.[24]

Adams also wanted a forum where ideas could be shared and discussed, and where writers could try their wings. So in 1977 he founded *The Journal of Pastoral Practice,* published through CCEF. As JPP's editor for

---

22. Westminster Theological Seminary, P. O. Box 27009, Philadelphia, Pennsylvania 19118.

23. Christian Counseling and Educational Foundation, 1803 East Willow Grove Avenue, Laverock, Pennsylvania 19118.

24. National Association of Nouthetic Counselors, 5526 State Road 26 East, Lafayette, Indiana 47905.

the next fifteen years, his purpose was to develop a journal that would ad-here to scholarly standards but would be "intensely practical" and would meet "the needs of men serving in the pastoral ministry."[25] This journal embodied a unique vision in at least three respects. First, counseling was not isolated from the rest of pastoral practice: preaching, Christian educa-tion, missions, worship, evangelism. The mere act of embedding private ministry in the context of a comprehensive vision counteracts the com-mon vision of counseling as discrete from the rest of the ministry of the Word of God. Second, the counseling articles (and counseling articles al-ways constituted the bulk of the journal's contents) took a distinctively biblical point of view. Third, the journal sought to be practical. It sought to address and influence practice, not simply theology or theory. In 1992 the name of the journal was changed to *The Journal of Biblical Counseling*. The concern to meet the needs of pastors has continued but has broad-ened to include the needs of trained lay people who seek to counsel biblically.[26]

Jay Adams, his writings, and the institutions he founded have led to a proliferation of biblical counseling ministries and training centers both in the United States and abroad. For example, a growing ministry for training lay people grew out of lectures Adams gave in Washington, D.C. (1973) when John Broger, a Christian layman active in ministry in the Pentagon, had a deep concern that discipleship address and solve the counseling issues in people's lives. He took Adams's materials and in 1974 founded the Biblical Counseling Foundation (BCF), which continues to grow as a ministry that trains lay people and pastors in discipleship meth-ods largely flavored by biblical counseling.[27]

Various local churches have founded biblical counseling ministries, taking many different forms: formal or informal, pastor or lay, focusing on congregational needs or reaching out to the community. Particularly note-worthy is Faith Baptist Church in Lafayette, Indiana. This church has founded a thriving counseling center and built church life around the con-cepts of progressive sanctification and mutual counsel that are at the heart of biblical counseling. Faith Baptist Counseling Ministries (FBCM) was started in 1977 by Rev. Bill Goode and Dr. Bob Smith. It has grown to

---

25. Jay E. Adams, *Journal of Pastoral Practice* 1, no. 1 (1977): 1.

26. *The Journal of Biblical Counseling*, 1803 East Willow Grove Avenue, Laverock, Pennsylvania 19118.

27. Biblical Counseling Foundation, P. O. Box 925, Rancho Mirage, California 92270.

offer training throughout the Midwest. Bill Goode has been the executive director of NANC since 1988, and FBCM has thus served as the location for the NANC offices. Faith Baptist Church has hosted the NANC national conference several times in recent years.[28]

The biblical counseling agenda has also become established in The Master's College and The Master's Seminary in California. In the late 1980s, John MacArthur and his co-laborers turned their attention closely to the issues of biblical counseling and secular psychology. They restructured the curriculum at both undergraduate and seminary levels to reflect a commitment to use biblical truth to explain people's needs and to offer them help. Two of Jay Adams's longstanding associates, Bob Smith (from FBCM) and Wayne Mack (from CCEF) have been instrumental in designing and building the program.[29]

The notion of doing distinctively biblical counseling has also been planted in a number of countries around the world. Whenever and wherever Christians counsel wisely in obedience to the Scriptures, biblical counseling happens, whether it is so titled or not. But it is a great advantage to identify self-consciously what one aims to do and to rally like-minded believers to the cause. For this reason, there are nascent biblical counseling movements in Germany, Switzerland, Great Britain, and South Africa, taking the form of associations and/or counseling and training centers.

QUESTIONS FOR THE TWENTY-FIRST CENTURY

One of the results of tracing the rediscovery of biblical counseling has been the challenge to think towards the future. Church history bears testimony to the uncertain fortunes of ministries and movements. Some thrive. Some miscarry early on. Some grow, then collapse. Some prosper awhile and then stagnate. Some go soft and drift into compromise. Some go the other way, becoming sectarian and self-righteous. Some are renewed when things look bleak. Some go off the tracks into error or irrelevancy. How can biblical counseling continue to grow in wisdom and stature as it faces the challenges of the future? Without doubt the biblical counseling

---

28. Faith Baptist Counseling Ministry, 5526 State Road 26 East, Lafayette, Indiana 47905.

29. The Master's College, 21726 West Placerita Canyon Road, P. O. Box 221450, Santa Clarita, California 91322-1450. The Master's Seminary, 13248 Roscoe Blvd., Sun Valley, California 91353.

movement faces three fundamental tasks through the 1990s and into the next century: (1) the task of defining, (2) the task of edifying, and (3) the task of evangelizing.

The Task of Defining

How will biblical counseling be defined? A creedal circle needs to be drawn delineating the boundaries of a biblical counseling confession of faith and practice. What commitments and practices mark one as a biblical counselor? What commitments and practices mark one as some other sort of counselor? Why does this next decade demand creedal development? Defining the boundaries is important for three reasons.

First, through the first twenty-five years of development Jay Adams's personal influence and his network of friendships provided a rough guide to the definition of biblical counseling. But the movement is growing rapidly, and the next generation will not necessarily know Jay Adams personally. The content of an allegiance to the biblical counseling vision and cause must be more precisely defined. Creedal definition and consolidation is a necessary phase of any healthy movement of reformation in the Church.

Second, the integration movement of Christian psychotherapists increasingly employs the adjective "biblical" and calls for theological renewal within their point of view. While we applaud any genuine increase of biblical consciousness and practice among integrationists, it remains to be seen whether the increase in Bible talk, God talk, and Jesus talk represents a substantive shift. In the meantime, the higher degree of verbal similarity between integrationist and biblical counseling has the potential to confuse many. Defining core biblical commitments will help weed out the theories and practices that claim to be biblical but deviate substantively from the Bible's teachings about people, about change, and about ministry.

Third, the biblical counseling movement from the beginning has pulled together an otherwise diverse group of Christians. We have never been monolithic, but have embraced Bible-believers of many shades: reformed, fundamentalist, evangelical. The founders and developers of biblical counseling have held diverse opinions on many specific counseling issues, as well as wider theological issues. What has held the movement together has been the judgment that these differences were secondary differences of application or emphasis, not matters of core commitment. Nailing down the primary areas of agreement becomes increasingly important as the movement expands. One way to phrase the boundary question is, "What is the size of the teapot within which there are allowable tempests?" Defining primary areas of agreement creates the freedom for the iron-sharpening-iron discussion of differences. The alternatives are either fragmentation or drift.

What are the common commitments? What are the rudiments of biblical counseling? Every reader of the Scriptures and of Adams's efforts to systematize the Scriptures would generate a slightly different list. Here we will highlight seven core elements that Adams rediscovered, articulated, and defended.

1. **God is at the center of counseling.** God is sovereign, active, speaking, merciful, commanding, powerful. The Lord and Savior, Jesus Christ, is the central focus of counseling and the exemplar of the Wonderful Counselor. The Word of God and the work of the Holy Spirit are foundational to all significant and lasting life change. The Word of God is about counseling, giving both understanding of people and methods of ministering to people. The Bible is authoritative, relevant, and comprehensively sufficient for counseling. God has spoken truly to every basic issue of human nature and to the problems in living. His Word establishes the goal of counseling, how people can change, the role of the counselor, counseling methods, and so forth. Christians have the only authoritative source for counseling wisdom: the Holy Spirit speaking through the Word of God. The fear of the Lord is the beginning of wisdom, and wisdom is the only worthy goal of counseling.

2. **Commitment to God has epistemological consequences.** First, other sources of knowledge must be submitted to the authority of Scripture. The sciences, personal experience, literature, and so forth may be useful, but may not play a constitutive role in counseling. Second, there is a conflict of counsel built into human life. Genesis 3, Psalm 1, and Jeremiah 23 are paradigmatic. Counsel that contradicts God's counsel has existed since the garden of Eden, challenging God's counsel and building from other presuppositions and towards other goals. Such false counsel must be noted and opposed. In particular, in our time and place, secular psychology has intruded into the domain of biblical truth and practice. Secular theories and therapies substitute for biblical wisdom and deceive people both inside and outside the Church. The false claimants to authority must be exposed and opposed.

3. **Sin, in all its dimensions** (e.g., both motive and behavior; both the sins we do and the sins done against us; both the consequences of personal sin and the consequences of Adams's sin) **is the primary problem counselors must deal with.** Sin includes wrong behavior, distorted thinking, an orientation to follow personal desires, and bad attitudes.

Sin is habitual and deceptive, and much of the difficulty of counseling consists in bringing specific sin to awareness and breaking its hold. The problems in living that necessitate counseling are not matters of unmet psychological needs, indwelling demons of sin, poor socialization, inborn temperament, genetic predisposition, or anything else that removes attention from the responsible human being. The problem in believers is remnant sin; the problem in unbelievers is reigning sin. Sin is the problem.

4. **The gospel of Jesus Christ is the answer.** Forgiveness for sin and power to change into Christ's image are the greatest needs of mankind. The orthodox gospel of Jesus Christ is the answer to the problem. Christ deals with sin: the guilt, the power, the deception, and the misery of sin. He was crucified for sinners, He reigns over hearts by the power of the Holy Spirit, and He will return to complete the redemption of His people from their sins and sufferings. These core truths must infuse the counseling process.

5. **The change process counseling must aim at is progressive sanctification.** While there are many ways of changing people, biblical counseling aims for nothing less than transformation into the image of Jesus Christ amid the rough and tumble of daily life. Change is not instantaneous, but progresses throughout life. This progressive view of sanctification has many implications. For example, the process of change is only metaphorically, not actually, healing. The metaphor is meant to capture the process of sanctification: ongoing repentance, renewal of mind unto biblical truth, and obedience in the power of the Spirit.

6. **The situational difficulties people face are not the random cause of problems in living.** These difficulties operate within the sovereign design of God. They are the context in which hearts are revealed, and faith and obedience are purified through the battle between the Spirit and the flesh. Influential aspects of one's life situation do not cause sin. Heredity, temperament, personality, culture, oppression and evil, bereavement, handicaps, old age, Satan, physical illness, and so forth are significant for counseling but are not ultimately causative of sin.

7. **Counseling is fundamentally a pastoral activity and must be church-based.** It must be regulated under the authority of God's appointed under-shepherds. Counseling is connected both structurally and in content to other aspects of the pastoral task: teaching, preaching, prayer, church discipline, use of gifts, missions, worship, and so forth. Counseling is the private ministry of the Word of God, tailored specifically to the individu-

als involved. The differences between preaching and counseling are not conceptual but only methodological. The same truths are applied in diverse ways.

These seven commitments have unified the biblical counseling movement. They have provided a framework within which many secondary differences—of Bible interpretation, of theological commitment, of setting for counseling, of personality—have been able to exist constructively rather than destructively. But there are numerous other issues that demand clear biblical thinking and firm commitment: the place of the past, the place of feelings, the biblical view of human motivation, the relationship of biblical truth to secular psychology, the place of suffering, how to apply various aspects of biblical truth and methods of biblical ministry to different kinds of problems, etc. Will biblical counselors draw the boundaries in the right places? Or will the lines be drawn too narrowly, creating a sectarian party spirit? Or will the lines be drawn too widely, inviting compromise and drift? Only within properly drawn creedal boundaries can energies for edification and evangelization be guided and released.

The Task of Edifying

How will biblical counselors develop greater skill in the cure of souls? How will we become wiser practitioners, thinkers, apologists, and Christian men and women? The task of edifying biblical counselors demands advances that are both exegetically sound and case-tried. It demands that we think well about many issues. One of the often ignored aspects of Jay Adams's work has been his repeated observation that his work is a starting place, and that much work remains to be done to build on the foundation.

Biblical counseling has been rediscovered. But perhaps it is more accurate to say that the *idea* of biblical counseling and the *call* to do biblical counseling have been rediscovered. This has brought into focus many fresh discoveries and new insights into the cure of souls. For example, the concern to specify counseling methodology (e.g., techniques of asking questions, building relationships, setting goals, speaking the truth, using homework, etc.) has produced helpful developments. And the concern to translate general biblical truths into a specific renewal of both inward and outward life (Rom. 13:12–14), tailor-made both to the counselee and the life situation, is refreshingly new. Will biblical counseling continue to develop intellectually and practically?[30] Or will we stagnate and turn yester-day's breakthroughs into tomorrow's formulaic-truisms and techniques?

The Task of Evangelizing

How will biblical counselors propagate the cause of biblical coun-seling? The task of persuasion must be undertaken with three distinct groups of people: (1) the great bulk of the believing Church, both in the United States and internationally; (2) the integrationist community here in the United States and abroad; and (3) the members of the secular psy-chological culture. Many people remain ignorant of the existence of biblical counseling, while others dismiss it on the basis of a caricature that bears no resemblance to anything the Bible teaches or anything wise counselors think and do. Biblical counseling needs evangelists and apolo-gists with sensitivities and passions for each of these communities. We have answers people need; answers that are better than those they have. Biblical counselors must think well, pray pointedly, and discuss actively to develop energetic and creative apologetic and evangelistic efforts to help people find these answers.

---

30. See D. Powlison, "Crucial Issues in Contemporary Biblical Counseling," *Journal of Pastoral Practice* 9, no. 3 (1988): 53–78, for specific areas with a growing edge.

Part II

The Theological Foundations of Biblical Counseling

4

The Scriptures and Biblical Counseling

Douglas Bookman

Epistemology is defined as "an inquiry into the nature and source of knowledge, the bounds of knowledge, and the justification of claims to knowledge."[1] It is the final element of that definition that is at stake here, the investigation into the broad and foundational question: "How do we *know* that what we *think* we know is in fact *true*?"

Any Christian who sets out to counsel another individual is aware that the counsel offered must be true. Counseling is by definition and impulse a helping ministry. It assumes one individual who is confronted with some measure of confusion, disappointment, or despair and a second person who endeavors to help by analyzing the counselee's situation, sorting out the issues involved, and then offering helpful and healing advice and direction. But the efficacy of all that any counselor undertakes to do is dependent at least on this one thing: that the analysis and counsel is true. Thus, any thoughtful consideration of the ministry of counseling must begin with the most basic of all philosophical questions, that question articulated by a Roman procurator two thousand years ago, "What is truth?"

Ever since its genesis as a distinguishable discipline almost four decades ago, the school of thought and ministry broadly known as Christian Psychology has been convulsed by the issue of its own epistemological

---

1. Paul Feinberg, "Epistemology," in *The Evangelical Dictionary of Theology* (Grand Rapids: Baker, 1984), 359.

construct. (That is, where should/can Christians go to find the *truth* necessary to help people who are hurting?) Because this discipline developed largely within the boundaries of evangelical Christianity, there has been a universal acknowledgement of the veracity of Jesus' answer to the question of truth when, as He addressed His heavenly Father in prayer, He stated simply, "Thy Word is truth."

But for most that answer alone does not suffice. The persuasion continues—articulated, justified, and applied in various ways—that there is truth that is at least profitable and perhaps even necessary to the counseling effort. This truth is to be discovered beyond the pages of Scripture. Counselors who are thus persuaded are anxious to affirm Jesus' simple but profound declaration, yet they feel compelled to qualify that affirmation with the proposition that Scriptural truths may (or even must) be supplemented by truths that have been discovered by human investigation and observation. This persuasion lies at the very heart of the integrationist impulse of Christian psychology.[2]

By all accounts, this integrationist tendency is rather recent in origin.[3] Throughout much of the twentieth century a spirit of mutual mistrust and even contempt existed between the worlds of secular psychology and Christian theology. But that hostility began to thaw in certain circles sometime in the middle of this century,[4] and by this last decade of the twentieth century there exists an obvious attitude of reconciliation

---

2. The term *integration*, used to denote the effort to define the relationship between theology and psychology and the limits to which the two may or may not be understood in concert with one another, is not entirely satisfactory, but it has become the term of choice in virtually every discussion of that issue. Fleck and Carter discuss the implications and delimitations of the term carefully, acknowledging that it is rather arbitrary and can be misunderstood, that there have been attempts to displace the term (with words such as synthesis or psychotheology), but that with proper qualifications it is the term that serves the most effectively and is employed almost universally. J. Roland Fleck and John D. Carter, eds., *Psychology and Christianity: Integrative Readings* (Nashville: Abingdon, 1981), 16. Compare J. Harold Ellens' rather acerbic critique of the term in "Biblical Themes in Psychological Theory and Practice," *Journal of Psychology and Christianity* 6, no.2 (1980): 2.

3. Fleck and Carter, in their introduction to *Psychology*, stress that "relating Christianity to the thought forms and intellectual understandings of a society and culture is not new at all," but that "the integration of Christianity and psychology is very new. In fact, it is almost totally post-World War II, with most of the substantive work done in the last fifteen years" (15). Further, they observe that "one reason for the newness of integration with psychology is obviously that psychology itself is still quite young as a science, its birth customarily dated from the founding of a laboratory by Wundt in 1879" (15).

4. In 1984, D. G. Benner wrote, "The last two decades have seen an enormous thawing in the climate of mistrust between Christianity and psychology." "Psychology and Christianity" in *Evangelical Dictionary of Theology*, ed. Elwell (Grand Rapids: Baker, 1984), 893.

between Christianity and psychology in many quarters. Indeed, many devotees of Christian psychology evidence a greater measure of fraternity with the secular psychological community than with those Christians who are compelled by their theology to reject the discipline of secular psychotherapy.[5]

Few would suggest, however, that this cordial and accepting spirit is evidence that the work of integration has been accomplished to everyone's—indeed, to anyone's—satisfaction.[6] In fact, the recurring theme in Christian psychological literature is that integration is a circle yet to be squared. The philosophical commitment to integration is unabated, and every integrationist model proceeds upon the assumption that in some sense and to some degree that task has been at least provisionally accomplished. Yet the task of integrating orthodox Christian theology with secular psychology, a task embarked upon with such heady optimism some twenty years ago, has proven itself disturbingly formidable. It is a Gordian knot yet untied.

The purpose of this chapter is to challenge certain working principles that impact evangelical attempts to integrate psychology and theology. However, it is necessary first of all to identify and define phases of the integration effort. We need to develop a workable integration model that honors our commitment to Scripture as well as our commitment to

---

5. Compare Ellens' characterization of those who reject integration as invalid. In his critique of the term *integration* he states that the term unfortunately implies "at its base the essentially American-Fundamentalist notion that truth comes only through the Christian Scripture, by the special revealing action of the Holy Spirit of God." He goes on to aver that "[t]hat notion is a residuum of 'Old-Time Fundamentalism' in the schizophrenic way it sets the natural and supernatural worlds at odds, the apocalyptic way it demarcates the domain of God and of the demonic, and the pagan suggestion that lies at the bottom of this dichotomy, i.e., that God does not live here but must invade alien territory to enter the domain of 'this world' and its scientific truth." Ellens, "Biblical Themes," 2.

6. To be sure, there are individuals who have struggled with the issue of integrating Christianity and psychology and are personally satisfied that they have produced an epistemological construct that suffices, at least for their own purposes. But each of these constructs is widely criticized and corrected by others within the community, and most of those constructs are acknowledged to be partial and even tentative. Further, the work of integrating any system of thought as multifaceted as Christian psychology with its counterpart in the secular world (which counterpart will be only more free-form given that it is not bounded by the delimiting factors native to biblical Christianity) is by definition a perpetually unfinished business. So this statement is not intended to be negatively critical. It simply needs to be affirmed that within the Christian psychological community the cart (models of counseling) has sometimes been allowed to run rather ahead of the horse (the epistemological construct that validates and controls the integrating impulse).

help people in the most effective way possible. Table 1 suggests such a model to properly relate theology and psychology.[7]

Table 1. A Suggested Construct for Building an Integrationist Model

THE BROAD ISSUE

How can the individual who is committed to the Bible as the Word of God, and who is determined to help people as effectively as possible (and who suspects that there is some help to be found in the discipline of secular psychology) fashion a working schema of integration that will honor both an allegiance to Scripture and a commitment to help others?

THE NECESSARY AND INTERDEPENDENT CONSTITUENT ISSUES
(To be read from the bottom up)

Phase Two: The Procedural Question

Issue Number Three: How are theology and psychology best integrated?

(This is a methodological issue. This question should only be addressed after the first two questions have both been answered affirmatively. This is where almost all of the integrationist work is being done today).

■ Waterline ■

Phase One: The Possibility Question

Issue Number Two: Should theology and psychology be integrated?

(This is an ethical issue. Not all things that can be done should be done. Is there any way in which the intrinsic virtue[s] and/or merit[s] of one discipline would be compromised or jeopardized by admixture with the other? Again, is there any intrinsic need or deficiency in theology that psychology can ameliorate? This question is moot unless the first question be answered in the affirmative.)

Issue Number One: Can theology and psychology be integrated?

(This is an ontological issue. That is, is there anything in the essence of theology that makes it constitutionally incompatible with psychology, or vice versa?)

Notice that this construct posits two phases in the integrating effort. Phase one deals with the possibility question; that is, is there any possibility that an adequate integrating model can be developed; if so, is there ethical justification for doing so? Phase two addresses the procedural question: given that it can be done, how is it best done?

Notice also that this construct is designed to emphasize that these constituent issues must be answered in a logical order. In fact, the arrangement in the table is intended to emphasize that the question that most immediately suggests itself in the discussion of integration is the third one, the one that is above the waterline. Yet it is invalid to address the third question without first settling the issues of the two questions below the waterline.

The evangelical community has produced an intimidating body of literature intended to defend the proposition that the integration of psychology and theology is at once virtuous and possible, and to define how that integration is best accomplished without emerging the two more foundational issues.[8] A survey of that literature suggests that three basic

---

7. Throughout this chapter the term *psychology* will be used with a deliberately narrow connotation, namely the talk therapy (or psychotherapy) that is intrinsic to models of counseling embraced within the Christian psychological community. This is not to suggest that the term *psychology* does not have a broader significance, or that the criticisms leveled herein would apply with equal force or legitimacy to all aspects of that broader discipline. But in the integrationist literature the term is used consistently with the narrower significance of talk therapy as employed in personal counseling, and thus for ease of understanding the same term will be employed here.

8. One of the most significant and seminal individual attempts to produce an integrative construct is that of G. R. Collins, *The Rebuilding of Psychology: An Integration of Psychology and Theology* (Wheaton: Tyndale, 1977). Collins focuses upon the worldview and presuppositions that prevail in secular psychology; he attempts to displace or amend those with elements of a thoroughly Christian worldview, thus redeeming the discipline from its own destructive foundation. For an early survey from within the Christian psychological community of the efforts to define a workable model of integration, see J. D. Carter, "Secular and Sacred Models of Psychology and Religion," *Journal of Psychology and Theology* 5 (1977): 197–208. Carter reduces the models of integration to four, differentiated primarily to the degree that they presume an intrinsic and implacable antagonism between the worldviews and/or the goals of secular psychology versus orthodox Christian theology. The *Journal of Psychology and Theology* is subtitled "An Evangelical Forum for the Integration of Psychology and Theology," and no issue is more often revisited in its pages than that of integration. An article entitled "The Popularity of Integration Models, 1980–1985," (16, no. 1 [1988]: 3–14) calculated that 43 percent of the articles published during that period (76 of 177 articles) addressed the issue. The entire Spring issue (8, no. 1 [1980]) is given to an assessment of the progress of the integrating efforts from the inception of the journal in 1973 to the date of that issue. Further, the collection of essays edited by Fleck and Carter, *Psychology*, is very helpful, although one is perhaps most struck by the variety of models suggested and the manifest dissonance between many of them. *Wholehearted Integration: Harmonizing Psychology and Christianity Through Word and Deed*, by Kirk E. Farnsworth (Grand Rapids:

approaches prevail in the effort to integrate psychology and theology. In the balance of this chapter we will consider each of those approaches.[9] Our study will be based on a twofold perception: (1) every one of the three approaches that are fundamental to the integrationist apologetic is seriously flawed in its validity and in its relevance to the issues at hand; and (2) in spite of those perceived weaknesses many in the evangelical world have embraced one of these as a sufficient rationale for the notion that the Scriptures alone are insufficient to help people who are hurting. Surely such a notion is not to be lightly embraced. The arguments appealed to in defense of that notion need to be carefully scrutinized.

THE TWO-BOOK APPROACH: CONFUSED AND DESTRUCTIVE

The fallacy of these approaches relates to issues one and two in table 1: Can and should theology and psychology be integrated? Among those integrationists who confess a high view of Scripture, this specific claim functions more often than all others as the fundamental apologetic for an affirmative reply to both of those issues. Indeed, this reply is so often and confidently asserted that it has taken upon itself the identity of an axiom: a truth so unassailable and self-evident as to demand only that it be expressed, never reasoned or defended. In reality, this truth-claim is the foundation upon which the evangelical superstructure of integration has been erected.

The Argument Identified

The two-book fallacy may be reduced to the following propositions:

Baker, 1985) has functioned as a watershed of sorts in the effort to define a workable schema for integration as well as to categorize the attempts. See also Larry Crabb, *Understanding People* (Grand Rapids: Zondervan, 1987), 25–73 for an attempt to produce an integrative model that honors a high view of Scripture. A more recent extensive attempt at an integrationist construct from a committed evangelical perspective is Stanton L. Jones and Richard E. Butman, *Modern Psycho-Therapies: A Comprehensive Christian Appraisal* (Downers Grove: InterVarsity, 1991). The most important critique of the integrationist effort by one not within the fold is that of David Powlison, "Integration or Inundation?" in *Power Religion*, ed. M. S. Horton (Chicago: Moody, 1992), 191–218. Also important is Powlison's "Which Presuppositions? Secular Psychology and the Categories of Biblical Thought," *Journal of Psychology and Theology* 12, no. 4 (1984): 270–78.

9. In the interest of integrity and fraternity, it is appropriate to acknowledge both the limitations of my expertise as author and the tentative character of this critique. I harbor no illusion that the questions and difficulties surrounding the integrationist effort will be solved in these pages. I am persuaded, however, that these three demand to be reexamined, along with the conclusion that is drawn from them.

The Axiomatic Assertion:
All truth is God's truth.

The Theological Formulation:
God has made Himself known via two channels: special revelation and general revelation.

Special revelation is the propositional truth recorded in Scripture.

General revelation is nonpropositional truth deposited by God in the created order of things. It must be investigated and discovered by mankind.

The Epistemological Conclusion:
Although the two channels of truth are distinguishable, both are in fact revelatory; thus truth accurately derived from the consideration of the natural order of things (general revelation) is just as true as that derived from Scripture.

The Integrationist Ramification:
Any defensible truth that is derived by means of psychological research into the order of humanity is truth derived from general revelation, thus truth derived from God, and thus truth as dependable and authoritative as truth exegeted from Scripture.

Consider just a sampling of the expressions of this basic apologetic element by integrationist theorists. James D. Guy, Jr., states,

> If integration is conceptualized as the search for truth concerning human nature, and God is identified as the source of this truth, the next logical issue involves the revelation of this truth. It has traditionally been held that God reveals this truth to us through both general and special revelation, with both nature and the Bible serving as expressions or representations of this truth. The disciplines of psychology and theology are attempts to discover and systematize truth by means of the study of the natural sciences and biblical revelation.[10]

Again, Fleck and Carter are quite explicit in this regard.

> Since God is the creator of the universe, all principles and laws have their origin in him. What is often called "nature" in science or philosophy is in reality God's creation. As his creation, nature and its laws reveal the Creator. Hence, theologians have referred to the picture of God in nature as general revelation because nature reveals God

---

10. James D. Guy, Jr., "The Search for Truth in the Task of Integration," *Journal of Psychology and Theology* 8, no. 1 (Spring, 1980): 28.

as a powerful and orderly creator. On the other hand, God is revealed in the Scripture and in Jesus Christ in a special way, i.e., special or particular details about God's person, nature, and his plan for human life and its relationship with him are revealed in Scripture. Hence, theologians refer to Scripture as special revelation.[11]

R. L. Timpe lays the same foundational rationale for the integration of theology and psychology.

> The task of integration involves an explicit relating of truth gleaned from general or natural revelation to that derived from special or biblical revelation, of interrelating knowledge gained from the world and knowledge gained from the Word. . . . The integration movement offers a rapprochement by proposing the adoption of two premises: 1) God is the source of all truth no matter *where* it is found; 2) God is the source of all truth no matter *how* it is found.
>
> To the integrationist, natural revelation supports special revelation instead of being a rival methodology. That is, if God is consistent (i.e., immutable) as the Scriptures suggest (e.g., Mal. 3:6), then knowledge based in revelation should parallel and complement that derived from reason. Both will complement that founded in replication and observation. Underlying this approach is a faith statement common to scientist and theologian alike: the laws that govern the operation of the world are discoverable.[12]

In the same vein, Ellens criticizes the "essentially American Fundamentalist notion that truth comes only through the Christian Scriptures"

---

11. Fleck and Carter, introduction in *Psychology*, 18.

12. R. L. Timpe, "Christian Psychology" in *Baker Encyclopedia of Psychology*, ed. David G. Benner (Grand Rapids: Baker, 1985), 166 (emphasis original). The implication seems to be that those who reject the validity of the integrationist effort would also reject the two rather tautological premises, evidently because of a suspicion that findings of "truth" by the methodologies of natural science would not "support special revelation." The notion seems to be that to deny that "knowledge gained from the world" can possess intrinsic authority tantamount to that of "knowledge gained from the Word" is also to question whether "the laws that govern the operation of the world are discoverable." This is, very frankly, a canard that only muddies the water in the current debate. In an unpublished paper read at a regional meeting of the Evangelical Theological Association in 1991, John H. Coe takes the charge a step further, arguing that the nonintegrationist fails in a stewardship God has given mankind to derive authoritative truth from nature, a stewardship reflected in the Old Testament sage's analysis of the natural order of things ("Educating the Church for Wisdom's Sake, or Why Biblical Counseling is Unbiblical," unpublished paper by John H. Coe, 1991).

because he feels it "devalues God's General Revelation in the world studied by the natural and social sciences" and thus "suggests that science, our reading of God's book in nature, is at war with the Christian Religion, our reading of God's other book, the Scriptures." Later in the same article Ellens avers,

> Theology and Psychology are both sciences in their own right, stand legitimately on their own foundations, read carefully are the two books of God's Revelation. They are not alien in any inherent sense. . . .
> Wherever *truth* is disclosed it is always *God's truth*. Whether it is found in General Revelation or Special Revelation, it is *truth* which has equal warrant with all other *truth*. Some truth may have greater weight than other *truth* in a specific situation, but there is no difference in its warrant as *truth*.[13]

Citations might be multiplied almost endlessly, but perhaps these will suffice to demonstrate the nature and importance of this specific rationale.[14]

The Argument Critiqued

The general revelation versus special revelation argument is appealed to in the integrationist epistemological construct to support the proposition

13. Ellens, "Biblical Themes," 2 (emphasis original). Ellens is actually criticizing the term *integration* here because he thinks the term suggests such a dichotomy. The canard only hinted at by Timpe (see former note) is by Ellens explicitly and caustically laid against all nonintegrationists. Of Jay E. Adams, Ellens remarks: "He apparently never even thought of the notion that all truth as God's truth, has equal warrant, whether truth from nature or scripture." Such a charge is simply ludicrous. Adams has written at copious lengths about this specific issue. (For a recent reference to the issue, see Adams' "Counseling and the Sovereignty of God," *The Journal of Biblical Counseling* 11, no. 2 [Winter, 1993]: 6.) But notice how, in the mind of Ellens, this rationale has attained the status of a first truth; if a person does not submit to its validity and its ramifications, it can only be because that person "never even thought of the notion"; the possibility that the notion is rejected because of a perceived flaw is not even entertained.

14. It is interesting to see the same perceived fallacy involved in integrative efforts not immediately related to psychology/theology. For instance, in building a case for integrating faith and learning in Christian higher education, Kenneth Gangel speaks of "natural revelation—science, mathematics, literature, music, etc." and goes on to say, "Many Christians tend to think of natural revelation only as the study of God's creation, but in reality all beauty is God's beauty just as all truth is God's truth." He distinguishes that category of "natural revelation" from "Special Revelation: Bible/Theology." "Integrating Faith and Learning: Principles and Process," *Bibliotheca Sacra* (April–June 1978): 102. This is not meant as a criticism of the point being made in the article; it is simply to state that this fallacious definition of the theological concept of general revelation invades other disciplines as well.

that integration can and should be done. However, that argument is crippled by the fact that the definition of general revelation, which is so foundational to the argument erected upon the term, is confused and erroneous on two counts: it misdefines the term *revelation*, and it misdefines the term *general*.

The term "revelation" is misdefined. This argument is flawed because it neglects the biblical concept that revelation is by definition nondiscoverable by human investigation or cogitation.

This is the teaching of Scripture regarding God's communication of truth, which we know as revelation (Isa. 55:9; 1 Cor. 2:11–14; 1 Tim. 6:15, 16; 2 Pet. 1:19–21), and that teaching has been acknowledged and cherished by evangelical theologians. Chafer distinguishes sharply between reason and revelation, asserting that "revelation by its nature transcends the human capacity to discover and is a direct communication from God concerning truths which no person could discover by himself."[15] Erickson succinctly defines revelation as "[t]he making known of that which is unknown; the unveiling of that which is veiled." Bancroft characterizes revelation as "that act of God by which He communicates to the mind of man truth not known before and incapable of being discovered by the mind of man unaided." Thiessen emphasizes that same element of revelation in his definition: "By revelation we mean that act of God whereby He discloses Himself or communicates truth to the mind; whereby He makes manifest to His creatures that which could not be known in any other way." Unger emphasizes this matter as well, characterizing the term "revelation" as "expressive of the fact that God has made known to men truths and realities which men could not discover for themselves." And Pache labors to make the point that "revelation is of necessity an act of God."[16]

---

15. Lewis S. Chafer, *Systematic Theology: Abridged Edition*, ed. John F. Walvoord (Wheaton: Victor, 1988), 1:63. Notice that revelation as being discussed here is a theological concept that "covers the semantic breadth of numerous biblical terms." Clark H. Pinnock, *Biblical Revelation* (Chicago: Moody, 1971), 29. B. B. Warfield discusses the range of terms in *The Inspiration and Authority of the Bible* (Philadelphia: Presbyterian and Reformed, 1948), 97–101. See also Bernard Ramm, *Special Revelation and the Word of God* (Grand Rapids: Eerdmans, 1961), 161ff.

16. Millard J. Erickson, *Concise Dictionary of Christian Theology* (Grand Rapids: Baker, 1986), 143; Emery H. Bancroft, *Christian Theology* (Grand Rapids: Zondervan, 1955), 35; Henry C. Thiessen, *Introductory Lectures in Systematic Theology* (Grand Rapids: Eerdmans, 1949), 31; M. F. Unger, "Revelation" in *Unger's Bible Dictionary* (Chicago: Moody, 1957), 922; and Rene Pache, *The Inspiration and Authority of Scripture*, trans. Helen I. Needham (Chicago: Moody, 1969), 13. Admittedly this is a superficial treatment of the nature of revelation, and indeed that subject has been much debated as to its essence and extent. Specifically, the struggle as to the relationship between general revelation and natural theology, especially as it erupted among Christian thinkers after the Enlightenment, might be germane to the issue at hand. Further, it is true that many theological definitions of the

Over against this concept is the view native to the two-book theory that general *revelation* is truth that God has embedded in the natural order and that people are responsible to extract from that order by investigation and cogitation. William F. English avers that

> the truths of general revelation are not delineated for us by God. Instead, they are "discovered" by fallible humans. At this point, it does not matter whether the "explorer" is a Christian or an atheist. Truths discovered in general revelation must be studied and examined for their trustworthiness, regardless of the religious beliefs of the giver.[17]

So there are two distinct models of revelation that we must consider: one posits that God has made known certain truths to mankind, which truths one could never have discovered for oneself; the other understands that God has somehow embedded a myriad of truths in the natural order and that people are capable of and responsible to ferret out those truths.

Now it is at this point that the intent of my argument is most liable to misunderstanding and thus must be carefully understood. First, let me affirm each of the following propositions:

1. God is the author and sustainer of the created order.

2. There are facts and realities and truths that by means of human investigation and cogitation are to be discovered in the created order, both natural and human.

3. The possibility exists that such humanly discovered and verified facts and realities are no less true than truth communicated in writing by God. (Indeed, the notion of degrees of truth, of some truths being more true than other truths, is definitionally erroneous.)

---

term *revelation* stop short of the element of nondiscoverability, affirming simply that the term means "the disclosure of what was previously unknown" (C. F. H. Henry, "Revelation, Special" in *Baker's Dictionary of Theology*, ed. E. F. Harrison [Grand Rapids: Baker, 1960], 457). But the element of nondiscoverability is usually latent in the discussion of the concept. At any rate, it can be argued that the biblical description of the history and the idea of revelation demands that nondiscoverability be acknowledged as a necessary element of the concept. Limitations of space forbid treatment of all the ancillary issues. The intent here is extremely narrow: simply to encourage the reader to confront what seems to be a basic contradiction in meaning between the orthodox understanding of the theological concept of revelation and the meaning assigned the term when it is employed as part of the rationale for the integrationist effort.

17. William F. English, "An Integrationist's Critique of and Challenge to the Bobgan's View of Counseling and Psychotherapy," in *Journal of Psychology and Theology* 18, no. 3 (1990): 229.

4. Many of the facts and verities discovered by human investigation into the created order can be employed to help people in many ways.

The issue, then, is not whether it is possible that truth might be discovered by human investigation of the natural and moral universe; rather, the issue is whether truth thus discovered can be assigned to the category of general revelation, and to prove that such material discovery can effect spiritual change.

My contention is that by reason of the proper definition of the theological category "general revelation" and by reason of the intrinsic and divine integrity and authority that must be granted to any truth-claim that is placed under that category, it is erroneous and misleading to assign to that category humanly deduced or discovered facts and theories. The issue is larger than appropriate taxonomy.[18] In fact, to assign such humanly determined truths to the category of general revelation introduces a twofold fallacy into the argument when it is used as a rationale for the integrationist position.

First, there is the fallacy that might be termed *falsely perceived validity*. Revelation is from God; thus it is by definition true and authoritative. To assign human discoveries to the category of general revelation is to imbue them with an aura of validity and consequent authority that they do not, indeed, they cannot merit. Thus, to assign a concept to the category of general revelation when that concept is in fact a theory concocted by a person is, in effect, to lend God's name to a person's ideas. That is fallacious, no matter the intrinsic truth or falsehood of the theory under consideration.

The second fallacy might be called *crippled accountability*. That is, once it is acknowledged that these theories are revelatory in nature, the issue of challenging them becomes moot. Much may be said about testing the ideas thus derived before acknowledging them as part of that august body of truth that God has communicated in the natural order of things, or about honoring the distinction in intrinsic authority between

---

18. In fact, the misdefinition being discussed here does involve an error with reference to taxonomy (i.e., the assignment of entities and concepts to appropriate categories). That error is the mistaken assumption that the categories of truth and revelation are coterminous. In fact, all revelation is truth, but not all truth is revelation. In other words, *truth* is a larger category than *revelation*; this is why we speak of revealed truth (as opposed to truth that is not ours by revelation but by investigation). This is not to disparage revealed truth; indeed, although revealed truth is not any more true than discovered truth, it is more dependable, simply because it is made known to us directly by God.

general and special revelation[19] but to craft an argument for integration based upon the equal merits and authority of general revelation and special revelation is functionally to short-circuit such efforts and to deny such distinctions. Very simply, if it is revelation, then God said it; if God said it, then it is true; when God speaks truth, mankind's responsibility is not to test that truth but to obey it. It is self-contradictory to insist that general revelation can include truths that must be "studied and examined for their trustworthiness."[20]

In summary, then, the integrationist rationale that arises from the claim that perceived truths established by human research constitute a subset of the category general revelation, and thus possess the authority and dependability native to revelation, is flawed first of all in its misdefinition of the term *revelation*. Inherent to the biblical concept of revelation is the idea of nondiscoverability, but the most dominant element of general revelation as construed in this rationale is that the facts to be granted the status of revelation are by definition the result of human research and observation.

The term "general" is misdefined. Second, the two-book theory is flawed in its misdefinition of the term *general*. In the articulation of the two-book argument, it is clear from the use of *general*, and sometimes from the accompanying explication and application of the concept, that the term is to be taken to signify "generic, nonspecific as to category or verifiability, cutting across a broad spectrum of loosely related topics." (This in contrast to special revelation, which is conceived to connote "narrow or specific as to category and focus, dealing with but one category.")

According to Fleck and Carter, for instance, general revelation is so called because it communicates the "picture of God in nature." The contrast to special revelation is represented thus: "God is revealed in the Scripture and in Jesus Christ in a special way, i.e., special or particular details about God's person, nature, and his plan for human life and its relationship with him are revealed in Scripture." Notice that it is because

---

19. For instance, English speaks of "the lesser truths of general revelation" (English, "Integrationist's Critique," 231). But this distinction between the lesser authority of general revelation and the greater authority of special revelation is an invalid and perilous distinction. To posit degrees of authority and dependability between various channels of revelation is dangerous. In fact, all revelation is from God, and thus all revelation is absolutely true and, assuming proper hermeneutical treatment, normative. Again, this error is born of a misdefinition of the idea of revelation.

20. English, "Integrationist's Critique," 229.

special or specific details are revealed in Scripture that "theologians refer to Scripture as special revelation."[21]

This is a critical misunderstanding of the connotation intended for the term *general* in this phrase. It makes the referent of the descriptive force of the term to be the content of the revelation thus described. In fact, as the term *general revelation* is historically and universally employed in evangelical theology, the term *general* is intended to characterize not the character of revelation under discussion but the audience to whom that revelation is available.

Ryrie describes the characteristics of general revelation as follows:

> General revelation is exactly that—general. It is general in its scope; that is, it reaches to all people (Matt. 5:45; Acts 14:17). It is general in geography; that is, it encompasses the entire globe (Ps. 19:2). It is general in its methodology; that is, it employs universal means like the heat of the sun (vv. 4–6) and human conscience (Rom. 2:14–15). Simply because it is a revelation that thus affects all people wherever they are and whenever they have lived it can bring light and truth to all, or if rejected, brings condemnation.[22]

So general revelation is general not because it deals with a broad and non-specific (that is, general) category of facts, but because it is accessible to all people of all time (that is, to people generally).

Again, *special* revelation is so called not because it makes known "special or particular details about God's person, nature, and his plan for human life,"[23] but because it is made known not generally but to specific individuals. Thiessen distinguishes special revelation as "those acts of God whereby He makes Himself and His truth known at special times and to specific peoples."[24] So the integrationist apologetic that takes the term *general* in

---

21. Fleck and Carter, *Psychology*, 18.

22. Charles C. Ryrie, *Basic Theology* (Wheaton: Victor, 1988), 28. Compare Erickson's concise definition of general revelation: Revelation which is available to all persons at all times . . ." (Erickson, *Concise Dictionary*, 143). Thiessen identifies the distinguishing element of general revelation as the fact that "it is addressed to all intelligent creatures generally and is accessible to all" (Thiessen, *Systematic Theology*, 32). Demarest defines general revelation as the "divine disclosure to all persons at all times and places by which one comes to know that God is and what he is like" (B. A. Demarest, "Revelation, General" in *Evangelical Dictionary of Theology*, (Grand Rapids: Baker, 1984), 944).

23. Fleck and Carter, *Psychology*, 18.

24. Thiessen, *Systematic Theology*, 35. Compare Erickson's definition: "God's manifestation of himself at particular times and places through particular events . . ." (*Concise*

general revelation as referring to the type of content that can be placed under that category, and therefore argues that all manner of sundry facts and realities derived by human investigation can thus be categorized, is rendered fallacious by its misdefinition of the term *general.*[25]

And that fallacy is ominous on two counts. First, it is perilous because it *expands the category* known as general revelation far beyond what Scripture allows. Demarest and Harpel define the extent of the truth that is divinely disclosed through the channel of general revelation as "(a) a metaphysical dualism—that a supreme Creator exists distinct from finite creatures; (b) an ethical dualism—that there is a difference between right and wrong; and (c) an epistemological dualism—that truth exists as distinct from error."[26] It is a category carefully restricted by the teachings of Scripture, and orthodox theology has honored the biblical bounds placed upon it. It is general in that it includes revelation available to all people, but it is not a general category sufficient to include all the discoveries and theories of human reasoning.

Again, the fallacy implicit in the definition of this term is destructive because it *eviscerates the character* of general revelation. That is, as described in Scripture, general revelation is truth that is manifestly set forth before all humanity (Rom. 1:17–19; 2:14, 15); it is truth so clear and irrefutable as to be known intuitively by all rational beings (Ps. 19:1–6; Rom. 1:19); it is truth so authoritative and manifest that when people, by reason of willful rebellion, reject that truth, they do so at the cost of their own eternal damnation (Rom. 1:20; 2:1, 15). For this seamless, flawless, and majestic tapestry of God-given truth is substituted a patchwork of "lesser" truths,[27] of truth

---

Dictionary, 144). Demarest characterizes special revelation by the fact that "God sovereignly disclosed His redemptive purposes to certain people." Bruce A. Demarest and Richard J. Harpel, "'Redemptive Analogies' and the Biblical Idea of Revelation," *Bibliotheca Sacra* (July-September 1989): 336.

25. This is not to insist that the misdefinition at hand proves that the category of general revelation could not be expansive enough to include all those perceived realities (though it is my persuasion that it cannot). The limits of the category of general revelation must be established by appeal to the Scriptures (see below). However, it needs to be emphasized that the misunderstanding concerning the term *general* is at the heart of the axiomatic use to which the phrase is put, and it is that axiomatic force that is entirely broken by the observation that the term is being misdefined.

26. Demarest and Harpel, "'Redemptive Analogies,'" 335. For a careful development of the dangers of expanding the category of general revelation, see Kenneth Kantzer, "The Communication of Revelation," in *The Bible: The Living Word of Revelation,* ed. Merrill C. Tenney (Grand Rapids: Zondervan, 1968), 62–69.

27. English, "Integrationist's Critique," 231.

that "is obtainable at least in part,"[28] truths that "are not delineated for us by God" but are "discovered by fallible humans" and thus must be "studied and examined for their trustworthiness,"[29] truth the consideration of which "hopefully results in a higher level of insight and understanding."[30] Surely such a concept of general revelation represents a ravaging of the biblical concept.

Not every integrationist apologetic employs the argument from the nature of general revelation, but most do. Further, the more thoroughly and visibly evangelical the apologist, the more likely that individual is to employ that argument. But it has been the contention here that the two-book approach is twice flawed. First, it is confused in its definition of the term *revelation*. By defining general revelation as that body of truth that is gained by human investigation and discovery, the argument is guilty of neglecting the element of nondiscoverability intrinsic to the biblical notion of revelation and supplanting that notion with its exact antithesis. Further, the approach is dangerous in that it attributes to the truth-claims of humanity an authority they do not and cannot possess, and renders it virtually impossible to bring those truth-claims under the authority of the one standard by which God demands that they be measured.

Second, the argument from the perceived authoritative character of general revelation is confused in its definition of the term *general*. By mistakenly taking that term to refer to the content of the category (rather than to the audience to which the revelation thus denominated is available), the apologists who employ this argument commit two fallacies that are destructive of orthodox theology: first, they expand the category to include all manner of truth-claims that have no right to be thus honored; and second, they eviscerate the character of revelation by including in the category truth-claims that are admittedly lesser than the truths of Scripture, which demand that finite and fallen people measure them to determine their validity, and which at best can possibly issue in a higher level of insight into the demands of living.

In summary, I am persuaded that, in the interest of validating the integrationist impulse and effort, many in the Christian psychological community have, wittingly or unwittingly, exchanged the biblical doctrine of general revelation for one of their own making. The evangelical world is entirely the loser in the bargain.

---

28. Stephen M. Clinton, "The Foundational Integration Model," *Journal of Psychology and Theology* 18, no. 2 (1990): 117.

29. English, "Integrationist's Critique," 229.

30. Guy, "Search for Truth," 27.

THE NO-BOOK APPROACH: CORRUPT AND DISHONEST

This perceived fallacy is not nearly so prevalent as the two-book approach, and it tends to be embraced by those with less of a commitment to the inerrancy of Scripture. However, as one moves forward in time this mentality is encountered with increasing frequency across the integrationist spectrum.

The Approach Identified

The no-book approach may be reduced to the following propositions:

The Axiomatic Affirmation:
All truth-sources are liable to produce error to the degree that fallible and preconditioned individuals are involved in accessing those sources.

The Theological Formulation:
Regardless of the intrinsic truthfulness and consequent authority of Scripture, any human application of Scripture presupposes the process of interpretation.

By reason of spiritual fallenness and cultural-gender preconditioning, individuals necessarily come to the interpretative task laboring under significant and crippling liabilities.

The Epistemological Conclusion:
All human knowledge is flawed by definition. There is no reason to be any more suspicious of science than of theology (i.e., of the theories and facts derived by human investigation and deduction than of supposed truths derived from Scripture) simply because Scripture is no less liable to the limitations of human participation than is any other truth source.

Regardless of the authority and/or verity of the truth source, human knowing of truth can only approach greater and greater levels of probability; certainty is presuppositionally unthinkable.

The Integrationist Ramification:
Negatively, any suggestion that finality or certainty might be imputed to any element of any model is mistaken.

Positively, the integrationists must be constantly testing and refining all of their findings and convictions, from the presuppositional to the methodological, in the hope that they can effect for themselves an ascending spiral of confidence and effectiveness.

This is rather a stark and perhaps disquieting expression of the fallacy under consideration. But, in fact, this is the essence of the position being taken by many in the integrationist community.

For instance, in addressing the question, "Can We Know the Truth?," Guy acknowledges that the Scriptures "reveal ultimate truth about mankind and our existence" but goes on to warn that "[a]ttempts to know the truth as it is revealed through the Bible are prone to the same errors and inaccuracies found in the observation and interpretation of truth as it is revealed through nature."[31] He argues from the "existence of numerous, conflicting, and constantly changing theories about truth" that "we are unable to fully know the truth since our knowledge is partial, at best."[32] This line of reasoning leads Guy to the following implication:

> Because we are unable to know the truth and our attempts to do so
> are prone to error, the conclusions of theology are prone to the same
> errors as those made when formulating the conclusions of science. Nei-
> ther set of theories about truth needs to have ultimate authority over
> the other. Assumptions about the truth as it is revealed in the Bible
> need not be regarded as authoritative over the assumptions of science.
> If God is, indeed, the source of all revealed truth, any apparent contra-
> diction is the result of error in observation or interpretation of that truth
> in the disciplines of science or theology, or both. Because error is prob-
> able in either field, diversity can be viewed as a stimulus for growth and
> development—a process which hopefully will result in higher levels of
> accuracy and understanding in the search for truth.[33]

Finally, in an attempt to put a happier spin on this rather discouraging epistemology, Guy concludes,

> There will be no single model of integration, nor will there be one
> set of therapeutic assumptions, techniques, or goals which are totally

---

31. Guy, "Search for Truth," 29. Guy has affirmed in the context that "God reveals . . . truth to us through both general and special revelation, with both nature and the Bible serving as expressions of this truth" (28). He regards the two as fully equal in authority and dependability. It is interesting that he employs the two-book argument at the axiomatic level, but his view of both "books" (nature and the Bible) manifests an impoverished understanding of the concept of revelation.

32. Ibid., 30. This entire article is a response to Collins's attempt to construct a model of integration (Collins, *Integration*). Guy's argument is that Collins has erred in supposing that any one model of integration could be intrinsically superior to all others.

33. Ibid., 31.

accurate and true. Christian psychologists are free to adopt any one of a variety of models and orientations as they seek to work out a personal integration within the scope of their own private ministries.[34]

Because of this type of conclusion, this mentality is here denominated the no-book fallacy. Simply, this construct leaves the counseling community with no book, no authority, no absolutely dependable source of truth, and no normative standard against which to measure the countless theories and models proffered today in the worlds of psychology and counseling.

Thorson posits this same epistemological limitation: ". . . the important fact that a divine revelation is the real *source* of our knowledge does not eliminate the purely epistemological problems of communication, interpretation, and comprehension, nor does it impart a special status of rational certainty to our knowledge itself."[35] Farnsworth articulates a similar mentality. Appealing to an article in which it is argued that "male dominance has tarnished even our best translations [of the Bible],"[36] from which he derives evidence of the inescapable preconditioning that inexorably discolors any understanding of even an authoritative text, Farnsworth concludes that "[i]n spite of the accessibility of the words of Scripture, reading them is not a matter of perfect perception. It is easy to forget that reading the Bible is a psychological-perceptual experience."[37] He goes on to add this methodological caveat.

> Since God reveals his truths in a variety of ways, various disciplines other than theology are needed to interpret the wide range of revelational data. Further, since all academic disciplines are subject to human error, no one discipline should be made subservient to any other. What I am

---

34. Ibid.

35. W. R. Thorson, "The Biblical Insights of Michael Polanyi, *Journal of the American Scientific Affiliation* 33 (1981): 132 (emphasis original).

36. B. Mickelsen and A. Mickelsen, "Does Male Dominance Tarnish Our Translations?" *Christianity Today* (October 1979): 23–29.

37. Kirk E. Farnsworth, "The Conduct of Integration," *Journal of Psychology and Theology* 10, no. 4 (1982): 311. Shepperson, in replying to the article by Farnsworth, makes mention of the "assumption that one's experiential base, conscious and unconscious, influences one's perception of theological and psychological truth" as part of his argument that theology should not exercise "imperialism" over psychology (Vance L. Shepperson, "Systemic Integration: A Reactive Alternative to 'The Conduct of Integration'," *Journal of Psychology and Theology* 10, no. 4 (1982): 326. Shepperson expresses delight that Farnsworth's article "indicates a willingness to evenly weigh multiple inputs from various disciplines."

not saying is that the Bible does not have functional authority over all other forms of revelation. What I am saying is that theology, as a human discipline, does not necessarily have functional authority over any other human discipline.[38]

The no-book approach becomes most manifest and alarming when it is employed in the development of an integrationist apologetic for the veracity and authority of truth derived from psychological research. First, it often becomes the means of effecting the *de facto* denial of the role the Scriptures have normally been expected to play in an evangelically oriented system of thought. For instance, in an attempt to frame a Christian epistemology, the following warning is issued.

> Revelation as a source of knowledge presupposes a transcendent supernatural reality. Christian education argues that truth gained through this source is absolute. However, one must realize that distortion of this truth is possible in the process of human interpretation. Therefore, the Christian must be careful not to become preoccupied with revelation and fail to use the other sources of knowledge available in seeking truth.[39]

Earlier in the article the author had affirmed the importance and uniqueness of Scripture, but here he cripples the role those Scriptures can play by reminding his reader that "distortion of this truth is possible in the process of human interpretation."[40]

---

38. Farnsworth, "Conduct," 311 (emphasis original). Notice again the axiomatic expression of the two-book fallacy in the use of the phrase "other forms of revelation" in reference to other human disciplines. This distinction between the Bible and theology, between the authoritative truth-source and the fallible accessor of that source, is vacuous; it will be discussed below.

39. Jimmy F. Sellars, "In Defense of a Christian Epistemology," *Christian Education Journal* 12, no. 3 (1992): 163. The "other sources of knowledge" that Sellars catalogues in the article are "reason, intuition, the senses, and the secondary source of testimony or authority" (163).

40. Compare James D. Foster and Mark Ledbetter, "Christian Anti-Psychology and the Scientific Method," *Journal of Psychology and Theology* 15, no. 1 (1987): 17, where after a discussion concerning "what is the most valuable way of knowing" they conclude, "While we can accept authority, intuition, and personal experience as valuable approaches to learning, we object when knowledge from these sources is presumed in some way to be superior to knowledge gained through observation, measurement, and experimentation." Earlier the authors had acknowledged that "the Bible is . . . an authority to Christians because of its revelatory nature" (11). This evisceration of the Scriptures' authoritative role comes full in Morton Kelsey's "Reply to Analytical Psychology and Human Evil," *Journal of Psychology and Theology* 14, no. 4 (1986): 282–84, in which the author argues that the

Second, the corrupting influence of the no-book approach is seen in the fact that this argument—which insists that though the Scriptures might indeed be absolutely true and authoritative, any human understanding of those Scriptures will necessarily be tarnished by limitations intrinsic to humanity—might be expected to result in a certain carelessness about the interpretation of Scripture. That is, if the interpreter knows that no matter how much effort is expended in the attempt, the work will always be so flawed *as to disqualify one's conclusions as a standard of truth,* the interpreter is left with no compelling incentive to heroic diligence in the stewardship of interpretation. Very simply, if the results of careful exegesis can possess no greater intrinsic authority than the results of sloppy exegesis, there is no reason to do careful exegesis.

Whether it is fair to anticipate this fall-out from the no-book mentality, readers must decide for themselves. But it is my observation that an alarmingly cavalier attitude toward exegesis does in fact surface with disturbing regularity in the writings of the no-book theorists.

For instance, in arguing for "nonrational" or "humanistic psychological and theological methodologies" that would "allow us to ask questions unrestricted by our natural scientific technology and rationalistic theological categories," Farnsworth makes some rather creative use of Scripture.

> The nonrational is the sensitivity of feeling that balances the sensibleness of rationality and that gives warmth and richness to the direction and maturity of reason. It is the direct preconceptual encounter with God that enables one to pray in silent expectancy . . . and without ceasing (1 Thessalonians 5:17). . . . This is what Jeremiah meant, saying, "But let the one who glories boast in this, that he understands and knows Me" (Jeremiah 9:24).[41]

In a reply to Farnsworth in the same edition of *Journal of Psychology and Theology,* Virkler chastens him for using the Scriptures "carelessly," and briefly examines the two passages appealed to by Farnsworth, concluding

---

"thinking and experience" of C. G. Jung "provide the best framework upon which to base the integration of psychology and theology" (282). Kelsey is responding to G. A. Elmer Griffin's "Analytical Psychology and the Dynamics of Human Evil: A Problematic Case in the Integration of Psychology and Theology,"(*Journal of Psychology and Theology* 14, no. 4 [1986]: 269–77), in which Griffin critiques a series of lectures at Fuller Theological Seminary in which Kelsey argued that Jung could best serve as the framework for integrating psychology and theology. The point is, of course, that the Scriptures have here been displaced by Jung as a framework for accomplishing integration.

41. Farnsworth, "Conduct," 312.

that "by no stretch of our exegetical imaginations" can those passages be used as Farnsworth had used them.[42] Farnsworth responds as follows:

> I can see how [Virkler], being an expert in the area of hermeneutics, could form a negative opinion about my hermeneutics, when he sees that we disagree on the meaning of certain portions of Scripture. Although I agree that this is in fact a minor criticism that does not detract from the validity of my integration model, I disagree that because we do not agree on the rendering of some verses of Scripture I am "careless" and he is not. There is no basis whatever in my article for such a judgment.[43]

He makes no attempt to defend his understanding of the passages through hermeneutical considerations; he simply asserts that he disagrees with his critic's understanding of those same passages. In fact, there is no defense of Farnsworth's use of those passages except this: the way he construes those biblical texts supports the point he is trying to make in the article. The prosecution rests.

The Approach Critiqued

The no-book approach is ultimately corruptive of the notion of epistemological authority, and thus of the possibility of functional absolutes in the moral realm. That is, the Scriptures (it is acknowledged) may (probably, do) possess intrinsic truth that will, in some entirely transcendental otherworld, exercise authority in the cosmic struggle of competing truth-claims. But because every human attempt to comprehend the meaning of those Scriptures is prejudged as crippled and crippling, and because in the contest of ideas appeal can be made only to human understanding of the Scriptures (as opposed to the raw material

---

42. Henry A. Virkler, "Response to 'The Conduct of Integration'," *Journal of Psychology and Theology* 10, no. 4 (1982): 332.

43. Farnsworth, "Responses to 'The Conduct of Integration': An Appreciative Reaction," *Journal of Psychology and Theology* 10, no. 4 (1982): 334. The "basis" in Farnsworth's article for Virkler's "judgment" of poor hermeneutics is simply the fact that Farnsworth makes the passages to which he appeals say something very different than, if not antithetical to, the plain meaning of those passages in their contexts. This is precisely the criticism lodged by Virkler, but it has no force whatever in the mind of Farnsworth. The suggestion is that, given the approach employed by Farnsworth, exacting hermeneutics have not only ceased to be a possibility, they have ceased to be a consideration.

of their intrinsic meaning), the Scriptures cannot functionally referee between competing truth-claims.

In a discussion of the idea that there is "running throughout Scripture" some "radical obscurity, or outright incoherence, or at least a Delphic[44]
sort of ambiguity," Packer comes to a similar conclusion concerning the
necessary implications of such a notion.

> Ought we then to conclude that when the Reformers affirmed the
> intrinsic clarity of Scripture in presenting its central message, they were
> wrong and that the many millions who down the centuries have lived
> and died by the light of what they took to be divinely taught certain-
> ties were self-deceived? Must we say that no such certainties are
> available to us, nor ever were to anyone? That is what this idea, if
> accepted, would imply.[45]

The Scriptures have often been thus characterized as intrinsically ambiguous and therefore nonauthoritative, but the charge has come from those
who would deny the high view of the inerrancy and authority of Scripture,
which has been a hallmark of evangelical theology.[46] To find the same pe-
jorative assessment of Scripture coming from the pens of those who claim
evangelical credentials "cannot but disturb."[47]

In fact, however, the notion that "purely epistemological problems of
communication, interpretation, and comprehension"[48] render the authority

---

44. The reference is to the Grecian Oracle at Delphi, a supposed soothsayer who
deliberately couched her prognostications in ambiguous pictures and phrases to eliminate
the possibility that any votary might challenge her accuracy.

45. J. I. Packer, "Infallible Scripture and the Role of Hermeneutics," in *Scripture
and Truth*, ed. Gerard Terpstra (Grand Rapids: Zondervan, 1983), 329. In this section of
his article (entitled "Has Scripture One Clear Message?"), Packer is directly addressing the
mentality at the base of the no-book mentality, namely the contention that "the method of
appeal and submission to Scripture, no matter how carefully pursued, is intrinsically unable
to produce certainty," and this because, as is claimed, "modern insight into the hermeneutical
process shows that different things are conveyed to different people by the same texts, depending on where those people are coming from and what experience and questions they
bring with them . . ." (328). After careful consideration of that mentality, Packer concludes that "such arguments as are currently offered to prove the intrinsic incoherence,
ambiguity, or unintelligibility of Scripture . . . are very far from successful" (332).

46. In introducing his discussion of what is referred to in this article as the no-book
mentality, Packer observes that "liberal theology has long maintained" such an attitude
toward the Scriptures (Ibid., 328).

47. Ibid., 329.

48. Thorson, "Biblical Insights," 132.

of Scripture an irrelevancy is flawed on at least three counts. First, it is logically fallacious and dishonest. Human language is being employed by the
detractor to insist that knowable thoughts cannot be communicated via human language. This is the skywriter who mounts to the heavens in a biplane
to scrawl across the horizon the message, "Human flight is impossible!" The
no-book theorist uses thousands of words to insist that words can mean nothing for certain. The thesis is disproven by its very articulation. As Pinnock
observes,

> The argument is fallacious and self-defeating. . . . On purely logi-
> cal grounds, if a person's interpretation is invalid simply because it is
> *his* interpretation, then the objector's opinion is wrong because it is
> *his* opinion.[49]

Second, the no-book mentality is a denial of the doctrine classically
known as the *perspicuity* of Scripture, defined as "clarity of thought, lucid-
ity," and identified as "one of the traditional attributes of Scripture."[50]
Hodge reduces the doctrine of perspicuity to the simple affirmation that
"The Bible is a plain book . . . intelligible by the people."[51] The Westminster Confession (1.7) articulates this doctrine as follows:

> All things in Scripture are not alike plain in themselves, nor alike
> clear unto all, yet those things which are necessary to be known, be-
> lieved and observed for salvation, are so clearly propounded and opened
> in some place of Scripture or other, that not only the learned, but the
> unlearned, in a due use of ordinary means, may attain unto a suffi-
> cient understanding of them.

Although in the history of Christian doctrine the canon of perspicuity, or clarity, was worked out in the context of an entirely different

---

49. Clark Pinnock, *Biblical Revelation* (Chicago: Moody, 1971), 99. The specific
argument to which Pinnock refers here is that which claims "that the interpretation of
any text is a matter of personal opinion, and that certain knowledge of what the Bible
says is impossible" (99). This is in a section in which Pinnock is contending for the clarity of Scripture, and that begins with the affirmation that "[i]t is necessary for Scripture,
if it is to be our authority, to be clear so that we can read and understand it" (97).

50. Richard A. Muller, *Dictionary of Latin and Greek Theological Terms: Drawn
Principally from Protestant Scholastic Theology* (Grand Rapids: Baker, 1985), 228. By "tradi-
tional attributes" Muller means that this is a characteristic traditionally attributed to
Scripture in Protestant theology.

51. Charles Hodge, *Systematic Theology: Abridged Edition*, ed. Edward N. Gross
(Grand Rapids: Baker, 1988), 92.

struggle,[52] the principles involved apply as well to the no-book mentality. Indeed, this doctrine of clarity (or perspicuity) stands in judgment upon any claim that the Bible is incomprehensible *for any reason relating to the character or accessibility of the Bible*. As Pinnock observes, "An obscure book could not perform the functions Scripture would perform. A denial of perspicuity is a denial of the *sola scriptura* principle itself."[53]

The evangelical community ought to regard with radical suspicion the tendency of the no-book theorists to cavalierly reject a concept as central to the Protestant tradition as the doctrine of the perspicuity of Scripture.

Third, the no-book mentality is denied by Scripture itself on several counts.

1. The Bible affirms that people will be held eternally accountable for disobeying the teachings contained therein (Ps. 50:16, 17; Prov. 13:13; Isa. 5:24: Luke 24:25; 2 Tim. 4:3, 4) and that obedience to those words will result in temporal and eternal blessedness (James 1:18; 2 Tim. 3:15, 16). It is absurd to suppose that God would promise to punish those who disobey, or to bless those who obey, words that by nature can at best attain only to "a Delphic sort of ambiguity."[54] Indeed, Jesus commanded His contemporaries to "search the Scriptures" (John 5:39), assuming that those hearers "were able to understand what the Old Testament said of the Messiah, although its teachings had been misunderstood by the scribes and elders and by the whole Sanhedrin."[55]

2. The messages and books of the Bible are addressed in context to people with the expectation that people will obey and understand. Indeed, in the narratives of the Bible, the generation who first received the messages are held accountable for their willingness to obey. Hodge insists that "it is the people who are addressed. . . . They are everywhere

---

52. The doctrine of perspicuity was articulated by the Reformers in denial of the Roman Catholic claim that "the Bible is obscure, and is badly in need of interpretation even in matters of faith and practice." According to Berkhof, the contention of the Reformers "was simply that the knowledge necessary unto salvation, though not equally clear on every page of Scripture, is yet conveyed to man throughout the Bible in such a simple and comprehensible form that one who is earnestly seeking salvation can, under the guidance of the Holy Spirit, by reading and studying the Bible, easily obtain for himself the necessary knowledge, and does not need the aid and guidance of the Church and of a separate priesthood." L. Berkhof, *Introductory Volume to Systematic Theology* (Grand Rapids: Eerdmans, 1932), 167. Compare the "modified" analysis of this Reformational struggle in G. C. Berkouwer, *Holy Scripture* (Grand Rapids: Eerdmans, 1975), 271–73.

53. Pinnock, *Biblical*, 99.

54. Packer, "Infallible Scripture," 329.

55. Hodge, *Systematic Theology*, 94.

assumed to be competent to understand what is written and are everywhere required to believe and obey what thus comes from the inspired
messengers of Christ."[56]

3. The message of Scripture was regarded as so plain that the recipi-
ents were commanded to "teach them diligently unto thy children" (Deut.
6:7) and unto "thy son's sons" (Deut. 4:9).

4. The Scriptures repeatedly claim to be plain and accessible.

> Scripture is a "light shining in a dark place (2 Pe 1:19). The "Father
> of lights" has given His Word to be a lamp to our feet and a light to
> our path (Ps 119:105). It is not inaccessible and hidden from us (Deu
> 30:11–14). We are commanded to read and search it (Jn 5:39; Ac 17:11).
> It makes wise the simple, revives the soul, rejoices the heart, enlight-
> ens the eyes (Ps 19:7,8). Scripture is clear because it is *God's*. If it were
> not clear, it would fail in its intention.[57]

Again, far from allowing the notion of their own intrinsic ambiguity,
Scriptures suggest that the denial of the clarity and thus of the authority of
the Bible is born of the impulse to reject God's authority, which in turn is
born of wicked rebellion (Prov. 1:29, 30; Isa. 30:9; John 3:20).

> Denial of clarity reflects a refusal to be bound by Scripture and a
> determination to follow one's own inclinations. Whenever a church
> or a theologian takes it upon himself to define truth without refer-
> ence to the objective authority of God's Word, he becomes demonically
> solipsistic.[58]

In sum, the no-book approach insists that, by reason of the limitations native to the human interpreter, no more can be said of the
dependability and authority of Scripture than can be said of any other
alleged truth source. This approach is a deconstructionist wolf in the
clothing of an evangelical sheep.[59] It is corrupt in its essence and in its
implications; it is dishonest in that it denies to the words of Scripture
the measure of plainness and meaning the theorists assume for their own

---

56. Hodge, *Systemic Theology*, 93.

57. Pinnock, *Biblical*, 98.

58. Ibid., 99. By "solipsistic" Pinnock means the spirit that regards nothing but self
as important.

59. See the discussion of "Deconstructionism" in Tremper Longman, *Literary Approaches to Biblical Interpretation* (Grand Rapids: Zondervan, 1987), 41–45.

words; it is antithetical to a doctrine that is cardinal to the theological tradition behind the evangelical movement; it is contradicted and condemned by the plain teachings of Scripture.

THE RULE-BOOK APPROACH: COMMENDABLE, BUT DANGEROUS

The distinction was made earlier between two phases of the integrationist effort: the possibility question (Can and should theology and psychology be integrated?) and the procedural question (How are theology and psychology best integrated?). The two approaches discussed above involve flawed reasoning at the possibility level. That is, they are advanced in defense of the notion that secular psychology can and should be appealed to in order to supplement the teachings of Scripture in the attempt to best help struggling people.[60]

On two important counts, this third approach is distinct from the first two. First, this mentality operates at the level of the procedural question, generally making no attempt to address the possibility question (i.e., the necessary and constituent issues that lay below the waterline).[61] Second, from the perspective of evangelical thought this construct involves no intrinsic fallacy of theology or logic;[62] indeed, it proceeds upon a sincere confession of a high view of inerrant Scripture characteristic of orthodox evangelical theology. It affirms the distinctive character and authority of all revealed truth, and it includes an honest commitment to honor that reality in the work of constructing a model of counseling. However, it will be argued that this approach to integration becomes fallacious when employed in the effort to reconcile theology and psychology.

---

60. The two-book fallacy argues that human findings can and should be appealed to because they fall under the broad(ened) category of general revelation, and thus have divine sanction; that is, the argument has force because it raises human findings to the level of Scripture. The no-book fallacy argues that human findings can and should be appealed to because, by reason of the limitations of the human interpreter of Scripture, theology can have no greater authority than human findings; in other words, this argument has force because it lowers the Scripture to the level of human discoveries. Each argument addresses the possibility phase of the integrationist effort; neither speaks to the procedural phase.

61. See table 1.

62. That is, it is valid and cogent as to logic, definition, and theology in all that it says. The argument here is that this approach is fallacious not in what it says but in what it *assumes*.

The Approach Identified

The rule-book approach may be reduced to the following propositions:

The Axiomatic Affirmation:

The Scriptures are uniquely and entirely the inerrant and authoritative Word of God.[63]

The Theological Formulation:

God has made Himself known through both general and special revelation. The only channel of special revelation available to us today is the recorded Scriptures. Thus, the only propositional and objective revelation of God available to us today is the Bible.[64]

The Epistemological Conclusion:

The Bible and the Bible alone must function for the believer as the only and sufficient rule for faith and practice.

The Integrationist Ramification:

All truth-claims that are the result of human cogitations, investigations, and theorizing must be subjected to the Word of God that alone will be allowed to pass judgment as to the veracity and applicability of those truth-claims. The Bible and the Bible alone will be granted the role of falsification; that is, if a truth-claim is discerned to contradict or compromise a truth established in Scripture, that competing truth-claim is to be adjudged false.[65]

---

63. Not all integrationists who employ the rule-book approach would embrace a view of Scripture as high as this, but such a view is in fact logically necessary to the mentality. Further, a mitigated view of the character of Scripture would only compromise the integrity of the rule-book approach, and here that mentality is being considered in its most viable expression.

64. In fact, rule-book theorists handle the issue of general revelation in distinguishable ways. Often, they commit the fallacy of identifying human discoveries, including those in the psychotherapeutic world, as belonging to that category (as in the two-book fallacy above). There is an intrinsic inconsistency in thus categorizing human discoveries as revelation and then positing that another form of revelation (the Bible) can sit in judgment upon those discoveries. But in this discussion the commitment to employing the Scriptures as a rule-book that alone can sit in judgment upon truth-claims from any other source will be taken at face value.

65. Some would strengthen the integrationist ramification at this point, insisting specifically that the believer ought to do more than utilize the Bible as a falsifier, that the believer ought to accept only that which the Bible explicitly affirms. But to say that all of the Bible is truth is not to suggest that all truth is in the Bible. Thus, it is difficult to insist that only that which can be proven true by an appeal to Scripture ought to be accepted. (For instance, water runs downhill; the Twins won the World Series in 1991.) Others have

In sum, this mentality accepts the Bible and the Bible only as the rule-book (thus the title used here). It posits simply that the Scriptures will rule on all truth-claims; they will function as the only authoritative arbiter in all epistemological questions.[66] As one apologist for this approach summarizes:

> Truth derived from the study of any segment of general revelation, whether psychology or any other field, is not as trustworthy as the truth found in the Scriptures. This is the reason that the integration-ist will filter psychological truth through biblical truth and will accept only that which is not contradictory to God's special revelation.[67]

---

insisted that the Bible contains all Truth (upper case), and all that people can discover is truth (lower case). Or the distinction is made between subjective versus objective truth, or metaphysical versus physical truth, or between truth and facts. But such distinctions seem entirely artificial. In fact, all truth is true, and people can discover and appreciate truth, even subjective/metaphysical truth (e.g., the soul-satisfaction that flows from self-sacrifice). Further, there does exist truth that is not explicitly stated in the pages of Scripture (e.g., the happy effect of a devoted pet in the life of a lonely, aged person). It might be argued that all important metaphysical/subjective truth is recorded in Scripture, and all that people can discover on their own is really of little consequence, but such a claim is untestable and after all of no real help. It is manifest that people can discover truth. But the question for the believer who encounters truth-claims from the world is simply this: "How do I know that what has been discovered is in fact truth?" That question can only be refereed by the Scriptures. Further, given the fact that all that is in the Bible is true, but that not all that is true is in the Bible (for instance, you believe that our solar system is composed of the sun and nine planets, though the Bible nowhere explicitly affirms that truth), that refereeing function cannot always be positive (truth-claim A can only be judged true if affirmed in Scripture). However, the Bible must always function negatively in a contest of ideas (that is, if truth-claim B compromises or contradicts any verity of Scripture it must be rejected, no matter how compelling it seems to be). This is what is meant by the phrase, "the role of falsification." For instance, although the psychotherapeutic world may insist that people suffer from a deficient view of their own importance, the Bible believer who recognizes that proposition as a contradiction of the scriptural teaching concerning the fallen state of all mankind is compelled to reject the notion.

66. Compare Robert C. Roberts, in an analysis of the counseling model of Carl Rogers: "Let me say at the outset that I consider it quite possible for pagan insights to help the church, if they are properly adapted. But we must be aggressively critical, testing the spirits, to make sure the gospel of Jesus, and the Christian life, are furthered by these pagan elements, and not hindered or contradicted by them." Carl Rogers, "Quiet Revolution: Therapy for the Saints," *Christianity Today* November 1985: 25.

67. English, "Integrationist's Critique," 229. Compare Gangel, "Integrating Faith," 106, where Gangel speaks of building a biblical-theological sieve through which to filter the "kinds of information which bombard [the student's] mental processes." English also uses the filter analogy to characterize the rule-book approach: ". . . the integrationist will filter psychological truth through biblical truth and will accept only that which is not con-tradictory to God's special revelation" (English, "Integrationist's Critique," 229). Perhaps the most aggressive and commendable (though, I would argue, nonetheless flawed) at-tempt to articulate a functioning rule-book model is that of Crabb, *Understanding People*, 25–73.

Surely this is an integrationist construct with which a believer who espouses a high view of Scripture can live! Indeed, this is the very stuff of maintaining a testimony in a fallen world. Is there any aspect of life in which culture does not confront the thinking believer with theories and mores and value-systems that must be challenged biblically? And is this rule-book mentality not the spirit in which that believer ought to respond to those challenges? It is my persuasion that the rule-book approach is precisely the mentality that should rule in the mind of believers as they seek to shine as lights in the midst of a crooked and perverse generation.

The Approach Critiqued

Why then has this mentality been denominated a fallacy here? Quite simply, my contention is that although the rule-book approach is legitimate as a basic approach to assessing the morality and veracity of the great body of the truth-claims offered by the world, it is fallacious to employ even this noble approach as a methodology for integration when a rationale in defense of the effort has not been provided. It is invalid to proceed to the procedural level without satisfactorily addressing the possibility issues, no matter the inherent merit of the construct employed at the procedural level.

It was stated earlier that my purpose in this chapter is to excite in the reader a willingness to revisit the issue of whether the integration of theology and psychology *can* or *should* be pursued. The literature would suggest that this issue of *moral rationale* is not much discussed today within the integrationist community; indeed, the existence of the rationale is the given upon which countless attempts are made to construct a coherent methodology of integration.

On the other hand, the one apologetic construct that is consistently invoked within the evangelical community of integrationists is that which appeals axiomatically to the two-book mentality, the notion that all human discoveries fall under the broad(ened) category of general revelation and thus must be acknowledged to possess the veracity and authority intrinsic to revelation. But the two-book approach was earlier demonstrated to be fallacious. If that is so, then the methodological superstructure has been deprived of its foundational rationale. That is, to the degree that the rule-book methodology (which dominates in the evangelical community) is dependent upon the two-book rationale (which has been demonstrated to be bankrupt), the requirements of a cogent integrationist approach have been compromised and the methodology itself is rendered suspect.

And it is for just this reason that the rule-book approach is here adjudged fallacious as a methodology to integrate theology and psychology. As indicated in table 1, it is at once foolish and dangerous to move to the procedural question without having satisfactorily addressed the possibility questions. The issue reduces itself here, then, to the integrity not of this specific integrationist method but of the integrationist impulse. No matter the merit of the method, if the impulse is either foolish or wicked, the effort demands to be abandoned. Frankly, it is my persuasion that the impulse is, in fact, both foolish and wicked.

To be sure, that sort of proposition will not be well received by many in the evangelical community. But is there not a cause? Is there not a reason to be suspicious of the presumption that either of the possibility questions can be answered in the affirmative? If the proposition before the evangelical house is that the integration of Christian theology and secular psychology can be done, then the affirmative can be carried only if the case can be made that those two disciplines can indeed by reconciled—disciplines that were so long openly and consciously hostile to one another, that build upon sets of presuppositions so evidently mutually exclusive, and that operate within worldviews so entirely foreign to one another.[68] The burden of proof is certainly upon those who would argue in the affirmative.

By the same token, if the proposition to be considered by the believing community is that the integration of Christian theology and secular psychology should be done, then the case must be made that there is some intrinsic inadequacy or imperfection in the Scriptures demanding that insights be gleaned from secular psychology that will redress those deficiencies and enable Christian counselors to more effectively help hurting people. But the Scriptures make explicit claim to sufficiency, especially with regard to issues of fruitful living (2 Tim. 3:15-17; 2 Pet. 1:3). Further, for hundreds of years the Christian world has rested secure in the confidence that those Scriptures are, in fact, fully sufficient in all of the vicissitudes and adversities of life. Surely these realities would leave any evangelical suspicious of the suggestion that any demerit or deficiency is intrinsic to those Scriptures.[69]

---

68. An article surveying Christian counseling ministries begins with the observation that "In March 1907, Sigmund Freud took on God, presenting a paper before the Vienna Psychanalytic Society in which he concluded that religion was a 'universal obsessional neurosis.' Ever after psychiatrists have seen religion as a symptom of problems, not a source of healing. No field has been more resolutely irreligious." Tim Stafford, "Franchising Hope," *Christianity Today* May 1992: 22.

69. A careful and extensive defense of the notion of the sufficiency of Scripture is to be found in John MacArthur, Jr., *Our Sufficiency in Christ* (Dallas: Word, 1991). See especially "Truth in a World of Theory" (73ff).

It might be responded that if the methodology is adequate (i.e., if the rule-book mentality genuinely and adequately honors the unique character of Scripture) it will suffice even if the possibility issues have not been addressed. Again, one might anticipate that if theology and psychology were indeed ontologically irreconcilable they would demonstrate themselves so in the effort to integrate them. But such a supposition is born of spiritual naïveté. In fact, there are some discomfiting moral realities that must be factored into this question: the reality that many of the notions of secular psychology, though contrary to Scripture, are nonetheless seductively attractive to the Adamic nature (e.g., the tendency to make victims of virtually all people, thus relieving them of moral responsibility for sin); the reality that if Christian psychotherapists accept the validity of secular psychology they make available to themselves professional status and affluence they almost certainly could not have known otherwise; the reality that even armed with the rule-book methodology many integrationists have embraced concepts that seem manifestly contrary to the plain teachings of Scripture.[70] These realities remind us that the injunction of the apostle that believers "make no provision for the flesh in regard to its lusts" (Rom. 13:14) does have application to this issue.

In sum, it is acknowledged that from the standpoint of one who confesses a high view of Scripture and who seeks to implement a thorough-going biblicist worldview, the rule-book mentality is an airtight integrationist methodology. But I have alleged that in the effort to integrate theology and psychology, that methodology has been employed imprudently and recklessly; my fear is that the damage done to the cause of authentic New Testament Christianity has been beyond measure. That indictment of recklessness arises from the observation that the effort has proceeded to the methodological phase without adequately addressing the issue of rationale. All would acknowledge that there is no virtue in doing well a task that is either foolish or wicked. If the attempt to integrate Christian theology with secular psychology is neither foolish nor wicked, then my criticism here is entirely off the mark. But because the evangelical integrationist community has not adequately addressed the epistemological issues "below the waterline," that effort has not been proven either wise or virtuous. Christian integrationists owe it to themselves, to their colleagues, to their patients, and to their Lord to produce a cogent and exegetically sound rationale for the impulse *before* they proceed to the matter of method.

---

70. See for instance John E. Wagner, "National Association of Evangelicals: Amplifying His Voice," *Christianity Today* May 1975: 45ff.

CONCLUSION

The tenor of this chapter has been almost entirely—perhaps, dis-turbingly—negative. We have examined three (sometimes overlapping) approaches currently utilized in the effort to integrate secular psychology and orthodox evangelical theology. First the two-book approach was con-sidered, which broadens the category of general revelation to include all those data that result from human investigation into the created order, thus imbuing the perceived realities of secular psychology with the status and authority of revelation. That approach was assessed as confused in its definitions and thus destructive of the authoritative role that evangelical theology has assigned to Scripture alone. Second, the no-book mentality was analyzed, which presupposes that the limitations and preconditioning common to all human beings so cripple their ability to access even an au-thoritative and dependable truth-source such as Scripture that theology itself can be no more dependable than any other source of knowledge. That mentality was characterized as corrupt in its theological presuppositions and conclusions, and as dishonest in its estimation of the character of Scrip-ture. Finally, focus was upon the rule-book approach, which honors Scripture as the only authoritative propositional truth-source available to-day and which acknowledges that the Scriptures alone must be granted the role of falsification in every contest of competing truth-claims to which they speak. That approach was recognized as commendable, with the ca-veat that even such a laudable approach should not be employed until it is established that the integration of psychology and theology is itself a vir-tuous and wise effort.

And yet, even in the face of this negative assessment of so much of what is going on in the world of Christian psychology, God forbid that this article would leave the reader with a sense of loss or despair. Even if these criticisms are valid, if secular psychology is in fact a "broken cistern that can hold no water," Christian counselors are in so sense impoverished. We simply need to be reminded that it is foolish to "forsake the fountain of living waters" that is to be found in the Word of God. In a word, the Scriptures are sufficient.

Almost twenty years ago, in an article in which he was exploring the dynamics of an integrationist construct that would honor the unique char-acter of Scripture, J. Robertson McQuilkin addressed the question, "To what extent do the behavioral sciences among evangelicals give evidence of being under the authority of Scripture?" In developing an answer to that pivotal issue, he issued a very sobering warning:

. . . the range of success in integrating truth derived empirically and truth revealed in Scripture (and, indeed, the interest in making such an integration) varies so widely in evangelical circles that no precise answer to my question is possible. Nevertheless it is very important to raise the question because the potential for good or evil is so great. A resounding affirmative should be possible: "The great majority of evangelical scholars in the behavioral sciences give consistent evidence of thorough integration with Scripture in control." If such an affirmation cannot be made with confidence, we are in great danger because of the pervasive power of humanistic thinking in our society and because of the subtlety with which Scripture's authority is eroded.

My thesis is that in the next two decades the greatest threat to Biblical authority is the behavioral scientist who would in all good conscience man the barricades to defend the front door against any theologian who would attack the inspiration and authority of Scripture while all the while himself smuggling the content of Scripture out the back door through cultural or psychological interpretation.[71]

McQuilkin then catalogued several examples of "cultural or psychological interpretation" that were being accepted by the Christian psychological community at that time, but that reflected a weak view of the authority of Scripture (skepticism toward the grammatical-historical interpretation of Scripture; denial of the moral wickedness of homosexuality; a genre of Christian literature instructing readers how to lead fruitful lives but making no appeal to the standard Christian graces nor to the power of the Holy Spirit; recommendation of cathartic ventilation at the expense of the virtue of self-control; the claim that a knowledge of the Gospel is unnecessary to salvation), after which he concludes, ". . . we are in great danger of the wide-scale subversion of Biblical authority by those who are committed to that authority on the conscious and theoretical level, but who through uncritical use of behavioral scientific methodology have unwittingly come under its control."[72]

---

71. J. Robertson McQuilkin, "The Behavioral Sciences under the Authority of Scripture," *Journal of the Evangelical Theological Society* 20, no. 1 (March 1977): 37.

72. Ibid., 41. McQuilkin struggles to define a strategy to protect evangelicalism from this tendency. He recommends that Scripture be in "functional control" over the theories and methods devised by the psychotherapist, an attitude that involves "not just mental assent to the thesis, which would make for theoretical or constitutional control, but acute awareness of the danger involved and a jealous commitment to the Bible first and last as the originating and controlling source of ideas about man and his relationships" (42). He suggests that one practical step to insure that control is that the Christian behavioral scientist also be trained in theology (43). This is interesting in contrast to James R. Beck, "The

That warning was issued in 1977. McQuilkin's fear was for "the next two decades." Unfortunately, the evangelical community may be ahead of schedule.

Role of Theology in the Training of Christian Psychologists," (*Journal of Psychology and Theology* 20, no. 2 [1992]: 99–109), in which Beck seeks to define some sort of apologetic for the idea of including theological training. He posits "three major roles theology can play in the training curriculum for Christian psychologists," and in developing the second of those he states, "When our quest for understanding thus leads us to the limits of psychology's ability to explain, the Christian can utilize theological understanding to help guide the ongoing search" (103). Rather a long way from McQuilkin's "jealous commitment to the Bible first and last as the originating and controlling source of ideas about man and his relationships"!

5

Counseling and the Sinfulness of Humanity[1]

John MacArthur, Jr.

No concept is more important to the gurus of modern psychology than self-esteem. According to the self-esteem credo, there are no bad people—only people who think badly of themselves.

For years, educational experts, psychologists, and a growing number of Christian leaders have championed self-esteem as a panacea for all sorts of human miseries. According to the purveyors of this doctrine, if people feel good about themselves, they will behave better, have fewer emotional problems, and achieve more. People with high self-esteem, we are told, are less likely to commit crimes, act immorally, fail academically, or have problems in their relationships with others.

THE BLIND FAITH OF SELF-ESTEEM

Advocates of self-esteem have been remarkably successful in convincing people that self-esteem is the solution to whatever ails anyone. One survey revealed that a majority of people view self-esteem as the single most important motivator for hard work and success. In fact, self-esteem ranked several points higher than a sense of responsibility or fear of failure.[2]

---

1. Adapted and abridged from *The Vanishing Conscience* (Dallas: Word, 1994).

2. Jerry Adler et al., "Hey I'm Terrific," *Newsweek* 17 February 1992: 50.

But does self-esteem really work? Does it, for example, promote higher achievement? There is plenty of evidence to suggest it does not. In a recent study, a standardized math test was given to teenagers from six different nations. Besides the math questions, the test asked the youngsters to respond yes or no to the question, "I am good at mathematics." American students scored lowest on the math questions, far behind Korean students, who had the top scores. Ironically, more than three-fourths of the Korean students had answered *no* to the "I am good at math" question. In stark contrast, however, 68 percent of the American students believed their math skills were just fine.[3] Our kids may be failing math, but they obviously feel pretty good about how they are doing.

Morally, our culture is in precisely the same boat. Empirical evidence strongly suggests that society is at an all-time moral low. We might expect people's self-esteem to be suffering as well. But statistics show Americans are feeling better about themselves than ever. In a survey conducted in 1940, 11 percent of women and 20 percent of men agreed with the statement, "I am an important person." In the 1990s, those figures jumped to 66 percent of women and 62 percent of men.[4] Ninety percent of people surveyed in a recent Gallup Poll say their own sense of self-esteem is robust and healthy.[5] Incredibly, while the moral fabric of society is unraveling, self-esteem is thriving. All the positive thinking about ourselves seems not to be doing anything to elevate the culture or motivate people to live better lives.

Can it really be that low self-esteem is what is wrong with people today? Does anyone seriously believe that making people feel better about themselves has helped the problems of crime, moral decay, divorce, child abuse, juvenile delinquency, drug addiction, and all the other evils that have dragged society down? Could so much still be wrong in our culture if the assumptions of self-esteem theory were true? Do we really imagine that more self-esteem will finally solve society's problems? Is there even a shred of evidence that would support such a belief?

Absolutely none. A report in *Newsweek* suggested that "the case for self-esteem . . . is a matter less of scientific pedagogy than of faith—faith that positive thoughts can make manifest the inherent goodness in any

---

3. Charles Krauthammer, "Education: Doing Bad and Feeling Good," *Time* 5 February 1990: 70.

4. Cheryl Russell, "Predictions for the Baby Boom," *The Boomer Report* 15 September 1993: 4.

5. Adler et al., "Terrific," 50.

one."[6] In other words, the notion that self-esteem makes people better is simply a matter of blind religious faith. Not only that, it is a religion that is antithetical to Christianity, because it is predicated on the unbiblical presupposition that people are basically good and need to recognize their own goodness.

THE CHURCH AND THE SELF-ESTEEM CULT

Nevertheless, the most persuasive proponents of self-esteem religion have always included clergymen. Norman Vincent Peale's "positive thinking" doctrine, which was popular a generation ago, was simply an early self-esteem model. Peale wrote *The Power of Positive Thinking* in 1952.[7] The book opened with these words: "Believe in yourself! Have faith in your abilities!" In the introduction, Peale called the book a "personal-improvement manual . . . written with the sole objective of helping the reader achieve a happy, satisfying, and worthwhile life."[8] The book was marketed as motivational therapy, not theology. But in Peale's estimation the whole system was merely "applied Christianity; a simple yet scientific system of practical techniques of successful living that works."[9]

Evangelicals, for the most part, were slow to embrace a system that called people to faith in themselves rather than faith in Jesus Christ. Self-esteem as Norman Vincent Peale outlined it was the offspring of theological liberalism married to neo-orthodoxy.

Time has evidently worn away evangelicals' resistance to such doctrine. Now many of the hottest-selling books in evangelical bookstores promote self-esteem and positive thinking. Even *Newsweek* has commented on the trend. Noting that self-esteem is considered "religiously correct" nowadays, the magazine observed:

> The notion [of self-esteem] may put off anyone old enough to remember when "Christian" as an adjective was often followed by "humility." But American churches, which once did not shrink from calling their congregants wretches, have moved toward a more

---

6. Adler, et al., "Terrific," 50.

7. Norman Vincent Peale, *The Power of Positive Thinking* (Englewood Cliffs, N. J.: Prentice Hall, 1952).

8. Ibid., viii.

9. Ibid., ix.

congenial view of human nature. . . . Chastising sinners is considered counterproductive: it makes them feel worse about themselves.[10]

Psychology and self-esteem theology have fed one another. And as evangelicals become more and more accepting of psychological counseling, they become more and more vulnerable to the dangers posed by self-esteem teaching. As even the *Newsweek* article suggests, those who are concerned primarily with self-esteem are hardly in a position to deal with human transgressions as *sin against God* or to inform people already comfortable in self-love and self-righteousness that they are actually sinners in need of spiritual salvation.

Here one's theology becomes intensely practical. These are questions that must be settled in the heart before the counselor can offer truly biblical counsel: Does God really want all people to feel good about themselves? Or does He first call sinners to recognize the utter helplessness of their own estate? Of course, the answer is obvious to those who let Scripture speak for itself.

UNDERSTANDING THE DOCTRINE OF TOTAL DEPRAVITY

Scripture, of course, teaches from beginning to end that all humanity is *totally depraved*. Paul says unredeemed people are "dead in . . . trespasses and sins" (Eph. 2:1). Apart from salvation, all people walk in worldliness and disobedience (v. 2). We who know and love the Lord once "lived in the lusts of our flesh, indulging the desires of the flesh and of the mind, and were by nature children of wrath, even as the rest" (v. 3). We were "separate from Christ, excluded from the commonwealth of Israel, and strangers to the covenants of promise, having no hope and without God in the world" (v. 12).

In those passages Paul describes the state of unbelievers as estrangement from God. It is that they *hate* God, not that they are intimidated by Him. In fact, Paul says, "There is no fear of God" in the unregenerate person (Rom. 3:18). Before our salvation, we were actually God's enemies (Rom. 5:8, 10). We were "alienated and hostile in mind, engaged in evil deeds" (Col. 1:21). Sinful passions, inflamed by our hatred of God's law, motivated all our living (Rom. 7:5). We were tainted by sin in every part of our being. We were corrupt, evil, thoroughly sinful.

---

10. Adler et al., "Terrific," 50.

Theologians refer to this doctrine as *total depravity*. It does not mean that unbelieving sinners are always as bad as they could be (cf. Luke 6:33; Rom. 2:14). It does not mean that the expression of sinful human nature is always lived out to the fullest. It does not mean that unbelievers are incapable of acts of kindness, benevolence, goodwill, or human altruism. It certainly does not mean that non-Christians cannot appreciate goodness, beauty, honesty, decency, or excellence. It *does* mean that none of this has any merit with God.

Depravity also means that evil has contaminated every aspect of our humanity—our heart, mind, personality, emotions, conscience, motives, and will (cf. Jer. 17:9; John 8:44). Unredeemed sinners are therefore incapable of doing anything to please God (Isa. 64:6). They are incapable of truly loving the God who reveals Himself in Scripture. They are incapable of obedience from the heart, with righteous motives. They are incapable of understanding spiritual truth. They are incapable of genuine faith. And that means they are incapable of pleasing God or truly seeking Him (Heb. 11:1).

Total depravity means sinners have no ability to do spiritual good or to work for their own salvation from sin. They are so completely disinclined to love righteousness, so thoroughly dead in sin, that they are not able to save themselves or even to fit themselves for God's salvation. Unbelieving humanity has no capacity to desire, understand, believe, or apply spiritual truth: "A natural man does not accept the things of the Spirit of God; for they are foolishness to him, and he cannot understand them, because they are spiritually appraised" (1 Cor. 2:14). In spite of all this, people are *proud* of themselves! Lack of self-esteem is not the issue.

Because of Adam's sin, this state of spiritual death called total depravity has passed to all mankind. Another term for this is *original sin*. Scripture explains it this way: "Through one man sin entered into the world, and death through sin, and so death spread to all men, because all sinned (Rom. 5:12). When, as head of the human race, Adam sinned, the whole race was corrupted. "Through the one man's disobedience the many were made sinners" (Rom 5:19). How such a thing could happen has been the subject of much theological discussion for centuries. For our purposes, however, it is sufficient to affirm that Scripture clearly teaches that Adam's sin brought guilt upon the entire race. We were "in Adam" when he sinned, and therefore the guilt of sin and the sentence of death passed upon all of us: "In Adam all die" (1 Cor. 15:22).

We might be tempted to think, *If I'm sinful by birth and never had a morally neutral nature, how can I be held responsible for being a sinner?* But our corrupt nature is precisely why our guilt is such a serious matter. Sin flows from the very soul of our being. It is because of our sinful nature that we commit sinful acts: "For from within, out of the heart of men, proceed the evil thoughts, fornications, thefts, murders, adulteries, deeds of coveting and wickedness, as well as deceit, sensuality, envy, slander, pride and foolishness. All these evil things proceed from within and defile the man" (Mark 7:21–23). We are "by nature children of wrath" (Eph. 2:3). Original sin—including all the corrupt tendencies and sinful passions of the soul— is as deserving of punishment as all our voluntary acts of sin. What is sin, after all, but *anomia*—"lawlessness" (1 John 3:4)? Or as the Westminster Shorter Catechism says, "Sin is any want of conformity to, or transgression of, the law of God" (q. 14). Far from being an excuse, original sin itself is at the heart of *why* we are guilty. And original sin itself is sufficient grounds for our condemnation before God.

Moreover, original sin with its resulting depravity is the *reason* we commit voluntary acts of sin. D. Martyn Lloyd-Jones wrote,

> Why is it that man ever chooses to sin? The answer is that man has fallen away from God, and as a result, his whole nature has become perverted and sinful. Man's whole bias is away from God. By nature he hates God and feels that God is opposed to him. His god is himself, his own abilities and powers, his own desires. He objects to the whole idea of God and the demands which God makes upon him. . . . Furthermore, man likes and covets the things which God prohibits, and dislikes the things and the kind of life to which God calls him. These are no mere dogmatic statements. They are facts. . . . They alone explain the moral muddle and the ugliness that characterise life to such an extent today.[11]

Salvation from original sin is only through the cross of Christ: "As through the one man's disobedience [Adam's sin] the many were made sinners, even so through the obedience of the One [Jesus Christ] the many will be made righteous" (Rom. 5:19). We are born in sin (Ps. 51:5), and if we are to become children of God and enter God's kingdom, we must be born again by God's Spirit (John 3:3–8).

In other words, contrary to what most people think—contrary to the presuppositions of self-esteem doctrine—men and women are not naturally good. Just the opposite is true. We are by nature enemies of God,

---

11. D. Martyn Lloyd-Jones, *The Plight of Man and the Power of God* (Grand Rapids: Eerdmans, 1945), 87.

sinners, lovers of ourselves, and in bondage to our own sin. We are blind, deaf, and dead to spiritual matters, unable even to believe apart from God's gracious intervention. Yet we are relentlessly proud! In fact, nothing is more illustrative of human wickedness than the desire for self-esteem. And the first step to a proper self-image is a recognition that these things are true.

That is why Jesus *commended* the tax-gatherer—rather than rebuking him for his low self-esteem—when the man pounded his chest and pleaded, "God, be merciful to me, the sinner!" (Luke 18:13). The man had finally come to the point where he saw himself for what he was, and he was so overcome that his emotion released in acts of self-condemnation. The truth is, his self-image had never been more sound than at that moment. Rid of pride and pretense, he now saw there was nothing he could ever do to earn God's favor. Instead, he pleaded with God for mercy. And therefore he "went down to his house justified"—exalted by God because he had humbled himself (v. 14). For the first time ever he was in a position to realize true joy, peace with God, and a new sense of self-worth that is granted by God's grace to those He adopts as His children (Rom. 8:15).

ALL HAVE SINNED AND FALL SHORT

Deep in our hearts, we all know something is desperately wrong with us. Our conscience constantly confronts us with our own sinfulness. Try as we might to blame others or seek psychological explanations for how we feel, we cannot escape reality. We cannot ultimately deny our own consciences. We all feel our guilt, and we all know the horrible truth about who we are on the inside.

We *feel* guilty because we *are* guilty. Only the cross of Christ can answer sin in a way that frees us from our own shame. Psychology might mask some of the pain of our guilt. Self-esteem might sweep it under the rug for a time. Other things—such as seeking comfort in relationships, or blaming our problems on someone else—might make us feel better, but the relief is only superficial. And it is dangerous. In fact, it often intensifies the guilt, because it adds dishonesty and pride to the sin that originally wounded the conscience.

True guilt has only one cause, and that is sin. Until sin is dealt with, the conscience will fight to accuse. And sin—not low self-esteem—is the very thing the gospel is given to conquer. That is why the apostle Paul began his presentation of the gospel to the Romans with a lengthy discourse about sin. Total depravity is the first gospel truth he introduced, and he spent nearly three full chapters on the subject. Romans 1:18–32 demonstrates the guilt of the pagans. Romans 2:1–16 proves the guilt of the moralist, who violates the very standard by which he judges others. And Romans 2:17–3:8 establishes the guilt of the Jews, who had access to all the benefits of divine grace but as a whole rejected God's righteousness nonetheless.

Since Romans 1 Paul has argued eloquently, citing evidence from nature, history, sound reason, and conscience to prove the utter sinfulness of all humanity. And in verses 9–20 of chapter 3, he sums it all up. Paul reasons like an attorney giving his final summation. He reviews his arguments like a prosecutor who has made an ironclad case against all humanity. It is a powerful and compelling presentation, replete with a charge, convincing proof, and the inescapable verdict.

The Charge

"What then? Are we better than they? Not at all; for we have already charged that both Jews and Greeks are all under sin" (Rom. 3:9). Paul's indictment thus begins with two questions: What then? or, "Is there any need of further testimony?" And, Are we better than they? or, "Can anyone honestly claim to live above the level of human nature I have been describing?"

"*Not at all*," he answers. Everyone from the most degenerate, perverted sinner (Rom. 1:28–32) to the most rigidly legalistic Jew falls into the same category of total depravity. In other words, the entire human race, without exception, is arraigned in the divine courtroom and charged with being "under sin"—wholly subjugated to the power of sin. All unredeemed people, Paul is saying, are subservient to sin, in thrall to it, taken captive to sin's authority.

Paul's Jewish readers would have found this truth every bit as shocking and unbelievable as it must be to those weaned on modern self-esteem doctrine. They believed they were acceptable to God by birth and that only Gentiles were sinners by nature. Jews were, after all, God's chosen people. The idea that all Jews were sinners was contrary to the beliefs of the Pharisees. They taught that only derelicts, beggars, and Gentiles were born in sin (cf. John 9:34). But Scripture clearly pronounces otherwise. Even David said, "I was brought forth in iniquity, and in sin my mother conceived me" (Ps. 51:5). "The whole world lies in the power of the evil one" (1 John 5:19). Modern humanity, weaned on self-esteem psychology, also finds it shocking to learn that all of us are by nature sinful and unworthy creatures.

The Proof

Paul, continuing his courtroom summation, goes on to prove from the Old Testament Scriptures the universality of human depravity:

> As it is written, "There is none righteous, not even one; there is none who understands, there is none who seeks for God; all have turned aside, together they have become useless; there is none who does good, there is not even one. Their throat is an open grave, with their tongues they keep deceiving, the poison of asps is under their lips; whose mouth is full of cursing and bitterness; their feet are swift to shed blood, destruction and misery are in their paths, and the path of peace have they not known" (3:10–17).

Notice how Paul underscores the universality of sin. In those few verses, he says "none" or "not even one" six times. No person escapes the accusation. "The Scripture has shut up all men under sin" (Gal. 3:22).

Paul's argument is constructed in three parts. First he shows *how sin corrupts the character*: "There is none righteous . . . there is none who does good, there is not even one" (Rom. 3:10–12). Here Paul makes six charges. He says that because of their innate depravity, people are universally evil ("none righteous"); spiritually ignorant ("none who understands"), rebellious ("none who seeks for God"), wayward ("all have turned aside"), spiritually useless ("together they have become useless"), and morally corrupt ("there is none who does good").

The verse Paul is quoting is Psalm 14:1: "The fool has said in his heart, 'There is no God.' They are corrupt, they have committed abominable deeds; there is no one who does good." The words at the end of Romans 3:12, "not even one," are an editorial comment from Paul, added to make the truth inescapable for someone who might otherwise think of himself as an exception to the rule—as is the common attitude of self-justifying sinners.

Notice, Paul does not suggest that some sinners might be prone to think worse of themselves than they ought to. The very opposite is true: "I say to every man among you not to think more highly of himself than he ought to think" (Rom. 12:3). Undue pride is the typical and expected response of sinners. Self-esteem teaching is the expression of that very pride. Making a savage feel good about himself only increases his deadliness.

Again, the utter depravity Paul is describing certainly does not mean that all people play out the expression of their sin to the ultimate degree. There are certainly some people who are good in a relative sense. They may have characteristics of compassion, generosity, kindness, integrity, decency, thoughtfulness, and so on. But even those characteristics are imperfect and sullied with human sin and weakness. No one—"not even one"—comes close to true righteousness. God's standard, after all, is absolute perfection: "You are to be perfect, as your heavenly Father is perfect" (Matt. 5:48). In other words, no one who falls short of the touchstone of perfection is acceptable to God! What does that do to self-esteem theology? How does one feel good about oneself when God Himself declares us worthy of wrath?

There *is* an answer to the dilemma, of course. God justifies the ungodly by faith (Rom. 4:5). Christ's own perfect righteousness is imputed to our account, so by faith we can stand before God clothed in a perfect righteousness that is not our own (Phil. 3:9). This does not speak of external works that we do. It is a superior righteousness, the totality of Christ's own righteousness, credited to our account. Christ, on our behalf, has already fulfilled the requirement of being as perfect as our heavenly Father is perfect. His virtue is assigned to our account, so God regards us as fully righteous.

But we are jumping ahead of the apostle's carefully arranged evidence. He adds a paraphrase also from Psalm 14: "The Lord has looked down from heaven upon the sons of men, to see if there are any who understand, who seek after God" (v. 2; cf. 53:3). Ignorance and depravity go hand in hand. But people are not sinful and enemies of God because of their spiritual ignorance; rather they are spiritually ignorant because of their sinfulness and their adversarial disposition toward God. They are "darkened in their understanding, excluded from the life of God, because of the ignorance that is in them, *because of the hardness of their heart*" (Eph. 4:18, emphasis added). In other words, because of their hatred of God and their love for their own sin, they reject the witness of God in creation and the testimony of their conscience (Rom. 1:19–20). This hardens the heart and darkens the mind.

The hard heart and darkened mind refuse to seek for God: "There is *none* who seeks for God." That again echoes Psalm 14:2. God invites the seeker and promises that those who seek Him with all their hearts will find Him (Jer. 29:13). Jesus also promised that everyone who seeks Him will find Him (Matt. 7:8). But the sinful heart is inclined away from God and does not seek Him. Without God's gracious, sovereign intervention, seeking and drawing sinners to Himself first, no one would seek and be saved. Jesus Himself said, "No one can come to Me, unless the Father who sent Me draws him . . . (John 6:44).

Rather than seeking God, sinners inevitably go their own way. Still using Psalm 14, Paul cites verse 3: "They have all turned aside"—or as Romans 3:12 has it, "All have turned aside." This is reminiscent of Isaiah 53:6: "All of us like sheep have gone astray, each of us has turned to his own way." Sinners are naturally wayward. Inherent in human depravity is an inescapable drift away from truth and righteousness. Sinners always lose their way: "There is a way which seems right to a man, but its end is the way of death" (Prov. 14:12).

The taint of sin further renders the sinner "useless" (v. 12)—translating a Greek word used to describe spoiled milk or contaminated food to be thrown out. Unredeemed people are unfit for any spiritual good, useless for righteousness, fit only to be thrown into the fire and burned (John 15:6). Their great need is not self-esteem or positive thinking, but redemption from their prideful sin.

In the next few verses Paul describes *how sin defiles the conversation*: "Their throat is an open grave, with their tongues they keep deceiving, the poison of asps is under their lips; whose mouth is full of cursing and bitterness" (3:13–14). One's true character inevitably becomes apparent in conversation. Scripture is filled with affirmation of this truth:

- "The mouth speaks out of that which fills the heart. The good man out of his good treasure brings forth what is good; and the evil man out of his evil treasure brings forth what is evil" (Matt. 12:34–35).

- "The things that proceed out of the mouth come from the heart . . . " (Matt. 15:18).

- "The mouth of the righteous flows with wisdom, but the perverted tongue will be cut out. The lips of the righteous bring forth what is acceptable, but the mouth of the wicked, what is perverted" (Prov. 10:31–32).

- "The tongue of the wise makes knowledge acceptable, but the mouth of fools spouts folly. . . . The heart of the righteous ponders how to answer, but the mouth of the wicked pours out evil things" (Prov. 15:2, 28).

- "Your iniquities have made a separation between you and your God, and your sins have hidden His face from you, so that He does not hear. For your hands are defiled with blood, and your fingers with iniquity; your lips have spoken falsehood, your tongue mutters wickedness" (Isa. 59:2–3).

- "They bend their tongue like their bow; lies and not truth prevail in the land. . . . Every neighbor goes about as a slanderer. And everyone deceives his neighbor, and does not speak the truth, they have taught their tongue to speak lies . . . " (Jer. 9:3–5).

Paul chooses more passages from the psalms to underscore the point:

- "Poison of a viper is under their lips" (Ps. 140:3).
- "There is nothing reliable in what they say; their inward part is destruction itself; their throat is an open grave; they flatter with their tongue" (Ps. 5:9).
- "His mouth is full of curses and deceit and oppression; under his tongue is mischief and wickedness" (Ps. 10:7).

Those verses, all written to condemn "the wicked," Paul applies to everyone. He is making the point that human depravity is universal. *All* are wicked. *Everyone* is guilty. *No one* can claim exemption from the charges Paul levels.

Moreover, he is illustrating how thoroughly sin pervades and permeates every aspect of our humanity. Note how completely sin contaminates the conversation: it defiles the "throat," corrupts the "tongue," poisons the "lips," and pollutes the "mouth." Evil speech, an expression of the wickedness of the heart, thus defiles every organ it touches as it "proceeds out of the mouth," defiling the whole person (Matt. 15:11).

Third, Paul quotes several verses to show *how sin perverts the conduct*: "Their feet are swift to shed blood, destruction and misery are in their paths, and the path of peace have they not known" (Rom. 3:15–17). Here Paul is quoting a passage from Isaiah. This is significant, because in these verses Isaiah was excoriating Israel for their sins against Jehovah. This was no denunciation of wicked pagans, but an indictment of religious people who believed in God: "Their feet run to evil, and they hasten to shed innocent blood; their thoughts are thoughts of iniquity; devastation and destruction are in their highways. They do not know the way of peace, and there is no justice in their tracks; they have made their paths crooked; whoever treads on them does not know peace" (Isa. 59:7–8).

The phrase "their feet are swift to shed blood" describes sinful humanity's penchant for murder. Remember, Jesus taught that hatred is the moral equivalent of murder (Matt. 5:21–22). The seed of hatred ripens and matures, and the fruit it bears is the shedding of blood. Sinners are naturally attracted to hatred and its violent offspring. People are "swift" in their advance toward such acts. We see this very clearly in our own society. An article in *Newsweek*, for example, recently reported that "a 12-year-old boy turn[ed] without a word and [shot] dead a 7-year-old girl because she 'dis'ed' him by standing on his shadow."[12]

In some of our larger cities, as many as two hundred murders will occur in a typical week. Drive-by shootings, drunken brawls, gang violence, family strife, and other crimes all contribute to the body count. If lack of self-esteem is the problem of the human heart, why, we must ask, is the murder rate on the rise so dramatically in a society where self-esteem is also growing? The answer is that low self-esteem is not the problem. On the contrary, pride itself is the very problem that leads to all sin, including hate, hostility, and killing. A love for bloodshed festers in the heart of sinful humanity. Remove the moral restraints from society, and the inevitable result will be an escalation of murder and violence—no matter how good people feel about themselves.

"Destruction and misery" further characterize the tendencies of depraved humanity. Again, no one familiar with the trends of modern society can deny the truth of Scripture on this point. The lid is off, and we can see clearly the true nature of the human heart. What else could explain our culture—where people are robbed, beaten, raped, or murdered for no reason other than sheer enjoyment? Wanton destruction is so much a part of society that we have become inured to much of it.

"Gangsta rap"—music that glorifies murder, rape, and drug use— now accounts for many of the hottest-selling albums on the record charts. The lyrics of most gangsta rap are indescribably vile. They mix violence, sexual imagery, and unimaginable profanity in a way that is repulsive and purposely offensive. Worse, they openly incite young people to join gangs, kill policemen, rape women, riot, and commit other acts of wanton destruction. Gangsta rap is big business. These recordings are not sold secretly out of the back of some hoodlum's car, but marketed openly in retail stores everywhere—with slick ad campaigns designed by executives in companies like Capitol Records. And the prime target for such products are kids younger than eighteen. A whole generation is being indoctrinated with these vices. Destruction and misery *are* in their path. And woe to those unfortunate enough to cross their path! In recent months several nation-

---

12. George F. Will, "A Trickle-Down Culture," *Newsweek* 13 December 1993: 84.

ally-known rap artists have been charged with violent crimes, including murder and gang rape.

Why is it that misery and despair are so characteristic of this modern age, even though humanity has made such remarkable advances in technology, psychology, and medicine? It is because depravity is at the very heart of the human soul. All these problems are so bound up in the human heart that no amount of learning and no measure of self-esteem will ever erase them. As science advances, people only become more sophisticated in their use of evil means. The destruction and misery wrought by human sin does not diminish; it accelerates. The history of this century, filled with world wars, holocausts, serial killers, escalating crime, and bloody revolutions, is graphic proof of that. Depravity is bound up in the human heart.

In other words, "the path of peace" is unknown to sinful humanity (Rom. 3:17). Though we hear much talk these days of "peace, peace," there is no peace (cf. Jer. 6:14).

Paul sums up the evidence for human depravity: "There is no fear of God before their eyes" (Rom. 3:18). There he returns to the psalms for a final quotation. Psalm 36:1 says, "Transgression speaks to the ungodly within his heart; there is no fear of God before his eyes." Human sinfulness is a defect of the human heart itself. Evil commands the heart of man. People's hearts are naturally attuned to wickedness. They have no native fear of God.

Fear of the Lord, of course, is the primary prerequisite to spiritual wisdom (Prov. 9:10). Moses commanded Israel, "You shall fear only the Lord your God; and you shall worship Him, and swear by His name" (Deut. 6:13). In fact, as Moses summed up the responsibilities of the Israelites, this is what he said: "And now, Israel, what does the Lord your God require from you, but to *fear* the Lord your God, to walk in all His ways and love Him, and to serve the Lord your God with all your heart and with all your soul, and to keep the Lord's commandments and His statutes which I am commanding you today for your good?" (Deut. 10:12–13, emphasis added). We in the New Testament era are likewise commanded to "cleanse ourselves from all defilement of flesh and spirit, perfecting holiness in the fear of God" (2 Cor. 7:1). We are to "honor all men; love the brotherhood, *fear God*, honor the king" (1 Pet. 2:17, emphasis added, cf. Rev. 14:7).

"The fear of the Lord is the instruction for wisdom" (Prov. 15:33). "By the fear of the Lord one keeps away from evil" (Prov. 16:6). "The fear of the Lord is a fountain of life, that one may avoid the snares of death" (Prov. 14:27).

We do not hear much about fearing God these days. Even many Christians seem to feel the language of fear is somehow too harsh or too negative. How much easier it is to speak of God's love and infinite mercy. But longsuffering, kindness, and such attributes are not the truths that are missing from most people's concept of God. The problem is that most people do not think of God as someone to be *feared*. They do not realize that He hates the proud and punishes evildoers. They presume on His grace. They fear what people think more than they care what God thinks. They seek their own pleasure, unmindful of God's displeasure. Their conscience is defiled and in danger of vanishing. "There is no fear of God before their eyes."

The fear of God, by the way, is a concept diametrically opposed to the doctrine of self-esteem. How can we encourage fear of the Lord in people and at the same time be obsessed with boosting their self-esteem? Which is the more biblical pursuit? The Scriptures speak for themselves.

The Verdict

Having presented a convincing case for total depravity, Paul makes the verdict clear: "Now we know that what things soever the law saith, it saith to them who are under the law: *that every mouth may be stopped, and all the world may become guilty before God*" (Rom. 3:19, KJV, emphasis added).

Here Paul blasted the assumption of those who believed that merely *having* the law of God somehow made the Jews morally superior to pagan Gentiles. The law carried its own condemnation against those who did not keep it perfectly: "Cursed is he who does not confirm the words of this law by doing them" (Deut. 27:26; cf. Gal. 3:10). "Whoever keeps the whole law and yet stumbles in one point, he has become guilty of all" (James 2:10). Merely having the law did not make the Jews any better than the rest of humanity.

The Gentiles, on the other hand, were accountable to the law written on their own consciences (Rom. 2:11–15). Both groups are proven in violation of the law they possess. The prosecution rests. There can be no defense. Every mouth must be stopped. The case is closed. Unredeemed humanity is guilty of all charges. There are no grounds for acquittal. The whole world stands guilty before God.

Self-esteem is no solution to human depravity. It aggravates it! The problems of our culture—especially the anguish that wracks individual human hearts—will not be solved by the deception of getting people to think better of themselves. People really *are* sinful to the core. The guilt and shame we all feel as sinners is legitimate, natural, and even appropriate. It has the beneficial purpose of letting us know the depth of our own sinfulness. We dare not whisk it aside for the faulty teachings of humanistic self-esteem.

I recently read an unusually clear-sighted article dealing with the myth of human goodness from a non-Christian perspective. The author, a Jewish social critic, writes,

> To believe that people are basically good after Auschwitz, the Gulag and the other horrors of our century, is a statement of irrational faith, as irrational as any [fanatical] religious belief. Whenever I meet people—especially Jews, victims of the most concentrated evil in history—who persist is believing in the essential goodness of people, I know that I have met people for whom evidence is irrelevant. How many evils would human beings have to commit in order to shake a Jew's faith in humanity? How many more innocent people have to be murdered and tortured? How many more women need to be raped?[13]

This article lists five consequences of the people-are-basically-good myth. Notice how they all contribute to the destruction of the conscience:

> The first such consequence is, quite logically, the attribution of all evil to causes outside of people. Since people are basically good, the bad that they do must be caused by some external force. Depending on who is doing the blaming, that outside force could be the social environment, economic circumstances, parents, schools, television violence, handguns, racism, the devil, government cutbacks, or even corrupt politicians (as expressed by this frequently heard foolishness: "How can we expect our children to be honest when the government isn't?").
>
> People are therefore not responsible for the evil they commit. It's not my fault that I mug old women, or that I cheat much of the time—something (chosen from the previous list) made me do it.
>
> A second terrible consequence is the denial of evil. If good is natural, then bad must be unnatural, or "sick." Moral categories have been replaced by psychological ones. There is no longer good and evil, only "normal" and "sick."
>
> Third, neither parents nor schools take the need to teach children goodness seriously—why teach what comes naturally? Only those who recognize that people are not basically good recognize the need to teach goodness.

---

13. Dennis Prager, "The Belief that People Are Basically Good," *Ultimate Issues* (January–March 1990); 15.

Fourth, since much of society believes that evil comes from outside of people, it has ceased trying to change people's values and concentrates instead on changing outside forces. People commit crimes? It is not values and character development that we need to be concerned with; we need to change the socioeconomic environment that "produces" rapists and murderers. Irresponsible men impregnate irresponsible women? It is not better values they need, but better sex education and better access to condoms and abortions.

Fifth, and most destructive of all, those who believe that people are basically good conclude that people do not need to feel accountable of their behavior to God and to a religion, only to themselves.[14]

That author, oddly enough, denies human depravity as well as human goodness. He believes people are neither good *nor* bad but choose their way in life. (At the outset of his article, however, he quotes Genesis 8:21: "The intent of man's heart is evil from his youth.")

Despite this inconsistency in the author's position, the article shows very clearly the dangers of the myth of human goodness.

The Church must safeguard sound doctrine by recovering the doctrine of human depravity. As J. C. Ryle wrote nearly a century ago,

A scriptural view of sin is one of the best antidotes to that vague, dim, misty, hazy kind of theology which is so painfully current in the present age. It is vain to shut our eyes to the fact that there is a vast quantity of so-called Christianity nowadays which you cannot declare positively unsound, but which, nevertheless, is not full measure, good weight and sixteen ounces to the pound. It is a Christianity in which there is undeniably "something about Christ and something about grace and something about faith and something about repentance and something about holiness," but it is not the real "thing as it is" in the Bible. Things are out of place and out of proportion. As old Latimer would have said, it is a kind of "mingle-mangle," and does no good. It neither exercises influence on daily conduct, nor comforts in life, nor gives peace in death; and those who hold it often wake too late to find that they have got nothing solid under their feet. Now I believe that the likeliest way to cure and mend this defective kind of religion is to bring forward more prominently the old scriptural truth about the sinfulness of sin.[15]

---

14. Prager, "People Are Basically Good," 15.

15. J. C. Ryle, *Holiness* (1879; reprint, Durham, England: Evangelical Press, 1991), 9–10.

You may be asking, on the other hand, *Does God want us to wallow in shame and self-condemnation permanently?* Not at all. God offers freedom from sin and shame through faith in Jesus Christ. If we are willing to acknowledge our sinfulness and seek His grace, He will wonderfully deliver us from our sin and all its effects. "There is therefore now no condemnation for those who are in Christ Jesus. For the law of the Spirit of life in Christ Jesus has set you free from the law of sin and of death" (Rom. 8:1–2). The liberation from sin those verses describe is the only basis on which we can really feel good about ourselves.

6

Union with Christ: The Implications for Biblical Counseling

David B. Maddox

Counseling is about change.[1] It is necessarily so because gospel ministry proclaims that in Christ there is a future hope and a present reality of

---

1. It is not within the scope of this chapter to present argumentation for the biblical teaching of the expected change of the regenerate, otherwise referred to as progressive sanctification. Yet, we should acknowledge that real, progressive change is fundamental to Reformed faith. Representative are the works of G. C. Berkouwer. For instance, in *Faith and Sanctification* (Grand Rapids: Eerdmans, 1952) he states that "faith is not merely an intellectual affirmation of a distant and alien righteousness but that it is a power which renews man and expresses itself in good works" (39). In a more recent work, J. P. Moreland suggests that any commitment to truth will include a "resolve to cultivate the mind as part of our discipleship under the lordship of Christ," in introduction to *Christian Perspectives in Being Human: A Multidisciplinary Approach to Integration,* ed. J. P. Moreland and D. M. Ciocchi (Grand Rapids: Baker, 1993), 8. In the same work, Robert Saucy abjures that, "It is significant that faith, which obviously entails thought, is nevertheless always associated even in the New Testament with the heart indicating that true believing is more than an intellectual activity" (36). The normalcy of life change has sparked not a little debate in recent years most commonly discussed under the banner of "lordship salvation." Lewis Sperry Chafer (*He That is Spiritual* [New York: Our Hope, 1918]) joined by his colleagues John Walvoord (*The Holy Spirit* [Grand Rapids: Zondervan, 1954]), Charles Ryrie (*Balancing The Christian Life* [Chicago: Moody, 1969]) and *So Great Salvation* (Wheaton: Victor, 1989), and Zane Hodges (*The Gospel Under Siege* [Dallas: Redencion Viva, 1981]) has led the contingency who hold to what may be described as the "normality of non-change." The reader would do well to become familiar with the works of John F. MacArthur, Jr. (*The Gospel According to Jesus* [Grand Rapids: Zondervan, 1988] and *Faith Works* [Dallas: Word, 1993]); John Murray (*Redemption, Accomplished and Applied* and *Principles of Conduct* [Grand Rapids: Eerdmans, 1955]); and Robert Belcher's excellent summary, *A Layman's Guide to the Lordship Controversy* (Southbridge, Mass.: Crowne, 1990).

renewal.[2] The concept of change is central to the gospel, as J. Gresham Machen states: "It is inconceivable that a man should be given this faith in Christ, that he should accept this gift which Christ offers, and still go on contentedly in sin. For the very thing which Christ offers us is salvation from sin—not only salvation from the guilt of sin, but also salvation from the power of sin."[3]

The counselor, as one who ministers the gospel of grace,[4] endeavors to move the counselee in a godward direction. Although all counselors take with them a culture of information from which they draw and get basic direction,[5] three fundamental assumptions that *biblical* counselors must maintain are: (1) God has created each person; (2) sin has prejudiced each person; and (3) God has made provision for each person to change. It is my intention in this chapter to discuss a subject I consider to have utmost theological importance and practical implications—union with Christ. It is my contention that the primary reality of change in salvation is comprehended by union with Christ.

BEGINNING ASSUMPTIONS ABOUT UNION WITH CHRIST

Godward change, which is at once distinct and yet inseperable from initial change wrought by union, is not an option because "real faith inevitably produces a changed life."[6] Paul said that whom God "foreknew He also predestined to become conformed to the image of His Son" (Rom. 8:29). Characteristically, Paul follows the great discourses of what God has accomplished in Christ (the indicatives) with Spirit-endorsed commands (the imperatives) to live in a "manner worthy of the calling with which [we] have been called" (Eph. 4:1). The imperatives of Ephesians (ch. 4–6)

---

2. Speaking of change in a chapter titled "On the Biblical Notion of 'Renewal,'" B. B. Warfield says that "This conception [change] is that salvation in Christ involves a radical and complete transformation . . . by virtue of which we become 'new men' (Eph. iv. 24, Col. iii. 10), no longer conformed to this world (Rom. xii. 2, Eph. iv. 22, Col. iii. 9), but in knowledge and holiness of the truth created after the image of God (Eph. iv. 24, Col. iii. 10, Rom. xii. 2)" in *Biblical Doctrines* (Edinburgh: Banner of Truth Trust, 1988), 439.

3. J. G. Machen, *What is Faith* (New York: Macmillan, 1925), 203.

4. Jay Adams rightly refers to counseling as the Church's "God-given task" in *A Theology of Christian Counseling* (Grand Rapids: Zondervan, 1979), x.

5. See David Powlison, "Which Presuppositions? Secular Psychology and the Categories of Biblical Thought," *Journal of Theology and Psychology* 12, no.4 (1984): 270–278.

6. MacArthur, *Faith Works*, 24.

follow the indicatives of the first three chapters of that same epistle.[7] Similarly, in Paul's epistle to Roman believers, his *magnus opus* of theology, the indicatives of chapters 1 through 11 form the foundation necessary for the imperatives of chapters 12 through 16. To the apostle, change is an assumed experience because it is preceded by, grounded in, and generated out of God's objective working—what Ridderbos terms the historical-redemptive working of God in Christ.[8] Ridderbos explains that "The imperative is grounded on the reality that has been given with the indicative, appeals to it, and is intended to bring it to full development."[9]

Although godward change is expected and grounded in the work of God in Christ, we must hasten to add that in this life change will never be complete. In terms that at first seem a bit surprising, Paul describes believers as those who "groan" in this life while waiting eagerly for the "adoption . . . the redemption of the body" (Rom. 8:23).[10] The consummation of the redemption must wait until that day when we will be fully transformed into the image of Christ (1 John 3:2). Meanwhile, we live in the age that falls between the "already" (which has the dual constituents of historical-redemptive and personal-appropriative) and the "not yet," or the final consummation that occurs when we will be ushered into the presence of Christ. Therefore, the Christian life is lived out between the "already" and the "not yet" of redemption, it is in this present age that we are called upon by God to be transformed (Rom. 12:2). In other words, we are to struggle against sin in the pursuit of godward change.

Hence, it is necessary that biblical counselors be equipped with the knowledge of the character of change (past, present, and future) in order to help counselees whose lives are suspended between the polarities of "already"

---

7. Berkouwer makes the significant statement: "There is never a stretch along the way of salvation where justification drops out of sight." *Faith and Sanctification*, 77.

8. Ridderbos explains this term: "The governing motif of Paul's preaching is the saving activity of God in the advent and the work, particularly in the death and resurrection of Christ. This activity is on the one hand the fulfillment of the work of God in the history of the nation Israel, the fulfillment therefore also of the Scriptures; on the other hand it reaches out to the ultimate consummation of the parousia of Christ and the coming of the kingdom of God. It is this great redemptive-historical framework within which the whole of Paul's preaching must be understood and all of its subordinate parts receive their place and organically cohere." *Paul: An Outline of His Theology* (Grand Rapids: Eerdmans, 1975), 39.

9. Ibid., 255.

10. J. Murray, *Romans* (Grand Rapids: Eerdmans, 1979), 307. Murray explains that the groaning in this passage is not "mere groaning under the burden of imperfection of the present but groaning *for* the glory to be revealed."

and "not yet." At the same time, the counselee is faced with the Bible-endorsed expectation that he or she become more like God *now* and yet confronted with the ever-present, active, antagonistic principle—sin.

God entered the dimensions of time and space in the incarnation to effect change in the environment of fallenness. Thus when we speak of change we must consider the doctrine of union with Christ, the doctrine that encompasses the past, present, and future of a believer's transformation. It swallows the indicatives and the imperatives and hence provides the answers to the *how* of change and the *why* of struggle. The counselor must know what the Bible teaches concerning union with Christ in order to understand *what* changes in salvation and *why* believers, who have been changed, sin. Because the counselor's position on those two issues will control how he or she responds to a counselee who is entangled in sin, the doctrine of union with Christ is an essential part of the biblical counselor's theological understanding. Out of the counseling comprehension of the three tenses of change (past, present, and future) will grow his or her method of counseling.

THE IMPORTANCE OF UNION WITH CHRIST

Union with Christ is at once a difficult and woefully neglected subject (the latter possibly explained by the former). Yet Sinclair Ferguson writes that union with Christ is "a doctrine which lies at the heart of the Christian life and is intimately related to all the other doctrines. . . . Union with Christ is the foundation of all our spiritual experience and all spiritual blessings."[11] And Murray observes that "Union with Christ is really the central truth of the whole doctrine of salvation, not only in its application but also in its once-for-all accomplishment in the finished work of Christ."[12] In addition, the respected theologian A. W. Pink introduces his work on union with this emphatic statement:

> The present writer has not the least doubt in his mind that the subject of *spiritual union* is the most important, the most profound, and yet most blessed of any that is set forth in the sacred Scriptures; and yet, sad to say, there is hardly any which is now more

---

11. S. Ferguson, *Know Your Christian Life* (Downers Grove, Ill.: InterVarsity, 1981), 92–93.

12. Murray, *Redemption*, 170.

generally neglected. The very expression "spiritual union" is unknown in most professing Christian circles, and even where it is employed it is given such a protracted meaning as to take in only a fragment of this precious truth. Probably its very profundity is the reason why it is so largely ignored in this superficial age.[13]

Counselors must emphasize the doctrine of union with Christ because it incorporates two key issues essential to understanding change and struggle. *First*, union with Christ is an all-encompassing doctrine. "It embraces the wide span of salvation from its ultimate source in the eternal election of God to its final fruition in the glorification of the elect."[14] *Second*, it is the one doctrine that embraces the factors of what Christ has accomplished (the indicative) and what believers are commanded to do (the imperative). Moule says that the gospel begins "in the indicative statement of what God has done," and before it goes on to the imperatives "to struggle" it confronts us with the imperative "to attach oneself (be baptized! be incorporate!)."[15] Configured between what God has accomplished in Christ and what we are to do in obedience, and possessed with a scope that extends from eternity past to eternity future, union with Christ is an indispensable doctrine in understanding change and struggle in people's lives.

THE REPRESENTATIONS OF UNION WITH CHRIST

In Scripture we find that union with Christ is taught through at least five metaphors.[16] *First*, is the union of a building and its foundation. In

---

13. A. W. Pink, *Spiritual Union and Communion* (Grand Rapids: Baker, 1971), 7.

14. Murray, *Redemption*, 165.

15. C. F. D. Moule, "The 'New Life' in Colossians 3:1–17" *Review and Expositor* 70, no. 4 (1973): 482.

16. The tedious labor of the biblical interpreter is further complicated when distinguishing literal from nonliteral usage, particularly when a given term is used in the NT both analogically and nonanalogically such as *body* and *flesh*. Serious error results when we fail to recognize metaphor or when we fancifully and unjustifiably insinuate it where it does not belong. Paul S. Minear cautions: "The whole history of Biblical interpretation might be told in terms of the process by which certain key images have, during successive periods in the history of thought, moved from the realm of relatively marginal metaphors into the realm of central and decisive concepts. Moreover, the opposite movement has always been in operation: a concept once deemed essential has moved toward the periphery of thought." *Images of the Church in the New Testament* (Philadelphia: Westminster, 1960), 18–19.

Ephesians, Paul speaks of Christ as the "corner stone." In Christ, "the whole building, being fitted together, is growing into a holy temple in the Lord; in whom you also are being built together into a dwelling of God in the Spirit" (2:21–22). Peter says that Christ is "a living stone, rejected by men, but choice and precious in the sight of God, you also, as living stones, are being built up as a spiritual house . . ." (1 Pet. 2:4–5). *Second,* union with Christ is pictured by union between man and wife. Paul's classic statement in Ephesians speaks to this metaphor, "For this cause a man shall leave his father and mother, and shall cleave to his wife; and the two shall become one flesh. This mystery is great; but I am speaking with reference to Christ and the church" (Eph. 5:31–32). *Third,* is the illustration of the vine and branches found in the gospel of John and again in Paul (John 15:1–5; cf. Rom. 6:5; Col. 2:6–7). *Fourth,* Paul uses the metaphor of the union between the members and head of the body. In his first epistle to the Corinthians he says that "the body is one and yet has many members, and all the members of the body, though they are many, are one body, so also is Christ" (1 Cor. 12:12). *Fifth,* and most significant, in Romans 5 and 1 Corinthians 15 Paul speaks of two corporate races under which all mankind is subsumed. One is the race of all unregenerate persons who are in Adam. That race is under the sentence of death. The second Adam, Christ, is the head of a second corporate race. In Romans, Paul "points to the bond that joins all the descendants of Adam with their progenitor, as the pattern and type of the communion between Christ and his own."[17] According to one commentator, in chapter five of Romans Paul recollects "what we human beings are, as members of Adam's lost race; everything human is sunk in sin and stands under the wrath of God. But, on the other hand, he has declared what we have become through Christ; by faith in Him we have been delivered from the dominion of wrath and received into the kingdom of righteousness and life."[18]

Thus, just as the solidarity existing between Adam and his posterity explains how death has passed upon all, so the solidarity between Christ and his posterity explains how the obedience of One has been reckoned as the obedience of many. Paul is acknowledging here what many have described as a "corporate personality."[19] Adam and the Messiah are pictured

---

17. Ridderbos, *An Outline,* 61.

18. A. Nygren, *Romans* (Philadelphia: Fortress, 1949), 210.

19. For this term see the Old Testament studies of H. W. Robinson and J. deFrain, *Adam and the Family of Man* (Staten Island, NY: Alba House, 1965). See also, G. C. Berkouwer, *Sin* (Grand Rapids: Eerdmans, 1971), 512ff. Saucy states that in what is termed

as the inclusive representatives of two humanities. Those who live in solidarity with the first Adam constitute one body; those in solidarity with the one new Man constitute another. These two bodies provide the only two solidarities that are open to mankind; in their inherent opposition lies the clue to the character of each. The chart below gives the distinctives of each.[20]

In Adam	In Christ
all die	all are living
death reigns	all reign in life
all sin	all are righteous
sin rules	grace rules
sin enslaves	Christ enslaves

THE CONSEQUENCES OF UNION WITH CHRIST

The Bible speaks of wonderful consequences of union with Christ. Yet I have noted how many who write about this union seem to drift in the wrong direction because they fail to maintain the distinction between the *consequences* of union and the *essence* of union.[21] Thus, rather than ad-

---

"corporate personality" we find the teaching that "the union of the individual and the community were such that the entire group could be conceived of as acting in the individual (e.g., the sin of Achan in Josh. 7:10–12). While this has something of a representative idea, it also has a certain reality of relationship which may be seen most clearly in the concept of 'being in Christ.' The union of all human beings with Adam by natural birth is thus analogous to the union of the new humanity with Christ. . . . In this concept of corporateness a real unity of mankind is affirmed without attempting to explain its exact nature." R. L. Saucy, "Theology of Human Nature," in *Christian Perspectives*, ed. Moreland and Ciocchi, 49.

20. Paul S. Minear, *Images of the Church in the New Testament* (Philadelphia: Westminster, 1960), 74.

21. For example, consider this statement: "The new nature and old nature are opposite dispositions toward God; the old nature is a disposition of enmity against God." R. E. Showers, *The New Nature* (Neptune, N. J.: Loizeaux Brothers, 1986), 9. Showers, while offering many helpful interpretations, appears to make no distinction between the consequences and the essence of union. For what I consider to be a more reasoned statement on the primary reality of change in salvation see G. E. Ladd, *A Theology of the New Testament* (Grand Rapids: Eerdmans, 1974). Ladd states, "The idea of the new birth is no different from the Pauline idea of being baptized into Christ and so entering into newness of life (Rom. 6:4). The metaphor is different—new birth, union with Christ—but the theology is the same. In Pauline thought, men become children of God by adoption rather than by birth" (290).

dressing what union is, they merely address what it produces. Albeit, while we are seeking to understand the meaning of union, it is important to acknowledge the normal consequences that result from it. We will not venture to examine all of these consequences, but will include three here that relate to our pursuit of the essence of change wrought in salvation.

Justification

The first consequence of union we will consider is justification. Ridderbos defines justification as that which "man requires in order to go free in the judgment of God and to know himself discharged from the divine sentence."[22] Paul puts it this way: "All those who believe . . . [are] being justified as a gift by his [God's] grace" (Rom. 3:22–24); again, Paul says, "A man is justified by faith apart from works of the Law" (Rom. 3:28). A classic text of justification is Romans 1:17 where Paul writes, "The righteousness of God [is] revealed from faith to faith: as it is written, those who are by faith, just, shall live" (author's translation). God *declares* the believer to be justified because He *imputes* (Rom. 3:28; 4:11ff) righteousness to the believer. "The underlying assumption of these passages is that Christ himself is the righteousness and that, by union with him or by some kind of relationship which we come to sustain to him, we gain property in that righteousness which he is."[23] It is important to note that the biblical doctrine of justification does not require a belief in the change of regeneration as being substantive or constitutional in nature.

New Life

In union with Christ, God restores us to relationship with Himself through the objective reality of justification. But salvation "does not consist only in a new relationship, but that a restoration of the whole of life in the most inclusive sense of the word results from it and has been given with it."[24] Thus Paul speaks of the righteousness of God accomplished in Christ as a "justification of life" (Rom. 5:18). To Paul, the two realms of existence (the realm of death and the realm of life) are at once decisive

---

22. Ridderbos, *An Outline*, 163–164.

23. Murray, *Romans*, 357. Properly understood then, justification is not a declaration that arises from God's mercy but from His justice. Having been united with Christ the believer is justly declared righteous.

24. Ridderbos, *An Outline*, 205.

and self-evident. That is, the good news of the Gospel resides in the declaration of life brought from death. In 2 Timothy 1:10 Paul says that Christ
has vanquished death and brought life and incorruptibility to light "through
the gospel." Because of its life-giving power, Paul calls the gospel the "word
of life" (Phil. 2:16). Elsewhere, Paul can actually speak of the gospel as an
"aroma of life and death" (2 Cor. 2:14–16).[25] The irreducible element of
gospel proclamation is that it is the declaration of life in Christ.

In union with Christ believers have been taken up into the new life
context of Christ. The concept of newness in Paul's writings is critical for
an adequate understanding of the essence of change and must be contemplated in distinction to what was old. In Ephesians 4:23–24, the "old man"
(*ho palaios anthrōpos*) is a view of the whole self in its fallenness.[26] Thus,
the old man is the autonomous man under sin. The theological significance of Paul's contrast and comparison of the new and old man is
poignantly expressed in the following discussion:

> Paul is seeking to express [i.e. speaking of the antithesis in 1 Cor.
> 5:6–8] the incompatibility between the previous life in sin and newly
> begun Christian life. . . . The thought is even more sharply put in
> the contrast between the old man and the new, Rom. 6:6; Col. 3:9;
> Eph. 4:2. . . . In Rom. 6 Paul says that he who is baptised is baptised
> into Christ's death. The service of sin is no longer possible."[27]

The new life context of the new man and the old life context of the
old man are mutually exclusive—they cannot coexist. Furthermore, the
change from old man to new man is an instantaneous work of the Holy
Spirit: "In Titus 3:5 the Holy Spirit is revealed as the agent who effects this
amazing change in a person. Apparently, here the continuing process of

---

25. Nygren, in his helpful commentary on Romans (Philadelphia: Fortress, 1949),
believes that the text that unlocks Paul's central theme in that epistle is 5:12–21. Comment-
ing on that passage he says, "The question to which Paul is here addressing himself is to
inquire what it is that has come about because Christ has been given to us. His answer (in
Romans 5.12–21) is clear: the new aeon, the aeon of life, has come upon us" (*Romans*, 20–
21). Ladd says that "Christ's death avails to transfer the believer from the realm of
indebtedness, of condemnation and death—the old aeon—to the realm of life in the new
aeon." *A Theology of the New Testament* (Grand Rapids: Eerdmans, 1974), 487.

26. C. E. B. Cranfield, *The Epistle to the Romans*, vol. 1, in *The International Critical
Commentary*, ed. J. A. Emerton and C. E. B. Cranfield (Edinburgh: T. and T. Clark, 1979),
309.

27. Heinrich Seesemann, *Theological Dictionary of the New Testament*, vol. v, ed. G.
Friedrich, trans. and ed. G. W. Bromiley (Grand Rapids: Eerdmans, 1967), 719.

the Spirit's work is not primarily in mind, but the instantaneous change which takes place at conversion. (Note the aorist tense: 'He saved us.')"[28] In the life context of the new man, the Holy Spirit rules. "The Spirit is not only the one under whose dominion the church may live, but he also enters into the actual existence of believers."[29] Even though progress is not in view in Titus 3:5, we must hasten to say that the work of the Spirit within the realm of new life marks the inception of renewing.[30] New life is a radical and instantaneous transformation, not of substance but from one life context to another.

The Spirit

The person who is united with Christ is also "in the Spirit" (Rom. 8:9). "To be 'in the Spirit' means to be in the realm that the Spirit created, where the Spirit blesses and gives new life."[31] The reality of that indwelling is first christological not anthropological. That is, the Spirit indwells Christ (1 Cor. 12:13), and by virtue of union with Christ those who believe participate in the Spirit. It follows then that one who is joined to Christ is joined to the Spirit (1 Cor. 6:17). On the subject of the primacy of Christ in relation to the Spirit's indwelling, Ridderbos makes this statement:

> The thought is not that the Spirit first shows himself to individual believers, brings them together into one whole, and thus constitutes the body of Christ. For in this way participation in Christ would follow upon sharing in the Spirit, whereas the church has been given precisely with Christ as the second Adam. The sequence is accordingly the reverse: those who by virtue of the corporate bond have been united with Christ as the second Adam, have died and been buried with him, may know themselves to be dead to sin and live to God, may also know themselves to be "in the Spirit." They are, because included in this new life-context, no longer in the flesh, but in the Spirit (Rom. 8:9).[32]

---

28. D. L. Norbie "The Washing of Regeneration" *The Evangelical Quarterly* 34, no. 1 (1962): 36.

29. Ibid., 222.

30. This issue is discussed further in chapter 7.

31. Ladd, *A Theology of the New Testament*, 483.

32. Ridderbos, *An Outline*, 221.

The Spirit indwells Christ and His Body, the Church. The ministry of Christ and the Spirit are so conjoined that being in Christ is described as being in the Spirit, and conversely, being in the Spirit is tantamount to being in Christ. In fact, and notably, all the expressions and realities of new life are attributed to the Spirit as well as to Christ. Newness of life, which is after the pattern of Christ's resurrection, coalesces into the "newness of the Spirit" (Rom. 7:6). Thus, new life is said to be a gift of the Spirit (2 Cor. 3:6), and the corresponding and progressing change generating from new life is at once the ministry of Christ and the Spirit (2 Cor. 3:18).

In Galatians 5:25 Paul says that "if we live by the Spirit (indicative) we will also walk by the Spirit (imperative). Union then, with its central characteristic of corporateness, pictures the Spirit indwelling the Church (Christ's Body), and as members of that new realm of existence we have been translated from the dominion of sin (which has been broken) into the dominion of Christ (which has been inaugurated, Col. 1:13). Thus, Spirit indwelling is not anthropological (spatial) but christological (corporate).[33] Therefore, the plural pronouns of 1 Corinthians 3:16 are not many individuals but, rather, are Pauline expressions of the corporate nature of the body of Christ—in which the Spirit dwells and in which we are incorporated through union.[34]

Synopsis

The union of the believer with Christ includes the christological blessings of justification, new life, and indwelling. Based on those foundational realities the believer receives further enjoyments from life in

---

33. If we miss the nuance of Paul's use of imagery from the Old Testament, we will have wrongly interpreted 1 Cor. 6.19. In that verse Paul is not speaking of the physical body as the material container of God. Fee says that "Paul now images the body as the *Spirit's* temple, emphasizing that it is the 'place' of the Spirit's dwelling in the individual believer's lives. In the same way that the temple in Jerusalem 'housed' the presence of the living God, so the Spirit of God is 'housed' in the believer's body. This is imagery pure and simple, in which the significance of the body for the present is being affirmed; it is not intended to be a statement of Christian anthropology, as though the body were the mere external casing of the spirit or Spirit." G. Fee, *First Corinthians* (Grand Rapids: Eerdmans, 1987), 264. The Spirit indwells the body of Christ and is a "gift in which believers share in virtue of their incorporation into the body" (Ridderbos, *An Outline*), 373.

34. That is not to say that the Spirit's ministry is not personal. Joy (1 Thess. 1:6); love (Col. 1:8); and unity (Eph. 4:3) are some of the personal benefits derived from the Spirit's ministry. The Spirit teaches us the Word of God (1 Cor. 2.14–16) and equips us for service (1 Cor. 12:4, 11).

Christ. In order to understand the essence of the change that occurs in salvation, we suggest that incorporation, not alteration, is the best description of this change. The realities of justification, new life, and indwelling do not necessitate belief in a change in man's essence because the Bible does not teach that they accomplish such change. People are declared—not made—righteous. In new life, a person is part of the new humanity in which Christ is the head. That person is joined to Christ, and because the Spirit indwells Christ, that person participates in Christ's gift to the Church, the Holy Spirit.

THE LANGUAGE OF UNION WITH CHRIST

In Christ

Union with Christ is frequently spoken of as "in Christ." So predominant is this phrase that it is virtually interchangeable with other NT expressions such as "salvation," and in particular, "new life." Thus we are not surprised to find Paul alternating among the expressions "in Christ," "in the Spirit," and "in the faith."[35] In Christ the old life has been finished once and for all time. "You have died and your life is hidden with Christ in God" (Col. 3:3).

But what does being "in Christ" mean?

> Some claim that something inside us as believers actually changes or a part of our person, "the spirit," which before was dead is made alive, and so we can look inside ourselves and see "a new life" there. Paul does say that we are a new creation, that we have new life, but he does not mean by this that a dramatic change, observable internally, has taken place in some part of us. He is referring, primarily, to our new status before God: because Christ is our representative and is alive, we too, being *in* Christ by faith, have life (italics his).[36]

---

35. "That which is at one time called living, walking, standing in Christ (Rom. 6:11; Col. 2:6; Phil. 4:1; 1 Thess. 3:8), and elsewhere living, walking in or by the Spirit (Gal. 5:25; Rom. 8:4), can also be called living, walking, standing in or by faith (Gal. 2:20; 2 Cor. 5:7; Rom. 11:20; 1 Cor. 16:13; 2 Cor. 1:24)." Ridderbos, *An Outline*, 233.

36. R. Macaulay and J. Barrs, *Being Human: The Nature of Spiritual Experience* (Downers Grove: InterVarsity, 1978), 82.

Through some 164 occurrences, Paul uses the phrase "in Christ" to signify that there is a correspondence between the work of God accomplished in Christ and the blessings believers receive. "In Christ is one of Paul's favorite terms for the new life, describing the deep, permanent and joyful relationship between the new Christian and his Lord, a life which can only be thought of in terms of a totally different form of existence."[37] In Ephesians chapter 1 Paul says that in Christ the believer is "chosen" (v. 4), "graced" (v. 6), "redeemed" (v. 7), "reconciled" (v. 10), "destined" (v. 11), and "sealed" (v. 13). God worked in Christ to effect the inauguration of a new dimension of existence, one that conquers the old dominion in Adam. Joined with Christ, believers are now members of that new humanity of which Christ is the head. The immediate result is that the "chosen in Christ" are blessed "with all spiritual blessings." In Christ, we are a new "creation" or a new person whose citizenship is in the new age or aeon. Newness is the description of being joined with Christ.

Baptism

In Romans 6:1–11 Paul uses the idiom of dying and rising with Christ to express the same truth as that found in the phrase "in Christ." United with Christ in salvation, the believer enters a new mode, and, even further, the "old has passed away." In Romans 6 Paul explains the meaning of this by claiming that in Christ believers have "died to sin" (6:1–2). "What the apostle has in view is the once-for-all definitive breach with sin which constitutes the identity of the believer. A believer cannot therefore live in sin; if a man lives in sin he is not a believer. If we view sin as a realm or sphere [aeon] then the believer no longer lives in that realm or sphere."[38]

Then in verse four Paul uses the term *baptism* to argue that death to sin is the fruit of being united with Christ. "Therefore, union with Christ, which baptism signifies, means union with Him in His death."[39]

Similar to the use of the phrase "in Christ," baptism (in nonsacramental usages) is nearly interchangeable with the thought of the union of believers with Christ (1 Cor. 12:13; cf. Gal. 3:27; Col. 2:11, 12). This intertwining of baptism with union in Christ is noted by Ridderbos: "For Paul,

---

37. G. Carey, *I Believe in Man* (Grand Rapids: Eerdmans, 1977), 87.

38. Murray, *Romans*, 213.

39. Ibid., 214.

what once took place in Christ has also taken place with the church. The 'in Christ' has its validity back into Christ's preexistence (Eph. 1:4), and reaches out to his parousia (Col. 3:4). But so far as the church is concerned, through baptism the 'once' becomes a 'here' and 'now.'" [40]

CONCLUSION

Since Christ's work of redemption, there have been two life dominions: that of Christ and that of Adam. While outside Christ, people are spiritually dead (Eph. 2:11-12), but inside Christ they have life with God and can experience spiritual blessing (Eph. 1:3-14) and death to sin (Rom. 6:1-11). Since blessing and death to sin are what God has accomplished in Christ, these must be appropriated personally through union with Christ. This is the union described by Paul as "in Christ" and "baptism."

We have argued that to understand the concept of union with Christ we need to consider in what sense we can say that change occurs in salvation. Futhermore, when Paul speaks of spiritual change he frequently uses metaphors. We have taken a brief look at five of these and have discovered that central to each image is the quality of corporateness. Scripture declares the believer in Christ to be "new"—a description of a person who is now a part of the new humanity that exists under the rule of Christ. The consequences of that union are manifold. Justification, new life, and indwelling of the Spirit are key fruits that issue from this relationship with God. These consequences are entirely consistent with the union aspect of Paul's imagery in that they, too, are derivatives of being joined to Christ.

From our inclusion into the new realm of Christ we are declared righteous; all that is descriptive of life is now ours, and because the Spirit indwells Christ, we are participants in that gift as well. And finally, Pauline terminology of union finds expression in phrases such as "baptism" and "in Christ." Baptism into Christ means death to sin because the old man has been crucified (Rom. 6:2, 6). On the positive side baptism brings "life unto God." The idiom of dying and rising, which baptism conveys, is a death to the old age and participation in the new age.

Redemptively speaking, the person who once lived in the old age has ceased to exist. In the language of Paul, that person "has passed away" (2 Cor. 5:17). "In Christ, the eternal Christ, who suffered, rose, ascended, who

---

40. Ridderbos, *An Outline*, 213.

is seated now at God's right hand supreme over all the forces of the universe: in Christ, in the heavenly sphere wherein He now abides, in the region of spiritual activities, all spiritual blessing is ours: in Christ God has blessed us.[41] It should be no surprise to us that Paul says that in Christ "man is a new creation." In Christ old things have passed (aorist) and the new has come (perfect).

As part of the race in Adam, the unregenerate person held to a world- and life-view that was anthropocentric (man-centered). Now, in Christ, the regenerate person lives life with a christocentric world- and life-view (Christ-centered). The primary reality of this change is a new relationship with God known in union with His Son. The foundational aspect of that change can be summarized in these words: "To know one's environment in a new way, and to be newly related to God through justification, is to live in a new world; a new set of relationships has come into being."[42] The new person is genuinely but not totally new. Hence, being "free from sin" and "sinless" are two very different things. In Christ, the new man has been freed from the dominion of sin. It is freedom from sin's dominion that is the basis for and gives explanation to the believer's continued fight against sin. Indeed, "the imperative is spoken because the indicative is true." [43] The old person is totally dead. But in neither case is the reality a matter of a change in substance, but, as we have shown, a matter of union with Christ. We, along with Murray, can conclude that

> sanctification involves . . . conformity to the image of God's Son, a conformity attained not through external imitative assimilation, but through an impartation of the fulness of Christ, an impartation which flows through a living organism that subsists and acts on an immensely higher plane than any form of organic or animate life with which we are acquainted in our earthly existence.[44]

The counselee's conflict with sin is to be interpreted in light of Paul's conflict in Romans 7:14–25. For in both, the source of tension is in terms of two colliding modes of existence or aeons. In Romans 7 the believer is at conflict because of his double situation brought about when he lives out the new age in the context of the old age (flesh).

---

41. J. A. Robinson, *Commentary on Ephesians* (Grand Rapids: Kregel, 1979), 25.

42. C. K. Barrett, *A Commentary on the Epistle to the Romans*, in *Harper's New Testament Commentaries*, ed. H. Chadwick (New York: Harper and Row, 1973), 174.

43. Murray, *Romans*, 241.

44. J. Murray, *Collected Writings* (Edinburgh: Banner of Truth Trust, 1977), II:304.

7

The Work of the Spirit and Biblical Counseling

John MacArthur, Jr.

A recent book titled *I'm Dysfunctional, You're Dysfunctional*, by Wendy Kaminer, debunks much of the mystique of modern psychology.[1] The author does not purport to be a Christian. In fact, she describes herself as "a skeptical, secular humanist, Jewish, feminist, intellectual lawyer."[2] Yet she writes as a bitter critic of the marriage of religion and psychology. She notes that religion and psychology have always more or less deemed one another incompatible. Now she sees "not just a truce but a remarkable accommodation."[3] Even from her perspective as an unbeliever, she can see that this accommodation has meant a change in the fundamental message Christians convey to the world. She writes:

> Religious writers would minimize or dismiss the effect of psychology on religion, fiercely denying that it has made doctrinal changes, but it does seem to have influenced the tone and packaging of religious appeals. . . . Christian codependency books, like those produced by the Minirth-Meier clinic in Texas, are practically indistinguishable from codependency books published by secular writers. . . . Religious writers justify their reliance on psychology by praising it for "catching up" to

---

1. Wendy Kaminer, *I'm Dysfunctional, You're Dysfunctional* (Reading, Mass.: Addison-Wesley, 1992).

2. Ibid., 121.

3. Ibid., 124.

some eternal truths, but they've also found a way to make the temporal truths of psychology palatable. Religious leaders once condemned psychoanalysis for its moral neutrality. . . . Now popular religious literature equates illness with sin.[4]

Some of the criticism Kaminer levels against evangelicals is unwarranted or misguided, but in this respect she is right on target: evangelicalism has been infiltrated by a worldly anthropology-psychology-theology that is diametrically opposed to the biblical doctrines of sin and sanctification. As a result of this accommodation, the Church has compromised and hopelessly muddled the message it is to proclaim.

Visit your local Christian bookstore and notice the proliferation of books on addiction recovery, emotional therapy, self-esteem, and other psychology-related topics. The language of such books carries a common theme: "look within yourself"; "get in touch with your inner child"; "explore the recesses of your past fears, hurts, and disappointments"; and "find the real answers to your problems within your own heart." Why? Because "the answers lie deep within."

Those books may sport logos from Christian publishers, but that kind of advice is not biblical and is unworthy of being labeled Christian. In fact, it sums up the very worst advice secular psychology offers.

Nowhere does Scripture advise people to seek answers by looking within. In fact, Scripture explicitly teaches us that we are sinners and should distrust our own hearts: "The heart is more deceitful than all else and is desperately sick; who can understand it? I, the Lord, search the heart, I test the mind . . ." (Jer. 17:9–10). Those who look within themselves to find answers are in a hopeless situation. Instead of answers, they get lies.

Psychology cannot solve this dilemma. Virtually all psychotherapy turns people inward, studying feelings, groping for suppressed memories, seeking self-esteem, scrutinizing attitudes, and generally listening to one's own heart. But emotions are hopelessly subjective, and our own hearts are deceitful. Only biblical counseling can offer reliable, authoritative, objective answers. And the objective truth of Scripture is the only tool God uses in the process of sanctification. Jesus Himself prayed, "Sanctify them in the truth; thy word is truth" (John 17:17).

Unfortunately, psychology and worldly therapies have usurped the role of sanctification in some Christians' thinking. Psychological sanctification has become a substitute for the Spirit-filled life. The notion is abroad

---

4. Kaminer, *I'm Dysfunctional,* 124–125.

within the Church that psychotherapy is often a more effective change agent—particularly in dealing with the most difficult cases—than the Holy Spirit who sanctifies.

But can psychotherapy possibly accomplish something that the Holy Spirit cannot? Can an earthly therapist achieve more than a heavenly Comforter? Is behavior modification more helpful than sanctification? Of course not.

THE PARACLETE

To understand the crucial role the Holy Spirit plays in meeting people's inner needs, we must go back to what Jesus taught His disciples when He first promised them He would send the Holy Spirit. It happened on the night Jesus was betrayed. His crucifixion was drawing near, and the disciples were fearful and confused. When Jesus spoke to them about going away, their hearts were troubled (John 14:1-2). In that hour of turmoil, they feared being left alone. But Jesus assured them that they would not be left to fend for themselves. He comforted them with this wonderful promise:

> "I will ask the Father, and He will give you another Helper, that He may be with you forever; that is the Spirit of truth, whom the world cannot receive, because it does not behold Him or know Him, but you know Him because He abides with you, and will be in you.
> "I will not leave you as orphans; I will come to you. After a little while the world will behold Me no more; but you will behold Me; because I live, you shall live also. In that day you shall know that I am in My Father, and you in Me, and I in you.
> "He who has My commandments and keeps them, he it is who loves Me; and he who loves Me shall be loved by My Father, and I will love him, and will disclose Myself to him."
> Judas (not Iscariot) said to Him, "Lord, what then has happened that You are going to disclose Your self to us, and not to the world?" . .
> Jesus answered and said to him, "If anyone loves Me, he will keep My word; and My Father will love him, and We will come to him, and make Our abode with him. He who does not love Me does not keep My words; and the word which you hear is not Mine, but the Father's who sent Me. These things I have spoken to you, while abiding with you. But the Helper, the Holy Spirit, whom the Father will

send in My name, He will teach you all things, and bring to your remembrance all that I said to you" (John 14:16–26).

"Helper" in verse 16 is the Greek word *paraklētos*, meaning someone called to another's aid. First John 2:1 applies the same term to Jesus Himself: "If anyone sins, we have an Advocate [*paraklētos*] with the Father, Jesus Christ the righteous." The word is sometimes transliterated into English as "paraclete." It describes a spiritual attendant whose role is to offer assistance, succor, support, relief, advocacy, and guidance—a divine Counselor whose ministry to believers is to offer the very things that so many people vainly seek in therapy!

The promises Jesus made with regard to the Holy Spirit and His ministry are staggering in their scope. Let's look at some of the key elements of this text.

A DIVINE HELPER

The word translated "another" is a key to understanding the nature of the Holy Spirit. The Greek text carries a precision that is not immediately evident in English. Two Greek words can be translated "another." One is *heteros*, which means "a different one, a different kind" as in, "If that style is not what you want, try another." *Allos* is also translated "another" in English, but it means "another of the same kind," as in, "That cookie was tasty; may I have another?"

Jesus used *allos* to describe the Holy Spirit: "another [*allos*] Helper [of the same kind]." He was promising to send His disciples a Helper exactly like Himself—a compassionate, loving, divine Paraclete. They had grown dependent on Jesus' ministry to them. He had been their Wonderful Counselor, Teacher, Leader, Friend, and had shown them the Father. But from now on, they would have another Paraclete—One like Jesus—to meet the same needs He had met.

Here, for the first time, Jesus gave the disciples extensive teaching about the Holy Spirit and His role. Note that our Lord spoke of the Spirit as a Person, not an influence, not a mystical power, not some ethereal, impersonal, phantom force. The Spirit has all the attributes of personality (mind—Rom. 8:27; emotions—Eph. 4:30; and will—Heb. 2:4) and all the attributes of deity (cf. Acts 5:3–4). He is another Paraclete of exactly the same essence as Jesus.

There was, however, a significant difference: Jesus was returning to the Father, but the Holy Spirit would "be with you forever" (v. 16). The

Holy Spirit is a constant, sure, trustworthy, divine Paraclete graciously given by Christ to His disciples to be with them forever.

A GUIDE TO TRUTH

It is noteworthy that Jesus referred to the Holy Spirit as "the Spirit of truth" (v. 17). As God, He is the essence of truth; as a Paraclete, He is the One who guides us into truth. That is why apart from Him, it is impossible for sinful beings to know or understand *any* spiritual truth. Jesus said, "The world cannot receive [Him], because it does not behold Him or know Him" (v. 17). Echoing that truth, Paul wrote, "To us God revealed [things which the world cannot see or understand] through the Spirit. . . . Now we have received, not the spirit of the world, but the Spirit who is from God, that we might know the things freely given to us by God. . . . But a natural man does not accept the things of the Spirit of God; for they are foolishness to him, and he cannot understand them, because they are spiritually appraised" (1 Cor. 2:10, 12, 14).

The unregenerate have no facility for spiritual perception. They cannot comprehend spiritual truth because they are spiritually dead (Eph. 2:1), unable to respond to anything except their own sinful passions. Believers, on the other hand, are actually taught spiritual truth by God Himself (cf. John 6:45). In fact, much of the Holy Spirit's ministry to believers involves teaching them (John 14:26; 1 Cor. 2:13; 1 John 2:20, 27); guiding them into the truth of Christ (John 16:13–14); and illuminating the truth for them (1 Cor. 2:12).

This promise of a supernatural Teacher had a special application for the eleven disciples. Often, Jesus' teaching was difficult for them to understand immediately. In fact, much of what He told them meant nothing to them until after His resurrection. For example, in John 2:22 we read, "When . . . He was raised from the dead, His disciples remembered that He said this; and they believed the Scripture, and the word which Jesus had spoken." John 12:16 says, "These things His disciples did not understand at the first; but when Jesus was glorified, then they remembered that these things were written of Him, and that they had done these things to Him." In John 16:12, Jesus said, "I have many more things to say to you, but you cannot bear them now."

After Jesus ascended to heaven, one of the crucial ministries of the Holy Spirit was to bring to the disciples' minds what Jesus had said and to teach them what He meant: "These things I have spoken to you, while abiding with you. But the Helper, the Holy Spirit, whom the Father will send in My name, He will teach you all things, and bring to your remembrance all that I said to you" (John 14:25–26). That means that the Holy Spirit enabled the disciples to recall the precise words Jesus had spoken to them—so that when they recorded them as Scripture, the words were perfect and error free. This assured that the gospel accounts were recorded infallibly, and that the apostolic teaching was unadulterated.

But this promise of our Lord also reveals the Holy Spirit as a supernatural Teacher who ministers truth to the hearts of those whom He indwells. The Spirit guides us into the truth of God's Word. He teaches us, affirms the truth in our hearts, convicts us of sin, and often brings to mind specific truths and statements of Scripture that are applicable to our lives. As we noted, "Things which eye has not seen and ear has not heard, and which have not entered the heart of man, all that God has prepared for those who love him . . . to us God revealed them *through the Spirit* . . ." (1 Cor. 2:9–10, emphasis added).

As a divinely indwelling teacher, the Spirit of Truth fills a function that no human counselor can even approach. He is constantly there, pointing the way to truth, applying the truth directly to our hearts, prompting us to conform to the truth—in short, sanctifying us in the truth (John 17:17).

THE INDWELLING PRESENCE

Look a little more closely at Jesus' words at the end of John 14:17: "He abides with you, and will be in you." Our Lord was promising that the Holy Spirit would take up permanent, uninterrupted residence within His disciples. It was not only that the Spirit would be *present with* them; the greater truth was that He would be *resident within* them permanently.

This truth of the permanently indwelling Spirit is one of the wonderful New Covenant realities. Ezekiel 37:14 foretold it: "I will put My Spirit within you, and you will come to life." In the Old Testament, the Holy Spirit was often present with believers, but He did not indwell them. Moreover, His presence seemed to be conditional; so David prayed, "Do not take Thy Holy Spirit from me" (Ps. 51:11).

In the New Testament era, however, believers have a permanently resident Paraclete, not *with*, but *within*. In fact, the indwelling presence of the Spirit is one of the proofs of salvation: "You are not in the flesh but in the Spirit, if indeed the Spirit of God dwells in you. But if anyone does not have the Spirit of Christ, he does not belong to Him" (Rom. 8:9).

Jesus' promise in John 14 that the Holy Spirit would reside within was not limited to the eleven apostles who were present that night. The Holy Spirit indwells every Christian. In verse 23, Jesus said, "If *anyone* loves Me, he will keep My word; and My Father will love him, and We will come to him, and make Our abode with him" (emphasis added). Paul, writing to the Corinthians, said, "Do you not know that your body is a temple of the Holy Spirit who is in you, whom you have from God, and that you are not your own?" (1 Cor. 6:19). Thus each believer enjoys the permanent, continuing presence of the Holy Spirit living within.

Union With Christ

In John 14:18–19, Jesus continued, "I will not leave you as orphans; I will come to you. After a little while the world will behold Me no more; but you will behold Me." Christ knew that within hours He would be crucified. His earthly ministry was coming to an end. But He reassured the disciples that He was not leaving them altogether. They would continue to behold Him.

What does that mean? In what sense would they be able to behold Him? There seem to be two key elements to that promise. First, He was reassuring them by implication that He would rise from the dead. Death would neither conquer Him nor end His ministry in their lives. Second, He promised, "I will come to you" (v. 18). That promise can be interpreted in various ways. Some see it as a reference to the Second Coming. Others view it as a promise that He would appear to them after He rose from the dead. In this context, however, this promise seems linked to the coming of the Holy Spirit to dwell within them. What Jesus seems to be saying is that He will be spiritually present in the disciples through the agency of the indwelling Holy Spirit. Compare this to the subsequent promise He gave just before He ascended: "Lo, I am with you always, even to the end of the age" (Matt. 28:20). In what sense is He "with" His chosen ones? And in what sense would they "behold" Him? The answer seems to be that He would also indwell them through the Holy Spirit.

This doctrine is known as union with Christ. John Murray wrote, "Union with Christ is really the central truth of the whole doctrine of salvation."[5] All believers are joined with Christ by the Holy Spirit in

---

5. John Murray, *Redemption—Accomplished and Applied* (Grand Rapids: Eerdmans, 1955), 161.

an inseparable union. Scripture sometimes speaks of this union as our being *in Christ* (cf. 2 Cor. 5:17; Phil. 3:9), and sometimes as Christ's being *in us* (cf. Rom. 8:10; Gal. 2:20, Col. 1:27). A few passages even merge the twin concepts: "Abide in Me, and I in you" (John 15:4). "By this we know that we abide in Him and He in us, because He has given us of His Spirit" (1 John 4:13).

As that last verse shows, our union with Christ is inextricably linked to the Holy Spirit's indwelling. It is through the Holy Spirit that we become one with Christ, and through the Spirit that Christ lives in our hearts. Those in whom the Spirit abides operate in a different dimension. They are alive to the spiritual realm. They commune with Christ. They move and participate in the life of the Spirit. They have the mind of Christ (1 Cor. 2:16).

Jesus continued His comforting words to the disciples in John 14: "In that day you shall know that I am in My Father, and you in Me, and I in you" (v. 20). Here He was emphasizing our spiritual union with Him and His own union with the Father. It seems evident that on this dreadful night when Jesus was about to be betrayed, the disciples still did not understand the mystery of Christ's relationship to His Father. Much less could they have grasped the concept of their own union with Christ. But Jesus told them that the time would come when they would begin to understand the richness of these realities: "In that day you shall know" (v. 20) seems to refer to the day of Pentecost, when the Holy Spirit came in power. What happened that day demonstrates the power of God's Spirit to teach us, to untangle our confusion, and to empower us for service. Peter suddenly stood up and began preaching with a power, a clarity, and a boldness that were foreign to him. It was as if everything suddenly fell into place spiritually for him. He had the mind of Christ and was immediately transformed from a cowering, confused disciple, into a fearless, forthright apostle. He was united through faith with Christ, filled with the Holy Spirit. He now had access to a power and a confidence that he had never shown before.

THE LOVE OF GOD

There is at least one more important aspect of Jesus' promise to His disciples on that final night. He told them, "He who has My commandments and keeps them, he it is who loves Me; and he who loves Me shall be loved by My Father, and I will love him, and will disclose Myself to him" (John 14:21). There Jesus echoes a statement He had made just a few verses earlier ("If you love Me, you will keep My commandments"—v. 15), then expands that truth into a promise of the Father's love graciously shown to those who follow the Son.

That passage describes the believer's relationship with the Father and the Son. We love Christ, so we keep His commandments. Those who love Christ are loved by the Father, and Christ manifests Himself to them. The Spirit's role is not explicitly stated here, but it is the Spirit within who empowers believers to love and obey Christ: "The love of God has been poured out within our hearts through the Holy Spirit who was given to us" (Rom. 5:5). It is not that God loves us *because* we love the Son. On the contrary, our love for Him is prompted by His grace to us. The apostle John says elsewhere, "We love, because He first loved us" (1 John 4:19).

Thus Christianity involves a supernatural relationship with the Trinity. The Spirit indwells the believer, kindling righteous desires and holy affections, pouring out the love of God in our hearts. The believer thus loves Christ and strives to obey Him. Moreover, both the Father and the Son pledge their love to believers, and Christ continually manifests Himself in that love. The believer, then, is the beneficiary of a loving relationship involving Father, Son, and Holy Spirit.

At this point in Jesus' discourse, Judas—not Judas Iscariot but the disciple who is also called Lebbaeus and Thaddaeus—spoke out: "Lord, what then has happened that You are going to disclose Yourself to us, and not to the world?" (John 14:22). Jesus answered, "If anyone loves Me, he will keep My word; and My Father will love him, and We will come to him, and make Our abode with him" (v. 23).

That answer simply reiterated what the Lord had said in verses 15 and 21. But Jesus continued: "He who does not love Me does not keep My words; and the word which you hear is not Mine, but the Father's who sent Me" (v. 24). The implication is clear: The Lord Jesus will not manifest Himself to those who are disobedient. Those who do not love Christ, who do not want Him, who refuse to obey His words, are cut off from any relationship or fellowship with Him.

Moreover, those who reject the Son reject the Father as well. When they turn from the commandments of Christ, they scorn the Father's Word. They cut themselves off from any of the spiritual benefits of fellowship with God.

That raises a question essential to the issue of biblical counseling. Can the biblical counselor offer meaningful help for non-Christians? If the counselee lacks all the spiritual resources Jesus has described; if the

Holy Spirit does not dwell within; if the person has no fellowship with the Father or the Son—can any amount of counsel ultimately help resolve the problems that brought the individual for help in the first place?

The answer seems obvious. Some superficial problems might be addressed by the application of biblical principles. For example, a husband might be encouraged to live with his wife in an understanding way (1 Pet.3:7), and the quality of that marriage might improve some. Or a young person struggling with submission to authority might learn the importance of complying with parents and authority figures, and thereby avoid some conflicts. But apart from the regenerating influence of the Holy Spirit, no amount of counseling can resolve the root problems. External conformity even to biblical law cannot undo the effects of sin.

Therefore, the biblical counselor's first priority is to determine whether the counselee is a believer. Those who are not must be shown their need for redemption first of all. That is, in fact, the way Jesus Himself modeled counseling. When Nicodemus came to Him by night, Jesus told him, "You must be born again" (John 3:7).

THE HOLY SPIRIT IN BIBLICAL COUNSELING

The new birth is the Holy Spirit's sovereign work (John 3:8). And every aspect of true spiritual growth in the life of the believer is prompted by the Spirit, using the truth of Scripture (John 17:17). The counselor who misses that point will experience failure, frustration, and discouragement.

Only the Holy Spirit can work fundamental changes in the human heart. Therefore, the Holy Spirit is the necessary agent in all effective biblical counseling. The counselor, armed with biblical truth, can offer objective guidance and steps for change. But unless the Holy Spirit is working in the heart of the counselee, any apparent change will be illusory, superficial, or temporary—and the same problems or worse ones will soon reappear.

At the outset of this chapter we spoke of the futility of looking within to find answers to our problems. And it is certainly true that those who focus on themselves, their childhood traumas, their wounded feelings, their emotional cravings, or other egocentric sources will never find genuine answers to their troubles.

The true believer, however, does have a Helper who dwells within. He is the Holy Spirit, who applies the objective truth of Scripture in the process of sanctification. Yet even He does not draw our attention inward, or to Himself. Instead, He directs our focus upward, to Christ. Jesus said, "When the Helper comes, whom I will send to you from the Father, that is the Spirit of truth, who proceeds from the Father, *He will bear witness of Me*" (John 15:26).

Ultimately, it is unto Christ that the counselee's focus must be directed. "Beholding as in a mirror the glory of the Lord, [we] are being transformed into the same image from glory to glory, just as from the Lord, the Spirit" (2 Cor. 3:18). That is the process of sanctification. And it is the ultimate goal of all truly biblical counseling.

8

Spiritual Discipline and the Biblical Counselor

Robert Smith

When we hear that a counselor has been involved in sexual sin with a counselee, we ask, "How did it happen? How could it have been prevented?" Then it is easy to add, "That will never happen to me!"

Perhaps we know a counselor who is excessively overweight and yet does an excellent job of counseling. Again a question comes to mind. "How can this person possibly help counselees develop discipline in their lives when he (or she) is obviously undisciplined?"

Such questions cause us to reflect on a basic necessity in the life of a biblical counselor—spiritual discipline. This is particularly true in light of Paul's warning that those who seek to restore another must be careful not to get caught up in the offender's sin. Biblical counselors must have a growing relationship with the Lord, must be growing both in knowledge of and obedience to the Word of God, and must be aware of their potential to sin.

RELATIONSHIP TO THE LORD

The biblical counselor must, of course, be born again; for how can counselors correctly use the Word of God unless they are indwelt by His Spirit? And how can counselors encourage others to change and grow in their relationship with the Lord unless they are a growing model of the changing power of the Gospel themselves? In the discussion that follows we will describe eight essential elements for maintaining a growing relationship with Jesus Christ.

Reading God's Word

To correctly apply the Word of God to counseling situations we must know it and practice it. We must read it and study it in order to apply it to our lives before we can use it effectively in the counseling room. A regular reading program can be a helpful structure to do this. There are many different ways to study the Bible and while one method will be productive for one person, a different method will be more productive for someone else. Counselors who study the Bible for sermon or Sunday school lesson preparation or Bible study instruction will find that the insights gained from that study will naturally spill over into counseling.

Scripture Memorization

Scripture memorization is an essential part of the counselor's relationship with God, as well as a means of increasing personal knowledge of the Word to be used with others. As the counselor applies memorized passages to daily life, he or she is able to help the counselee use them effectively also. The Bible is the Spirit's Sword and the counselor must have that Sword available and ready to use at a moment's notice, not only in personal practice but also in the counseling sessions.

It is helpful to use a guided program in Scripture memorization. As you memorize Scripture, try to memorize passages rather than individual verses (other than Proverbs) in order to avoid using verses out of context. Memorize verses that are useful in your own life and verses that teach doctrines applicable to counseling problems. In his book, *What To Do On Thursday*, Dr. Adams includes an excellent list of verses for memorization that are particularly beneficial for counseling.[1] .

Prayer

Counselees often have a wrong view of prayer. In order to help them understand prayer, counselors need to have a correct understanding of prayer, and they need to practice prayer.

---

1. Jay Adams, *What to Do On Thursday* (Nutley, N.J.: Presbyterian and Reformed, 1982), 31–49.

Why do we need to pray? The Bible gives many reasons, but three are particularly important. First, God commands it (Col. 4:2; 1 Tim. 5:17). Second, Christ modeled the example of prayer for us (Mark 1:35; Luke 6:12). If He, the sinless perfect One prayed, how much more should we pray? Third, since Christ taught us to pray we can assume He wants us to pray—prayer is an act of obedience and worship of God (Matt. 6:5-9).

Prayer is basically one-way communication with God. We do not expect Him to speak to us in a mystical way in prayer because He has already spoken through His Word. If we want to hear Him, we must "search the Scriptures."

We must also remind ourselves (and frequently our counselees) that God responds to prayer with answers other than an immediate yes. For example, in Acts, Paul's request to go to Rome as a preacher was answered a different way. He went instead as a prisoner, with all expenses paid by the Roman government! Sometimes answers to prayer are delayed. George Mueller prayed for a man all his life and never experienced the answer to his prayer. Years after Mueller's death the man was saved.

In order to establish a habit of prayer it is helpful to schedule a time to pray. When you pray, use your time efficiently by praying from a prayer list. Some items on the list may be prioritized for daily prayer and others will be scheduled for weekly prayer. Praying every day for a need is not as important as praying regularly. And recognize that a long prayer time has no merit simply because it is long. On some days, when crises, and other responsibilities take over your schedule, your structured prayer time may be reduced to praying on the run. But on other days you can return to your schedule of regular prayer.

The ministry of counseling is impossible without the Spirit's guidance in understanding the Word. Counselors must seek His help in prayer to understand and rightly utilize the Sword of truth in dealing with counselee's problems. In gathering data we need the Spirit's help to correctly piece it all together. And we must continually depend on the Holy Spirit to help with counselee's problems. Change will occur in counselee's lives in proportion to their understanding of the biblical principles that apply to their situation. And although wise counsel from a counselor may produce external change, it will not be permanent change. Only the Spirit can give the necessary insight and motivation for permanent change. So counselors must pray that the Spirit will work in their counselee's lives and must pray that their own lives will be examples of obedience to biblical principles and constant growth in the knowledge of the Word of God.

Here are two observations on prayer by Jay Adams:

Prayer is a resource that Satan doesn't possess and the flesh knows nothing of it. Yet it is yours—a powerful asset which the Lord warns you not to neglect. Of course faithful prayer is difficult, as the disciples discovered and as we all know. And right here many battles are lost. People who know the Word, whose minds are fixed on the right goals and who want to win the war within, nevertheless fail because they do not pray.

It is important to have the Spirit's aid in praying as well as in the battle itself. . . . If God provides for all aspects of the battle, including the very prayer with which you call on Him for provision, then make no mistake—there is no excuse for failure. You cannot even plead that you do not know how to pray![2]

Relationship with a Local Church

Maintaining a relationship with a local body of believers is an essential part of the counselor's relationship with the Lord. This relationship is mandated in the Bible. Of approximately 110 references to the church in the New Testament over 90 refer to the local church. In the New Testament, believers quickly united with the local assembly (Acts 2:41, 47). Thus if we attempt to minister apart from the local church we are ignoring God's view and purpose of the church.

There are many benefits for the counselor who maintains a relationship with a local church. One of the benefits is the preaching of the Word. This is where the counselor is fed apart from personal study. No believer can be in the Word too much to need the preaching of the Word. An irregular relationship with a local church will only diminish the counselor's spiritual growth and, thus, his or her counseling ministry. Another benefit of maintaining close ties with a local church is that this provides accountability—accountability for discipline, repentance, and restoration. A counselor who is a member of a local church accepts this protection and declares submission to biblical principles in all aspects of life.

Submission to the authority of other church leaders is particularly important for counselors. In this way they model submission to the Word of God and to imperfect leadership for counselees who must also be encouraged to submit to authority that is not perfect. Those who refuse to submit to local church leadership miss all the blessings God promises in

---

2. Jay Adams, *The War Within* (Eugene, Or.: Harvest House, 1989), 87–88.

biblical submission and have no answer to those in similar situations who come to them for counsel.

Worship

Worship is mandated for the believer and thus must be an important part of the counselor's life. Worship is not an experience or a warm feeling, it is a cognitive awe and reverence of the Holy God that focuses on Him. Without worship it is easy to minimize sin and to fail in spiritual growth that would please God. Worship makes us aware of our own spiritual needs.

The church is the biblical place for corporate worship. The music, the order of service, and all that is done should focus toward the sermon, which is designed to help the listeners accomplish the ultimate act of worship: daily obedience to God.

Worship includes praise and thanksgiving for what the Lord is doing both in the counselor's life and in the lives of counselees. Praise and thanksgiving can help to prevent discouragement when dealing with difficult problems. Such problems then become an opportunity to praise God for what He has done and can do.

Theological Correctness

Since the basis of nearly every counseling problem is a doctrinal problem, a correct understanding of theology is essential for the biblical counselor. This does not mean that we can find the answers to counseling problems in a theology textbook. The Bible is our textbook, and if we understand the Bible correctly we will adhere to a correct theology.

It is particularly important in biblical counseling for the counselor to understand the correct theology of sin. So many counseling problems are a direct result of sin, yet, frequently, counselees minimize sin; they do not understand the doctrine of sin, how bad sin is, how pervasive it is, what God thinks about it, or what they must do about it. Theological correctness is necessary in other counseling situations also. For example, when a husband does not love his wife as he should because he does not understand the doctrine of Christ: His love for the Church, His demonstrations of that love, and His driving desire to obey the Father. In all counseling problems involving a conflict with another person, there is evidence of failure in that person's relationship with God.

Theological correctness is also essential to understanding biblical counseling as opposed to other forms and philosophies of counseling, such as those who attempt to manipulate others—even God—using the Bible, or those who claim that the Bible is insufficient and that modern counselors must add their wisdom to the Bible. A correct understanding of the theology of the Bible helps sort out these issues.

Goal of Christ-Likeness

Romans 8:28–29 teaches that the goal of all believers is to become more like Christ. All that happens in a person's life is divinely orchestrated to help that person become more like God's Son. Certainly this must be a priority goal in the counselor's life.

Stewardship

Believers are stewards of all that God has entrusted to them. There is nothing we have that God has not given to us and entrusted us to use for His glory. This includes spouse, children, abilities, possessions, ministry. In entrusting them to us, He expects us to use them faithfully for His glory.

RELATIONSHIP TO OTHERS

Evangelizing Others

A biblical counselor must be an evangelist, because God's Word commands believers to evangelize (Matt. 28:19–20; Mark 16:15; Acts 1:8). But beyond this, without evangelism there is no need for counseling, since the nonbeliever cannot be counseled biblically. Adams correctly states that we can only do precounseling of nonbelievers to prepare them for salvation through the counseling relationship.[3] Thus, the counselor must be able to show people, from the Bible, how they can obtain the gift of eternal life. A counselor who is not grieved about the eternal destiny of lost souls is missing the primary focus of Christ's life and of all ministry.

Success in evangelism is not measured by results, but by the careful and accurate presentation of the Gospel. This includes all the facets that

---

3. Jay Adams, *A Theology of Counseling* (Grand Rapids: Zondervan, 1979), 309–325.

lead up to being able to present the gospel. One who is building bridges of relationships to others is successful in evangelism even though no gospel presentation has been made. Being all things to all men to enhance the presentation of the gospel is essential and part of the success. However, it is also true that if one works only on bridge building and never carries the message over the bridge (perhaps because of personal failure, such as fear or neglect), then this is not success either.

Evangelism is particularly important for biblical counseling because unless the counselee experiences (or has experienced) saving faith, there cannot be much further progress in the counseling process. The counselor may use the Bible to help people improve their situations, but must always tell unsaved counselees that they will never achieve all the success God desires because they do not have the help of the indwelling Spirit. They will settle for far less than the Spirit's goals since they cannot understand His Word. Success in such instances might be defined as an improvement in the circumstances, but could not be considered as change for the glory of God. In the process of solving daily problems, the counselor must not overlook the greater problem of the counselee's eternal destiny.

Discipling Others

Biblical counseling is simply an extension of discipling. There is no sharp distinction between the two. Discipling might be described as teaching basic Christian principles to a believer, whereas counseling is using those principles to deal with specific situations in a person's life. The most productive counseling grows out of the ministry of discipling a person after salvation, of teaching that individual the basic principles of living the Christian life. Biblical counselors who want to see lives change must be aggressive disciplers.

Serving Others

Jesus did not come to this earth to be served, but to serve (Matt. 20:28). If the One who created came to serve those who were created, how much more should those who were created be willing to serve. The ministry of counseling must not focus on generating an income, but on serving. Service to others is essential in establishing integrity and authenticity in biblical counseling. The counselor must be a servant in the home, in the church, even in positions of leadership.

Dealing with Criticism

One of the best means to handle criticism successfully is to approach it as a learning situation. Become a student of your critic, especially when you believe you are innocent of the criticism. Although the natural response when we believe we are innocent is to defend ourselves or try to make the accuser see that we are innocent, it is better to learn how the critic reached the conclusion. We need to ask what the accuser observed that caused him or her to make the accusation. The answers to that question can inform us how we look or sound to others with whom we communicate. We may have been totally innocent in our thoughts and motives, but inadvertently communicated something different.

For example, you may be accused of being angry with a counselee. As you reflect on the previous counseling session, you may not remember any anger or distress with the person during the discussion. But when you ask what made the person think you were angry, you learn that as you were talking you were scowling, you appeared restless, and your voice became somewhat firmer than usual. The counselee interpreted these nonverbal responses as demonstrations of anger. Although you were not angry, you can understand why the counselee felt that you were angry, and you can determine to take more care to monitor your voice and facial expressions in the future.

When you are challenged, do not run but determine to learn from the conflict. Your best defense is to ask the critic to defend the criticism as you attempt to learn from it. Proverbs 29:1 warns about ignoring reproof and in 2 Samuel 16, David saw his critic Shemei as being directed by God for his benefit. We need to remind ourselves that God is in control of our critics and could have prevented the criticism if He thought that was best. When He allows it, it is for our benefit and the benefit of our critic. By observing how we learn rather than defend, the critic sees a biblical response.

The best defense of innocence is to allow the facts to prove it, and the only facts are those that can be observed. We can ask a challenger for the facts behind an inferred conclusion and ask how the conclusion is legitimate, at the same time reminding the person that conclusions about *attitudes* based on those facts are only inferences and cannot be treated as facts. By showing we are not afraid to have our innocence carefully examined, we produce the best defense of our innocence, even when the accusation threatens our integrity. First Peter 2:12 and 3:16 teach that a godly character is the best defense against false accusation. If you have nothing to hide or to be ashamed of, let the quality of your character be closely examined. Your godly character will prove your innocence.

PERSONAL RELATIONSHIPS

Marriage

The Bible teaches that marriage is a picture of the love of Christ for His bride—the Church—and the submission of that bride to her Lord. The biblical counselor's marriage must be an example of this relationship. If counselors do not apply biblical principles to make their marriages successful, they will not be in a position to help counselees with their marriages. We cannot expect other couples to build a biblical marriage if we have not built one ourselves.

A spouse's companionship is God's provision to help prevent wrong relationships with counselees. God has ordained that our needs for intimacy be met only through the marriage relationship and through a relationship with His Son. Although no marriage is completely free of problems, the counselor's marriage must be an example of how sin-cursed people live in biblical harmony with one another, even in difficult times. Counselors must first successfully minister in their homes if they are to effectively demonstrate Christian principles for living to counselees.

Family

The counselor's first ministry is to his or her spouse and family. We cannot help other parents with their children if we are not spending time properly training and disciplining our own children. We must bring them up in the nurture and admonition of the Lord (Eph. 6:4). The time we spend with our children should include fun times (doing what they want) as well as times of direct spiritual teaching. If we are not fun to live with, we may need to look for ways to grow and change (Eccl. 9:9).

RELATIONSHIP TO SELF

Galatians 6:1 warns restorers (counselors) to be aware of their own lives—they must be growing in their relationship to Christ. Counselors should be characterized as people who are growing and changing. No counselor is perfect, for perfection is impossible, but we are to be growing more like Jesus Christ who is perfect. Here are four important concepts to consider in relationship to self.

Potential to Sin

Counselors must take a realistic view of themselves and their potential to sin. This is part of the warning in Galatians 6:1, for though we are regenerated, we still live under the curse of sin. This means that we are capable of committing the same sin as nonbelievers. To believe anything else is not only theologically erroneous but is naive and potentially dangerous. Keeping this fact in mind, we must take great precautions to make it very hard to sin (Matt. 5:28–30).

For example, if your sexual relationship with your spouse is not all you hope for, be alert to your potential to be tempted in this area. Work on serving and ministering to your spouse and thank God for the good qualities in her or him. When you see failure, recognize that God is using this to make you more like Christ. When you are tempted to think of a sexual relationship with a fictional person or a real person, recognize such thoughts as sin and immediately replace them with biblical thoughts. If you find yourself attracted to a counselee, recognize that such thinking and feeling is violating your marriage covenant. Then take every precaution necessary to remove yourself from tempting situations with that counselee.

Response to Sin

A counselor who sins must do just what counselees do: repent and change by developing a specific plan to change. It is extremely important not to form a habit of becoming comfortable with sin. No matter how small or big, sin must stop. As counselors who study the Word of God, we need to be alert to the Spirit's teaching about sin that applies to our lives.

When we are confronted with sin in our lives, we cannot ignore it. If we are guilty we must repent and change. If we are innocent, we must consider why God would allow us to be accused of the sin. Perhaps we need to be more consistent in adhering to protective guidelines to prevent that sin in our lives.

Personal Discipline

In 1 Corinthians 3:17 believers are commanded not to defile their body, which is the temple of the Holy Spirit. This admonition would include the injunction to take proper care of the body. Taking proper care of our bodies includes getting sufficient sleep, exercising daily, and disciplining ourselves to maintain a balanced weight.

Sleep. Most people need between seven and eight hours of sleep each night. Very few people can function well on less than this on a regular basis, and very few of those who think they can, actually do. Counselors should not let busy schedules keep them from getting adequate sleep. Sufficient rest is as important as all the other physical aspects of the body. Without adequate rest, fatigue makes it difficult to concentrate, especially when studying or listening to a counselee.

Exercise. Taking proper care of our bodies also includes adequate physical exercise. Numerous medical studies have confirmed the necessity of exercise for maintaining good health as well as the long-range benefits of exercise to mental and physical health. Not only does it keep our bodies functioning well, but exercise helps to reduce stress and thus lessens the risk for illness. Counselors need to develop a daily habit of exercise and at least some physical exertion. It will clear the mind and provide extra energy.

Weight. Maintaining a balanced weight level is also an important health factor. For many counselors who have desk jobs that do not require much physical exercise, this requires extra measures of self-discipline and determination, not only in choosing a balanced low-fat diet but in burning excess calories through exercise. Keeping our weight under control is a necessity, for how can a counselor insist that a counselee be disciplined in various areas of his or her life when the counselor is not disciplined in the very basic areas of diet and weight control?

Total Life View

A biblical counselor must see all of life from God's perspective. No event in the counselor's life or the counselee's life is isolated from God—He has total and complete control of everything. Nothing in this world is out of control. The Scriptures teach that every facet of life is under His control and He is using it for His glory and our benefit (Rom. 8:28–29). We can rest assured that "God never pursues His glory at the expense of the good of His people, nor does He ever seek our good at the expense of His glory. He has designed His eternal purpose so that His glory and our good are inextricably bound together."[4]

---

4. Jerry Bridges, *Trusting God* (Colorado Springs: NavPress, 1989), 25–26.

9

The Godward Focus of Biblical Counseling

Douglas Bookman

By definition, the biblical counselor is one who is persuaded of and allegiant to a Christian worldview. That is, one who functions within a frame of reference that consciously sees all of the realities and relationships of life from a perspective that is biblically coherent and consistent, and thus honors the God of Scriptures. The one element of such a worldview that most dramatically distinguishes it from all pretenders is the commitment to a theocentric perspective on all of life and thought. Thus any model of counseling that is authentically biblical will be framed, designed, and executed in happy submission to the biblical demand that our lives be lived out entirely for the glory of God! In short, biblical counseling is animated by a godward focus.

The temptation today, even within the Christian community, is to do otherwise, to conduct counseling with a primary focus on someone or something other than God. But the biblical counselor must be committed to a preeminently godward focus in counseling. Why? There are three basic reasons: (1) because God demands it; (2) because the natural exaltation of self is destructive; and (3) because the soul-satisfying life God intends for His children can only be found through Jesus' spiritual paradox—deny self and focus on God.

THE MORAL IMPERATIVE

Simply stated, a godward focus must be zealously maintained in biblical counseling because God demands that it be so. In one of the Old

Testament's most precise articulations of the covenant-keeping nature of God, YHWH declares through the prophet Isaiah,

> Thus says God the LORD,
> Who created the heavens and stretched them out,
> Who spread out the earth and its offspring,
> Who gives breath to the people on it,
> And spirit to those who walk in it, . . .
> "I am the Lord, that is My name;
> I will not give My glory to another,
> Nor My praise to graven images."
>
> Isaiah 42:3, 8

Later in the same section of prophecy, as YHWH foretells the mighty deliverance He will accomplish on behalf of His covenant people, He reiterates this profound reality: "For My own sake, for My own sake, I will act; for how can My name be profaned? And My glory I will not give to another" (Isa. 48:11).

God, who has made Himself known in Scripture, is jealous for His own glory (Deut. 4:24). He is a sovereign God who demands that people acknowledge Him as God and honor Him as the Creator and Sovereign of all the universe. This moral imperative to honor God is most often communicated in Scripture in contexts relating to God's glory. The Hebrew term for "glory" is *chabod*, which basically means "to be heavy, weighty."[1] Deriving the idea of glory, dignity, or personal worth from the concept of weightiness is typical of Hebrew progression of thought. To the Semitic mind, honor or dignity cannot be reduced to a purely ideal quality; rather, those concepts depend for their significance upon the concrete concept of something "weighty in a man which gives him importance."[2] Although the term *chabod* is used with various literal connotations in the OT, the concept most often conveyed by the term is that of a weighty person: one who is honorable, impressive, and worthy

---

1. John N. Oswalt, "Chabod," in *Theological Wordbook of the Old Testament*, ed. R. L. Harris, G. L. Archer, Jr., B. K. Waltke (Chicago: Moody, 1980), 1:426. With all of its derivatives the term occurs 376 times in the Old Testament. Its most concrete usage is as the title for the theophanic glory-cloud that appeared as Israel departed Egypt (Ex. 13:22) and that indwelt the tabernacle (Ex. 40:34); *chabod* is used at least 45 times in the Old Testament of this visible manifestation of God.

2. Gerhard von Rad, "*Chabod* in the Old Testament," in *Theological Dictionary of the New Testament*, ed. G. Kittel (Grand Rapids: Eerdmans, 1964), 2:235.

of respect.[3] This connotation prevails in more than half the occurrences of the term in the OT.[4]

Thus, the biblical notion of glory involves more than intrinsic dignity or value; it includes the visible representation of that intrinsic value. For example, *chabod* connotes not only a rich man's dignity and standing in his community but the riches that demonstrated his dignity (i. e. livestock, silver, and gold in Gen. 13:2; the wealth Jacob carried away from Laban in Gen. 31:1);[5] not only the honor of the priestly office but the distinctive garments worn by the priests to manifest the dignity of their office (Ex. 28:2, 40);[6] not only the unique and infinite splendor and majesty of the person of YHWH, but the ineffable physical glory-cloud that testified of His covenant-keeping nature and sovereign rule in the midst of His people.[7] In sum, the term *chabod* speaks not only of intrinsic dignity and worth but of the external and tangible manifestation of that worth.

Thus when YHWH insists that He "will not give His *glory* to another" (Isa. 42:3; 48:11), there is more at stake than the intrinsic worth of His sovereign person. Based on God's use of the term *glory* in those statements, we conclude that His demand is not only that we personally acknowledge His unique dignity and infinite perfection but that we consciously and publicly parade those majestic realities. Indeed, it is the stewardship of every child of God not only to embrace the truths that God has revealed concerning Himself but to deliberately and consistently

---

3. Two times in the Old Testament it is used of literal weightiness: Eli the priest is described as "heavy" in 1 Sam. 4:18, and the hair of Absalom is portrayed as "heavy on him" in 2 Sam. 14:26. Again, the term may be used of "slowness or dullness" as in a heavy (or hardened) heart (Ex. 7:14; 8:15, 18; 9:7); or of ears (Isa. 6:10), a tongue (Ex. 4:10), or eyes (Gen. 48:10) that are dull and insensitive. Again, it may signify severity, as when used of work (Ex. 5:9), slavery (1 Kgs. 12:10), warfare (Judg. 20:34), or a yoke (2 Chron. 10:4, 11).

4. Oswalt, "Chabod," 426.

5. Note, such material wealth is referred to by the noun *chabod*, not because the term has a primary sense of riches, but because the riches were conceived of as giving the individual some distinctive honor. Thus the basic concept is that of weightiness, or that which distinguishes an individual, setting him or her apart from others.

6. Notice that the word "glory" in these verses is *chabod*.

7. Payne says of the glory-cloud, "[A] man of *kavodh* carries weight in the eyes of his fellows (Gen. 45:13). God's *Kavodh* is, therefore, the visible extension of His divine perfection." J. B. Payne, *The Theology of the Older Testament* (Grand Rapids: Zondervan, 1962), 46. The term is transliterated in the Old Testament name Ichabod, which was given to a child born just after his mother learned that the ark of the covenant had been captured by the Philistines and that the glory-cloud had departed from Israel (1 Sam. 4:21); the term *ichabod* involves a rare usage of the Hebrew particle, but is best understood as meaning "no glory."

order every aspect of life to display the grace, justice, and faithfulness of God, to whom that child belongs.[8]

To clarify this concept, consider how God publicly maintained His glory (i.e., His reputation) in various narratives of the Old Testament. For instance, the drama of deliverance from Egypt, which culminated in the miracle of the Red Sea, was carefully framed by YHWH so that He would "be honored through Pharaoh and all his army, through his chariots and his horsemen" (Ex. 14:17, 18).[9] The ten plagues that immediately and causally preceded the Red Sea experience were so ordered and timed by YHWH that the Pharaoh gradually steeled himself to Moses' demands. All of which prepared the way for Pharoah's command—a command as militarily and spiritually stupid as any in history—that his chariot forces pursue the fleeing Israelites across the miraculously dried up Red Sea. When Moses stretched out his hand over the sea and the waters covered the Egyptians, God did indeed get glory upon Egypt. And He answered the arrogant question posed by the Pharaoh some months earlier, "Who is this YHWH that I should obey his voice to let Israel go?" (Ex. 5:2). In effect, by miraculously delivering Israel from Egypt, YHWH confronted the world of that day, and of centuries to come, with the indisputable evidence of His might and His character. (Compare the reaction of Rahab in Josh. 2:9-14 and the flawed remembrance of the Red Sea evinced by the Philistines some four hundred years later in 1 Sam. 4:8.)

Again, when the southern kingdom of Judah was taken captive to Babylon, the name of YHWH was in severe jeopardy of being disreverenced. God had covenanted with Israel that if they persevered in rebellion and disobedience He would cause them to be taken captive by a "nation of fierce countenance" (Deut. 28:49ff; cf. 1 Kgs. 8:46). And yet, given the universal superstition of the time that if one nation were defeated by another it was because the gods of the victorious nation were more powerful than those of the vanquished, God's name was in danger of being dishonored if He kept that promise of judgment upon His covenant people. But God intervened to publicly preserve His glory through the man Daniel.

---

8. These two aspects of the concept of God's glory are sometimes distinguished as *intrinsic* glory (that which is inherent to God) and *ascribed* glory (the conscious acknowledgement of God's glory by rational creatures). See for instance John F. MacArthur, Jr., *The Ultimate Priority* (Chicago: Moody, 1983), 128-30.

9. Notice that the word translated "honored" in both verses 17 and 18 by the NASB is the verb from of *chabod* in the Hebrew.

As a young man, Daniel was taken captive by King Nebuchadnezzar in the first stage of Judah's deportation to Babylon (ca. 606 B.C., cf. Dan. 1). Later, God enabled Daniel to provide the content and interpretation of the Babylonian monarch's dream, but only after all of the king's pagan soothsayers had confessed their absolute inability to do so (Dan. 2). Thus YHWH was publicly honored as Nebuchadnezzar acknowledged the power of the God worshiped by Daniel and his friends (Dan. 2:46, 47).

Some decades later, the prophet interpreted another dream for the king. This time King Nebuchadnezzar wrote a decree to be read throughout all the kingdom that told the story of his own madness and thus honored Daniel's God as "the Most High . . . who lives forever." The king's decree concludes with this encomium of praise to YHWH:

> For His dominion is an everlasting dominion,
> And His kingdom endures from generation to generation.
> And all the inhabitants of the earth are accounted as nothing,
> But He does according to His will in the host of heaven
> And among the inhabitants of earth;
> And no one can ward off His hand,
> Or say to Him, "What hast Thou done?"
>
> > Daniel 4:34, 35

Thus did Nebuchadnezzar publicly and universally declare the glory of YHWH.[10]

The historical examples from Scripture could be multiplied, but with these the point is made: when YHWH insists He will not share His glory with another, He wants us to understand not only that He possesses such personal majesty, but also that it is His sovereign will that His majesty be publicly displayed. It is His concern and must be our concern.

Obedience and Fallenness

There are profound implications to this mandate to deliberately and publicly reflect the God whom we serve. It means that the children of God

---

10. Notice that it was precisely this captivity in Babylon and the subsequent deliverance effected through the Persian, Cyrus, that was in view when YHWH declared in Isaiah 48:11, "For my own sake . . . I will act . . . and My glory I will not give to another."

are under Scriptural obligation to see themselves as vehicles of God's glory, as mirrors with which the Sovereign of the universe has chosen to reflect His glory, as conduits to display Him before a watching world. It is morally imperative that believers frame their lives, order their priorities, fashion their relationships, and discipline their souls in ways appropriate to this relationship and responsibility.

Of course, the infernal fly in the ointment is the fallenness of mankind. Although it is cosmically appropriate for human creatures to content themselves with playing the moon to the Creator's sun and to be satisfied with the privilege of reflecting YHWH's glory (even though in so doing they are confessing that they have no glory of their own), people are not willing to do so. Indeed, it is the stuff of fallenness to be offended by God's claim that He alone is worthy of honor, and instead to exalt oneself, to thrust oneself onto the throne of one's private universe. The Luciferian rebellion is reiterated moment by moment in the souls of the unredeemed offspring of Adam when they, in effect, intone the most cardinal credo of fallenness:

> I will raise my throne above the stars of God,
> And I will sit on the mount of assembly
> In the recesses of the north.
> I will ascend above the heights of the clouds;
> I will make myself like the Most High.
>
> Isaiah 14:13, 14[11]

It might be argued, in fact, that this proclivity to exalt self is the essence of sinfulness. As Strong observes,

> Sin, therefore, is not merely a negative thing, or an absence of love to God. It is a fundamental and positive choice or preference of self instead of God, as the object of affection and the supreme end of being. Instead of making God the centre of his life, surrendering himself unconditionally to God and possessing himself only in subordination to God's will, the sinner makes himself the centre of his life, sets himself

---

11. There is much discussion today as to whether the fall of Lucifer is referenced in Isaiah 14 (and/or in Ezekiel 28). I am persuaded that in those passages conscious reference is made to that primordial insurrection, but the point being made in the text here will stand even if the characterization of Isaiah 14 is in context restricted only to the wickedness of the king of Babylon.

directly against God, and constitutes his own interest the supreme motive and his own will the supreme rule.[12]

This is the flesh that even in the believer sets its desire against the Spirit (Gal. 5:17); the lofty thing that raises itself up against Christ (2 Cor. 10:5); the old self that has been corrupted in accordance with the lusts of deceit (Eph. 4:22).

It is in such a moral universe that biblical counselors must minister—indeed, must consciously conceive of themselves as ministering. On the one hand, the omnipotent Creator and Sovereign of the universe demands that finite humans honor Him as such, and it is altogether appropriate that He receive that honor. On the other hand, every fallen person, whether unredeemed or redeemed, is possessed of an Adamic nature that longs to be like God, that compels each one of us to usurp the place of honor and dominion that rightly belongs only to God, despite the fact that it is altogether inappropriate that any person receive such honor.

God Alone Is God

By reason of these two factors, biblical counselors must constantly and consciously arm their spirit, inform their instruction, and constrain their counselees with a commitment to glorify God and God alone. Such a commitment will compel us to exult in the truth that God alone is God, and to acknowledge joyfully that every creature of God is under sacred obligation both to resist the temptation to exalt self and to honor God as God!

All of this might be more simply expressed in this short rendering: **God is God, and I am not!** God alone is eternal; He knows the end from the beginning, and thus He is able to comprehend exactly how all things will in fact "work together for good"—no matter how distressing some

---

12. A. H. Strong, *Systematic Theology* (Valley Forge, Penn.: The Judson Press, 1907), 572. This in a section in which Strong is arguing "the essential principle of sin to be selfishness." He insists that selfishness is "not simply the exaggerated self-love which constitutes the antithesis of benevolence, but that choice of self as the supreme end which constitutes the antithesis of supreme love to God" (567). Although there are various suggestions as to what constitutes the essence of sin in Scripture (unbelief, hardness of heart, pride, sensuality, fear, self-pity, jealousy, greed, etc.), Strong's point is well taken: given that love of God and man together constitute the whole law (Matt. 22:37-39; Rom. 13:8-10; Gal. 5:14; James 2:8), it is reasonable to conclude that love of self, which thus exalts self above God and above others, constitutes the fundamental violation of God's law (2 Thess. 2:3, 4). For other biblical arguments in defense of thus defining the essence of sin, see Strong, 572.

of those things might seem to us (given that we can know only today, and that but haltingly and partially). God alone is sovereign; we can depend on Him to order the affairs of the moral universe so as to silence the great accuser of the brethren and to cause His children to grow in the grace and knowledge of the Lord Jesus Christ. God alone is true altogether; His word is life and light, and thus are we eternally well-advised to cast ourselves entirely upon His promises and to find in His word (and in His word alone) all things that pertain to life and godliness—even though we will be set upon from every quarter by theories and truth-claims that contravene the Word of God and are so seductive as to be alluring almost beyond resistance.

But **God is God, and I am not!** Therefore, God deserves to be honored, worshiped, trusted, feared, and loved as God. Our responsibility and privilege is to glorify Him—to enhance His reputation in the minds of rational creatures, to live our lives and order our days so that all who encounter us will have a higher regard for God than they might have had they never encountered us! But our besetting temptation is to glorify self—to live life as if we were the center of the universe, as if the enhancement of our reputation were a meritorious pursuit, as if our contentment were the greatest good of the cosmos. That is why every believer must continually be confronted with the demand that God be honored as God. And that is why biblical counseling must be framed by a conscious, undeviating commitment to the glory of God!

SELFISH PREDISPOSITIONS RESULT IN DESTRUCTION

A conscious commitment to a godward focus in biblical counseling is also imperative because destructive consequences are certain to follow when people exalt themselves rather than God. This truth is particularly significant in biblical counseling, because so many who seek our help have, in fact, plunged themselves into just such destruction. They have fulfilled the longing to aggrandize self, and the price to be paid for such spiritual rebellion is the most profound tragedy of the human soul. In short, the temptation to exalt self is at once terribly seductive and certainly destructive.

Jonah: Tempted, Fallen, Restored

The prophet Jonah struggled with the temptation to exalt himself over God, to pursue his own desires rather than obey God's commands, and he lost that struggle. The prophet high-handedly rejected God's word and became so morally inept that he convinced himself he could run from the presence of God. He discovered in rather dramatic fashion, however, that YHWH was no stranger to Joppa or to the sea lanes that led to Tarshish. The result of the prophet's rebellion was three days and three nights in the belly of a great fish!

Jonah did come to repentance, of course, and his prayer of contrition and confession is recorded in Jonah chapter 2. In that prayer Jonah called out in distress after he had been cast into "the deep, into the heart of the seas" (2:3). He bemoaned the fact that because of his own wickedness he found himself in the "great deep" with seaweed wrapped about his head (2:5). Even as he was "fainting away," as the breath of life was about to slip from him, he "remembered the LORD," fastened his soul's eye upon the temple in which YHWH had placed His name (2:7), and acknowledged his foolishness and sin. Then God responded by rescuing the prophet from the great fish.

In Jonah's psalm of repentance (Jon. 2:2–9) we find a brief statement that speaks directly to the issue at hand: "They that observe lying vanities forsake their own mercies" (v. 8 KJV). In other words, sin is both seductive and destructive.

Sin: Deceptive and Delicious

In speaking of the seductive nature of sin, Jonah acknowledged that he had "observed lying vanities." The Hebrew verb translated "observe" means "to give themselves up to" or "devote themselves to."[13] It suggests dogged determination or clinging to something in spite of influences to do otherwise.[14] The lying vanity Jonah clung to was "false love for his country, that he would not have his people go into captivity, when God would;

---

13. S. C. Burn, *The Prophet Jonah* (London: Houghter and Stoughton, 1880; reprint, Minneapolis: Klock and Klock, 1981), 130. Compare Pusey's representation of the verb as meaning "to diligently watch, pay deference to, court" in E. B. Pusey, *The Minor Prophets: A Commentary* (Grand Rapids: Baker, 1950), 1:410.

14. The verb is *shamar*, "to keep, guard, observe, give heed." Austel states that the basic idea of the root is "to exercise great care over" and that this meaning "can be seen to underlie the various semantic modifications seen in the verb" in H. J. Austel, "Shamar," *Theological Wordbook of the Old Testament* (Chicago: Moody, 1980), 2:939. Pusey emphasizes the fact that the verb means more than just to *do* vanities; it has to do with "they who observe, guard vanities, or lies, they, into the affections of whose hearts those vanities have entered; who not only do vanities, but who guard them, as loving them, deeming that they have found a treasure." Pusey, *Minor Prophets*, 1:410.

would not have Nineveh preserved, the enemy of his country."[15] But the phrase "lying vanities" is more generic, it encompasses "all things which man makes into idols or objects of trust."[16]

> Human devices contrary to the will of God are "lying vanities;" empty, they bring no satisfaction; lying, they promise peace and safety, but bring misery and horrible troubles. So Eve found, so Pharaoh, so Israel when they went after the ways of the heathen. So Jonah himself. So all who forsake the Fountain of living waters and hew out to themselves broken cisterns that can hold no water. Worldly devices to get happiness apart from God are indeed "vanity of vanities."[17]

With regard to the destructive nature of sin, Jonah acknowledges in his prayer that by clinging to empty, self-serving lies he had forsaken his "own mercy"; he had forfeited the goodness and grace that God longed to bestow upon him.

> In God is salvation; out of him is destruction. There is something appalling in the doom which is here described as overtaking those who, when the Saviour may be found, turn their back upon him, in order to seek and to serve other gods. Such are said to "forsake their own mercy." They act against their highest interests; they refuse the richest blessing; they abjure their truest Friend.[18]

Keil develops this same thought with reference to Jonah's warning concerning "forsaking one's own mercy":

---

15. Pusey, *Minor Prophets*, 1:410. To understand something of the cruelty and greed of Assyria is to begin to comprehend Jonah's anxiety to see that country destroyed, but none of that reduces the guiltworthiness of Jonah's rebellion and flight.

16. C. F. Keil, "The Twelve Minor Prophets," in *Biblical Commentary on the Old Testament*, ed. C. F. Keil and F. Delitzsch (Grand Rapids: Eerdmans, 1949), 1:403. There is some debate as to whether Jonah was criticizing the idolatrous religion of the pagans who had cast him overboard or his own wickedness in resisting YHWH. That the noun translated "vanities" is sometimes used with reference to idols is employed as an argument in favor of the contention that Jonah's focus is upon the pagan rituals of the sailors. But the spirit of his prayer demonstrates that the prophet is speaking here of his own sin. Perhaps the reference to "lying vanities" includes the admission that in resisting God he was treating his own desire for the destruction of Nineveh as an idol to be worshiped.

17. G. T. Coster, "Jonah," in *The Pulpit Commentary*, ed. H. D. M. Spence and J. S. Exell, 22 vols. (Grand Rapids: Eerdmans, 1958), 55.

18. J. R. Thomson, "Jonah," in *The Pulpit Commentary*, ed. H. D. M. Spence and J. S. Exell, 22 vols. (Grand Rapids: Eerdmans, 1958), 47.

The soul of man cannot be satisfied with husks. For God's servants to follow them is to forsake their own mercy. It is for the prodigal son to change the father's house for the society of rioters and harlots: "Many sorrows shall be to the wicked: but he that trusteth in the Lord, mercy shall compass him about" (Ps. 32:10). The way of duty is ever the way of safety, peace, and comfort; neglected duty is a sure forerunner of trouble; an evil conscience can never be the harbinger of sweet content.[19]

The significance, then, of Jonah's confession is simply this: those who stubbornly cling to seductive lies deprive themselves of the mercy and goodness God longs to shower upon them. From the belly of Sheol (2:2), Jonah acknowledged the God-dishonoring wickedness and soul-destroying foolishness of his stubbornness and repented.

"Lying Vanities": Empty, Self-Serving Lies

Jonah obeyed a lie. That lie was two-fold: (1) he believed that his desire for the destruction of Nineveh was more worthy than YHWH's desire for the repentance of that city; and (2) he believed that he could actually flee from the "presence of YHWH" (1:3). It is difficult to accept that Jonah actually *believed* that lie; he was, after all, a true prophet of YHWH (2 Kgs. 14:25). It defies credulity to suggest that a ministering prophet was persuaded that his desire transcended the command of God in worthiness or importance, or that such a spokesman for God consciously conceived of YHWH as a local deity so bound by space that a person could escape His presence by taking ship. But the issue whether Jonah actually believed the lie and whether he would have consciously affirmed the credibility of its claims, is moot; the historical fact, recorded in the Bible, is that he obeyed the lie. Jonah confessed that because of his own desires ("lying vanities": empty and self-serving lies) he rendered himself so spiritually foolish that he behaved as if the lie were true ("they that observe": cling to, embrace, cherish in spite of all influences to the contrary) and thus brought suffering upon himself.

The horrifying spiritual reality of Jonah's experience is this: the power of a lie is not intrinsic in its inherent credibility but in its attractiveness. The pivotal moral issue is not whether people will believe the lie but whether they will obey it! The father of lies learned in the Garden that a lie of

---

19. Keil, "Minor Prophets," 403.

almost infinite implausibility ("in the day that ye eat . . . ye shall be as gods") will seduce if it is sufficiently tantalizing ("good for food . . . pleasant to the eyes . . . to be desired to make one wise"). In short, a lie is powerful not because it is deceptive but because it is delicious.[20]

To make the same point from a different perspective, a lie is effective only because of our selfish predisposition, because as fallen creatures we are so bent upon pandering to our own desires that we will render ourselves so spiritually foolish as to obey a lie we would never consciously affirm. But that selfish predisposition is in every case destructive. When people determine to abandon what they know to be the truth in order to embrace a beguiling lie, they forsake God's mercy. That is the testimony of the prophet Jonah.

Anyone who counsels will, by the nature of that ministry, confront people who have obeyed seductive lies, and who have forsaken their own mercy. They have obeyed lies because of their selfish predisposition. In other words, they have rejected a godward focus in favor of a self-ward focus, and the result has been spiritual, emotional, physical, and/or relational destruction. They are living in the middle of Jonah 2:8, but their only hope is found in Jonah 2:9. They have set their eyes upon themselves and have brought havoc into their lives. We must confront them with this wickedness and challenge them to set their eyes upon God, to obey His word, to live their lives for His glory, and in this to confess and experience that "Salvation is of the Lord"!

Lying Vanities in Christian Counseling

The tragedy in the contemporary marketplace is that many models of Christian counseling are based on theories more accurately subsumed under the error of Jonah 2:8 ("lying vanities") than under the truth of Jonah

---

20. Compare the observation of Eliphaz that man "drinks iniquity like water" (Job 15:16); Solomon's observation, "Like a dog that returns to its vomit is a fool who repeats his folly" (Prov. 26:11, quoted by Peter in 2 Pet. 2:22); Jeremiah's rebuke of his contemporaries because their feet "loved to wander" (Jer. 14:10); Hosea's application of his own unhappy domestic experience, as he rebukes his countrymen because they "direct their desire toward their iniquity" (Hos. 4:8); Jesus' condemnation upon people because they "loved darkness rather than light, because their deeds were evil" (John 3:19); and Paul's statement that people will be deceived by the man of sin because they "did not receive the love of the truth" but took "pleasure in unrighteousness" (2 Thess. 2:10, 12). The univocal testimony of Scripture is that the root cause of sin is not confusion but rebellion, that people obey wicked impulses not because those desires seem morally noble or spiritually credible but because their hearts long to do evil (Rom. 1:18–25).

2:9 ("Salvation is of the Lord!"). Wittingly or not, some counselors have proven themselves to be blind leaders of the blind; they have acquiesced to ear-tickling notions that are sub-biblical and God-dishonoring—notions that only make people more comfortable in their wickedness.

It is distressing to contemplate the catalogue of "lying vanities" that have insinuated themselves into sundry models of "Christian" counseling: models that legitimize a narcissistic preoccupation with self; models that fabricate a dimension to the human psyche that cannot be proven to exist, but the acknowledgment of which has the insidious practical effect of making individuals the victims of forces for which they cannot be held accountable, and thus of denying that people are morally responsible for the way they act, think or feel; models that validate the notion that finite creatures have a right to be angry with the infinite Judge of the universe (who has, in fact, assured us that He will do right, Gen. 18:25), and that there can be spiritual and therapeutic benefit to expressing such an attitude of rage against God; models that speak of emotional healing and growth in relationships and in maturity while deliberately eschewing any appeal to the Holy Spirit or to the standard graces vouchsafed us by God.

All of these are lies! They are not intellectually compelling to anyone operating within a scriptural worldview, but because they make people comfortable in their sin they are extremely seductive. Furthermore, because it is a fixed reality of the moral universe that all who observe lying vanities will *always* forsake their own mercy, these lies are also destructive.

For both the counselor and the counselee, the means to counter these destructive lies is to make a deliberate and practical commitment to focus on the glory of God. This was the delivering discovery of the prophet Jonah. When he focused on his selfish desires he found himself in a mess, but when he recognized the destructiveness of his selfish predisposition, when he confessed the enslaving character of the lying vanities he had embraced, when he acknowledged that in clinging to those vanities he had forsaken God's goodness and brought destruction upon himself, Jonah found release. Millions have followed his example—people who would happily confess that all the glory and praise for the relief they found belongs to God alone.

The Dynamics of Jesus' Spiritual Paradox

Well into His eighteen month ministry in Galilee, when opposition had increased dramatically and it was apparent that time was short, Jesus called to Himself the twelve men He had authorized as apostles.

He empowered them to work miracles as proof of that authorization and then dispatched them to "preach, saying, 'The kingdom of heaven is at hand!'" (Matt. 10:7). Anticipating the difficulties His apostles would encounter, however, the Lord armed them with a promise as enigmatic as it was blessed. It was a paradoxical promise, at once the most rudimentary governing principle of the moral universe as framed by God and the greatest stumbling stone to mortals, who insist on defining that moral universe based on finite perspectives and distorted human values. What was that paradoxical promise? "He who has found his life shall lose it, and he who has lost his life for my sake shall find it" (Matt. 10:39).

On three other occasions recorded in the Gospels, Jesus proclaimed this principle. Some weeks after the Lord had authorized the apostles, He traveled with them to a remote area known as Ceasarea-Philippi. There He told them for the first time that He would suffer many things of the Jewish leaders and would die (Matt. 16:21). The disciples were horrified. Then Jesus followed this unhappy revelation with the warning that they, too, would have to be willing to take up a cross, deny themselves, and follow Him (Matt. 16:24; Mark 8:34; Luke 9:23). As part of that challenge, Jesus said,

> For whoever wishes to save his life shall lose it;
> and whoever loses his life for My sake and the gospel's shall save it.
>
> Mark 8:3

And again, in the midst of His final trip to Jerusalem for the Passover feast, Jesus confronted His antagonists, the Pharisees, with this cryptic warning.

> Whoever seeks to keep his life shall lose it,
> and whoever loses his life shall preserve it.
>
> Luke 17:33

Finally, during the final passion week, Jesus addressed "certain Greeks" who had sought Him out. Contemplating His own impending death, Jesus said:

> He who loves his life loses it;
> and he who hates his life in this world shall keep it to life eternal.
>
> John 12:25

On at least four different occasions, while addressing three different audiences, our Lord uttered this hard saying. To finite humans, these are difficult words—paradoxical at best, nonsensical at worst. But they are, in fact, the words of the Savior Himself, and they are words that communicate a truth central to His teaching about living successfully.

Losing Life—Finding Life

To understand Christ's promise we need to consider two nuances of the word *life* that are at stake.[21] The warning is that whoever wishes to save his or her life (i.e., temporal, material life) will lose it (i.e., eternal blessedness). The promise is that whoever is willing to lose life (again, temporal matters) for the sake of the Savior will, in fact, find life (again, eternally significant matters). Indeed, Hort insists that "this 'paradoxical' saying gets its point from the fact that men call by the name of 'life' that which is not truly life: 'he that wishes to save his 'life' (i.e. life in the narrower sense) will lose his true 'life' (i.e. life in its highest sense)".[22] Morison acknowledges this same distinction; he paraphrases the warning: "In grasping at the shadow he shall infallibly lose the substance."[23]

The statement is paradoxical, then, only because people do not comprehend what constitutes real life. They are fully persuaded that life consists in the things that a person has; Jesus says it does not (Luke 12:15). They live under the delusion that satisfaction lies in accomplishing goals, establishing a reputation, exercising great power, and amassing much wealth; Jesus states simply that the person who learns to hunger and thirst after righteousness is blessed, because that person will be filled (i.e., satisfied, Matt. 5:6). The soulish individuals, who have persuaded themselves that happiness and contentment are to be found in the present world, are compelled by the force of their own abominable logic to set their eyes on this world.

But the dynamic of Jesus' spiritual paradox constrains us to focus on the glory of God rather than upon the gratification of our own desires. The rationale for such a selfless ethic is as uncomplicated to the eye of faith as it is inscrutable to the natural man; it is as compelling to one impelled by the Spirit as it is repugnant to one controlled by the flesh. That

---

21. In every one of these passages the word translated "life" (NASB) is *psuche*, the Greek term most often translated "soul." The reference is not to the soul/spirit (i.e., the immaterial aspect of man) as opposed to the body (the material aspect); rather, Jesus is making reference to the "principle of life generally." F. J. A. Hort, *Expository and Exegetical Studies* (Minneapolis: Klock and Klock, 1980; Grand Rapids: Kregel Publications, 1987), 122.

22. Hort, *Expository and Exegetical Studies*, 122.

23. J. Morison, *A Practical Commentary on the Gospel According to St. Matthew* (Boston: N. J. Bartlett, 1884; reprint, Minneapolis: Klock and Klock, 1981), 291.

rationale is simply this: "Whoever loses his life for My sake and the gospel's sake shall save it!" In other words, the only way to find a fruitful and contented life is to give one's self away to God ("My sake") and to others ("the gospel's sake").

It might be argued that there is egocentrism latent in this ethic, that giving one's life away with the motive of getting it back is only selfishness once removed. But this argument is based on the mistaken notion that God is displeased if people are happy, that God wants them to be miserable, and, thus, that it is morally inappropriate for anyone to long for or strive for happiness. In fact, God is a good and loving God who yearns for His creatures to find the soul-satisfaction He has provided for them. The univocal testimony of Scripture is that God's heart longs for each person to find contentment. Indeed, God so loved the world that He gave His own Son in order to provide such soul-satisfying peace. Wickedness lies not in the desire to find contentment of soul but in the determination to find it at the expense of God's standards and mandates. God takes immeasurable delight in those who determine to obey Him and by means of that obedience to know the peace that transcends human comprehension.

Focusing on God

So we see again the necessity of a focus upon the glory of God in the ministry of counseling. Tragedy will certainly befall people who live each day in an attempt to find satisfaction, for in that very effort they will lose it! When these soul-sick individuals come to us for counseling, we need to encourage them to honor the dynamic of Jesus' spiritual paradox; that is, to redirect their focus, to set their soul's gaze first of all upon God and then upon those about them, and then to order their lives in ways consistent with that focus. Lamentably, the effect of much counseling today is to reinforce the counselee's focus upon self. Exegetical and theological acrobatics are attempted to justify this strategy, but such efforts notwithstanding, this counsel is twice grievous: it is explicitly condemned by the Scriptures, and it is disastrous to the counselee.

How much wiser and God-honoring it is to acknowledge the authority of Jesus' person and the truth of His words, and to prove the life-changing power of the spiritual paradox He gave to us.

The way of self-crucifixion and sanctification may seem foolishness and waste to the world, just as burying good seed-corn seems waste to the child and the fool. But there never lived the man who did not find that, by sowing to the Spirit, he reaped life everlasting.[24]

In sum, the spirit of the biblical counselor must be like that expressed by the psalmist David: "Be thou exalted, O God above the heavens; let thy glory be above all the earth "(Ps. 57:5, KJV). Indeed, the primary goal of the counselor must be to see this same spirit functioning as the controlling attitude in counselee's lives. Only as a person's heart becomes overwhelmed with the desire articulated by the psalmist and is consumed with the prayer, "Be thou exalted, O God," is that person going to know the peace God longs to give to His children.

The realities of the moral universe demand that I live my life out in every way for His honor rather than for my own; after all, God is God, and I am not! But the deepest need of my soul also constrains me to honor God as God, to submit to His standards and cherish His instruction; only as I thus hunger and thirst after righteousness will I be filled. Indeed, as Tozer has reminded us:,

> There is a logic behind God's claim to preeminence. That place is His by every right in earth or heaven. While we take to ourselves the place that is His the whole course of our lives is out of joint. Nothing will or can restore order till our hearts make the great decision: God shall be exalted above.[25]

---

24. J. C. Ryle, *Expository Thoughts on the Gospels: John* (Greenwood, S. C.: Attic Press, 1965), 2:333.

25. A. W. Tozer, *The Pursuit of God* (Camp Hill, Penn.: Christian Publications, 1982), 104.

Part III

The Process of
Biblical Counseling

10

Developing a Helping Relationship with Counselees

Wayne A. Mack

Biblical counseling is about solving people's problems. It is about discovering the causes of their problems and then applying biblical principles to those causes. Sometimes, even well-intentioned counselors err, however, by counseling without cultivating the key element of *involvement*.[1]

Consider the approach of this counselor described in *The Christian Counselor's Casebook* by Jay Adams:

> Clara comes to you stating that she has filed for divorce on the grounds of mental and bodily cruelty.
>
> Clara returns for the third session. "I tried to get him here but he had *other* things to do," she begins. "You know what his other things are, of course. I told you all of them."
>
> "I don't want to hear such charges behind Marty's back," you respond. "This continuing hostility toward him, even though you told

---

1. We could discuss at length the necessity of the counselor's involvement with Christ for only when he or she has a vital, intimate relationship with the Lord can counseling be truly effective (cf. Matt. 7:3–5; Acts 4:13; 1 Cor. 11:1). But this chapter will primarily discuss the counselor's involvement with the counselee, an involvement intended to develop and maintain a facilitative relationship between the two. Ultimately and preeminently the purpose for that involvement is to enhance the counselee's involvement with Christ. This vertical dimension is what makes biblical counseling different from all other forms of counseling.

him you forgave him, seems to indicate that you made little or no attempt to bury the issue and start afresh. I don't think that you understand forgiveness. You . . ."

"Forgive him! You know there is a limit. After he has beat me, and his drinking away our money maybe, but when I came home and found him in my bed with that woman, I can never bury that! He is just an immature, immoral, animalistic pig," she declares.

You tell her that it will be necessary for her to change her language about her husband and that you are here to help but not to salve her self-righteous attitude and listen to her ever-increasing charges against her husband.

"Why are you siding with him? I'm the one that belongs to this church!" She breaks into tears.[2]

Why did that session deteriorate into near hopelessness before it had hardly begun? Although most of what the counselor said was probably true, the session turned sour because the counselor took, what I call, the auto mechanic approach to counseling.

When someone leaves a car for repair, the mechanic pulls out the shop manual, puts the car through various diagnostic tests, then repairs the problem according to the manual. Some counselors, I fear, treat people this way. They are interested only in finding out what the problem is and what the book says to do about it. Then they immediately try to fix the problem with little regard to their relationship with the counselee.[3]

This approach to counseling is faulty because it regards the counselee as a mechanism, while the biblical counselor is trying to help a whole *person*. This is not to say, of course, that the person should be emphasized to the extent that his or her problems are disregarded. A genuine care and concern for the individual will compel us to deal with the person and the problems. The point is, counselors cannot allow themselves to become exclusively *problem-oriented*. Rather, they need to be *person-oriented*, then the treatment of problems that flows from that emphasis will be set in the proper context.

The counselor in Clara's case failed because he was too problem-oriented in his approach. Apparently, he had done little to establish

---

2. Adapted from Jay Adams, *The Christian Counselor's Casebook* (Grand Rapids: Zondervan, 1974), 186.

3. Unfortunately, the counselor who does this lends validity to the criticism that biblical counselors merely "throw out Bible verses" or "shove Scripture down people's throats." As we will see later in this chapter, that kind of "biblical" counseling is patently not biblical.

involvement with his counselee. He had not endeavored to develop a facilitative relationship that would assure her of his concern. He could have taken time to listen to her and sympathize with the pain she was experiencing, but, instead, he jumped right in and addressed her sin.[4] Almost immediately, Clara viewed him as an enemy or opponent rather than an ally. And as long as she viewed her counselor this way, his counsel would mean little to her. His words might be truthful and appropriate to her situation, but she would reject them.

Proverbs 27 says, "Faithful are the wounds of a *friend*" (v. 6); and "A man's counsel is sweet to his *friend*" (v. 9, emphasis added). We are most receptive to counsel from those we know are with us and for us. They can speak to us frankly about our faults, and though we may be annoyed temporarily, we soon realize that they are only trying to help us because they are concerned for us. On the other hand, if someone whom we perceive as a stranger or an enemy criticizes us, we tend to react defensively and with suspicion about their motives.

In counseling, as in any other relationship, we must remember that *our impact and influence in people's lives is usually related to their perception of us.* That is why involvement is so important to the counseling process. Usually, the counseling process is truly effective only when an acceptable level of involvement has been established.[5]

With that in mind, let us consider three ways that counselors can develop involvement with counselees. The facilitative relationship must be built on the foundations of *compassion*, *respect*, and *sincerity*.

INVOLVEMENT THROUGH COMPASSION

Involvement is established when people know that we sincerely care for them.

---

4. Clara's sin in the situation was of utmost importance and needed to be dealt with as the counseling continued. But by taking the approach he did, the counselor gave Clara the impression that he did not consider her husband's sin to be very serious, which immediately created a wall between them because of her preoccupation with her husband's hurtful actions.

5. Of course the counselor cannot *make* the counselee view him or her as a friend or ally. Some people we work with may be so predisposed against us that nothing we do will reverse this attitude. Our responsibility is simply to do whatever we can to be the kind of person that deserves their respect and trust.

Two Impressive Examples of Compassion

Jesus. Undoubtedly, the greatest counselor of all times was our Lord Jesus Christ. Isaiah the prophet told us, "His name shall be called Wonderful Counselor" (9:6) and that upon Him would rest "the spirit of wisdom and understanding, the spirit of counsel and strength" (11:2). One of the keys to Jesus' success as a counselor was His intense compassion for men and women, which is apparent throughout the gospel accounts of His life and ministry.

The book of Matthew tells us that "seeing the multitudes, He felt compassion for them, because they were distressed and downcast like sheep without a shepherd" (Matt. 9:36). Jesus suffered with the needy multitudes. He felt for them and cared for them. His compassion permeated all of his attempts to meet their needs (Matt. 9:35, 37–38). Far from being a cold-hearted, auto mechanic type counselor who merely attacked problems and treated people like statistics, Jesus was motivated by compassion for them.

Mark 3:1–5 says that when Jesus noticed a man with a withered arm in the synagogue, He became angry and grieved at the Pharisees for their lack of sensitivity toward the man. Jesus showed compassion for the man by healing him of his malady.

A rich young ruler came to Jesus seeking eternal life, but left without it because he loved his riches too much to give them up. Mark 10:21 says that "looking at him, Jesus felt a love for him." Even when Jesus had to tell people what they did not want to hear, He did so with compassion.

One day Jesus was walking with His disciples when a funeral procession passed nearby (Luke 7:11–15). The only child of a widow had died, and Christ stopped to comfort her: "And when the Lord saw her, He felt compassion for her, and said to her, 'Do not weep.'" Then He proceeded to raise her boy from the dead.

Jesus' compassion caused Him to shed tears of sorrow and grief. Luke 19:41 records that Jesus wept over Jerusalem as He predicted the judgment of God that would soon fall upon it. In John 11:33–35, when Jesus saw Mary's grief over the death of Lazarus, "He was deeply moved in spirit, and was troubled," and He wept. Mary and all the others Jesus interacted with throughout His ministry knew how much He cared for them. That is one of the qualities that made Him the Wonderful Counselor. He did not just observe problems and dispense platitudes—He epitomized the compassion that every counselor needs.

Paul. Another compassionate counselor was the apostle Paul. Many people think of Paul only as a staunch defender of the faith and a brilliant theologian. They fail to realize that he also was a compassionate man who cared deeply for people. In Acts 20:31 he reminds the Ephesian elders, "Night and day for a period of three years I did not cease to admonish each one with tears." The Greek word translated "admonish" (*nŏuthĕtĕ[ma]ō*) can also be translated "counsel," and it most often means "to correct or to warn." Even when Paul rebuked them for their sin, his tears communicated a genuine, caring, and loving heart.

Paul's great love for his fellow Jews is also shown in Romans 9:1–3. There he says, "I am telling the truth in Christ, I am not lying, my conscience bearing me witness in the Holy Spirit, that I have great sorrow and unceasing grief in my heart. For I could wish that I myself were accursed, separated from Christ for the sake of my brethren, my kinsmen according to the flesh." Paul was willing to burn in hell if that would save other Jews! Surely you and I have a long way to go before we match that kind of compassion.

In 2 Corinthians 2:4, Paul refers to a strong letter of admonishment he had previously written to that church: "For out of much affliction and anguish of heart I wrote to you with many tears; not that you should be made sorrowful, but that you might know the love which I have especially for you." Later he speaks of the "daily pressure" of concern he feels for all the churches and then says, "Who is weak without my being weak? Who is led into sin without my intense concern?" (2 Cor. 11:28–29). Paul identified with the problems and weaknesses of his "counselees" to the extent that it seemed he experienced them himself.

The Thessalonian church received an especially moving expression of Paul's love for them: "We proved to be gentle among you, as a nursing mother tenderly cares for her own children. Having thus a fond affection for you, we were well-pleased to impart to you not only the gospel of God but also our own lives, because you had become very dear to us" (1 Thess. 2:7–8).

Paul cared for people, and people knew that he cared. His heart was "opened wide" to them (2 Cor. 6:11). That is why he could be so straightforward in addressing their faults without alienating them. If we are to be effective counselors, we must have this same kind of compassion.

How to Develop Genuine Compassion

Perhaps you are questioning whether you have the kind of compassion Jesus and Paul had, or perhaps you are wondering how to develop such compassion. Fortunately, the Bible does not merely give us these examples, it tells us how we can emulate them. The following suggestions about developing compassion toward others are taken from Scripture.

Think about how you would feel if you were in the counselee's position. Many passages that refer to Jesus' compassion state first that he "saw" the people or He "looked upon" them. For instance, Matthew 9:36 says, "*Seeing* the multitudes, He felt compassion for them" (emphasis added). And the account of the mourning widow states, "When the Lord *saw* her, He felt compassion for her" (Luke 7:13).[6] These verses indicate that Jesus looked thoughtfully at others who were experiencing difficulty; He put Himself in their place and intentionally tried to feel what they were feeling. His compassion for them arose from this empathy. Hebrews 4:15 says that even now in heaven He is "touched with the feeling of our infirmities" (KJV).

Consider again the case of Clara. She quickly concluded that her counselor was not sympathetic with her. All she sensed from him was condemnation. He needed to listen to her complaints and concerns before he tried to understand how she felt. Before responding, he could have asked himself, "What would it be like for me to come home to a wife who was wasting all of our money on alcohol? What would it be like to have a wife calling me names, scratching me, and throwing things at me? What would it be like to have a wife who didn't care about what I thought or what I said? What would it be like for me to come home and find my wife in my bed with another man? How would I feel? What emotions would I be experiencing?"

This is where the counseling process must start. And although the sin problems must be addressed and solved, in most cases, effective counseling cannot occur until the counselor has shown the counselee the compassion of Christ by identifying with his or her struggles.

Think of the counselee as a family member. Paul says in 1 Timothy 5:1–2, "Do not sharply rebuke an older man, but rather appeal to him as a father, to the younger men as brothers, the older women as mothers, and the younger women as sisters." When I counsel, I deliberately try to imagine how I would treat one of my close relatives. I ask myself, how would I talk to them? How would I proceed if this were my mother or my father or my brother or my sister sitting across the desk from me? In reality, our counselees *are* our spiritual brothers and sisters, and our heavenly Father demands that they be treated as such.

Think about your own sinfulness. Galatians 6:1 instructs and cautions counselors: "Brethren, even if a man is caught in any trespass, you who are spiritual, restore such a one in a spirit of gentleness; *each one*

---

6. Cf. Matt. 14:14; Luke 10:33; 15:20.

looking to yourself, lest you too be tempted" (emphasis added). When we become aware of sin in the counselee's life, we must always remember that we are not immune to sin ourselves; we can fall into it just as easily as anyone else. No one has done anything that we could not do, but for the grace of God. If we keep this in mind we will avoid becoming self-righteous or condescending toward those who sin. Instead, we will reach out to them in compassion just as Jesus did to the adulterous woman (John 8:1–11).

Think about practical ways to show compassion. In reality, compassion is not so much an emotion as it is a choice of the will. Even if we do not feel like being kind to someone, we can still be kind (cf. Luke 6:27–28). Often, feelings of love for others follow the decision to act in a way that pleases and benefits them. Use the following questions to help you determine whether you are demonstrating genuine compassion toward your counselees:

Have you told your counselees that you care for them? (Phil. 1:8)

Have you prayed for them and with them? (Col. 4:12–13)

Have you rejoiced and grieved with them? (Rom. 12:15)

Have you dealt with them gently and tenderly? (Matt. 12:20)

Have you been tactful with them? (Prov. 15:23)

Have you spoken graciously to them? (Col. 4:6)

Have you continued to love and accept them even when they have rejected your counsel? (Mark 10:21)

Have you defended them against those who mistreat and accuse them? (Matt. 12:1–7)

Have you forgiven them for any wrong they have done to you? (Matt. 18:21–22)

Have you been willing to meet their physical needs if necessary? (1 John 3:17)

INVOLVEMENT THROUGH RESPECT

Not only do people need to know that we care for them, they also need to know that we respect them. Webster defines respect as "deferential regard" and "considering another worthy of honor." The Bible lauds this quality repeatedly. Romans 12:10 says that we are to "give preference to one another in honor"; Philippians 2:3 commands "with humility of mind let each of you regard one another as more important than himself"; and 1 Peter 2:17 tells us to "honor all men."

To return once more to the example of Clara, the counselor failed her miserably in this regard. His conversation with her communicated only disrespect, which undoubtedly was a major reason their relationship deteriorated.

In cases when a counselee shows little respect for the counselor, it may be because the counselor has shown little respect for the counselee. It is a matter of reaping what the counselor has sown. So when those we are trying to help fail to look to us for guidance (as we think they should), the first question we need to ask ourselves is, "Have I honored them as God commands me to?"[7]

How to Show Respect to a Counselee

There are several ways the counselor can show respect that will help establish involvement with the counselee:

Use proper verbal communication. We can show respect both in the way we talk to our counselees and in the way we talk about them. In 2 Timothy 2:24–25 Paul says, "The Lord's bond-servant must not be quarrelsome, but be kind to all, able to teach, patient when wronged, with gentleness correcting those who are in opposition, if perhaps God may grant them repentance leading to the knowledge of the truth." Rude or harsh speech is never condoned in Scripture, even when one is speaking the truth (cf. Eph. 4:15). Proverbs 16 says that "sweetness of speech increases persuasiveness" (v. 21) and "pleasant words are a honeycomb, sweet to the soul and healing to the bones" (v. 24). So the method of verbal communication is important in showing respect to a counselee.

Use proper nonverbal communication. Showing respect involves what we say with our mouths and what we do with the rest of our bodies. Leviticus 19:32 says, "Rise in the presence of the aged, show respect for the elderly" (NIV). In the Old Testament, etiquette required that a young person stand when an older person entered the room. It was a nonverbal way of saying, "I honor you; I respect you." Such nonverbal communication is

---

7. Of course not every counselee will respond with the proper respect for us even if we do all we can to respect them. In some cases, we may deal with people who simply respect no one. But we still must exemplify a godly honor for them and trust that God will use our example to convict them of their own pride.

as important to God today as it was then because it reveals what we think of others.

The acronym S-O-L-V-E-R is a useful device for remembering several nonverbal ways to show respect for a counselee:

S——squared shoulders. Face counselees in a way that indicates you are alert and giving them all your attention.

O——open stance. Relax your arms, hands, and shoulders as if to say, "I am here to receive whatever you want to communicate. You have access to me."

L——lean forward slightly. This shows interest in what the person is saying to you.

V——vocal quality. Maintain a volume and intensity in your speech that is neither abrasive nor hard to hear. Always let your voice reflect tenderness and compassion rather than anger and irritation.

E——eye contact. Look at people, especially when they are speaking. Do not stare at them so that they are uncomfortable, but show your interest in what they are saying by giving them your rapt attention.

R——relational posture. Coordinate all your body, head, and facial movements in a way that is most conducive to the comfort of the counselee. Your posture should not be stiff and robotic, but neither should it be so totally relaxed that the person thinks you are about to go to sleep.[8]

In all of these forms of nonverbal communication, maintain a balance so the counselee does not perceive you as either uptight or indifferent—both perceptions can build a wall between the two of you that will interfere with the counseling process.

Take the counselee's problems seriously. Never minimize the problems presented by your counselees. You may think, "This is so trivial—why are they making a big deal out of it?" But while it may seem trivial to you, it is extremely important to them, or they would not be discussing it with you. When you take their problems seriously, you communicate respect. On the other hand, if you make light of their problems you will alienate them from the beginning and will remove any hope they had that you could help them.

---

8. Adapted from Gerard Egan, *The Skilled Helper: Model Skills and Methods for Effective Helping* (Monterey: Brooks/Cole, 1986), 76–77.

Trust your counselees. First Corinthians 13:7 says that love "believes all things." Applied to counseling, this means that we should believe what our counselees tell us, until the facts prove otherwise. We should also believe that they have entered counseling because they want to please God more. Presumptive suspicion is a worldly attitude, not a Christian one (Phil. 2:3).

Note what one psychology textbook says about Gestalt therapist Fritz Perls:

> Perls . . . expresses his skepticism about those who seek therapy and indicates that not very many people really want to invest themselves in the hard work involved in changing. As he points out, "Anybody who goes to a therapist has something up his sleeve. I would say roughly ninety percent don't go to a therapist to be cured, but to be more adequate in their neurosis. If they are power mad, they want to get more power. . . . If they are ridiculers, they want to have a sharper wit to ridicule, and so on."[9]

As believers, we cannot approach counseling with such a cynical attitude. Although at times people will come to us with insincere motives, we should not allow ourselves to think they are insincere without good reason.

Express confidence in the counselee. The Corinthian church had more problems than any church Paul wrote to, yet he told them, "I rejoice that in everything I have confidence in you" (2 Cor. 7:16). No matter how many weaknesses our counselees have, if they are believers we need to convey the attitude that we are confident they will respond well to counseling and will grow through it.

Scripture states that "God . . . is at work in [us believers], both to will and to work for His good pleasure" (Phil. 2:13); and Jesus said, "My sheep hear My voice, . . . and they follow Me" (John 10:27). So we should have an attitude of confidence that believers will respond positively to the directives of our Lord. And we should communicate this confidence to our counselees. The apostle Paul followed this practice with people. He counseled believers about serious problems in their circumstances and in their lives, yet with only one exception (the letter to the Galatian church), his teaching, reproof, correction, and admonition were accompanied with expressions of confidence and respect.

---

9. Gerald Corey, *Theory and Practice of Counseling and Psychotherapy* (Monterey: Brooks/Cole, 1977), 179.

Welcome the counselee's input. We can show respect for our counselees by asking them to evaluate the sessions and suggest improvements. We can say to them, "God has brought us together, and He not only wants to use me in your life, He also wants to use you in my life." This also means that we must receive any negative input without becoming defensive or irritated. We can view criticism or complaints as an opportunity to model the godly responses we want counselees to develop in their lives.

Maintain confidentiality. A final way to show respect to counselees is to guard their reputations as much as possible without disobeying God. Unfortunately, confidentiality is not always possible (or desirable) in light of Jesus' commands. In Matthew 18:16–17 He says that if a brother is sinning and proves unwilling to listen to private rebuke, we should "take one or two more with you, so that by the mouth of two or three witnesses every fact may be confirmed. And if he refuses to listen to them, tell it to the church." Jay Adams added these comments to those verses:

> The implication of this biblical requirement to seek additional help in order to reclaim an offender is that Christians must never promise absolute confidentiality to any person. Frequently it is the practice of Bible-believing Christians to give assurances of absolute confidentiality, never realizing that they are following a policy that originated in the Middle Ages and that is unbiblical. . . .
>
> Is it right, then, to refuse any confidentiality at all? No, confidentiality is assumed in the gradual widening of the sphere of concern to other persons set forth in Matthew 18:15ff. As you read the words of our Lord in that passage, you get the impression that it is only reluctantly, when all else fails, that more and more persons may be called in. The ideal seems to be to keep the matter as narrow as possible. . . .
>
> What then does one say when asked to keep a matter in confidence? We ought to say, "I am glad to keep confidence in the way that the Bible instructs me. That means, of course, I shall never involve others unless God requires me to do so." In other words, we must not promise *absolute* confidentiality, but rather, confidentiality that is consistent with biblical requirements.[10]

Biblical confidentiality is essential in building a relationship of trust between counselor and counselee.

---

10. Jay Adams, *Handbook of Church Discipline* (Grand Rapids: Zondervan, 1986), 30–32. See also George Scipione, "The Limits of Confidentiality in Counseling," *Journal of Pastoral Practice* 7, no. 2.

INVOLVEMENT THROUGH SINCERITY

The kind of relationship we want to develop with our counselees can exist only when they know that we are genuine and honest. Paul described his ministry as "not walking in craftiness . . . but by the manifestation of truth commending ourselves to every man's conscience in the sight of God" (2 Cor. 4:2). Commentator Philip E. Hughes wrote concerning that verse, "So far from being marked by subterfuge, self-interest, and deceit, however, Paul's ministry was one in which the truth was manifested, openly displayed, outspokenly proclaimed (cf 3:12f.), in such a manner that none could gainsay the genuineness and sincerity of his motives."[11]

We must be like Paul in our counseling, having no hidden agendas or disguised motives, but openly revealing the truth about who we are (and even what we are thinking) to those we seek to help.[12] Only then will they be able to trust us through the process.

How can we be sincere and honest in our counseling? Scripture indicates the following methods:

Be honest about your qualifications. It is easy for counselors to misrepresent their credentials to counselees in an attempt to gain respect and confidence. But while this motive may be legitimate, the method is not. Even the great counselor Paul, who had every right to throw around his title of Apostle, more often referred to himself as merely "a servant of Christ" (Rom. 1:1; Phil. 1:1; Titus 1:1; etc.). We should follow his humble example and represent ourselves in a similar way to our counselees. Certainly we must never exaggerate or otherwise deceive them about our qualifications. A relationship of trust will be highly unlikely if they find out we have lied to them!

Be honest about your own weaknesses. Being open about personal problems and struggles is an effective way for counselors to demonstrate sincerity to counselees. Paul told the Corinthians, "When I came to you, brethren, I did not come with superiority of speech or of wisdom, . . . I was with you in weakness and in fear and in much trembling" (1 Cor. 2:1-3). He

---

11. Philip E. Hughes, *The Second Epistle to the Corinthians*, in *The New International Commentary on the New Testament*, ed. G. D. Fee (Grand Rapids: Eerdmans, 1962), 124.

12. This, of course, does not mean that we should tell our counselees everything about ourselves or volunteer everything we are thinking at any given time. Nevertheless, a willingness to share our thoughts and experiences with them is a good indicator of the godliness of our attitudes toward them, toward ourselves, and toward God. Reluctance to be open and transparent, even when appropriate and helpful, may indicate pride and a fear of man.

did not present himself as somebody who always had it all together. He was honest about his weaknesses and fears. When he wrote to the Corinthians again, he told them that during a time of affliction he and Timothy had been "burdened excessively, beyond our strength, so that we despaired even of life" (2 Cor. 1:8).

This was the man who said in 1 Corinthians 10:13 that God would never allow us to be tempted beyond what we are able to bear. Yet he admitted that there was a time when he was so burdened he did not think he could take it anymore. This is one of the reasons Paul was such a great counselor: he was able to proclaim the truth firmly without leaving people under the impression that he was perfect or unable to relate to their failings (cf. Rom. 7:14–25).

Of course we need to be careful that our self-disclosure is not inappropriate in nature or in duration (we do not want to make our counselees think that we need counseling more than they do!), nor should we spend an inordinate amount of time talking about our problems when counselees come to receive help for theirs. But an appropriate openness shows sincerity, which helps to establish involvement. Whatever we do, we must never pretend to be something we are not.

Be honest about your goals and agenda. Generally speaking, it is advisable and fitting to let counselees know from the beginning what we are trying to do and how we intend to do it. We need to be honest about our counseling methods and standards. We need to make it clear that God and His Word are our source of authority. We must let them know that we approach counseling this way because we are convinced that God's way of describing problems, identifying their causes, and solving them is superior to any other way.

Occasionally, people come to me wanting their problems to be labeled and interpreted, and solved psychologically. My frequent response to this request is something like this: "I want to serve and help you and I am firmly convinced that the best way to do that is God's way. I am resolutely committed to the Scriptures as my sole authority because I believe God knows far better than anyone else what our problems are, why we have them, and what to do about them. So because I am a Christian who is convinced that God's way of understanding and dealing with problems is far superior to any other way and because I want to give you the best help available, my method will be based on the Scripture. If you want a different approach, you will have to secure another counselor. For the Lord's sake and for yours, I cannot approach counseling in any other way." Over the years, as I have responded to people in this way, most of them have appreciated my honesty and have stayed for help. From the very start counselees know I will be honest with them and this enhances our relationship.

We must never be like many non-Christian therapists, who hide their true intentions and play games with people in order to get them to change. Jay Haley is one such therapist:

> A third tactic [of Haley's counseling approach] is the encouraging of usual behavior. In this case resistance to the advice can only result in change. For instance, asking a domineering woman to take charge of the family will often highlight her interaction and result in her wanting to recede more into the background. What is important in Haley's approach is the question of control. If the therapist tells the domineering woman to lead, she is no longer leading but following the instructions of the therapist. . . . Like the Zen Master the therapist induces change in the client by the use of paradox.[13]

Any type of reverse psychology like this is unacceptable for the biblical counselor—it only creates barriers to the desired involvement with the counselee.

Be honest about your limitations as a counselor. When we make mistakes or have difficulty knowing how to proceed in a particular case, we should admit it. Paul told the Galatians that he was "perplexed" about them (Gal. 4:20; 2 Cor. 4:8), and in 2 Corinthians 12:20 he writes, "I'm afraid that when I come again my God will humiliate me before you." Now that is being honest! Paul knew and admitted that he was fallible as a minister, an admission that revealed his sincerity and enabled people to trust him.

What role does establishing a facilitative relationship with a counselee play in the counseling process? Scripture underscores its significance by exhortation and example, and what Scripture teaches, counseling experience illustrates. Here, for example, is one counselee's evaluation of some of the factors she considered most helpful in her counseling experience:

> For me the content of the counseling in many ways was secondary. Often it was who the counselor was that laid the foundation for whether I could trust, accept, and do what was presented during counseling.
>
> It was a big step for me to be under the tutelage of a male. My relationships with both men and women had been so bad that I didn't

---

13. Vincent D. Foley, *An Introduction to Family Therapy* (New York: Grune and Stratton, 1974), 84–85.

trust anyone, although it was worse with men than with women. A counselor needs to be trustworthy. For me some of the hardest things in my life did not hit the table until long after I knew my counselor. Much of that was simply because I needed to know that no matter what was happening, he could be trusted. I had many experiences with people who didn't believe me when I told them certain things were happening in my life. I assumed that most people were like that, and feared that they all were. So I did not easily trust anyone. Time was needed and I needed to see that this counselor believed in me. I needed to see that he trusted me. I don't mean to suggest that he never had the right to question the validity of my situation (in fact he did), but I simply needed to see that I was going to be trusted, accepted, and believed in.

On one occasion I walked out on the counselor and slipped back down the slide, yet he was patient with me. He hurt with me and even in the midst of my own failings, I sensed the respect from him that helped me start climbing the ladder again. My counselor's credibility was built over the long haul—he continued to love when I did not love and tried to run.

One counselor I've had seemed to have the answers too available on his cuff. At times he responded too quickly and gave the impression of having a canned approach. I left feeling that he didn't sense the difficulty that existed and the time needed for rebuilding. Whereas my counselor seemed much more sensitive to my own hurts, and although he didn't hesitate to confront me with hard truths, he did it in ways that I knew without a doubt that he loved and cared for me and my growth in Christ.

One other element I needed and looked for was whether or not I was accepted. Even when things would seem to go from bad to worse, did he still accept me? This didn't mean that he condoned everything I had done or still did. It didn't mean that he never rebuked or reproved me or called on me to repent, but it did mean that he did it in a loving and gracious way so that I knew he was my friend and not my enemy. It also meant that my counselor affirmed me when possible— he commended and complimented as well as challenged.

As this letter illustrates, those who come for counsel are often scrutinizing the counselor to see if he or she is someone who can be trusted. Only if the counselor proves to be trustworthy, can a helping relationship be established that will make the counseling process a mutually profitable experience.

Though God sometimes chooses to accomplish His work through unlikely ways and unlikely people, the Bible emphasizes (and the counselee's letter illustrates) that God usually changes lives in a situation where a relationship of concern and trust exists between the helper and the one who needs help. As biblical counselors, we must do all we can to wrap the content of our counseling in a package of compassion, respect, and honesty.

11

Instilling Hope
in the Counselee

Wayne A. Mack

Biblical change cannot take place without hope—especially in the difficult situations we face as counselors. People who have had life-shattering experiences like divorce, a death of a loved one, or a loss of a job need hope. People who have faced the same problem for a long time need hope. People who have sincerely tried to solve their problems and failed need hope. People who have compounded their initial problems with other unbiblical responses need hope. People whose problems have been wrongly described need hope, and people whose hopes have been dashed repeatedly need hope. If we want to help any of these people, we must make sure that inspiration and hope are operative elements in our counseling.

THE BIBLICAL EMPHASIS ON HOPE

The role of hope in the process of sanctification cannot be underestimated. Consider what Scripture says about its many contributions to that process:

Hope produces joy that remains even through the most difficult trials (Prov. 10:28; Rom. 5:2–3; 12:12; 1 Thess. 4:13).

Hope produces perseverance (Rom. 8:24–25).

Hope produces confidence (2 Cor. 3:12; Phil. 1:20).

Hope produces effective ministry (2 Cor. 4:8–18).

Hope produces greater faith and love (Col. 1:4–5).

Hope produces consistency (1 Thess. 1:3).

Hope produces increased energy and enthusiasm (1 Tim. 4:10).

Hope produces stability (Heb. 6:19).

Hope produces a more intimate relationship with God (Heb. 7:19).

Hope produces personal purity (1 John 3:3).

Since the Bible places such emphasis on the role of hope in spiritual growth, it must be a strong emphasis in our counseling as well.

CONTRASTING TRUE AND FALSE HOPE

Most counselors, both Christian and non-Christian, realize that people with problems need hope. Unfortunately, however, the hope that many counselors provide is a false hope that rests on an unbiblical foundation and will inevitably crumble (Prov. 10:28; 11:7). It is important to understand the difference between this false hope and the true hope that the Bible describes.

Characteristics of False Hope

False hope is based on human ideas of what is pleasurable and desirable. Many people think that their problems will disappear if they can just get what they want—and sometimes counselors encourage them in that error by promising or intimating that their desires will be satisfied. This is a serious mistake, because God never promises us that we will get everything we want, nor does He even tell us that getting what we want will make us happy. Often what we want is *not* what is best for us, and a name-it-and-claim-it approach to our desires only compounds our problems. When a certain lady came for counseling concerning severe financial difficulties, her counselor discovered that her problems resulted from this kind of thinking. She had visited a car dealership, walked around a Lincoln Town Car seven times, laid hands on it, and "claimed" it from the Lord. God did not provide the money to pay for it, of course, and now she was in dire straits financially.

This is an extreme example, but many people cling to similar false hopes. They think, "If I could just get married, my problems would be solved," or "If I could get a better job, I would be nicer to live with." Unfortunately, the objects of their desire are physical rather than spiritual and temporal rather than heavenly. Because God has not promised them freedom from tribulation in this world (John 16:33; cf. James 1:2–4), they become disillusioned when they do not get what they want.

False hope is based on a denial of reality. I once counseled a young man who wanted to make his living as a musician. Some of his friends encouraged him in this pursuit because they did not want to hurt him. But, in reality, he did not have any musical ability. He thought he did, but he did not. So as a counselor I needed to point him in another direction rather than perpetuate a false hope.

I also remember a young lady whose husband left her and whose well-meaning friends continually told her they were sure he would come back. When she asked me about this in counseling, I had to say repeatedly, "I don't know. What I do know is that God can use this in your life to make you a greater woman of God, and if that happens you have benefited from the situation. I wish I could tell you for sure that your husband is going to come back, but I cannot do that."

"All my friends tell me my husband will come back," she said to me once, "and every time I come here, instead of encouraging me, you discourage me." I then asked her why she kept coming back to me for counseling, and she replied that it was because she knew I would tell her the truth. Deep inside she knew that her friends were bending reality in an attempt to comfort her, and that provided no true comfort.

False hope is based on mystical or magical thinking. Sometimes Christians place their hope in fanciful ideas that have no biblical substance. For example, some people's approach to daily devotions is "a verse a day keeps the devil away." They read their Bible every morning as a magical rite to ward off trouble. If they happen to miss their devotions one time, they suffer throughout the day in fear.

Certainly we should begin the day with God by having devotions in the morning, but we must recognize that there is no mystical power in that activity. In fact, Bible reading (and even memorization) only benefits us when we understand and apply the Scriptures to our lives. Only the person who "looks intently" at the Word and is an "effectual doer" of the Word will be blessed in what he or her does (James 1:25).

False hope is based on an unbiblical view of prayer. One of the questions on the personal inventory sheets we use in counseling[1] is "What have

---

1. See sample of Personal Data Inventory form on page 387.

you done about your problem?" Under that question, counselees will some-times write that they have prayed about it and nothing else. When we talk with them further, we find that they believe prayer is all God requires them to do. One such man, who was having constant problems with sexual sin, was angry at God because God had not taken away his problems in re-sponse to his prayer.

This can be called the "quarterback approach" to spirituality—we pass the ball or hand it off to God (by praying) and expect Him to run it across the goal line without any help from us. But such an approach only creates a false hope, because God never promised that we could reach the goal of godliness without strenuous personal effort (1 Tim. 4:7b). We need His divine strength to succeed (John 15:5), and that is where prayer comes in, but prayer alone will seldom solve our problems.

In Matthew 6:11 Jesus said that we should pray, "Give us this day our daily bread." But in 2 Thessalonians 3:10 Paul says, "If any one will not work, neither let him eat." These two commands are not contrary, for while we are to pray that God will provide the things we need to live, we must not expect them to fall from heaven. We need to work for them with the strength God gives us. So even the hope we place in prayer can be false if we hope that prayer alone will take care of everything.

False hope is based on an improper interpretation of Scripture. Many Christians suffer from the errors of eisogesis, the practice of reading per-sonal meaning into a text rather than drawing the author's true meaning out of it (exegesis). Another way to describe this practice is "lucky dip-ping" or seeking guidance and hope by reading random verses in Scripture and assigning meaning to them regardless of their context.[2] This approach leads to a misunderstanding of what the Bible actually teaches and to dis-illusionment when the supposed promises do not come true.

A woman who had gotten involved in an extramarital affair came to me for counseling, and I found that one of the causes leading to her sin was a false hope based on misinterpreted Scripture. Several years before, her father had threatened to leave her mother and she found refuge from her fears by reading Matthew 18:19, "If two of you agree on earth about anything that they may ask, it shall be done for them by My Father who is in heaven." This woman found a Christian friend who agreed with her

---

2. Two classic examples of this are people who open a Bible and read whatever verse their eyes first notice, or those who swing a finger over a page with their eyes closed and let it fall on the verse God wants them to read that day. People who do this often end up trying several times because they first happen upon an inappropriate verse such as Exodus 16:36: "Now an omer is a tenth of an ephah."

that her father should stay with her mother, and they prayed and expected God to keep them together. Her hopes were dashed, however, because her father left her mother anyway. In the woman's mind God had failed to keep His Word, and her faith was severely damaged. Doubt and bitterness toward God grew in her heart until finally she broke her marriage vows and got involved with another man.

Unfortunately, her hope was based on a misinterpretation of Scripture. Matthew 18:19 is part of a passage discussing church discipline (vv. 15–20) and has no direct application to prayer.[3] God never had promised her that He would keep her father and mother together simply because she and her friend agreed together in prayer. Showing her that her hope had been false and that God had not been unfaithful to His Word was an important step in bringing her back to holiness.

As counselors, we need to challenge the hopes that people hold when we are concerned that they might be false. When we do, however, we need to realize that the response we receive may be rather unpleasant. While true hope usually holds firm even when someone challenges it, those who hold a false hope tend to get upset when their hope is called into question. An example of this phenomenon is the story of Micaiah the prophet in 2 Chronicles 18. He prophesied against King Ahab's confidence that Israel could conquer the Arameans (a hope that had been bolstered by four hundred men who claimed to be prophets), so Ahab had him thrown into prison (vv. 16–19; 26). Micaiah suffered only because he had the courage and concern to challenge the king's false hope.

Micaiah was right, by the way—the Israelites were routed and Ahab died in the battle. We must be careful not to provide false hope as a temporary comfort, and we must be willing to examine and challenge the basis of our counselees' hopes. We must not allow them to build hope on an unbiblical foundation that will topple when the storms come (cf. Luke 6:47–49).

Characteristics of True Hope

Now that we understand some characteristics of false hope, we can contrast these with what the Bible says about true hope.

True hope is a biblically based expectation of good. In other words, it is biblical hope, an expectation based on the promises of God. Romans

---

3. For a discussion of the contextual meaning of this verse, see John MacArthur, Jr. *Matthew 16–23* (Chicago: Moody, 1988); or William Hendriksen, *The Gospel of Matthew* (Grand Rapids: Baker, 1973).

4:18 says about Abraham, "In hope against hope he believed, in order that he might become a father of many nations, according to that which had been spoken, 'So shall your descendants be.'" His hope was grounded on the promises given to him by God (cf. 2 Pet. 1:4).

Notice also that his hope was a *believing* hope—not a mere speculation. Today we often use the word *hope* to refer to something that may or may not happen. We say, "I hope my friend comes to visit tomorrow." But the biblical meaning of the word *hope* is different—it is more like "I know my friend is coming over tomorrow, and I can't wait to see him." That is why I say true hope is an *expectation*. It is based on the promises of an Almighty God, and there is no doubt that it will be rewarded. Consider this definition of biblical hope from *The New International Dictionary of New Testament Theology*:

> The hope of faith, . . . is a concrete personal expectation. Despite the "not yet" of the realization of salvation, it looks forward confidently though not without tension. However, Yawheh, for whom it waits, is not like us men. Since he knows, promises, and brings to pass what the future holds for his people, hope attains unparalleled assurance in the realm of revelation. Despite everything which at present runs counter to the promise, the one who hopes trusts God for his faithfulness' sake not to disappoint the hope he has awakened through his word (Isa. 8:17; Mic. 7:7; Ps. 42:5).[4]

True hope is the result of true salvation. In Scripture hope is always tied to the new birth by the Holy Spirit and personal faith in Christ. Consider these verses:

> Blessed be the God and Father of our Lord Jesus Christ, who according to His great mercy has caused us to be born again to a living hope . . ." (1 Pet. 1:3.)

> Since we heard of your faith in Christ Jesus and the love which you have for all the saints; because of the hope laid up for you in heaven, of which you previously heard in the word of truth, the gospel (Col. 1:4–5).

> Of this church I was made a minister according to the stewardship from God bestowed on me for your benefit, that I might fully carry

---

4. Colin Brown, ed., *The New International Dictionary of New Testament Theology* (Grand Rapids: Zondervan, 1976), 240.

out the preaching of the word of God, that is, the mystery which has been hidden from the past ages and generations; . . . which is Christ in you, the hope of glory (Col. 1:25-27).

Paul, an apostle of Christ Jesus according to the commandment of God our Savior, and of Christ Jesus, who is our hope (1 Tim. 1:1).

Those last two passages clearly say that Christ Himself is our hope. His person is the sum and substance of it. So how can someone have true hope if they do not love and trust in Jesus Christ? It simply is not possible, and we have to remember as counselors that we cannot affirm the hopes of anyone who has not been born again by the Spirit of God.

True hope is holistic in focus. By holistic we mean that true hope does not merely focus on the *part* (an individual life) but also the *whole* (God's plan for the universe). It finds encouragement in the eternal as well as the temporal and in the intangible as well as the tangible. Instead of being concerned only with what happens in one's life, true hope is concerned with what happens in the lives of others and whether God receives glory in the events that transpire.

The apostle Paul was a tremendous example of a man whose hope was holistic in focus. Read these verses carefully and consider what they reveal about his attitude:

> Now I want you to know, brethren, that my circumstances have turned out for the greater progress of the gospel, so that my imprisonment in the cause of Christ has become well known throughout the whole praetorian guard and to everyone else, and that most of the brethren, trusting in the Lord because of my imprisonment, have far more courage to speak the word of God without fear (Phil. 1:12-14).

> For I know that this [more bad circumstances] shall turn out for my deliverance through your prayers and the provision of the Spirit of Jesus Christ, according to my earnest expectation and hope, that I shall not be put to shame in anything, but that with all boldness, Christ shall even now, as always, be exalted in my body, whether by life or by death (Phil. 1:19-20).

> But even if I am being poured out as a drink offering upon the sacrifice and service of your faith, I rejoice and share my joy with you all (Phil 2:17).

> Remember Jesus Christ, risen from the dead, descendant of David, according to my gospel, for which I suffer hardship even to imprisonment as a criminal; but the word of God is not imprisoned. For this reason I endure all things for the sake of those who are chosen, that

they also may obtain the salvation which is in Christ Jesus and with it
eternal glory (2 Tim. 2:8–10).

Paul's hope did not rest simply on what happened to him personally.
He saw himself as a part of a great and glorious movement of God, through
which people were being brought to Jesus Christ and the Church was being edified. He placed his hope in the Kingdom purposes of God in this
world. So if furthering God's plan involved suffering on Paul's part, that
was all right with him. His hope did not waver when he faced imprison-
ment, slander, and even death because he was more concerned with God's
glory than with his personal comfort. What happened to him was of little
importance compared to the bigger picture.[5]

Joseph and Job are two Old Testament illustrations of the holistic
aspect of true hope. Joseph's hope remained solid even when he was sold
into slavery, lied about, and thrown into prison—and the reason it did is
revealed in his famous statement in Genesis 50:20. There he told his treach-
erous brothers, "As for you, you meant evil against me, but God meant it
for good in order to bring about this present result, to preserve many people
alive." And even though Job lost everything he had and never knew the
greater purposes God had in mind for his suffering, he said, "Though He
slay me, I will hope in Him" (Job 13:15) and, "As for me, I know that my
Redeemer lives, and at the last He will take His stand on the earth" (Job
19:25).

The Christian's cup in this world is never half empty—it is always
half full. Christians are never in a no-win situation, but always in a *no-lose*
situation, because even though we may not understand God's reasons for
whatever happens to us, we can know that He is accomplishing a grand
divine plan that will ultimately glorify Him and benefit us.[6] "The steps of
a man are established by the Lord" (Ps. 37:23); "God causes all things to
work together for good to those who love God, to those who are called
according to His purpose" (Rom. 8:28); and He "works all things after the

---

5. Paul's attitude is especially meaningful in light of the integral part he played in
the foundation of the Church. It would have been easy for him to focus on avoiding prison
or death, with the idea in mind that God had called him to apostleship and therefore needed
Him to complete the divine plan. But even Paul was expendable, and he knew it. Like
him, we should never compromise the truth because we think we are too important to
suffer the consequences of standing for it.

6. This includes even the most wicked intents and actions of mankind. See Acts
2:22–23 where Peter says that the crucifixion of Christ was foreordained by God—certainly
that was the vilest, most sinful event in world history, yet it produced more good than any
other event ever will.

counsel of His will" (Eph. 1:11). True hope focuses on the glorious plans of a God who says, "My purpose will be established, and I will accomplish all My good pleasure" (Isa. 46:10). Therefore, this hope is never shaken, even through unpleasant circumstances.

True hope is realistic. Romans 8:28 says that all things work together for good, but it does not say that all things *are* good. Even though true hope expects good to eventually come from trials, it does not try to deny the reality of sin and suffering, or the pain they cause.[7] True hope does not preclude tears and grief, nor does it rest on an illegitimate perception of personal capabilities. Notice in Romans 4:19 that Abraham "contemplated his own body, now as good as dead since he was about a hundred years old, and the deadness of Sarah's womb." Then verses 20–21 say, "*Yet*, with respect to the promise of God, he did not waver in unbelief, but grew strong in faith, giving glory to God, and being fully assured that what He had promised, He was able also to perform" (emphasis added). Abraham's hope was not based on an unrealistic view of his own capabilities (or Sarah's) but, rather, on God's ability to do what was humanly impossible. Likewise, true hope for us is not created by denying or twisting reality but by accurately considering it and basing our hope in God's power.

True hope must be renewed daily. God does not inject people with a huge dose of hope that will last for years. Our hope corresponds with the gradual work of sanctification that God is doing in our lives, so it cannot be sustained unless we allow that work to continue every day. In 2 Corinthians 4:16 Paul says that he does not lose hope because "though our outer man is decaying, yet our inner man is being renewed day by day." Only as Paul saw the work of renewal going on in his life each day could he have true hope. So we, too, must maintain a consistent relationship with God so that our hope will remain.

True hope is inseparable from a diligent and accurate study of God's Word. Psalm 119:49 says, "Remember the word to Thy servant, in which Thou hast made me hope," and Psalm 130:5 says, "I wait for the Lord, my soul does wait, and in His word do I hope." Scripture is the means by which God gives hope. Remember the experience of the two disciples on the Emmaus Road in Luke 24? They were walking along together,

---

7. Christian Science and the Word/Faith movement essentially deny the reality of bad circumstances (such as sickness). For more information on Christian Science, see Walter Martin, *The Kingdom of the Cults* (Minneapolis: Bethany, 1985). For more information on the Word/Faith error, see D. R. McConnell, *A Different Gospel* (Peabody, Mass.: Hendrickson, 1988); and John F. MacArthur, Jr., *Charismatic Chaos* (Grand Rapids: Zondervan, 1992).

despondently discussing the murder of Christ and how their hopes had been crushed by that event. But after the risen Jesus (unrecognized by them) came alongside and "was explaining the Scriptures" to them, they said, "Were not our hearts burning within us while He was speaking to us?" (Luke 24:32).

Their heaviness was lifted and their hope renewed by an increased understanding of the Word of God. The same thing happens to believers today who faithfully read and study the Bible, and without that diligent pursuit there can be no true hope.

True hope is a matter of the will. Hope is a choice, just as hopelessness is a choice. We can choose either to have hope or not to have hope. First Peter 1:13 says, "Fix your hope completely on the grace to be brought to you at the revelation of Jesus Christ." That is a command from God—therefore we must have the ability (with the help of the Holy Spirit) to choose and to do what it says. God does not give us commands that we cannot keep, contrary to the implication made in the following article, published recently. The article claimed that the idea of helplessness was an important contribution of psychology to the Church, and then said this:

> "There is an implication in all of [our critics'] writings that people are able to choose what is right," says [psychologist] Henry Cloud. "There is a total denial of the fact that we are sold into slavery." Psychotherapists constantly indict the evangelical church for failing to grasp people's helplessness. They suggest Evangelicals—especially those from a fundamentalist background—have deified willpower, as though a sinking person can pull himself up by his own bootstraps.[8]

This is a caricature of what biblical counselors believe, because choosing what is right through the power of the Holy Spirit is far different from pulling oneself up by one's own bootstraps (cf. John 15:5). Also, that emphasis on helplessness only produces an enslaving *hopelessness*. What hope do we have if we are unable to choose what is right?[9] Contrary to the claims in that article, the Bible does say we have the ability to choose what is

---

8. Tim Stafford, "The Therapeutic Revolution," *Christianity Today* 37, no. 6 (1993): 24–32.

9. The practical implications of that quote are frightening. It implies that a person with problems *must* have the help of another person (besides God) to choose what is right, and also that the only person who can help is someone who has knowledge beyond that revealed in Scripture. Counselors who persuade people of such helplessness will only succeed in making them dependent upon their counsel.

right (1 Cor. 10:13; Phil. 2:12; 4:13), which also applies to our responsibility to hope.

There are times when we need to choose to place our hope in God and in His Word by turning to His resources and focusing our minds on His promises. We need to choose to view our circumstances from a hope-filled perspective rather than a hopeless one.

True hope is based on knowledge. Romans 5:2–3 says, "We exult in hope of the glory of God. And not only this, but we also exult in our tribulations, knowing that tribulation brings about perseverance. . . ." James 1:2–3 says, "Consider it all joy, my brethren, when you encounter various trials, knowing that the testing of your faith produces endurance." Paul and James say that true hope is based on what we know, not on *how we feel*. If that were the case, we could never have hope during painful trials! The more truth we understand from God's Word, the more hope-ful we will be even in the worst circumstances. But if we base our hope on feelings, it will crumble.

HOW TO INSPIRE HOPE

Now that we have learned how to distinguish between true and false hope, let us consider how we can help to produce true hope in the people we counsel.

Help People to Grow in Their Relationship with Christ

Because Jesus Christ Himself is our hope (1 Tim. 1:1), an intimate relationship with Him is essential to true hope. Therefore, we need to do everything we can to insure that our counselees have this relationship. In some cases this may require evangelism. Those counselees who are avow-edly non-Christians must be told that there is no true hope for them until they are born again by the Spirit of God (John 3:3, 36).[10] And sometimes even professing Christians need to be taught about the nature of true sal-vation before they can have hope.

If we are doubtful whether a counselee has entered into a genuine relationship with Christ, then we need to ask questions along those lines

---

10. For more information on this issue, see Jay Adams, "What To Do When You Counsel An Unbeliever," in *A Theology of Christian Counseling* (Grand Rapids: Zondervan, 1979), 309–326.

and challenge the person in that area. One such case would be someone who seems to have a *historical* relationship with God rather than a *personal* one. When asked if they are Christians, these people will often say, "Yes, I accepted Jesus as my Savior when I was four," or "Yes, I believe Jesus died on the cross for me." However, they do not say anything pertaining to a present, vital relationship with God. They do not talk about how they are obeying Him each day or how close they have grown to Him.[11]

Another situation in which professing Christians may need to be challenged about their salvation is when the trials they face begin to destroy their faith. People who do not have a true relationship with Christ may coast along fine until pressures come. Then the weakness of their faith and the invalidity of their profession is revealed (Luke 6:46–49).[12]

Not only do we need to help people begin a relationship with Christ but we must also provide hope to true Christians by helping them strengthen their relationship with Jesus Christ. Many Christians lack hope simply because they lack maturity in their interaction with Christ and His Word.

An illustration of this is a woman who came to me some time ago for counseling. She was having problems with an intense, debilitating, and irrational fear. She heard voices and saw things that made her think Satan and demons were harassing her. Paralyzed by this fear, she did not want to leave the house, go to church, or be involved in other normal activities. She was able to sleep at night only if she wore a certain leather coat and vinyl hat. Her husband, who accompanied her to the counseling session, had not experienced any of the alleged phenomena.

Her problems made me think of Daniel 11:32: "The people who know their God will display strength." This verse says that a deep personal rela-

---

11. For an excellent discussion of both the nature of true faith and the danger of false profession, read John F. MacArthur, Jr., *The Gospel According to Jesus* (Grand Rapids: Zondervan, 1988); and *Faith Works: The Gospel According to the Apostles* (Dallas: Word, 1993).

12. This is not to say that if a person falters in faith during trials we can automatically conclude that he or she is not a Christian. Proverbs 24:10 says, "If you are slack in the day of distress, your strength is limited." There could be several reasons for the limit on someone's strength. It could be that the person has true faith but has let it become weak (like the disciples at times in the gospels). On occasion, Jesus spoke of their "little faith." Sometimes weakness in faith is due to the fact that the individual is a young believer, or it could be that the person has neglected the spiritual disciplines that strengthen faith (Rom. 10:17; 2 Pet. 1:5–9; Eph. 3:16–19; Heb. 3:12, 13; 10:24, 25). Weakness in faith also happens when people take their focus off the Lord and allow themselves to become spiritually dull (Dan. 11:32; Heb. 12:2; Rev. 2:1–7). Or, in some instances, a person is weak because he or she has no true faith and therefore no power to stand during hard times. Because weak faith can be symptomatic of various things, biblical counselors must seek to discover what it signifies and address that particular need.

Instilling Hope in the Counselee 201

tionship with God gives us strength and delivers us from fear (cf. 1 John 4:18), which raised a question in my mind about her relationship with God. So I asked both the husband and wife to read sections from the book of Mark every day as a homework assignment and to write down what they learned about Jesus as a person. And I told them, "I don't want you just to record historical facts, but I want you to interact with the material and let Jesus reveal himself to you through your reading."

This is what the husband wrote about Mark 2:

> The most telling verse of this chapter to me is verse 17. It is not the healthy who need a doctor but the sick. I have not come to call the righteous but sinners. Isaiah 53:6 says all we like sheep have gone astray, each of us has turned to his own way and the Lord has laid on Him the iniquity of us all. For me there is reassurance for forgiveness. I am a sinner. We all are. Christ came for us all, not because of our righteousness but because of our sins. If I were really righteous I wouldn't need Christ, but I'm not, I'm simply sinful. I need Him. The most revealing aspect of God's immense love is shown here. It's as if He said I know that you are sinful but I love you so much that a part of Me, My Son, will live among you. He'll die for you. So great is My power that I'll raise Him from the dead. Believe in Me and by believing in Him and you will have eternal life. If God loves me so much in spite of my sin, how can I doubt? How can I not enjoy the fruits of life that He would have me sample? The inner peace that He gives, the flowers in the spring, the green grass, the sun and the rain, life with Christ really is fantastic. Lord, help me to share this gift with others.

That paragraph intimated that this man had a real and personal relationship with Christ. Now consider his wife's notes on the same passage:

> In Capernaum Jesus forgave a paralytic. When his sins were forgiven Jesus told the man to pick up his bed and walk home, which he did and the scribes were amazed. After Jesus talked to a large crowd of people, He went to Levi's house. Here Jesus and the disciples ate and drank with the tax collectors and the scribes wondered why Jesus would do that. He said that those who were sick needed a physician and that He came so that sinners might repent. I believe that Jesus felt the people in Levi's house needed him. Another name for Levi is Matthew and he became one of Jesus' disciples. John and the Pharisees wanted to know why the disciples did not fast as they did. They were told that the Jewish fast was a practice or ritual and the disciples

did not fast for they felt it would take the joy from their faith. But he said there would be a time when the disciples would have to fast.

It was apparent to me from those notes that her relationship with Christ needed to be strengthened, because to her He was more a historical figure than a friend. So for a number of weeks I focused on helping her know Him better. As she came to know Christ in a deeper and fuller way, I observed dramatic changes in this woman. Gradually, her fears began to disappear and her confidence grew as her relationship with the Lord developed. Where there had been fear, there was hope, because she had come to know the One who gives hope.

Teach People to Think Biblically

Both false hope and a lack of hope spring from an ignorance or misunderstanding of God's truth. If we understood the Scriptures perfectly and all our thoughts were in line with it, we would never suffer from either of these maladies. So if we want our counselees to have hope, we must help them to think biblically about various aspects of their lives.

Think biblically about the specific situation. I once counseled a man who was in despair because he was unable to sleep at night. In the course of our counseling, we looked at several passages in Scripture that pertain to sleep.[13] Like many people, he did not know that the Bible speaks to this problem, and I discerned his hope growing as we studied a number of passages that referred to sleep. We need to show people that the Word of God speaks specifically about their problem, rather than merely quoting abstract passages that have general applications. Knowing that God gives specific instruction for our personal situation is a tremendous source of hope.

Think biblically about God's character. We can provide hope for counselees by enlarging or correcting their concepts of God. People often lack hope simply because they have erroneous concepts of God. They may view Him as a cruel disciplinarian and, therefore, lack hope because they think they will never be pleasing to Him as long as they struggle with sin. On the other hand, they may view Him as an all-forgiving "nice guy," and they lack hope because they let sin run rampant in their lives. Whatever the errors may be in a counselee's concept of God, that person will benefit and gain hope by learning to think biblically about Him.

---

13. Ps. 3:1–6; 4:1–8; 127:2; Prov. 3:13–16; 19:23; Eccles. 5:12.

Think biblically about the possibilities for good. Sometimes people lack hope because they see only the negative side of their circumstances and fail to recognize the potential for good that exists in every situation. They only see the problems and the pain; they do not see what God wants to accomplish through the situation. We need to help them realize that when God pushes us out of our comfort zone, He does so for the purpose of our growth and development. James 1:2 says, "Consider it all joy, my brethren, when you encounter various kinds of trials." Why does James say to consider trials to be joy? Because he is a masochist? No, he says that because we can know "that the testing of [our] faith produces endurance . . . " (vv. 3–4). As Jerry Bridges wrote,

> Paul and James both say that we should rejoice in our trials because of their beneficial results. It is not the adversity considered in itself that is to be the ground of our joy. Rather, it is the expectation of the results, the development of our character, that should cause us to rejoice in adversity. God does not ask us to rejoice because we have lost our job, or a loved one has been stricken with cancer, or a child has been born with an incurable birth defect. But he does tell us to rejoice because we believe He is in control of those circumstances and is at work through them for our ultimate good.[14]

When people understand and believe that even the darkest cloud has a silver lining, they are inspired to have a tremendous hope that will sustain them through any difficulty.

Think biblically about the divine resources. We can provide hope for people by helping them to understand and appropriate the resources God has given them. People lose hope because they do not think they have the ability to handle whatever they are facing. But God's Word says that "in all these things we overwhelmingly conquer through Him who loved us" (Rom. 8:37), and that "God is able to make all grace abound to you, that always having all sufficiency in everything, you may have an abundance for every good deed" (2 Cor. 9:8). As Christians realize that they can do all things through Christ who strengthens them (Phil. 4:13), they will have a blessed confidence in the face of any struggle.[15]

---

14. Jerry Bridges, *Trusting God: Even When Life Hurts* (Colorado Springs: NavPress, 1988), 175.

15. For an excellent discussion of the sufficiency of our spiritual resources, see John F. MacArthur, Jr. *Our Sufficiency in Christ* (Dallas: Word, 1991).

Think biblically about the nature and cause of the problem. During the years that I have been involved in counseling, I have encountered many people who have lost hope because they have adopted an unbiblical psychological diagnosis of their problem. In some instances, this has occurred because someone else has given them the diagnosis. On other occasions they have read something, seen a television program, listened to a radio program, or taken a psychology course and decided they are suffering from a particular kind of psychological problem. They fail to realize that what is called a diagnosis is only a descriptive identification that someone has decided to use as a label for certain kinds of observable human behavior or experience. And while the descriptive word or phrase may sound intelligent and meaningful, it does not describe the cause or nature of the problem.

This is clear when we compare how diseases are diagnosed with how psychological problems are usually diagnosed. In medical science, if a patient has certain symptoms, the physician may suspect a certain disease. But before giving a definitive diagnosis, various scientific tests are performed (blood tests, x-rays, etc.) to confirm or negate the diagnosis. Then on the basis of scientific evidence, the physician can say either the patient has or does not have a certain disease. This diagnosis is not based solely on symptoms but on demonstrable proof or evidence concerning both the cause and nature of the problem.

Contrary to what many people seem to think, this is not the case in secular psychology. In psychology it is assumed that because a person has certain feelings, behaves and thinks in certain ways, or has certain symptoms for a prescribed period of time, that person has a certain psychological problem, even though the cause of the problem has not been proven—and in most cases cannot be proven by scientific methods. Without demonstrable evidence derived from hard facts about the cause and nature of a person's problems, it is deduced that certain symptoms indicate a specified psychological malady. This unproven (and in most cases unprovable) decision is then offered and frequently accepted as an indisputable and unquestionable diagnosis.

Unfortunately, when people believe that the nature of their problem is psychological, rather than spiritual, several things can happen: (1) in their attempt to resolve their difficulties, they bypass Christ and the Bible and look primarily (sometimes exclusively) to drugs or the ideas and concepts of secularistic psychology for solutions; or (2) they begin to think of Christ as a cosmic psychologist whose primary purpose for coming was to fix their psychological problems, help build their self-esteem, deliver them from codependency, or meet their ego needs; or (3) they lose hope and descend into despair because many of these psychological labels carry with them the idea of fixedness (this is what I am and it cannot be changed); or (4) they become discouraged because these unbiblical labels subtly or overtly encourage people to think that the primary solution to their difficulties is humanistic in nature—they must do it on their own (they can and must change themselves) or others, preferably experts, must do it for them.

So, many people try to change by relying on their own efforts or the help of others, and they fail. They come to realize that neither they nor any other human being can provide the power to break the slavery of sinful ways of thinking, feeling, and acting and enable them to think, feel, and live differently. When problems are viewed as primarily psychological in nature, we encounter people whose hope is dissipated, people who doubt that change can ever happen.

On the other hand, hopefulness blossoms when people begin to realize that their problems are basically spiritual: they are somehow linked to sin. Indeed, acknowledging that personal and interpersonal problems are related to sin[16] is truly good news, because then there is plenty of hope. Why? Because the primary reason Christ came into the world was to deliver us from the penalty and ruling power of sin (and, eventually, from the presence and possibility of sin). The clear Bible message is this: (1) Jesus is "the lamb of God who takes away the sin of the world" (John 1:29) ; (2) "[This] is a trustworthy statement, deserving full acceptance, that Christ Jesus came into the world to save sinners" (1 Tim. 1:15); (3) "You shall call His name Jesus, for it is He who will save His people from their sins" (Matt. 1:21); (4) He "gave Himself for us that He might redeem us from

---

16. Not only proactive sin, but reactive sin, i.e., unbiblical responses to the manifestations, expressions, or results of sin in our world; not necessarily nor primarily sinful actions but unbiblical attitudes, desires, thoughts, concepts, ideas (Prov. 4:23; James 1:13-16); not necessarily presumptuous or deliberate sins but also sins of ignorance, or secret sins (Ps. 19:12-14; Luke 12:46, 47; 1 Tim. 1:13); not merely sins of commission but sins of omission (1 John 3:4; Rom. 3:23); not merely behavioral sins but motivational sins or idolatrous sins where the primary focus of life is to please and serve self or other people, where the main concern, confidence, and desire of life is something or someone other than God, where as Romans 1:25 puts it: "They worship and serve the creature rather than the Creator" (Heb. 4:12; Rom. 1:18-32; 1 Cor. 10:1-13; Jer. 17:5-10; Ezek. 14:1-9). Sin may be defined as any thought, action, reaction, response, attitude, ruling desire, motive, choice, feeling, or habit pattern that is contrary to the revealed moral will of God in the Bible, whether known by the person or not, and whether deliberately and consciously chosen or committed as a habitual pattern of response. (See also Rom. 7:21-25; 14:23; Ps. 51:5; 58:3; Eph. 2:1-3; 4:17-22; Mark 7:21-23; Gal. 5:19-21; James 4:17; Heb. 4:12, 13; Exod. 20:1-17; Matt. 5:17-7:28).

every lawless deed and purify for Himself a people for His own possession, zealous for good deeds" (Titus 2:14).

The good news of the Bible is not that Christ Jesus came into the world to be a cosmic psychologist, to cure all our psychological ills, but that He came into the world to provide deliverance from the penalty and ruling power of sin (Rom. 6:1–23). The good news is this: there is hope for full deliverance from the penalty of sin and substantial deliverance from the ruling power of sin and its effects.

This biblical perspective of our basic problem comes loaded with hope for people who are struggling with unbiblical patterns of thinking, desiring, feeling, and living. This perspective is freeing, liberating, and encouraging; it is biblical, and it is true! It tells people that though their personal and interpersonal problems are serious and intense, there is hope for change because Christ Jesus came into the world to provide deliverance from condemnation and corruption, from guilt and pollution, and from the penalty and reigning power of sin in their lives. It tells people that in Christ Jesus they have all the resources they need to escape the corruption in the world and to live godly, fruitful lives characterized by moral excellence, knowledge, self-control, perseverance, brotherly kindness, and Christian love (2 Pet. 1:3–8).

Think biblically about what they say. Language is a tool God has chosen to use in communicating with us. Words are important to Him. If we are doing biblical counseling, we need to help our counselees think and talk biblically about their problems. To do this we need to use biblical terms, rather than psychological terms, to describe people's problems. Psychological terms tend to direct the counselee's thinking away from Christ and His Word, whereas the use of biblical words such as sin, fear, anger, worry, lying, lust, bitterness, coveting, envy, and jealousy direct thinking toward the Scriptures.

Counselors also need to be aware of the unbiblical language counselees may use to describe their difficulties. Here are three examples of the hope-diminishing language a counselee may use:

1. **"I can't."** These two words usually mean one of three things: "I won't"; "I don't understand my resources in Christ"; or "I don't know how to do what the Bible tells me to do". When someone repeatedly says "I can't," the counselor needs to explore precisely what the person means by those words and then follow up with the appropriate biblical response.
   For example, if "I can't" signifies overt rebellion against God, the counselee needs to understand and acknowledge that rebellion. The

counselor will want to use appropriate motivational strategies to help the counselee choose obedience to Christ. If a counselee is a Christian and the "I can't" means the person does not think he or she is able to obey biblical directives, the counselor will need to remind the individual of the resources that are available in Christ and will need to explain how to use those resources. Still further, if the "I can't" of a believer indicates a lack of practical know-how or skills to put biblical directives into practice, the counselor will want to help that person gain the skill to put God's instructions into practice.

2. **"My wife makes me mad."** This is a false and hopeless statement. It is false because the wife did not cause the sinful anger—the husband chose to be angry in response to her actions. Such a statement implies that the husband is a victim of the wife's actions and that he cannot help himself. According to the Bible, this is false. The husband needs to understand and believe that if he is a Christian, with God's help he can learn to respond correctly in spite of his wife's provocation.

3. **"I've tried everything, and it hasn't worked."** When people believe they have exhausted every alternative without success, the inevitable consequence is a sense of hopelessness. So we must question whether they have, in fact, tried everything and suggest to them some things they have not tried. It is likely that people who say they have tried everything have only done what was convenient to them. It may also be that they have an unbiblical understanding of or expectations about the results of doing things God's way. Then too, they may have unrealistic and unbiblical ideas of timing; they may be looking for a "quick, easy fix", expecting immediate results. Or they may have been doing the right thing for the wrong reasons: not because it was right or because God wanted them to but primarily because they wanted to be released from hardship and difficulty.

When we hear counselees make these types of statements we need to help them discern the reasons behind their unbiblical language and provide hope for them by correcting their misconceptions.

Provide Godly Examples for Counselees

Another way we can inspire our counselees is to demonstrate hope through our own lives and the lives of others.

Our own example of hope. Many people who seek counsel need to see hope modeled before they can experience it themselves, and what better person to model hope for them than the counselor? The counselor's biblically based attitude of hope will inspire hopefulness in the counselee. From the beginning we must show them that even if their situation is extremely difficult, we believe that God "is able to do exceeding abundantly beyond all that we ask or think" and that "with man this is impossible but with God all things are possible" (Eph. 3:20; Matt. 19:26). We should commend people for their willingness to seek counsel, be liberal with sincere praise, and encourage them with Paul's words: "I am confident of this very thing, that He who began a good work in you will perfect it until the day of Christ Jesus" (Phil. 1:6).

The example of hope in others. We can give people hope by showing them how others faced similar situations and handled them successfully. They need to know that they are not alone and that they are not the first person to experience such trials (1 Cor. 10:13). It can help counselees to read specific examples in Scripture of Christians who endured similar circumstances (and worse), or to talk to others who have experienced such situations. God can use the hope they see in the lives of others who have suffered to strengthen their own hope.

Romans 15:4 explains how God produces an attitude of hopefulness: "Whatever was written in earlier times was written for our instruction, that through perseverance and the encouragement of the Scriptures we might have hope."

The people Paul was writing to certainly experienced difficult circumstances. Paul was asking them to refocus and reorient patterns of thinking and behaving that were based on centuries of teaching and tradition. It was a costly form of self-denial. With good reason, Paul recognized that some of these people were discouraged. He knew that they would never have the desire or ability to make the necessary changes without hope. Thus, he wrote this verse to build up their hope.

Note carefully the three things this verse tells us about how hope is generated. First, it reminds us that Scripture must always play a central role in developing hope. "Whatever is written" refers, of course, to what was written in the Scripture. Hope comes through the encouragement of the Scriptures. Second, this verse indicates that the Scriptures promote perseverance and encourage a hopeful attitude through the example of others who have faced similar circumstances and have overcome them. Verse three calls attention to the example of Christ. Hope is developed as we realize that others, even Christ the Son of God, experienced hardship, denied Himself, and responded in the way that God asks us to respond. And third, the text suggests that the Scriptures generate hope by removing the surprise element from what is happening. That is, while things may be out of *our* control, they are definitely *not* out of God's control. In fact, what happens to us is exactly what God has said would happen. When properly understood through the Scriptures, we begin to realize that things are happening just as the Scriptures indicated they would. This builds hope, because it helps us to realize that God is in charge, that things are not happening by accident, that what is happening has meaning and purpose, and that God is present to sustain and support us in the midst of our difficulties.

Yes, hope is a powerful change agent. With hope people are inspired to do positive things, but without it they will flounder and fail. Mark it down and note it well: When people are not changing through our counseling efforts, perhaps they do not have hope—a solidly based biblical hope. We must never underestimate the importance of hope in the counseling process. For while we recognize that God is the ultimate hope giver (who provides hope through His Son, by His Spirit, and in His Word), at the same time, we realize that He also uses men and women to inspire and encourage the hopeless to find their hope in Him.

12

Taking Counselee Inventory: Collecting Data

Wayne A. Mack

When Eli saw Hannah's lips moving but heard no sound, he assumed she was drunk and condemned her without so much as smelling her breath! In reality, her problem was far different than he had interpreted it to be—she was praying for a child. Job suffered a similar misunderstanding. His counselors, who never asked questions or gathered information, assumed they knew his problem from the very start. Even when Job tried to correct their misconceptions with pertinent facts they stubbornly stuck to their theories. They could not interpret Job's problem accurately, because they never gained enough information about it. And because of that, their counsel to him only made his situation worse and added to his distress.

We must be careful that we do not make this mistake in our counseling. If we attempt to interpret people's problems before we gather adequate data, we will only add to their difficulty rather than relieve it. James 1:19 says, "Be quick to hear, slow to speak . . ." and nowhere is that command more important than in counseling.

In Proverbs 18:2 we read that "the mind of the prudent acquires knowledge and the ear of the wise seeks knowledge." The wise person seeks and acquires knowledge—not assumptions, speculations, or imaginations. And knowledge has to do with facts. The verse suggests that getting those facts will require the use of our minds (in planning) and the use of our ears (in listening). Accurate biblical counseling must include an organized method of gaining information that incorporates substantial times of listening to the counselee. It is particularly helpful in the initial stages of counseling to encourage the counselee to do much of the talking.[1]

Here is a counseling case that illustrates the importance of taking inventory of the counselee.

> Violet is now 54 years old. She is a Christian, lives with her son and his wife, and for many years has complained of depression. She does little or nothing else, but does still attend church regularly. Yet every week she comes home more upset and gets more depressed than before.
>
> In this first session she has admitted to bitterness and resentment that she connects vaguely with church attendance. She claims to be lonely, says she daydreams, and on her Personal Data Inventory hints at an undisclosed problem: ". . . and, there is a difficulty that I could mention only to God." Initial inquiries about this matter are met with hesitance, reluctance to speak, evasion, and embarrassment.[2]

Sometimes counselees will quickly reveal much of what you need to know. In fact, the greatest challenge with these counselees may be to convince them to listen. But most are more like Violet. She is holding something back, and the counselor cannot help her without addressing the difficulty that she "could mention only to God." To be effective, the counselor must first gather enough information to adequately understand the person and the problems.

With people like Violet, that may be easier said than done. They may feel embarrassed about their problems and are reluctant to share them with anyone. They may also be concerned that the counselor will look down on them, ridicule them, or betray their confidence. Perhaps all of this has happened to them before, and they are worried that it will happen again if they reveal too much. Like the city of Jerusalem, these people have built a wall around themselves. But do you remember the twelve gates of Jerusalem? The walls people build around their lives also have gates, and it is our job as counselors to find a way into the "city" through those gates. If we come to one gate and find it closed, we must

---

1. Pastors, in particular, may find it difficult to listen to counselees. Gifted in teaching and accustomed to speaking from the pulpit, a pastor tends to take a one-sided approach in counseling. Pastors need to be aware of the differences between preaching and counseling and take care not to approach them in the same way.

2. Jay Adams, *The Christian Counselor's Casebook* (Grand Rapids: Zondervan, 1974), 16. Used by permission.

try another until we find an open gate and gain access into the real thoughts, hopes, and fears of the counselee.[3]

THE KINDS OF DATA TO GATHER

What information do we need to be able to help people with their problems? We need to gather data in at least six areas: physical, resources, emotions, actions, concepts, and historical.

Physical Data

Physical problems can both contribute to and proceed from spiritual problems. The success of our counsel will sometimes be dependent upon understanding a particular aspect of someone's health. In 2 Corinthians 4:16, Paul implies that when "our outer man is decaying," our inner man tends to lose heart. There is a close connection between the two—the inner man can affect the outer man and vice versa. Thus we must be aware of any physical problems of our counselees if we desire to solve the inward problems they face.

In the following paragraphs we will discuss five aspects of our physical lives that can influence our spiritual health:

1. **Sleep.** Irregular sleep patterns can be caused by spiritual problems (such as anxiety, laziness, or guilt) or they can contribute to spiritual problems. Dr. Bob Smith writes this about sleep loss:

> From the sleep studies conducted it has been learned that the average individual needs approximately seven to eight hours sleep per night. In most cases, those who regularly require amounts in excess of this need to be explored for the possibility of depression. . . .
>
> "Scientists do not yet understand what lies behind our basic requirement for sleep, but this much they have made clear: Sleep is one of the most essential needs of man, and we sacrifice it at considerable peril to our bodies and minds.
>
> "Few of us would seriously consider going very long without food, yet hunger is hardly as serious as protracted sleep loss. A man can

---

3. This process is usually related to the development of the facilitative relationship we discussed in chapter 10. Counselees with walls built around themselves want to know that they can trust the counselor before they will share the concerns that are central to their problems.

survive starvation for over three weeks. But deprive him of sleep for that time and he will disintegrate and become psychotic. . . .

"Today's man-on-the-move is like the wreckless gambler who loses his shirt and then plays on with borrowed money. The sleepless American—feeling the angry pinch of fatigue and the erosion of his well-being—begins living in the red, using the 'pep' offered by well-advertised drugs that propel the body and mind onward with energies that are not really there."

All the while, however, there lurks a day of reckoning, "when symptoms can no longer be denied: agonizing fatigue, irritability, lapses in attention, withdrawal, fading judgment, erratic behavior, and even a weakening of ethical standards."[4]

That is why we need to find out how much sleep our counselees are getting. And we may find that some of their problems will lessen immediately once they begin to practice regular sleep habits.

2. **Diet.** The old saying, "You are what you eat," is partly true. We need to be aware of what our counselees eat, because nutritional imbalance can affect behavior. For example, stimulants such as sugar and caffeine can affect people in a pronounced way.[5] If you are dealing with a person who is nervous and hyperactive all the time, you will want to find out the quantity of stimulants they are consuming. Other individuals experience allergic reactions to dietary agents and so forth. In short, we must not ignore the diet factor.

3. **Exercise.** In counseling, it may be necessary to address the amount of physical activity people are involved in. Ecclesiastes 5:12 says, "The sleep of the working man is pleasant," and that verse was written in a day when most people earned their living by the sweat of their brow. Today in our culture, demanding physical labor is less common; most of our occupations

---

4. Robert Smith, M.D., "Sleep," *The Journal of Pastoral Practice* 4, no. 2 (1980): 36–43, citing Julius Segal, Ph.D., "Missing Sleep Dangerous," *Family Practice News* 2, no. 17 (1972).

5. Following is an excerpt from an article written by Arnold Fox, M.D. called "Caffeine—Unexpected Cause of Fatigue": "Simply put, caffeine is nothing more than a cruel hoax you play on yourself. You take in caffeine to give yourself a 'lift.' You get the lift—but you also set yourself up for fatigue, anxiety, and depression. Fatigue, followed closely by anxiety and depression, is the most common complaint we physicians hear from our patients. Although there are many causes of fatigue, one of the most common, and most often overlooked cause is 'caffeinism'—the consumption of caffeine" (*Let's Live* [April 1982]: 19–20). For other information on the effects of caffeine, see Bob Smith, "Caffeine," *The Journal of Pastoral Practice* 1, no. 1 (1977): 95–96.

call for the use of the mind more than the body. So for many of us the exercise we need to stay healthy must be a planned event in our free time, and that can often be overlooked to our detriment.

A lack of exercise can actually produce or heighten anxiety. The daily stress we face causes our bodies to produce chemicals (like adrenalin) that provide energy and even tighten up our muscles. Physical activity is one way God has designed for this everyday tension to be released, and without that activity our bodies can be affected negatively, and our moods may suffer as well. Gathering information about a person's activity level—how much exercise he or she gets—can be a significant factor in counseling people who struggle with anxiety or other ungodly emotions. Frequently, I have found that a homework assignment requiring regular exercise significantly helps counselees to relax.[6]

4. **Illness.** Sickness can sometimes be caused by personal sin (Ps. 32:3–4; 38:3; Prov. 14:30; 1 Cor. 11:30).[7] But sickness that is not caused by personal sin can also be an important factor in the struggles and temptations our counselees face. For instance, viral infection, hepatitis, mononucleosis, diabetes, and hypothyroidism are all associated with depression. In many cases, when Christians suffer from those conditions their depression symptoms may simply be a consequence of the exhaustion and discomfort caused by the malady. So we must not assume that in every case depression is a direct result of personal sin—it may be relieved or eliminated simply by the correct diagnosis and treatment of a medical problem.

5. **Medication.** Various medications, both prescription and over-the-counter, cause side effects that are harmful to one degree or another. These drugs can contribute to ongoing problems, especially if the individual is not aware of the possibility of side effects. Some cases of mild depression, for example, may be solved simply by finding out what medication the person has been taking and whether it might be causing side effects that are contributing to the depression. A counselor must learn to gather pertinent data and look for possible connections between problematic experiences and medication.[8]

---

6. When you do advise counselees to exercise, however, suggest that they be involved in a form of exercise that is noncompetitive, otherwise they may compound their stress rather than release it. Some people are so competitive they cannot participate in sports without being obsessed with winning. It is important to understand the individual's tendencies in this area in order to design an exercise plan that will be helpful.

7. For some helpful discussions of this truth, see S. I. McMillen, *None of These Diseases* (Old Tappan, N. J.: Revell, 1973); Smith, "Caffeine," 79–92; and Jay Adams, *Competent to Counsel* (Grand Rapids: Zondervan, 1970), chapter 7.

A useful tool for this process is *The Physician's Desk Reference*. This book, available through bookstores and some doctors' offices, contains a listing of all medicines on the market and describes the physiological dynamics of the drug, indications for use, possible adverse reactions, potentially dangerous side effects, and other accompanying symptoms it may cause.[9] Although it is not our place as biblical counselors to prescribe and deprescribe drugs, we can put ourselves in a better position to address some problems by learning what medicine a counselee has taken.[10]

Resources

A second area of data concerns the resources that the counselee has at his or her disposal. What resources does that person have that can aid in the counseling process, and what lack of resources might hinder the process?

The most important resources, of course, are the spiritual ones, so we must first find out if a counselee possesses these resources. In other words, is he or she a Christian? If not, the person has no spiritual resources to work with.[11] Thus, early in the counseling process it is important to ask questions pertaining to a person's spiritual condition. In some cases, when a counselee professes to be a Christian it may be necessary to question that person further to establish the validity of that profession.[12] When we are fairly certain that a counselee is born again we need to discover the extent

---

8. Many times a counselor who suspects this will not be able to confirm it alone but will need to advise the counselee to ask a physician about a possible connection.

9. Doctors are issued a new book each year by the drug companies and often will pass along the previous year's book to a counselor who asks for it.

10. For further reading on this issue, see Bob Smith, "The Use of Drugs in Counseling," *The Biblical Counselor* (May 1992): 1, 4.

11. Romans 8:7-8 says that "the mind set on the flesh [the mind of the unsaved person] is hostile toward God; for it does not subject itself to the law of God, for it is not even able to do so; and those who are in the flesh cannot please God." And 1 Corinthians 2:14 says that "a natural man [again, someone who is unsaved] does not accept the things of the Spirit of God; for they are foolishness to him, and he cannot understand them, because they are spiritually appraised."

12. It is not our place to pronounce judgment upon the spiritual state of those who profess to know Christ (1 Cor. 4:5; James 4:11-12), so we must treat them as believers unless they ascribe to doctrinal heresy, are guilty of continuing, flagrant, ungodly conduct (2 John 9-11), or are placed under discipline by the church (Matt. 18:17). But if their responses and conduct cause us to question the validity of their profession, we certainly can and should challenge them to examine their spiritual condition (2 Cor. 13:5). Some materials that are helpful in this process are John MacArthur, Jr.'s tape series *Examine Yourself* (Grace to You) and chapter 5 in his book *Saved Without A Doubt* (Wheaton: Victor Books, 1992).

of his or her Christian growth, because a person with greater spiritual maturity will find it easier to make use of available resources in Christ than a person who is a new Christian.

Counselors also need to gather information about other kinds of resources that can affect the spiritual dimension: intellectual, educational, experiential, and social.[13] Any one or all of these can be an important piece in the puzzle of an individual's problems.

Emotions

Emotions are like smoke detectors.

One night as I was relaxing in the family room, my children were trying to cook something on the stove in the basement. Apparently, some cooking oil spilled over the side of the pan and caught fire, igniting the top of the stove and sending flames high into the air. The smoke detector blared a high-pitched warning and I was able to throw a blanket over the flame and smother it before it did any major damage.

Emotions are like that smoke detector: they are not the primary problem but are warnings of the primary problem. Imagine if I had silenced the smoke detector with a hammer and gone back to relax in my chair—the house would have burned down! I had to take care of the source problem, the fire. Likewise, some people (and, unfortunately, some counselors) seek to eliminate negative emotions such as depression, anxiety, fear, or rage by attacking the emotions themselves through medication or behavior therapy. But they fail to address and eliminate the "fires" in the basement of their lives—the underlying problems that disturb their emotions.

The smoke detector analogy illustrates another truth about emotions: they should never be ignored. What if I had responded to the smoke alarm by slipping in some ear plugs? I would have lost more than my house! Likewise, counselors must recognize the significance of emotions. God has given them to us as outward indicators of what is happening in our hearts, and they are often inextricably linked to the problems we face.

Through the power of the Holy Spirit, Christians have the ability to control their emotions and do what God wants them to do regardless of how they feel (1 Cor. 10:13). On the other hand, emotions are powerful

---

13. Social resources are particularly important because there may be people in the counselees' environment (such as church or family) who can be enlisted to help with their problems. Many counselors miss such opportunities simply because they fail to gather the appropriate data.

enough to make it much harder to do what is right. Consider the first murder in Genesis 4:1–8, for instance. Most likely it would never have happened if Cain had not become "very angry" (v. 5). His anger was the result of sinful pride and could have been eliminated through repentance, but without repentance his anger provided the impetus for the most heinous of crimes. That is why we must ask questions about how our counselees feel and be sensitive to the effects those emotions have on their lives.

Actions

A fourth area to consider in gathering data is actions. We need to consider what our counselees do and what they do not do.[14] The Bible makes a close connection between our actions and other aspects of our lives. Actions have a profound effect on our spiritual, emotional, and physical health. Again consider Cain, who was not only angry but also depressed. God said to him, "Why has your countenance fallen? If you do well, will not your countenance be lifted up? And if you do not do well, sin is crouching at the door" (vv. 6–7). Cain sinned by bringing an inappropriate sacrifice to the Lord (v. 3), and the rest of the chapter indicates a direct correlation between that action and every part of his life. One disobedient action affected his relationship to God, produced various negative emotions, and led to further sinful action against his brother.

Time and again the Bible emphasizes the importance of our actions:

- "How blessed is the man who does not walk in the counsel of the wicked, nor stand in the path of sinners, nor sit in the seat of scoffers! But his delight is in the law of the LORD, and in His law he meditates day and night. And he will be like a tree firmly planted by streams of water, which yields its fruit in season, and its leaf does not wither; and in whatever he does, he prospers" (Ps. 1:1–3).

- "Who is the man who desires life, and loves length of days that he may see good? Keep your tongue from evil, and your lips from speaking deceit. Depart from evil, and do good; seek peace, and pursue it" (Ps. 34:12–14).

---

14. The Bible speaks not only of sins of commission but also sins of omission. God is concerned that we exert a positive influence on those around us through good deeds (Matt. 5:13–16; Eph. 4:22–32; James 4:17).

- "Why do you call Me, 'Lord, Lord,' and do not do what I say? Everyone who comes to Me, and hears My words, and acts upon them, I will show you whom he is like: he is like a man building a house, who dug deep and laid a foundation upon the rock; and when a flood rose, the torrent burst against that house and could not shake it, because it had been well built. But the one who has heard, and has not acted accordingly, is like a man who built a house upon the ground without any foundation; and the torrent burst against it and immediately it collapsed, and the ruin of that house was great" (Luke 6:46–49).

- "Blessed are those who hear the Word of God, and observe it" (Luke 11:28).

- "One who looks intently at the perfect law, the law of liberty, and abides by it, not having become a forgetful hearer but an effectual doer, this man shall be blessed in what he does" (James 1:25).

God's commands are not merely demands, they are invitations—invitations to fullness of life. They are not merely obligations, they are opportunities. They are not merely precepts, they are promises. "I set before you the way of life and the way of death," God says (Jer. 21:8; cf. Deut. 30:15, 19). The way of life requires obedience to the commands in His Word, and the way of death is assured by disobedience to them. Counselors who take God's commands seriously must realize the relationship between obedience to God and all aspects of life and must gather data about a counselee's actions to see if they are in line with the Word of God.

Concepts

We must also gather data about the counselee's concepts. *Concepts* refers to what Hebrews 4:12 describes as "the thoughts and intentions of the heart." This includes personal convictions, attitudes, expectations, desires, and values. It includes what or whom people are trusting, fearing, listening to, and depending on; what or whom they are serving in life (Matt. 6:24); what or who their functional gods are; and what or who controls them and calls the shots in their lives. As important as actions and emotions are, in a sense they are secondary to the conceptual area of life because what we think and desire (our thoughts and intentions) ultimately determines how we act and feel.

Here are several passages that reinforce this truth:

Mark 7:18–23. After listing numerous sins of action, such as "fornications, thefts, murders, adulteries, deeds of coveting and wickedness" (vv. 21–22), Jesus says, "All these evil things proceed from within and defile the man." His intention was to teach the Jews that sin is an inner problem, one that runs much deeper than surface behavior. It is a heart problem. And the term *heart* in Scripture is often used interchangeably with the word *mind* (cf. Gen. 6:15; Heb. 4:12). They both refer to the inner part of us that influences how we will act. This dimension of life must be addressed if lasting change is to take place.

Romans 12:1–2. In this passage Paul exhorts the Romans how to respond to the doctrinal truth he shared with them in Romans 1–11. It serves as a good summary of the entire process of spiritual growth that makes up the Christian life: We are to be "transformed by the renewing of our mind, that we may prove what the will of God is, that which is good and acceptable and perfect." If we want to see lives transformed we must understand what is going on in people's minds and focus on that as we seek to help them change.

Galatians 5:16–21. Verses 19 through 21 of this passage list some of the more common actions and emotions that constitute "the deeds of the flesh." Ungodly actions and reactions such as immorality, strife, enmities, disputes, dissensions, drunkenness, carousing, jealousy, and outbursts of anger are included in this extensive, though not exhaustive, catalog of behavioral and emotional sins. Verse 16, which refers to "the desires of the flesh," takes us behind outward behaviors to a deeper level and gives us another important perspective for understanding people and their problems. Understanding people not only requires an understanding of their deeds, it involves a knowledge of the *desires* that motivate their deeds. According to Paul, ungodly desires are the engine that drives ungodly deeds. The ungodly actions and feelings of people are related to and rooted in their ungodly, idolatrous thoughts and desires.

Ephesians 4:22–24. This is another well-known passage that summarizes the process of spiritual growth. In verse 22 Paul says to "lay aside the old self," and in verse 24 he says to "put on the new self." But the key to that process of change is in verse 23: "Be renewed in the spirit of your mind." We cannot eliminate unbiblical practices and cultivate biblical practices until our minds are being renewed.[15]

---

15. Second Corinthians 10:4–5 contains another often overlooked reference to the mind. Here Paul talks about the intense spiritual warfare we are involved in, and then says we fight it by "taking every thought captive to the obedience of Christ." And in James 4:1–6, describing why people do the ungodly things they do, James says that the source of these problems is in our "pleasures (desires) that wage war in [our] members" (v. 1), in our lusts (v. 2), in our idolatry or spiritual adultery (v. 4), and in our pride (v. 6).

Few truths are more essential to biblical counseling. Many counselors wonder why they see only temporary change in the lives of counselees, who, they observe with frustration, return to the same sins shortly afterward. In most cases, the reason is that the minds or hearts of those counselees have not been renewed. They experienced mere behavioral change because of the influence of someone who manipulated them through psychological tricks or pressured them week after week to conform. But when that external pressure is gone, their unrenewed minds quickly revert back to plotting the sins that their bodies are more than willing to carry out.

If we want to practice true biblical counseling, we must gain as much information as we can about our counselees' thoughts and desires so we can correct their misconceptions and help them to have "the mind of Christ" concerning their problems (cf. 1 Cor. 2:16).

Historical Data

Securing historical data about counselees and their problems is another important part of taking inventory. Historical data refers to information about people's present and past life-context—the external circumstances in their lives, the influences or pressures they have experienced or are experiencing, how they have been sinned against, their frustrations and hardships, their failures, temptations, temporal blessings, successes, comforts, wealth, etc.[16]

Some counselors, who have an unhealthy preoccupation with the past, believe that everything in a counselee's present life is somehow connected to the past. As a result they tend to transfer responsibility from the counselee to those who mistreated him or her long ago. But this is a dangerous tendency that must be avoided.[17] Yet we cannot allow ourselves to ignore the past, because what has happened in the past does affect our counselees, especially if it involves patterns of sin or has somehow provided them with an excuse to blame others for their problems.[18]

---

16. Issues that need to be addressed include family of origin, marital history, other significant relationships, problems in school or family, and possible physical or sexual abuse. We need to be concerned about any shaping experience from the past—especially those that the counselee believes are important.

17. For further reading about errors concerning the past, see John Bettler, "Toward A Confession of Faith on the Past," and Steve Viars, "Handling the Past Biblically," both in *The Biblical Counselor* July 1993: 1–4.

18. Some passages that refer to the effect of our past on our current lives are Gen. 25:27–28; 26:1–5; 2 Chron. 22:1–4; Prov. 5:22–23; 22:6; Jer. 13:23; Eph. 6:4; Col. 3:21; 2 Tim. 1:5; 3:15; and 1 Pet. 1:18.

I once talked with a young man who could not get along with his boss, although there were no apparent or objective reasons for the conflict. It was only when I started asking him about his previous work experience that I obtained a clue to the problem. When I asked him about each of his former jobs and how he perceived previous bosses, he responded negatively about every one of them. Then I asked him about his relationship with his father while growing up and discovered that he had extensive problems with his father. This indicated to me that, most likely, this man had never learned how to respond to authority—an insight that provided direction for questions and counsel from that point on.

In that case, it was primarily the man's own sin in the past that was contributing to his current problems. In other instances, the sins of others in the past can contribute to a counselee's problems. When people have been abused, mistreated, or neglected, they are usually tempted to blame the abuser for their problems and to respond negatively to anyone who reminds them of that person. The biblical counselor does not approach such situations by ignoring what occurred in the past, but listens attentively to their history, identifies with the pain they have experienced, then lovingly and patiently deals with their sinful responses and seeks to refocus their attention on their resources in Christ and His way of dealing with their past.[19]

In addition to taking historical inventory of people's lives, biblical counselors will also want to gather current data. What is presently occurring in their lives is equally important to what occurred in the past. Biblical counselors should never excuse or justify ungodly behavior in themselves or others because of past or present circumstances—God's Word is unequivocal about that.[20] Nevertheless, giving accurate, appropriate, and sensitive biblical counsel will require some understanding of the present context in which people live and respond. We must understand how people are being sinned against as well as how they are responding sinfully.[21]

---

19. We should be willing to listen to the history of those we counsel, if for no other reason than it is important to them. If we conclude from the start that their past is irrelevant and show no concern about it, it will be extremely difficult to establish the necessary facilitative relationship between counselor and counselee (see chapter 10).

20. Cf. Num. 11–23; Deut. 24:16; Prov. 6:30–31; Luke 6:27–38; Rom. 12:17–21; 14:10–12; Gal. 6:5; James 1:2–5; and 1 Pet. 1–5.

21. Cf. Gen. 3:1–4; 4:1–14; 12:10–20; 14:14–23; 22:1–14; 26:1–7; 1 Kgs. 19:1–28; Ps. 3:1–2; 73:1ff; Prov; 1:10–19; 13:20; 22:24–25; 30:7–9; 1 Cor. 15:33; 16:10; 2 Cor. 1:8–9; Gal. 2:11–12; 1 Tim. 2:1–2; 2 Tim. 2:16–18; Heb. 10:24–25; Rev. 2 (vv. 2, 3, 9, 13, 15, 19–20, 24); 3:8–9, 15–17.

Counsel given without the acquisition of life-context information may be irrelevant, inappropriate, clinical, sterile, and even hurtful. Without pertinent historical and current facts, biblical counselors may make the same mistakes that Job's counselor's made and actually add to the distress of counselees. To use the words of Job, they may be guilty of tormenting, insulting, crushing, and wronging people—the very people they are trying to help (cf. Job 19:1–3). In their attempt to do good, they may actually do evil (cf. Rom. 14:16).

To avoid these mistakes, biblical counselors must observe what is being done to people, what is going on around them, as well as what that person is doing, feeling, and desiring. They will want to acquire and process information about marriage and family situations, living conditions, relationships, church involvement, occupation or school situations, finances, and any other pressures, problems, joys, or successes that are relevant to the lives of their counselees.

How to Gather Data

We have discussed the importance of gathering data and how this is significant to the process of accurate biblical counseling. Now we need to consider methods for gathering the data. The primary methods we will discuss are: (1) using personal data inventory forms, (2) asking good questions, and (3) observing halo data.

Using Personal Data Inventory Forms

A helpful sample of a personal data inventory form (PDIF) is provided in the appendix of this book. This form can be a useful tool in the initial stages of counseling for the following reasons:

1. Requiring that counselees complete a PDIF indicates a counselor's concern for thoroughness.

2. The form provides constant access to basic information that the counselor may forget or neglect to cover during the counseling sessions.

3. The information helps to prepare the counselor for the counseling sessions. It will often reveal the initial direction the counseling should take.

4. Completing the form helps counselees think about the issues that will be discussed.

5. Discussing information from the form with the counselee can provide a natural and appropriate entry point into the counseling session.

Even when a counselor is working with someone familiar, it is wise to use the PDIF. Invariably, the form provides new and significant information.

Asking Appropriate Questions

In addition to the PDIF, the amount of data the counselor gathers will depend largely on the quantity and quality of questions he or she asks. While compassion and concern for the counselee should determine quantity, the following guidelines can help to develop quality questions.

1. **Appropriate questions are thoughtful and gracious.** If questions are not asked in an appropriate manner the counselor's efforts to gather data will be in vain. The Bible says, "Let your speech always be with grace, seasoned, as it were, with salt" (Col. 4:6). We need to ask questions in a way that sets our counselees at ease and does not put them on edge. One way to do this is to explain to them initially that you will be asking questions and gathering information in order to help them.

Another way to ensure a gracious manner is to ask questions using an advance-and-retreat method. That is, when the counselor senses the counselee becoming apprehensive or uncomfortable with a line of questioning, he or she backs off that issue temporarily and explores another. Perhaps later in the session or in another session the counselor will return to that issue.

2. **Appropriate questions are relevant.** All questions should relate to issues the counselor is seeking to address; they should not serve merely to satisfy curiosity. Like the young widows mentioned in 1 Timothy 5:13, counselors can sometimes become "gossips and busybodies" when they become privy to information they do not necessarily need to know. Irrelevant questions can also send people down rabbit trails in the discussion and distract them from the real issues at hand. So to keep counselees focused and to save precious time always ask questions that are relevant to the problems of the counselee.[22]

3. **Appropriate questions produce facts.** The following case illustrates the kinds of questions that do *not* produce significant information:

---

22. An exception to this rule would be when the counselor senses that the discussion is getting too heavy and decides to lighten it up by allowing the counselee to respond to something different for a few moments.

Bruce and Maggie appear with their daughter, Karen. The pastor is surprised; he expected only the parents.

Counselor: "Why are you here, Karen?" (Shrug of shoulders)

Maggie: "I asked her to come. She and I can't get along and it is wrecking our home."

Counselor: "Do you see a problem between you and Mom?"

Karen: "Um, yes."

Counselor: "Would you say there's animosity between you and Mom?"

Karen: (Hesitating, then) "Much!"

Counselor: "Why is there this problem with Mom?"

Karen: "I don't know."

Counselor: "Do you have this problem with anyone else?"

Karen: "No."

Counselor: "Karen, you know you are to honor your mother. It is sin not to. Do you see this as sin?"

Karen: "Yes."

Counselor: "Why haven't you made a move to right this situation?"

Karen: "I don't know how."[23]

The counselor in that situation gathered embarrassingly little data in the conversation because he failed to ask questions that produce facts.

First, notice that he asked several questions that began with the word *why*. Instead, he should have made an effort to ask more *what* questions. Generally, *what* questions produce much more information than *why* questions, which will often receive only the answer that Karen gave twice—"I don't know." Counselors will see better results in data gathering by asking questions like: What is your problem? What is happening? What do you mean? What have you done about it? What has helped? What has made it worse? What do you think about it?

Other helpful questions start with the word *how*: How do you feel? How have you acted? How have you reacted? How have you tried to resolve it? How long have you had the problem? How often have you had it? How can I be of help?[24]

Another problem with the counselor's questions to Karen was that the rest of his questions were closed-ended, which means they could be

_____

23. Adams, *Casebook*, 90.

24. A study of the questions Jesus asked in the gospels reveals that He asked *what* questions much more often than *why* questions. For instance, in Mark 8–10 Jesus asks twenty questions; seventeen of them are *what* questions.

answered sufficiently with a yes or no.[25] Rather, he should have asked more open-ended questions, so that the counselee could not answer with a yes or no, but would have to provide further information. Following are some examples of these two types of questions:

Closed: Do you want to get married?

Open: What are your thoughts about marriage?

Closed: Do you love your husband?

Open: How would you describe your attitude toward your husband?

Closed: Are you satisfied with your job?

Open: What do you like or dislike about your job?

Closed: Do you get along with your parents?

Open: What kind of relationship do you have with your parents?

We need to be conscious of the kinds of questions we ask in counseling; we need to choose them carefully so that they will provide the most information possible. Here are some examples of useful questions to ask in each of the six categories of data:

Physical

Generally speaking, how would you describe your present and past physical health?

Tell me about your sleep patterns.

What is involved in the work you do?

If you could change four things about your work, what would you change?

Give me a description of what you do in a typical day in your life.

Resources

Tell me about the most important persons in your life, and why they are so important to you.

---

25. This kind of question is helpful in certain circumstances, such as when you want to get a commitment from a counselee, when you need to clarify what you think he or she has been saying, and when the counselee is getting uncomfortable (because closed-ended questions are usually less threatening than open-ended questions).

Share with me the relationships in your life that give you the most joy; the most sadness or heartache.

When you have a problem, what do you usually do?

Tell me about the persons in your life with whom you feel comfortable sharing your private thoughts and feelings?

Tell me about your relationship with God: how it began, how it has developed, how important it is, where God fits into the total picture of your life or the picture of what is happening to you now, what you are doing to strengthen your relationship with God.

Describe what your church means to you.

When you have had problems in the past, what has helped you most in resolving them?

What are some of your greatest resources, strengths; greatest deficiencies/weaknesses?

What are your Bible reading and prayer practices?

Emotions

What are some emotions that you frequently experience?

How do others see you emotionally?

If you were able to change anything about yourself emotionally, what would you want to change?

Give me a few examples of times when you were extremely . . . (angry, happy, sad).

How do you feel about what is happening in your life right now?

If I had tape-recorded what you have just said and played it back to you, what emotions would you hear?

Actions

As you look back over your life, what are some of the things you have done that were worthwhile?

What are some of the things you wish you could undo?

As you look at your life right now, what are some of the things you think you are doing that are right? that are wrong?

Tell me some of the ways you see yourself growing as a Christian.

Tell me some of the ways you could improve as a Christian; in your relationship with Christ; as a testimony for Christ.

Tell me how you have helped other people; been a hindrance to other people.

When you think of the Ten Commandments, which ones do you have the greatest problem with?

Concepts

What do you see as your most pressing problem?*[26]

Do you have any idea why the problem has become so severe?*

What do you think about the way you have been handling the problem?*

What does all of this tell you about yourself?*

Do you have any idea why criticism is so hard for you to handle?*

If I had a tape recorder and could record your thoughts at this moment, what would I hear?*

What happens inside your head when I give you a suggestion about handling a problem?*

What do/did you want, desire, seek, aim for, pursue, hope for?*

What are your goals, expectations, or intentions?*

Where do you look for security, meaning, happiness, fulfillment, joy, or comfort?*

What do you fear most? What do you tend to avoid?*

What would make you happy?*

What brings out the worst or best in you?*

What or who rules or controls you in the nitty gritty of life? To what or whom do you listen?*

In what or whom do you place your functional trust? What drives you? In what or whom do you set your hope?*

When you are pressured or tense, where do you turn? Where do you find relief? How do you escape?*

Historical

When did you first begin to experience this problem?

Tell me what was happening in your life when. . . .

Tell me about your relationship with the Lord over the years: the high points and low points.

As you look back over your life, what are the happiest and saddest experiences you have ever had?

---

26. Those questions followed by an asterisk are adapted from David Powlison's class notes.

Tell me about some of the most positive influences in your life; the most negative influences in your life.

Tell me about your marriage, your family, your church, your work, etc.

If you could change anything about circumstances in your life, what would you change?

What is going on in your life that brings you the most pleasure? The most pain or distress?

What external pressures are you presently experiencing?

Observing Halo Data

Counselors can also learn about counselees through *halo data*, or information that is communicated in nonverbal ways. This includes both nonverbal behavior and paralinguistic communication.

1. **Nonverbal behavior.** Genesis 3:8 says that "the man and his wife hid themselves from the presence of the LORD God among the trees of the garden." Adam and Eve had never fled from God before, and this action revealed something important about what they were feeling. They did not have to say one word for us to know that they were experiencing the guilt and fear of sin. Likewise in counseling we can learn much from the actions of our counselees during the sessions.

Sometimes their faces will exhibit expressions that clearly reveal anger, sorrow, or other emotions. Sometimes they will move the chairs closer to the desk or farther away from it when they enter the room. Sometimes couples will move their chairs away from each other. Sometimes families will arrange themselves in a way that shows who is getting along and who is not, or which child is favored by the parents. Counselees may squeeze their chair handles or look at the floor every time the counselor mentions a particular issue. Some counselees will be late to the sessions every time. All these things (and many more) can reveal information that will be useful to help counselees change.

2. **Paralinguistic communication.** This type of halo data has to do primarily with the manner in which our counselees speak—not what they say, but *how* they say it. Does their tone of voice communicate hope, or does it communicate hopelessness? Does it communicate anxiety or peace? Anger or forgiveness? Love or hate? Interest or indifference? And does their voice portray them as rude, inconsiderate, manipulative, or give other

negative impressions that could be contributing to their interpersonal struggles? Paralinguistic communication also involves what counselees are willing to talk about and what they refuse to talk about. Sometimes the issues they hesitate to talk about are the very issues at the source of their problems.

Both types of halo data are especially important to notice in regard to how counselees relate to their counselors, because they probably treat others the same way they treat the counselor, and others probably perceive them in the same way that the counselor does. Never underestimate the importance of this kind of observation—it can provide as much information as merely concentrating on what the counselee says.[27]

CONCLUSION

Some other ways to gather data effectively include assigning homework specifically designed for this purpose,[28] talking with others who have a relationship with the counselee, and taking accurate notes for review as counseling proceeds.[29]

The importance of becoming skillful in taking inventory can hardly be overestimated. To a large degree, all other elements of the biblical counseling process depend on it. How we effectively build involvement with our counselees and inspire hope in them will be determined and directed by what we learn about them and their problems.

Understanding and counseling people biblically is a challenging and rewarding responsibility. But sloppiness or neglect in gathering date can undermine the whole process. That is why biblical counselors need

---

27. Halo data can also provide material for questions: "When I asked you that question you seemed upset. Could you help me to understand what bothered you about the question?" "You seem angry with me today. Is there something I have done to upset you?" "You seem a little preoccupied. What are you thinking about?" In many cases the questions inspired by halo data yield key information.

28. For examples of data-gathering homework, see Wayne A. Mack, *A Homework Manual for Biblical Living*, 2 vols. (Phillipsburg, Penn.: Presbyterian and Reformed, 1979); Wayne A. Mack, *Your Family God's Way* (Phillipsburg, Penn.: Presbyterian and Reformed, 1991); and Wayne A. Mack, *Preparing for Marriage God's Way* (Tulsa, Ok.: Hensley, 1987).

29. I suggest that this be done during the session in a limited way—write down important phrases, statements, or ideas for future recollection, reflection, and development. After the session is concluded, the counselor may want to take a few minutes to reflect, evaluate, and record any other significant information. That would also be a good time to plan tentatively what will be done in the next session.

to develop expertise in this endeavor. We need to work carefully and prayerfully at improving our inventory-taking skills as though our effectiveness as a counselor depended on it—because from a human point of view, it does!

13

Interpreting Counselee Data

Wayne A. Mack

In the last chapter we discussed the process of gathering data. Now we turn to the challenge of using that data. No matter how much information we obtain about our counselees, it is of no value unless we use it to draw conclusions about what is happening in their lives. We must not only interpret that data ourselves, but in many cases must also help our counselees to reinterpret it, because they may already have drawn wrong conclusions about their situations.

The process of biblical counseling we discuss in the following chapters depends upon an accurate interpretation of the counselee's problems. If the counselor's interpretation is wrong, the instruction, inducement, and implementation will be wrong as well. An accurate understanding of the meaning of the collected data provides strategic direction for the entire counseling process.

The Definition of Interpreting Data

What do we mean by interpreting data? This process involves two basic elements: accurately analyzing or conceptualizing the data and explaining it to the counselee. In other words, one aspect of interpretation involves what goes on in our minds as counselors. We must analyze the data gathered during the inventory phase so that we can understand it from a biblical viewpoint. And we must decide what should be done about the problems according to Scripture. The second facet of interpretation involves what we say to our counselees about their problems. Our interpretation of the situation is not complete until we interpret it *for them.* We must explain our analysis and conceptions to the counselee in such a way that he or she understands the real nature and causes of the difficulties from a biblical perspective. In many instances, progress is not made in counseling simply because the counselor did not identify the problem correctly, or did not explain it adequately so the counselee could agree with the interpretation and follow the counsel. In such a situation, two different interpretations of the problem exist—the counselor's and the counselee's—and these work against each other.

So when we discuss interpretation of data we must consider not only how the counselor should think about the problems but also how the counselor should communicate those conclusions to the counselee.

THE PROCESS OF INTERPRETING DATA

The biblical counselor can best achieve the goal of accurate analysis and clear explanation by following these four steps: (1) gather adequate data, (2) interpret the data, (3) formulate a working interpretation of the data, and (4) test the validity of the interpretation.

As these steps are explained throughout this chapter, you may think, "This process is going to take a tremendous amount of time and effort!" Yes, it will take much time and effort. People are complex, and a simplistic approach to helping them almost always fails. We are not like Jesus, who knew immediately the thoughts of people when He walked the earth. We certainly cannot take one look at someone and tell that person what he or she needs. In most cases, we will not even be able to talk to people once and tell them what they need. The process of interpretation can be somewhat lengthy and extensive. And although with experience a counselor is able to reach conclusions in less time, we must never get to a point where we are not willing to think long and hard about each person's problems.

Before we begin discussing the steps in the process of interpretation, consider the following case study, which will serve as an illustration throughout the rest of this chapter:

> "Feelings of inferiority have made me sick physically and generally impotent as a person," says Gus. "I've tried to do as you said, but I just can't." At a previous session you asked Gus to seek the forgiveness of

his father for several admitted offenses against him. Gus is now in his fourth session and the one assignment that has been given for the past two weeks still remains uncompleted. "You 'can't,' really means you 'won't,' doesn't it?" is your reply. "No, I just can't do anything," he responds. "I'm not a quitter or anything, but I can't do that. I want to; I know I should and if I had more ego strength, I might be able to do so."[1]

First, consider this case from Gus's perspective. How is he interpreting the problem? He believes that he does not have the ability to complete the homework assignment or otherwise overcome his problems. He sees himself as a victim who does not bear responsibility for his actions. He cites "feelings of inferiority" and a lack of "ego strength" as the cause of his impotency to do what is right.

We can see that Gus's counselor needs to interpret the problem biblically and communicate that interpretation to Gus. As we discuss this process in the following pages, we will provide some suggestions for interpreting Gus's situation in a way that will be helpful to him and glorifying to God.

Gather Adequate Data

The first step in the interpretation process is to make sure we have gathered enough data. Let's apply each category we discussed in chapter 12 to Gus's situation.

Physical. What does Gus mean when he says he is sick physically? When did this illness begin? How much sleep is he getting? Has he been to a doctor to see if there is anything wrong organically? What does he mean by the word *impotent*?[2]

Resources. Is Gus a Christian? Has he been taught from the Scriptures concerning his sufficiency in Christ? What kind of relationship does he have with other family members?[3] Does he have godly friends who can

---

1. Jay Adams, *The Christian Counselor's Casebook* (Grand Rapids: Zondervan, 1974), 162.

2. Perhaps Gus is evaluating himself wrongly in light of what other people can do physically, instead of recognizing that they may have different constitutions. He may think he cannot be useful or successful because he does not have the physical strength that others have.

3. Their involvement may be helpful, even crucial, for Gus to repair the broken relationship with his father.

encourage him and help him? Are his friends part of the problem or the solution? Does he lack social skills? Is he comparing his abilities and skills to others and thus concluding that he is inferior? How is he involved in church? Does he have a pastor or other shepherds who would be able and willing to help him?

Emotions. Is Gus excitable or indifferent? Does he harbor bitterness, resentment, or anger? Is he fearful? Is he angry with his father or afraid of him? Is he fretting about his problems? What does he mean by "feelings of inferiority"? Does he understand the biblical purpose and role of emotions? What role do emotions or feelings play in Gus's life; in his decision making; in what he does and does not do; in how he views and interprets himself and situations? How much confidence does he put in the accuracy and validity of his feelings?

Actions. Has Gus attempted anything the counselor or (more important) God is asking him to do? If so, what happened? What other things has he not done or is he not doing because he lacks "ego strength"? What would he like to do if he had more "ego strength"? He said that he is "not a quitter"—What are some of the things he has stuck with and carried through to completion? In what ways is he not living biblically or failing to fulfill his biblical responsibilities? What is he currently achieving in any area of his life?[4]

Concepts. How does Gus define the term *ego strength*? How does he believe he should go about getting more of that? What does he think it takes for a person to be successful? What is his view of the nature of the Christian life? What are his expectations? Who is he seeking to please and serve? How does he think God would describe his problem? Would God say feelings of inferiority have made him impotent and generally sick as a person?[5] What does he think would satisfy him? Does he understand what the Bible says about true success? What are his functional gods at this point in his life? To what voices is he listening? What are his cravings? What are his ruling desires? Who is Gus worshiping? On whom is he depending for the resources to live the Christian life and do what God wants him to do?

---

4. If Gus has accomplished some tasks in his life, and especially if he is successfully carrying out responsibilities in other areas, we can challenge his claim that he lacks "ego strength." We can build on his successful completion of past and present tasks to challenge and encourage him.

5. The reason for questioning Gus about what he thinks God would say is to encourage him subtly to think through his presuppositions rather than blasting him with the truth (cf. Eph. 4:15). We would need to encourage Gus to think on his own and help him to come to the conclusion that he is seeing things differently than God sees them.

History. How long has Gus had these "feelings of inferiority," and is there some event in his life connected with them? Is there one particular event through which he is seeing his entire life? How has his perceived lack of ego strength affected his life through the years? Is the problem with his father due to a series of things that have happened? When did those things develop? What is his job history? Are there other authority figures he has had problems with at his job; at school? When he was required to do difficult things in the past, how did he respond? What escapes has Gus previously used to evade responsibility?

Interpret the Data

This second step is the most difficult aspect of the process of interpretation because it involves thinking through the meaning and implications of the inventory data. After asking the counselee numerous questions, the counselor needs to answer some questions. The following questions are helpful for this part of the interpretive process.

What biblical category best describes the person I am counseling? We need to avoid the dangers of stereotyping or over-generalizing when we evaluate people, but we must also realize that the Bible does speak of various categories into which people fit to one degree or another.

Is this person saved or unsaved? Every person falls into one of these two categories, and as we discussed in chapter 12,[6] those who are saved have resources available that unbelievers do not. So we must consider what the data suggests about whether the counselee is a true believer. What does the data suggest about the person's relationship with Christ? Is it genuine and growing? Does the person spend time with the Lord in consistent prayer and Bible study? Is there any indication that this person's relationship with God is merely historical, meaning that the individual clings to a past decision for assurance without evidence of God's current work in his or her life? Do the convictions belong to that person, or are they borrowed from parents or friends? Your approach to the other phases of counseling, particularly instruction and inducement, will depend heavily on your interpretation in this area.

Is this person spiritually mature or immature? A second way of evaluating counselees is to assess whether they are spiritually mature or immature. Hebrews 5:11–14 mentions these two categories:

---

6. See page 215.

"Concerning him [Melchizadek] we have much to say, and it is hard to explain, since you have become dull of hearing. For though by this time you ought to be teachers, you have need for someone to teach you the elementary principles of the oracles of God, and you have come to need milk and not solid food. For everyone who partakes only of milk is not accustomed to the word of righteousness, for he is a babe. But solid food is for the mature, who because of practice have their senses trained to discern good and evil."

This passage teaches that spiritual maturity is more than what someone knows—it is what they put into practice. Mature Christians are able to discern between good and evil because they have practiced consistent godliness. On the other hand, immature Christians are described as those who have been taught many truths but have not practiced them sufficiently. By that definition even people who have been saved for many years may be immature. Their heads may be filled with scriptural facts and information; they may be able to recite verses and creeds forward and backward: they may even be skilled in discussing theology, but they are not mature because they have not lived out those truths.

Evaluating whether your counselees are mature or immature will determine to some extent the depth of the instruction you can give them—whether it should be "solid food" or merely "milk."[7] It will also help you to know how much you should focus on instruction, because if the person you are dealing with is a mature Christian, he or she will primarily need encouragement and support. Mature Christians with problems often know what needs to be done; counseling becomes simply a matter of helping them to do what they already know is right. Immature Christians, on the other hand, often require extensive instruction before they are ready to take the steps necessary to solve their problems.

Is this person unruly, fainthearted, or weak? In 1 Thessalonians 5:14, the apostle Paul provides a third way of evaluating counselees. He mentions three categories of people and the general approach we should take in dealing with each of them: "And we urge you, brethren, admonish the unruly, encourage the fainthearted, help the weak, be patient with all men."

The first type of person mentioned is the "unruly." In the original Greek this word (*ataktos*) means to be out of step, to be defiant and rebellious. It speaks of people who are disrespectful, self-willed, and stubborn. They are obviously set against doing what God wants them to do. Paul

---

7. Cf. 1 Cor. 3:1–2; Heb. 5:12–14.

says to "admonish" these people (i.e. warn them). He also says in Titus 3:10 that we should reject a factious person after a first and second admonition. If these people do not respond to our warning and merely want to argue, then we would be wasting our time to continue counseling them. And Proverbs 26:4 says, "Do not answer a fool according to his folly, lest you also be like him.[8] We do not want to allow such people to influence us in a negative way by drawing us into useless arguments or other unprofitable discussion. Therefore, we must simply warn them that the path they are choosing can end only in judgment from God, and that we are available to help them when they are open to counsel.

The second category of people mentioned in this passage are the "fainthearted." That Greek word, *oligopsuchos*, literally means "small-souled." It refers to people whose souls have shriveled up. They have become discouraged, weary, or despondent. Their problems do not stem from rebellion or obstinacy but from a feeling of defeat and a lack of ambition. Instead of warning them or otherwise confronting them, Paul says that we should encourage them.

I believe it is significant that Paul did not say, "Admonish the fainthearted." Faintheartedness is not necessarily sin; people can end up in that category simply because of difficult trials and disappointments that cause them to struggle with discouragement. Gus may be in that situation. And because of that possibility, his counselor should have been more hesitant about rebuking him before the problem had been adequately interpreted. Sometimes I fear that we biblical counselors are too quick to label discouragement a sin and call for repentance from people when we should first show them compassion and provide encouragement.

The third group of people mentioned in 1 Thessalonians 5:14 are the "weak." The Greek word translated "weak" (*asthenes*) means "without strength" and is used most often to describe those who are physically limited. It is also used in a general sense to describe people who are simply deficient in some way.[9] Their deficiency may be a lack of education, opportunities, or finances, or perhaps a physical problem. These people sometimes find it harder to do what is right because of their "weaknesses." According to Paul, they need more than encouragement: they actually need someone to come alongside and help them to do what they need to do.

---

8. Other passages in Proverbs that speak of the fool are 9:7; 13:20; 14:7; 17:10, 12; 22:10; 23:9; 26:3–5, 12; and 27:22.

9. Paul uses the term to refer to those who are considered deficient in 1 Cor. 1:27: "God has chosen the weak things of the world to shame the things which are strong."

The Greek verb for "help" (*antechomai*) can also be translated "support" or "hold to" (cf. Matt. 6:24). Some people have never had anybody be faithful and committed to them. They are accustomed to being criticized, neglected, and deserted in their time of need. They have never heard anyone say, "I am committed to you. I am going to be your friend through thick and thin, and I am not going to give up on you." They need to sense that someone sincerely loves them and is willing to support them regardless of their deficiencies.

What biblical language best describes the problems this person is experiencing? The Bible not only contains categories of people, it also labels various kinds of behavior. So we need to identify the terms the Bible uses to describe each problem we face in counseling. This will help us in finding the scriptural insight we need about the causes of the problem and the solutions; it will also help us to think in biblical terminology throughout the process. So ask yourself, "What biblical words, labels, or categories could be used to describe the various problems this person is experiencing?"

For example, in Gus's case it is apparent that he has a problem with "confidence in the flesh" (cf. Phil. 3:3). He believes that the solution to his problems is to gain more "ego strength." But the Scripture says a believer can do all things *through Christ who strengthens us* (Phil. 4:13, emphasis added), and Paul wrote in 2 Corinthians 12:9–11 that God's power operates in our weakness. The Bible teaches that we are only in a position to experience God's power and strength when we understand how weak we are, because that is when we abandon hope in our own resources and rely entirely on God. Our confidence should never be in our own strength, but in His. So Gus is looking in the wrong place when he places his confidence in the flesh. He needs to learn to place His confidence in the Lord.

What insights does the Bible provide about the proximate causes of such problems? The Bible speaks directly to the reasons behind what people do. When we are dealing with a specific problem in counseling, we need to find out if Scripture gives some clues to its cause. There may be examples of people who were in similar situations and experienced similar problems, or there may be direct references to the behavior and its causes. Here are some examples of both to consider.

- **Conflict**
  James 4:1–2 teaches that people who cause fights do so because they are selfish. They become dissatisfied and angry because they want their own way and are not getting it. They view others as

merely helps or hindrances in accomplishing what they desire, so they misuse others to get what they want.

- **Instability**
  According to James 1:8, one of the causes of instability is "double-mindedness." That term describes a person who is not truly submitted to the Lordship of Jesus Christ. He is "trying to serve two masters" in the sense that he claims to follow Christ, but something else takes priority over Him (cf. Matt. 6:24). This split focus results in an unstable life.

- **Lying**
  In Genesis 18:1–15, Abraham lied because he was ruled by fear, and many counselees who struggle with lying have the same root problem. They are controlled by fear of being hurt, fear of rejection, fear of failing, fear of losing the respect of people, etc. But merely telling those people to stop lying is a superficial and ineffective way of dealing with their problem. In such cases, we need to address the controlling fear they are experiencing before their problem can be solved.

- **Confusion**
  If we are working with a counselee who seems confused or disorganized, one of the possibilities is the person is committing the sins of jealousy or selfish ambition. James 3:16 says that where those sins exist, "there is *disorder* and every evil thing" (emphasis added.) Dealing with a counselee's confusion or lack of organization may not be sufficient; we may have to go deeper and address issues of the heart before we can help that person.

- **Fear**
  First John 4:18 says, "There is no fear in love; but perfect love casts out fear, because fear involves punishment, and the one who fears is not perfected in love." When people struggle with inordinate fears, it may be because they lack an understanding of God's love or (even more often) they lack love for others. Fear is often caused by selfishness. We experience it when we focus on ourselves rather than on serving the Lord and ministering to others. But fear disappears when we become more concerned about the good of others than about what happens to us.[10]

---

10. Proverbs 1:33 also reveals something about fear (and instability and insecurity)—it says that those things are often the result of not listening to or obeying God's Word.

- **Insecurity**

  When people exhibit behavior that we would call insecurity (or even paranoia), we often tend to think that is because they have been mistreated by others or because they lack self-confidence.[11]. But Proverbs 28:1 provides an interesting insight into that behavior. It says, "The wicked flee when no one is pursuing, but the righteous are bold as a lion." Some who exhibit insecurity do so simply because they have been involved in sin and bear guilt from it. Those who make a practice of deceit, for example, will often be extremely guarded and hesitant in their speech—because they have to be careful not to contradict lies they have told. However, those who always speak the truth will generally be more confident and secure in talking to others, because they do not have to worry about being found out.

- **Bizarre Behavior**

  Scripture contains numerous examples of bizarre behavior that lend insight into why some people act the way they do. For instance, in 1 Samuel 21:10–15 David deliberately feigned insanity to deceive others. Some people today do so for the same reason. They do not want to be held responsible for their actions, and they know that if they act in a bizarre manner, others will expect much less of them. They may have found that they are cared for and catered to when they act that way. (In my counseling experience I have had many people who exhibited bizarre behavior tell me later that they did so intentionally to get attention. In some cases, they have practiced this kind of behavior so often that it has become a habit pattern that is basically an unplanned, automatic, reflex reaction— it has become a way of life.)[12]

  Another scriptural example of bizarre behavior is king Nebuchadnezzar of Babylon who was transformed into a raving lunatic and acted more like an animal than a man (Dan. 4:28–33). This oc-

---

11. *Paranoia*, a Greek word found in 2 Peter 2:16, is translated "madness" or "foolishness." It is a combination of two Greek words: one means "to be at or by the side of" and the other refers to the mind. So, literally, a person experiencing paranoia is a person who is "by the side of his or her mind" or "out of his or her mind." That person is not viewing things realistically, rationally, accurately, and is not in touch with reality. As a result, the individual may experience panic attacks and delusions and act in other bizarre ways.

12. Cf. Prov. 5:22; Jer. 13:23; 22:21; and Eph. 4:22.

curred as part of God's judgment upon him because of his pride.[13] And notice that the solution to his bizarre behavior was a divinely granted repentance (vv. 34ff).

- **Worry or Anxiety**
  When we encounter people who claim they have so much going on in their lives that they cannot cope with it all, we can remind ourselves of Martha in Luke 10:38–42 and ask if their situation might be similar to hers. Martha interpreted her problem as having too much work to do, but Jesus pointed out that her problem was that her priorities were not right. She should have been worshiping Him rather than worrying about temporal things and judging her sister.

- **Judgmentalism**
  Third John 9–10 mentions an extremely critical and schismatic man named Diotrephes. And in those verses John tells us the root cause of Diotrephes' behavior, saying that "he loves to be first" or to have the preeminence. This man's pride needed to be dealt with before he would stop creating factions in the church.

As you can see from these examples, the Bible provides a wealth of insight into why people do what they do. The biblical counselor must be committed to searching God's Word continually for help in interpreting the causes of a counselee's problems.

What does the data suggest about the relationship of the various problems to each other? When dealing with several problems in a particular case, we need to ask questions like, "Which came first, the chicken or the egg?" Suppose you are counseling a person who is experiencing anxiety and also having difficulty sleeping at night. Is the anxiety making it difficult for the person to sleep, or is the lack of sleep influencing the anxiety? We all know that when we lose sleep it is much harder to handle problems than when we are well rested. When we are tired, our problems seem gigantic. On the other hand, failure to handle stress biblically can also cause sleep loss. Is one the root and the other the fruit? Is one the cause and the other the result? These questions are important to determine the structure and emphasis of our counseling.

Also, we need to notice if there are certain patterns running through a particular case. Does a lack of self-control, an improper response to

---

13. Another example of bizarre behavior resulting from sin and the judgment of God is found in Deut. 28:28–29.

authority, or some other single problem keep recurring in the person's life? It may be that a common denominator will turn out to be a key to every other aspect of the situation.

What hindrances to biblical change exist in the counselee's life? First, we must find out whether he or she has a proper understanding of biblical change. I have found that many people really do not understand how change comes about from a biblical perspective. They are expecting God to zap them (usually in response to prayer) and supernaturally take their problem away or eliminate their desire to do wrong. Unfortunately, they do not understand what the Bible has to say about the role of self-discipline in sanctification, and they need to be taught this before true change can take place.[14]

Biblical change can also be hindered when the cart is put before the horse. In Gus's case, he has not been able to ask forgiveness from his father at the counselor's direction, probably because he harbors bitterness against his father. This internal issue must be dealt with before he will be able to reconcile the relationship.

Here are some other questions that can help ascertain what hindrances need to be cleared away in counselees' lives:

Does the data indicate why they have not been able to resolve the difficulties on their own?

How do they view the problem? What is their understanding of the problem?

Have they failed to change because they do not want to, or because they do not know how?

What factors in their environment may be exacerbating the problem?[15]

What erroneous ideas are contributing to the problems?

What rewards are they receiving for their behavior? In other words, do they perceive the results of their behavior to be beneficial in some way, or are others encouraging it in some way?

---

14. For an excellent discussion of the role of personal discipline in the process of spiritual growth, see John MacArthur, Jr., "A Balance of Faith and Effort," in *Our Sufficiency in Christ* (Dallas: Word Publishing, 1991).

15. For instance, Prov. 22:24–25 says, "Do not associate with a man given to anger; or go with a hot-tempered man, lest you learn his ways, and find a snare for yourself." You may encounter a counselee struggling with anger who is surrounded by a lot of angry people. A change in environment and companions may be an important part of the solution.

What does the data indicate about the person's expectations and desires for the counseling process? We need to find out why our counselees are coming to us for counseling. Sometimes a husband really does not want to be there, but his wife has laid down an ultimatum. Or maybe their pastor has insisted, but they are determined not to change just to prove the pastor wrong. We also need to know if our counselees are looking for a quick-fix or are expecting a long process with numerous meetings. Have they come to achieve change, or are they simply looking for sympathy?

What does the data indicate about any possible organic or physiological factors?[16] It is important to learn whether our counselees have seen a physician, and if so, what conclusions the doctor reached. In some cases people have genuine medical problems (such as irregular thyroid function, diabetes, or a tumor) that negatively affect their thought patterns and behavior. In these cases the counselor must work with the physician to correct the physical problem and must counsel the person about the biblical response to sickness and suffering.

Counselors are also likely to encounter people who think their problem is physical when there is no proof that this is the case. They go to one or more physicians and have multiple tests, yet no documentable organic cause for their problem is discovered. Although the possibility of an organic cause can still exist, it is likely that the problem is not physiological. Even when a physician does diagnose a medical problem, we must not necessarily assume that the diagnosis is accurate, because some diagnoses are based strictly on the report of symptoms by the patient—symptoms that can be the result of wrong thinking and behavior rather than the result of an organic cause. For instance, I have counseled people whose problems were rooted in personal sin, but because of the guilt of that sin, they were experiencing such symptoms as multiple aches and pains and even hallucinations.[17]

What does the data indicate about the person's motive for wanting to change? If a wife wants to change simply because she wants her husband to change and make her life easier, then she has a wrong motive. If someone wants to change simply to win the approval or acceptance of other people, then this motive is wrong. Lasting change will not be produced unless the counselee's motive is to please and glorify God (cf. 2 Cor. 5:9; 1 Cor. 10:31).

---

16. See H. R. Lewis and M. E. Lewis, *Psychosomatics* (New York: Viking, 1972).

17. Drugs can be very misleading in this area. If medication seems to be helping someone, that does not necessarily mean the problem is organic. The medication may alleviate some of the symptoms but still not solve the root problem. So the fact that drugs are helping does not necessarily prove that the cause is organic.

Have I ever experienced a similar situation or similar problem? As a counselor, you should ask yourself how your own experiences can help you to interpret what is happening in each of your cases. Recalling how you felt may help you to empathize with your counselees, and objectively considering the dynamics of your experience may provide insight into the causes of their problems. You can ask yourself, "When I am in a situation similar to this person's, what am I tempted to do? How am I tempted to respond? What am I tempted to think? How do I feel or how am I tempted to feel? What do I want, desire, crave, or demand in a situation like this? What do I think about doing as a possible way of escape? To whom or to what do I turn? On what or on whom do I depend for deliverance?"

Have I counseled someone previously with similar problems? Sometimes a previous counseling experience can help to interpret a current case. However, we must exercise caution when using personal experience or the experience of others to make judgments about the nature of another counselee's problems. Two cases that appear similar may actually be quite different. Since Scripture indicates that none of us fully understands what another person is experiencing (cf. Prov. 14:13, 19), we must be careful not to assume that two people have the same underlying causes for similar problems. Nevertheless, since Scripture also tells us that "no temptation has overtaken you but such as is common to man" (1 Cor. 10:13), we would be foolish to ignore the possibility of some commonalities.

Formulate a Working Interpretation

After we have thought through the data by asking pertinent questions about it, the third step of the interpretation process is to use our answers to the questions to draw tentative conclusions about the case. They must be tentative conclusions because they have not yet been tested; nevertheless, it is still important to develop them. The counseling process will continue indefinitely unless we begin at some time to identify possible problems and solutions.

Determine Possible Reasons for the Problem. In light of the data you have analyzed and your knowledge of Scripture, identify possible explanations for the counselee's problems. In Gus's case, for example, there are several possibilities: perhaps Gus does not understand biblical change and is waiting for God to zap him with the desire and power to obey; perhaps he is too proud to admit his sin and ask his father for forgiveness; perhaps he is fearful of embarrassment or rejection and thus is concerned more for his own feelings than for his father's good.

Gus's counselor should weigh each of these possibilities (and others) and then decide the further direction of counseling (particularly the instruction) on the basis of which possibility best fits the data. The counselor would then need to test the validity of that interpretation, but before we discuss that step, there is another issue that must be addressed if we are to have any hope of formulating a helpful interpretation.

Consider the Counselee's Heart. As the counselor reflects on the questions and their answers, a primary purpose should be to identify what is going on in the counselee's heart. According to the Word of God, sinful behavior is merely an outward indication of problems in the heart. A survey of some of Scripture's teaching about the heart will show us how important this is.

- "The LORD is near to the brokenhearted, and saves those who are crushed in spirit" (Ps. 34:18).

- "Create in me a clean heart, O God, and renew a steadfast spirit within me. . . . The sacrifices of God are a broken spirit; a broken and a contrite heart, O God, Thou wilt not despise" (Ps. 51:10.17).

- "Thy word I have treasured in my heart, that I may not sin against Thee" (Ps. 119:11).

- "Watch over your heart with all diligence, for from it flow the springs of life" (Prov. 4:23).

- "As in water face reflects face, so the heart of man reflects man" (Prov. 27:19).[18]

- "The heart is more deceitful than all else and is desperately sick; who can understand it? I, the LORD, search the heart, I test the mind, even to give to each man according to his ways" (Jer. 17:9–10).

- "For from within, out of the heart of men, proceed the evil thoughts, fornications, thefts, murders, adulteries, deeds of coveting and wickedness, as well as deceit, sensuality, envy, slander, pride and foolishness. All these evil things proceed from within and defile the man" (Mark 7:21–23).[19]

---

18. There are seventy-two references to the heart in the book of Proverbs.

19. Other representative passages indicating the crucial significance of the heart are Gen. 6:5; 8:21; Deut. 5:29; 6:5; 10:12; 11:13; 26:16; 30:6; 1 Sam. 16:7; 2 Chron. 19:3; 30:19; Ezra 7:10; Ps. 27:3; 28:3; 76:5; 101:4; 140:2; Prov. 3:1–6; 6:14; 6:18; 6:25; 7:24; 11:20; 12:2; 15:13–15; 16:23; 20:9; 21:2; Matt. 5:8; 9:4; 12:33; 23:26; Luke 16:15; Acts 5:3; 16:14; Rom. 1:21; 1:24; 2:5; 8:7; 10:9–10; Eph. 3:17; 4:17; Heb. 3:8–15; 8:10; 10:16; 10:22; and James 3:8.

Two additional passages, one in the Old Testament and one in the New, deserve special comment because of what they reveal about the importance of the heart.

In Ezekiel 13 and 14 God speaks sternly to the elders of Israel about the judgment He is going to bring upon them. He warns them that judgment is coming and tells them that it is coming in part because of their evil conduct, but primarily because of what is happening in their hearts. Four times in chapter 14 the Lord refers to the fact that they had set up "idols in their hearts" (vv. 3, 4, 5, 7). These people outwardly claimed to be devoted to Jehovah, but in their hearts they were worshiping, serving, fearing, and depending on other gods. So it is with us when we act in unbiblical ways. The primary problem is not our behavior; our hearts have turned from worshiping, serving, fearing, and depending on the true God.

In 1 Corinthians 10:6–7 Paul recounts the events of another time that judgment fell on the Israelites and says that "these things happened as examples for us, that we should not *crave* evil things, as they also *craved*" (emphasis added). Then he exhorts his readers, "Do not be idolaters, as some of them were." Following those statements about desires and idolatry, Paul describes the sinful behavior of the people—their immorality and their grumbling. I do not believe it is an accident that Paul refers to their idolatrous cravings before he speaks of their sinful activity. He knew that the Israelites' problem was not merely a behavioral one; it was a heart problem that manifested itself in their behavior.[20]

Because biblical counselors recognize the preeminent place of the heart in the process of understanding and helping people, they will be concerned primarily about what people are thinking, worshiping, trusting, and seeking to please.[21] They will seek to identify the desires or pursuits that have become idols in the life of the counselee. In many instances, identifying

---

20. When Moses describes the incident Paul was referring to (Num. 11), he focuses on the hearts of the people as well. Verses 4 and 34 both mention "greedy desires" as the source of their sin.

21. First John 2:14–16 provides some clear and helpful direction to biblical counselors for interpreting the motivations of counselees. This passage identifies the three primary areas of heart idolatry: the lust of the flesh (inordinate, controlling desires for sensual pleasure, for ease and comfort, for physical gratification; cf. Gen.3:6; 19:33, 35; Eccles. 10:16, 17; Luke 21:34; Prov. 23:29–35; 23:20, 21; 21:17; Num. 11:1–34; Rom. 13:11–14); the lust of the eyes (covetousness and greed, a controlling desire for profit or for material things: cf. Prov. 28:22, 23; Josh. 7; 1 Kgs. 21; Eccles. 4:8; 5:9–11; Deut. 15:19; 1 Sam. 25:11; 1 Tim. 6:9, 10; Col. 3:5; Matt. 6:18–34); and the pride of life (inordinate ruling desires to be great in one's self and for self, to be accepted and approved, to have power and be in control, to be recognized and respected, to be regarded as successful; Rom. 12:3; Jer. 45:5, 6; Isa. 10:7–11; 37:12,

and casting down these functional gods will be a significant factor for promoting biblical, God honoring change.[22]

Test the Validity of Your Interpretation

This fourth and final step of the interpretation process is necessary because our initial conclusions should be tentative. We must always recognize that, as human beings, we are finite and fallen, and therefore may misinterpret the situation. Even if we are relatively confident that we have an informed biblical understanding of the nature and causes of someone's problems, our conculsions should still be tested and validated. The following steps can help the counselor to validate interpretive conclusions.

1. Review mental and written notes to confirm that information acquired provides a factual basis for the conclusions. Prayerfully think through the data again to make sure you are not reading into it your own assumptions or opinions. Do not "shoot from the hip"—let the facts lead you to your interpretations (cf. Prov. 18:2, 13, 15).

2. Consider the possibility that there may be other ways of interpreting or understanding what is happening in the person's life. Ask yourself, "Could there be other alternatives? Am I missing something? Is there another explanation?"

3. Solicit additional information, knowing that more information may lead to a different perspective. Continue to gather data in the counseling sessions. Have your counselees keep journals. (e.g. The counselee describes each occurrence of a certain behavior during the week.) Carefully analyze these journals looking for patterns, themes, and other information that may validate or invalidate your interpretation. Secure additional data from other knowledgeable parties. Invite them

---

13; Ps. 10:3, 4; Prov. 25:27; 29:25; 3 John 9, 10; Judg. 9:1–21; Matt. 23:5; 6:1–6; 21:15; Amos 6:1–6; Acts 12:23; Luke 18:11; Prov. 27:2; 30:13; Dan. 4:20–27; 1 Sam. 25:36; Prov. 13:10; 16:5; 28:25; Gen. 3:16). It is often profitable to determine whether a counselee is falling prey to the lust of the flesh, the lust of the eyes, or the pride of life. For a helpful exposition of those areas of sin, see J. Cotton, *An Exposition of 1 John* (Evansville: Sovereign Grace Publishers), 190–205.

22. See T. Keller, "Puritan Resources for Biblical Counseling," *The Journal of Pastoral Practice* 9, no. 3 (1988): 11–41 for an excellent treatment of idolatrous desires.

to a counseling session, have them fill out specialized inventory forms, call them on the telephone, or visit them.[23]

4. Without mentioning names or identifying details (normally), discuss the case with other experienced biblical counselors and ask for their viewpoint and suggestions. What flaws do they see in your interpretation? Do they think you may be overlooking some things? Do they agree that the facts support your conclusions?

5. Lovingly, gently, and prudently explain your interpretation to the counselee and ask for feedback that would either confirm, invalidate, or provide an alternative to your interpretation. My practice is to carefully and prayerfully present my tentative conclusions to the counselee along with an explanation of supporting facts about my conclusions acquired from counseling and biblical insights. Sometimes I share this with my counselees in a straightforward way and then ask for their response to my interpretation. Other times I present the facts to them—highlighting themes and patterns and the biblical insights or examples that may apply—and ask them what they think those facts may indicate about the nature and causes of their problems. I decide which of these approaches to take based on my observations of the spiritual, emotional, and physical condition of the counselees, their personalities, their learning style, and the strength or weakness of my relationship with them.

When you test the validity of your interpretation in these ways, you may find that it fails the test, but do not be discouraged. You have eliminated a possibility and are closer to the right conclusion. You do need to rethink the data, however, and perhaps spend time determining where your interpretation was off the track. You will probably need to gather more data at this point.

If your interpretation tests positive but the counselee does not agree with it, then your job is to lovingly provide instruction so that he or she can learn to think biblically about the situation. (We will discuss biblical instruction extensively in the next chapter.)

CONCLUSION

Interpreting counselee data is both a science and an art. It is a science in that it deals with facts—facts from the Scripture and facts about

---

23. Always inform the counselee that you are doing this. In most cases it is best to ask for the counselee's permission.

counselees and their world—that require much research, investigation, and analysis. In this chapter, we have provided numerous suggestions for achieving this scientific aspect of interpretation.

But we must also realize that interpretation is an art as well. One does not become a good artist by merely possessing an aptitude for art, or even by learning the mechanics of artistic procedure. One becomes a good artist by practicing what is learned. So it is in the discipline of biblical counseling. Becoming an effective counselor involves not only spiritual giftedness and knowledge of the science of interpreting data but a continual practice of those principles until they become second nature. After you study the information in this chapter, you will want to continually put that information into practice as you seek to understand the Scriptures and the people God wants you to help. That is how you will become highly skilled in both the science and the art of biblically interpreting counselee data.

14

Providing Instruction through Biblical Counseling

Wayne A. Mack

Two mistaken ideas about counseling instruction are prevalent. One is the idea that counseling is all instruction—that is, if someone has a particular problem, all we need to do is find the Bible verses that apply to it and give the person a sermon on the subject. Hopefully we have countered that idea sufficiently in the previous chapters by showing the importance of other aspects of the counseling process, such as involvement and inventory.

A second mistaken idea is that counseling involves little or no instruction. Those who hold to this idea believe that people know the answers to their problems and that counselors should simply ask questions, listen, and otherwise provide support for them. In other words, they believe that if we build a strong relationship with our counselees, they will find their own solutions and work out their problems without having us tell them what to do.

But this approach to counseling is unbiblical, for Scripture makes clear that instruction plays a necessary part in every person's spiritual growth and that it is indispensable in the process of solving problems.[1] So if we want to help people change, we must be skilled in biblical counseling instruction—and we must make it an important part of our counseling.

---

1. Cf. Prov. 6:23; Matt. 22:29; Eph. 4:11–12; 1 Thess. 4:13; 1 Tim. 4:6, 11, 16; 2 Tim. 2:16–18; Titus 1:10–11.

THE NATURE OF COUNSELING INSTRUCTION

Since instruction is a vital part of biblical counseling, we need to know what kind of instruction is necessary. In order to be pleasing to God and helpful to our counselees, our instruction must meet three basic requirements: (1) it must be biblically based, (2) it must be biblically accurate, and (3) it must be biblically appropriate.

Instruction Should Be Biblically Based

When we say that our instruction should be based on the Bible, we mean that all the information we impart to our counselees to help them change should proceed from Scripture. It should be based on the Bible *alone*, and never on mere human ideas or observations. Why? Because the Bible is a practical, comprehensive, trustworthy, and thoroughly adequate source of truth, whereas human knowledge is unable to effectively address the problems that we face in life.

The Bible is practical. The Bible is not simply a theological treatise expounding upon esoteric doctrinal subjects—it is a lamp to our feet and a light to our path (Ps. 119:105). It was given to teach us how to live each day in a way that pleases God, and it was given to help us solve our problems. As Henry Ward Beecher said, "The Bible is God's chart for you to steer by, to keep you from the bottom of the sea, and to show you where the harbor is, and how to reach it without running on rocks and bars."[2]

The Bible is comprehensive. Scripture should be the sum and substance of our counseling instruction, because it deals with *all* the issues of life that are necessary for us to understand. Second Peter 1:3 says, "His divine power has granted to us everything pertaining to life and godliness, through the true knowledge of Him who called us by His own glory and excellence." The knowledge Peter speaks of is limited to the realities described in Scripture; thus he is saying that *everything* we need to know to live successfully is found within the pages of God's Word.[3] Some people react incredulously to that statement, but that is what the Bible says. Second Peter 1:3 is either true or it is not—and if it is not true, then the whole Bible could be called into question.

---

2. Quoted in F. S. Mead, ed., *The Encyclopedia of Religious Quotations* (Westwood, N. J.: Revell, 1965), 24.

3. Second Timothy 3:16–17 teaches the same truth when it says that Scripture is able to make us "adequate, equipped for *every* good work."

But we know that second Peter 1:3 is true. Scripture contains all the information necessary to "life and godliness," and in-depth study of its contents is rewarded with insights into even the most complicated human experiences. What happens all too often in counseling, however, is that the counselor assumes that the Scripture does not speak to the particular problem of a counselee, and therefore, the counselor abandons the Word prematurely and seeks input from the ideas of men. If such counselors would proceed on the assumption that 2 Peter 1:3 is true, they would see complex problems as a challenge to deepen their understanding of theology and grow in their knowledge of how it applies to specific situations.

I have spent my life trying to help people, and I have never encountered a case in which an application of scriptural principles was not relevant, sufficient, and superior to anything the world has to offer. This is not to say we should simply throw Bible verses across the desk at our counselees, but it does mean that the only goal of our instruction should be to communicate *biblical* truth that relates to their problems. The truth of 2 Peter 1:3 certainly indicates that any secular psychological research or theory is unnecessary (at best) in the process of helping people change spiritually (just as insights gleaned from pagan religions would be).

The Bible is trustworthy. A third reason our instruction should be based solely on the Bible is that it is the only book that deals with the practical problems of life in an absolutely reliable and trustworthy fashion. When we instruct our counselees from Scripture, we can know without question that, if applied, it will change their lives for the better. No other source of information and insight can inspire that kind of confidence.

Consider what the Psalmist says about the biblical counselor's textbook:

- "The judgments of the LORD are true; they are righteous altogether" (Ps. 19:9).
- "Forever, O LORD, Thy word is settled in heaven" (Ps. 119:89).
- "I esteem right all Thy precepts concerning everything . . ." (Ps. 119:128).
- "The sum of Thy word is truth, and every one of Thy righteous ordinances is everlasting" (Ps. 119:160).

Jesus echoed the Psalmist when he declared, "Thy Word is truth" (John 17:17). These and similar verses teach us that everything the Bible says is true. But they also yield a biblical epistemology that casts suspicion on any claims about human nature or spiritual truth that are not taught by Scripture.[4] According to that epistemology, we as humans cannot discover absolute truth apart from the special revelation of God.[5] An observation made or opinion developed without referencing God's Word may be true, but we cannot be certain that it is true because we are finite and fallen creatures. Let's consider this concept further.

1. *The Finiteness of Man.* One reason we cannot know anything absolutely apart from God's revelation is that we are finite. Our knowledge is necessarily limited because there is only so much we can observe and only so much we can understand. And unless we know everything, we cannot know anything for sure about the ultimate issues of life and its meaning (on our own), because we always may discover something new that will disprove what we know.

This idea is illustrated by the familiar story of four blind men who were walking along and bumped into an elephant. One of them hit the leg of the elephant and concluded that it was the base of a large tree. The second encountered the trunk and thought it was a fire hose. The third walked into the tail and thought it was a rope. And the fourth slammed into the side of the elephant and decided that it was a wall. They had all bumped into the same object, but because of the limitations on their observation each thought it was something different. And we can reach conculsions just as faulty when we rely on our own observations and insights without referring to God's Word, because like those blind men we can comprehend only part of the whole. God, on the other hand, is infinite in His knowledge and understanding. As Isaiah 40:14 asks rhetorically, "With whom did He consult and who gave Him understanding? And who taught Him in the path of justice and taught Him knowledge, and informed Him of the way of understanding?" There is no limitation to the wisdom of God. He says, "I am God, and there is no other; I am God, and there is no one like Me, declaring the end from the beginning and from ancient times things which have not been done" (Is. 46:9–10).

---

4. Epistemology is the area of philosophy commonly called "the science of knowing," which seeks to answer the questions "How do we know?" and "What can we know?"

5. R. Pratt, Jr. writes, "*All* that can properly be called truth, not just so called 'religious truth' resides first in God and men know truly only as they come to God's revelation of Himself as the source of truth, for it is God who teaches man knowledge (Ps. 94:10). . . . This dependence of man on God in the area of knowledge does not mean that men are without true ability to think and reason nor that they are 'programmed' by God in analogy to the way computers 'know.' Men do actually think, yet, true knowledge is dependent on and derived from God's knowledge as it has been revealed to man." *Every Thought Captive* (Phillipsburg, N. J.: Presbyterian and Reformed Publishing, 1979), 17.

God knows the end from the beginning. He knows the past, the present, and the future. He understands every part of us and every part of our world perfectly. And He has been pleased to reveal His truth to us in His Word. That is why we must instruct our counselees from that sufficient repository of truth and never forsake it for the severely limited ideas of man.[6]

2. *The Fallenness of Man.* Another reason we cannot know anything absolutely apart from Divine revelation is that we are fallen creatures. The Bible teaches that our minds have been adversely affected by sin to the point that even if we observe something accurately, we are likely to interpret it wrongly. Our sinful minds tend to distort truth, and the only way we can think rightly is to allow the Holy Spirit to renew our minds (Rom. 1:18–32; 12:2; Eph. 4:23). This is achieved only by learning to look at life through the lens of Scripture.

Because of our finiteness and our fallenness, then, we are unable to ascertain truth unless God has revealed it to us. We have no standard by which we can evaluate whether something is true or false except the Word of God. Thus while we can be confident that whatever we share with our counselees from the Word of God is true, we should have a healthy skepticism about any theory or insight that does not proceed from Scripture.[7] If it is not taught by the Word of God, it may be error.

The Bible is adequate. Our counseling instruction should be based on the Bible alone because "all Scripture is inspired by God and profitable for teaching, for reproof, for correction, for training in righteousness; that the man of God may be adequate, equipped for every good work" (2 Tim. 3:16–17). Those verses clearly say that we have everything we need in the Word of God to make us adequate or *complete* (another translation for the Greek word). We do not need to be more than adequate, and we cannot add anything to completeness. As J. C. Ryle wrote,

> The man who has the Bible, and the Holy Spirit in his heart, has everything which is absolutely needful to make him spiritually

---

6. See chapter 4 for more information about epistomological issues.

7. This certainly applies to anything written by an unsaved person, such as a secular psychologist, because even when an unsaved person makes a basic observation about the world or reiterates an idea taught by Scripture, there is still a dangerous tinge of falsehood to what that person says. Richard Pratt, Jr. writes, "We may speak of such statements as false because they are not the result of voluntary obedience to God's revelation. . . . Beyond this, the statements are falsified by the non-Christian framework of meaning and therefore lead away from the worship of God. If nothing else, the mere commitment to human independence falsifies the non-Christian's statements" (ibid.).

wise. . . . He has the well of truth open before him, and what can he want more? Yes! though he be shut up alone in a prison, or cast on a desert island, . . . if he has but the Bible, he has got the infallible guide, and wants no other.[8]

If we truly believe those inspirational words, we will never be tempted to think that we need to study human theories outside of Scripture in order to be able to provide helpful instruction for our counselees. Instead, we will cling to the only infallible guide for that endeavor—the Bible. It is practical, comprehensive, trustworthy, and adequate.[9] Make it your goal to study it zealously, meditate on it deeply, and communicate it accurately. And never sell it short by assuming it does not speak to a particular issue; never forsake it for "cisterns that can hold no water" (Jer. 2:13). If we are faithful to God's Word, He will be faithful to us by empowering our ministry and producing fruit in the lives of our counselees.

Instruction Should Be Biblically Accurate

Not only should our instruction be biblically based, but it should also be biblically accurate. If we do not take care to understand the Word of God accurately, we may end up giving instruction that sounds biblical but, in reality, is not. Paul tells us in 2 Timothy 2:15, "Be diligent to present yourself approved to God as a workman who does not need to be ashamed, handling accurately the word of truth." The verse implies that we can inaccurately or wrongly handle the Word of God, and to avoid doing that we must be "diligent." It takes hard work to accurately interpret the Scriptures and instruct others from them.[10]

Here are some suggestions to help guard against misusing the Scriptures and to ensure that our instruction is indeed accurate.

Know the meaning of biblical words. Some words in Scripture are not used in common, ordinary language today, and others that are used

---

8. J. C. Ryle, *Practical Religion* (Cambridge: James Clark, 1959), 81.

9. A contemporary book that contains helpful discussions of these attributes of Scripture is Noel Weeks, *The Sufficiency of Scripture* (Carlisle, Penn.: Banner of Truth, 1988). See also John MacArthur, Jr., *Our Sufficiency in Christ* (Dallas: Word Publishing, 1991).

10. Two other verses that emphasize the danger of using the Scriptures inaccurately in our ministry to others are 1 Tim. 1:8 where Paul says that "the Law is good if one uses it lawfully" and Mark 7:13 where Jesus speaks of those who make void the Word of God by adding to it their own traditions.

commonly have a different meaning than they do in the Bible. We need to take care not to read our understanding of a particular word into a text and assume that is what the Bible means.

For example, when we use the word *hope*, it means something very different from the biblical word. When a girl has a hope chest, she is longing for things that may or may not happen in the future. And we say, "I hope it doesn't rain today," when the clouds indicate that it is likely to do so. There is much uncertainty in our use of the word hope. But this is not so in Scripture—there the word hope speaks of a confident anticipation of an event that *will* most certainly come to pass.[11]

Two biblical words we seldom use in our everyday speech are *justify* and *justification*. I cannot remember the last time I heard somebody use either of those words other than in a theological discussion. Many people, therefore, have no idea what those words mean. If they have heard the word *justify*, it has probably been used in the sense of, "He was trying to justify himself" (meaning that he was making an excuse), and that is not what Scripture means when it talks about justification.

Sanctification, repentance, propitiation, regeneration, meekness, and even *wisdom* are all examples of important biblical words that are not commonly used and thus are often misunderstood. An effective biblical counselor must be able to explain the meaning of such words to counselees to help them understand what they read in Scripture. A comprehensive Bible dictionary or *Vine's Expository Dictionary of New Testament Words* are useful tools for this purpose. The latter book, and its Old Testament counterpart, provide meanings of words in the original Greek and Hebrew languages.[12]

Determine the meaning of a verse (passage) within its context. Instructing someone with verses taken out of the proper context can be as damaging as adding to the Scriptures. Although the idea the counselor is trying to communicate may be true, careless techniques of interpretation can set a bad example for counselees.

Proverbs 23:7 is an example of a verse that is commonly lifted out of its context for counseling purposes.[13] In the King James Version that verse

---

11. See chapter 11, page 190–99 for a further discussion of this concept.

12. Two other tools that would be helpful are A. T. Robertson, *Word Pictures in the New Testament*, 6 vols. (Nashville: Broadman, 1930); and *The New International Dictionary of New Testament Theology*, 3 vols. ed. Colin Brown (Grand Rapids: Zondervan, 1975).

13. This is a pertinent example because the book of Proverbs is one of the few books in Scripture where we normally do not have to worry about context (because it is made up of mostly short, unrelated sayings). But this example proves that even when we are quoting a proverb, we need to examine the context to see if we are using it correctly.

says, "As a man thinks in his heart, so is he." Commonly, this is interpreted to mean that our thought life determines who we are, or that whatever we think about we will become. Thus many Christian books (even many on counseling) will emphasize the importance of one's thoughts by referring to this verse.

It is certainly true that thoughts are important and that they do influence our character greatly, but that is not what Proverbs 23:7 is saying. Look at the verse in its full context: "Do not eat the bread of a selfish man, or desire his delicacies; *for as he thinks within himself, so he is.* He says to you, 'Eat and drink!' But his heart is not with you. You will vomit up the morsel you have eaten, and waste your compliments" (Prov. 23:6–8, emphasis added). The helpful insight for counseling from that verse is entirely different from the one commonly perceived. It reveals that sometimes a person's actions are really not the same as that person's thoughts. People may think one way and behave another for the purposes of deception and manipulation. So if we want to know the truth about someone's character, we cannot judge merely on the basis of actions; we would have to find out what that person is thinking.

If I want to instruct my counselees about the importance of their thought lives, I take them to Romans 12:2 or 2 Corinthians 10:5, because those verses, in their contexts, are discussing that issue. I do not want to go to a verse like Proverbs 23:7 that is not speaking about that issue, because I am as concerned about teaching a correct method of interpreting the Scriptures as I am about teaching specific biblical truth. And if I use the Scriptures loosely by making them say whatever I want them to say, I am teaching my counselees an illegitimate method of Bible interpretation. The Bible is God's book, and we must be careful to represent each part of it with the meaning God intended for that part. Also, every text of Scripture has only one intended meaning. It may have many applications, but it has only one meaning. Therefore, we need to discover the one meaning of the text before we apply it in the lives of our counselees.[14]

Interpret every passage in harmony with the rest of Scripture. Not only is the immediate context surrounding a phrase or verse important, but the larger context of the whole Bible is also crucial in understanding

---

14. When we approach a passage, we need to ask the questions "What is the Holy Spirit trying to communicate in this passage?" and "What does He want to accomplish through it?" And rather than just launching into our study of a passage assuming we are able to ascertain its meaning, we ought to pray, "Holy Spirit, this is Your book, You gave it to us. Please help me to understand this part of it correctly. Help me to learn what You meant to say in it."

the meaning of a particular passage. Scripture never contradicts itself, so if we find something in one passage of Scripture that seems to be out of accord with what other passages have to say about that subject, it is likely that our understanding of the differing passage is wrong.

For example, in 1 Corinthians 15:29 Paul speaks of those who are "baptized for the dead." Based on that verse the Mormon Church encourages people to be baptized for the dead. The problem with this interpretation (besides the fact that 1 Corinthians 15:29 is an obscure and difficult passage) is that the rest of the Word of God says a lot about baptism without ever mentioning baptism by proxy. And other theological considerations negate the possibility that Paul could be teaching this Mormon practice (cf. Luke 16:26; Heb. 9:27).

Another example is the husband I once counseled who thought he had absolute authority over his wife. He told me that he believed his wife was obligated to do whatever he told her, even if what he told her to do was sinful.

"Do you mean that if you were to tell your wife to shoot somebody, she would be obligated to do it?" I asked him.

"Well, I would never do that," he answered. "But yes, if I told her to do it, then she would have to do it."

"On what do you base that?" I asked.

"I base that on Ephesians 5 where it says that the wives are to submit to their husbands in everything," was his reply. "And everything means everything."

However, other passages in Scripture make it clear that Paul did not mean "everything without exception" in that passage. "Everything you can do without sinning against God" is closer to his meaning. The only absolute authority in a Christian's life is the Lord; a husband's authority is secondary and is derived from the Lord Himself. So if a husband tells his wife to sin against God, she will have to respond to him as the apostles did when they told the Jewish authorities, "We must obey God rather than men" (Acts 5:29).[15]

If that husband had understood the Reformation principle of *analogia scriptura* (Scripture interprets Scripture), he would not have erred so griev-

---

15. Governmental authority is similar to a husband's. First Peter 2:13 says, "Submit yourselves to every ordinance of man" (KJV), but it was the author of that book who led the stand against the authorities in Acts 5. For a thorough discussion of the submission required of a wife, see *Rediscovering Biblical Manhood and Womanhood*, ed. John Piper and Wayne Grudem (Wheaton: Crossway Books, 1991); and Wayne A. Mack, *Strengthening Your Marriage* (Harmony, Penn.: Presbyterian and Reformed, 1977).

ously in his theology on that issue. Likewise, counselors must take care to instruct people accurately by comparing each passage with the rest of God's revelation.

Biblical instruction must be Christocentric and evangelical in emphasis. Counseling instruction should always be focused on Christ and the glorious truth of His gospel (or evangel). Charles Spurgeon used to say that every text in the Word of God is like the roads in England. He said if you followed the roads in England far enough, eventually they would all bring you to London. And if you follow every text in Scripture far enough, it will eventually lead you to Jesus Christ. Martin Luther said that the Bible is the royal chariot in which Jesus rides, and the swaddling clothes in which He is wrapped. He also said, "Faith is, as it were, the center of a circle. If anybody strays from the center, it is impossible for him to have the circle around him, and he must blunder. The center is Christ."[16]

Christ is the Word (John 1:1), and He is the central focus of the Word. Therefore, our counseling instruction is not biblical unless it exalts Jesus Christ. It is not enough for us to espouse certain principles and regulations for living, because that would be pure behaviorism. If our counseling is truly biblical, people should not come away from it saying merely, "The Bible is a wonderful book"—they should also come away saying, "What a wonderful Savior we have." We should labor in all of our instruction to point our counselees to Jesus Christ, and we will be successful in this if we can help them to behold "the Lamb of God who takes away the sin of the world!" (John 1:29).

Use instruction that is action-oriented. Our instruction will not be biblically accurate unless its purpose is to produce godly actions. It is not enough merely to provide information or to communicate facts to our counselees. Our goal is not to encourage them to learn Scripture so they can win theological arguments—we want the truth we teach them to change their lives and make them more like Christ.

In Colossians 1:9 Paul says, "We have not ceased to pray for you and to ask that you may be filled with the knowledge of His will in all spiritual wisdom and understanding." Why did he ask that they would be instructed about God's will? Verse 10 says, "So that you may walk in a manner worthy of the Lord, to please Him in all respects, bearing fruit in every good work." And when Jesus gave the Great Commission, He told us not merely to pass on information about Him to others but to be "teaching them to observe all that I commanded you" (Matt. 28:20).

---

16. From *Luther's Works*, vol. 54 (Philadelphia: Fortress Press, 1967), 45.

Our goal in giving instruction should be the same as that of Paul and Jesus. If it does not challenge our counselees to godly action, it is not truly biblical. Biblical counselors would do well to follow the advice Martyn Lloyd-Jones gave to preachers:

> Having isolated your doctrine in this way and, having got it quite clear in your own mind, you then proceed to consider the relevance of this particular doctrine to the people who are listening to you. The question of relevance must never be forgotten. . . . You are not an antiquary lecturing on ancient history or on ancient civilisations, or something like that. The preacher [and counselor] is a man who is speaking to people who are alive today and confronted by the problems of life; and therefore you have to show that this is not some academic or theoretical matter which may be of interest to people who take up that particular hobby, as others take up crossword puzzles or something of that type. You are to show that this message is vitally important for them, and that they must listen with the whole of their being, because this really is going to help them to live."[17]

Emphasize both the positive and negative dimensions of biblical change. Biblical change is always a two-factor process—it involves both "putting off" and "putting on" (Eph. 4:22–32). For our instruction to be biblically accurate, we must not merely tell people what they should not do but also what they *should* do, and vice versa. We need to help them replace old, sinful habits with godly ones. Because biblical counselors see the necessity of addressing sin in the lives of counselees, they can focus too much on the negative aspect of "putting off." They tell counselees, "Don't do this," or "Stop doing that," but, unfortunately, this leaves a vacuum in counselees' lives because they do not know the positive counterpart: what they should do. On the other hand, we would be equally wrong in some cases to simply exhort our counselees to do good. It may often be necessary to find out what sins are keeping them from doing what is right before we can instruct them in that regard (cf. Heb. 12:1). We must consistently strive to balance the positive and negative aspects of instruction.

Distinguish between divine directives and human suggestions. Our counsel will not be biblically accurate if we confuse God's principles with our own ideas. Yet we can fall into this temptation easily in trying to help people. For instance, some pastors have misrepresented Hebrews 10:25 in

---

17. D. Martyn Lloyd-Jones, *Preaching and Preachers* (Grand Rapids: Zondervan, 1971), 76.

a sincere attempt to get people to come to church more often. While the verse simply says that it is wrong to be "forsaking our own assembling together, as is the habit of some," pastors quote it to encourage their members to be in church not only Sunday morning, but also Sunday night, Wednesday night, and every other time there is a service.

True, every Christian needs to be involved in the services of the church, and I believe we need to be there as often as we possibly can. I also believe that in some counseling cases we need to encourage people to attend every service because that will help meet their particular spiritual needs. But we cannot conclude that anyone who does not come to every service is unspiritual and disobedient to God. That would be a human idea added to Scripture, because Hebrews 10:25 does not say, "Go to every service." It simply says, "Do not forsake the assembling." We can fulfill that command without being at every service, and in some cases it is best for the individual not to attend every service. For instance, a woman who has an unsaved husband may find that he objects to her being out on Sunday or Wednesday evenings, and it may be God's will for her to be at home ministering to him on those nights (cf. 1 Pet. 3:1–6).

Another example of confusing divine directives with human suggestions would be a counselor who quotes Ephesians 5:16 ("making the most of your time, because the days are evil") and tells counselees that they need to schedule every hour each week by filling out a block diagram. This type of procedure may be helpful to a particular counselee, but the counselor should not require it of every person or otherwise imply that God requires every one to adhere to a time schedule. On the contrary, the counselor should be careful to communicate that the schedule is the counselor's suggestion; it is not a divine imperative. The counselor may explain that this is one possible application of the truth of Ephesians 5:16, but that the verse itself is teaching only that we should use our time wisely.

We need to understand the distinction between God's truth and man's ideas, and we also need to be careful not to read any application of a text into the meaning of the text itself. Both are important steps toward ensuring the biblical accuracy of counseling instruction.

Instruction Should Be Biblically Appropriate

Counseling instruction should not only be biblically based and biblically accurate, but it should also be appropriate for each particular counselee in both content and method.

The content of instruction should be appropriate. I have seen some counselors prepare beforehand what they are going to say to a counselee, and then proceed to share that instruction without confirming that it is relevant to the person's needs. This is a waste of time, because even though the counsel may have been biblical and accurate, it did not contribute to the process of change in that particular case. In order to avoid this error, we must be aware of pertinent aspects of each counselee's situation and use that information to tailor the instruction accordingly.

First, our instruction should be appropriate to the counselees' *immediate concerns*. Although we may feel that they need a certain instruction (which they are not aware of and are not asking for), it is best to instruct them initially about the issues they have raised, and then build a bridge to the crucial issues we believe need to be addressed. Begin where they are and lead them to where they ought to be.

We also need to consider our counselees' *emotional conditions*. We may need to determine what instruction they can handle emotionally at a particular point in counseling. For instance, someone who is upset emotionally is usually not ready to hear strong rebuke nor to respond to it properly. (That was true in the case of Clara in chapter 10.) In such cases, we should seek first to bring the counselee to a point of emotional stability before we confront that individual more directly.

Biblically appropriate instruction also takes into account the *spiritual maturity* of counselees. Hebrews 5:12–14 makes clear that some Christians are immature and can receive only spiritual "milk," but others are mature and can handle "solid food." And just as a math teacher cannot take a student from number counting to calculus in one giant step, so we cannot expect a counselee who is used to spiritual baby food to manage a filet mignon. With those who are not spiritually mature, we need to gradually and gently build up to deep truths.

Finally, in order for our instruction to be appropriate we must be aware of our counselees' *receptivity to counsel*. Jesus said, "Do not give what is holy to dogs, and do not throw your pearls before swine, lest they trample them under their feet, and turn and tear you to pieces" (Matt. 7:6). There may be times when you are presenting truth to your counselees and you discern that they are resistant to it. At that point it is prudent to back off from that particular line of instruction rather than beating them over the head with it or ending up in fruitless debate (cf. Titus 3:9–10). If you discuss another issue with them for a while, perhaps God will open their hearts in the previous area and you can return to it later in that session or in another.

The method of instruction should be appropriate. Counseling instruction needs to fit the counseling situation, particularly in the method of communicating that instruction. Jesus, the master counselor and teacher, used many different methods of instruction (cf. Matt. 5:1–2; 16:13–20; 21:19–21), as did the apostles (cf. Luke 1:3–4; Acts 20:31). Biblical counselors have many methods of communication at their disposal, methods that are consistent with the biblical model of those great teachers. Some of the instruction will be done in the counseling session and some can be done outside of the session through various types of homework.[18] The following list presents a variety of ways to communicate the truth of Scripture to counselees:

lecture:	Counselor gives instruction from the Scriptures about a particular issue in the session.
observation:	Counselees observe counselor or someone else who is a good model in the areas where they struggle.
experience:	Counselees learn by doing.[19]
research:	Counselees complete study assignments on topics that are relevant to their problems.
discussion:	Counselees talk openly about the issue with the counselor and other knowledgeable people.
questions:	Counselor uses the Socratic method to lead counselees to a conclusion through their own responses.
reading assignments:	Counselees read assigned books (or listen to tapes) and write down what they learned. (This can be done during the counseling session or as homework).
evaluation:	Counselees evaluate and assess a statement, idea, or practice.

---

18. See chapter 12, footnote 26.

19. This is such an important method of instruction that it is really not optional. Scripture teaches that we cannot truly learn without doing (cf. James 1:22–25), and so it is never enough for us to simply heap information on our counselees. We need to give them opportunities (in the sessions and through homework assignments) to put the knowledge that they are acquiring into practice.

self-disclosure:	Counselor relates personal experiences relevant to counselees' problems.
illustration:	Counselor uses examples to help counselees understand a truth or to challenge them to think more deeply about it.
role-playing:	Counselor acts out instances of interaction between people to demonstrate examples of effective communication and the consequences of poor communication.
interviews:	Counselees are encouraged to ask questions of people who are knowledgeable in a particular area or who have otherwise excelled in it.

Using a wide variety of instructional methods is helpful because people learn in many different ways, and some people learn better in one way than another. For instance, some learn better listening to tapes than they would reading a book; others learn far more through observation than they would in either of those ways. The counselor should try to identify the method or methods of instruction that seem to be most beneficial for each counselee.[20]

HOW TO DEVELOP A KNOWLEDGE OF SCRIPTURE

The Bible is God's fully furnished medicine cabinet; it contains the remedy for all the spiritual problems we face in life. But just as no one medicine will cure all of our physical problems, so no one passage in the Word of God will cure all of our spiritual problems. A good physician or pharmacist has to know which medicine to use for each health problem, and biblical counselors must know what portions of the Word of God to apply to each counselee's problem. Therefore, in order to be effective, a biblical counselor must have a thorough knowledge of the Scriptures.

While there are numerous ways a counselor can develop a knowledge of Scripture even while involved in counseling, we suggest these

---

20. The following verses would be helpful for a further study of the biblical manner of instruction: Prov. 15:1, 4; 16:21, 24; Acts 20:31; Gal. 6:1; 1 Thess. 4:9–10; 1 Tim. 3:3; 4:6; 5:1–2; 6:2, 13; 2 Tim. 1:6; 2:16–17, 23–24; 4:1; Titus 2:6–9, 15; 3:1.

three: (1) develop a topical work list, (2) produce a personalized chain-referenced Bible, and (3) utilize training resources.

Develop A Topical Work List

Over the years, I have accumulated a wealth of valuable information in a simple notebook. I started this project by writing the names of specific problems or issues that I wanted to understand at the top of blank sheets of notebook paper. As I encountered new problems in counseling, I added more pages to the notebook. Then as I read and studied the Word of God, or listened to others teach and learned something that applied to one or more of those problems, I wrote that biblical reference or insight on the appropriate page. After many years of compiling these notes, I now have at least one page of biblical information about almost any problem that I encounter in counseling. This topical work list has proven to be both a tremendous stimulus for learning, as well as a helpful resource for instruction.[21]

Produce a Personalized Chain-Referenced Bible

When you complete a topical study of a particular issue in Scripture, make a prioritized list of the appropriate verses beginning with the verse you want to refer to first when you deal with that particular issue. Find that verse in your Bible and in the margin next to it write verse number two and so on. With this system you can walk through the pertinent passages on a particular issue any time you need to.

For example, suppose you are trying to help someone who is having trouble sleeping, and you want to instruct them initially by showing them what Scripture says about sleep. If you have created a counselor's chain reference for that subject, you can open your Bible to the first verse about sleep. (It would be helpful to have an index of "first verses," perhaps in the front of your Bible.) After you read that first verse and discuss it, you can then turn to the reference of the second verse and do the same with that passage. Using this chain-referenced system you can work your way through strategic Bible verses on the subject of sleep.

---

21. It is helpful to accumulate ideas for homework assignments in a similar fashion. Place a list of assignments that relate to a particular problem in a notebook next to biblical information on that problem so those ideas will be easily accessible in the counseling session.

Utilize Training Resources

Your knowledge of Scripture and how to use it in counseling can grow by learning from others. Helpful resources include organizations that are devoted to biblical counseling, such as The Master's College and Seminary, the National Association of Nouthetic Counselors, and the Christian Counseling and Educational Foundation.[22] These organizations offer training seminars and conferences each year, and NANC and the Christian Counseling and Educational Foundation publish periodicals about biblical counseling.[23]

Books about biblical counseling are another valuable resource. Also, check local libraries for commentaries, systematic theologies, and other reference works. Audio tapes and video tapes can also provide beneficial information for the counselor and some can serve as homework for counselees.[24]

CONCLUSION

Let me share two final suggestions concerning instruction in counseling. First, the biblical counselor should be extremely hesitant to give instruction on biblical issues that he or she has not studied. If we do not know about something, we should never act as though we do. What we should say in that instance is, "I am not sure what the Bible teaches about that subject, but I will do some research on it and share with you what I discover next week." Do not be embarrassed if you are not sure about a particular issue. Seek help from books and other counselors and take the opportunity to learn and grow in that area.

The second suggestion is that the counselor should practice team counsel whenever possible. Of course this is not always possible because of the lack of counselors and the prevalence of problems, but it is certainly a

---

22. NANC's address is 5526 SR 26 East, Lafayette, Indiana 47905. Two of CCEF's east coast addresses are 2299 Brodhead Road, Bethlehem, Pennsylvania 18017 and 1803 East Willow Grove Avenue, Laverock, Pennsylvania 19118. There is also a west coast Christian Counseling and Educational Foundation located at 3495 College Avenue, San Diego, California 92115.

23. NANC publishes *The Biblical Counselor* (monthly), and CCEF publishes *The Journal of Biblical Counseling* (quarterly; formerly known as *The Journal of Pastoral Practice*).

24. See chapter 20 for a more complete listing of resources for counselor development as well as resources for counselees.

good idea. One of my former students wrote this note after I had sat in on a counseling session with him. I think it states well the benefit of team counseling.

> I found it very helpful when you interacted with us toward the end of the session. It first showed me how you deal with this kind of situation and it also helped the counselee to understand the concept much more clearly after you had explained it to him in your way. This made me really think about team counseling. I can imagine that in many difficult cases team counseling could be of great help. I think that as an observer you often see things that the one involved in counseling misses. I sometimes think that I still miss too much data because I'm too concentrated on my interaction with the counselee. I think that one of the hardest parts in counseling is to interact well with the counselee at the moment and still be able to conceptualize what's going on in the whole counseling process.

If you can team up with another biblical counselor or conduct a training program in which the students are able to participate in sessions, you will find that a second person's input can be most helpful to the process of instruction. We need to challenge ourselves to communicate biblical truth clearly and consistently. Above all, we must always remember that "the goal of our instruction is love from a pure heart and a good conscience and a sincere faith" (1 Tim. 1:5).

15

Biblical Counseling and Inducement

Wayne A. Mack

Change does not occur by chance but by choice. Many people talk about wanting to solve their problems and change for the better, but only some are willing to make the commitment necessary to accomplish those things. Proverbs 14:23 says, "In all labor there is profit, but mere talk leads only to poverty." Biblical counseling must take people beyond talk to action, and an essential part of that process is *inducement*.

Defining Inducement

In biblical counseling the term inducement means to motivate counselees to make biblical decisions conducive to change. This motivation includes the following processes:

1. *Help counselees to accept personal responsibility for their desires and motivations, thoughts, attitudes, feelings, words, and actions.* Counselees need to stop blaming circumstances and people for their problems; they need to realize that through the resources available in Christ they can change .

2. *Bring counselees to the realization that biblical change involves personal choice.* People will never change until they decide they want to change. In fact, the reason people fail to change, when God has provided the resources for change, is often because they have decided to remain in a defeated state. When they say "I can't," they really mean "I won't."

3. *Promote a concern about heart sins as well as behavioral sins.* Godly, biblical change in behavior must always begin with a change in the heart. God calls us to rend our hearts not merely our garments; to purify our

hearts as well as to cleanse our hands; and to honor and seek Him with our hearts not only our lips. He wants us to repent about heart sins (thoughts, attitudes, desires, motives, intentions) and not just be sorry for unbiblical actions or reactions. Nothing less than heart repentance and heart change will please God and produce change that is genuine and lasting.[1]

4. *Secure a commitment from counselees to put off the desires, thoughts, and actions that hinder biblical change and to replace them with ones that promote biblical change.* To a great degree, counseling is truly successful only when this goal is achieved.

All that we have discussed in the last five chapters finds its culmination in the goal of encouraging counselees to commit themselves to biblical thoughts and behavior in every area of their lives. In counseling, we may have been faithful in implementing all the previously described principles, yet inducement may still prove difficult. Hopefully, this chapter will serve as a guide for the biblical counselor as he or she seeks to overcome such difficulties and secure a godly commitment from the counselee.

Defining Commitment

What is the biblical commitment we are seeking from our counselees? A biblical commitment will include at least six factors. These are described below under the acronym A-C-C-E-P-T.

A—*Acknowledge personal responsibility for thoughts and actions.* Counselees will not be able to change as long as they excuse, blame, rationalize, or defend their sinful behavior. We must help them to understand that regardless of their circumstances. If they are Christians, they can respond biblically through the power of the Holy Spirit.

C—*Choose to look at circumstances in the past and present from a biblical point of view.* Human wisdom and feelings often hinder people from looking at things the way God wants them to. They need to interpret their circumstances through the lens of Scripture rather than through their own opinions and emotions.

C—*Commit to eliminate whatever hinders biblical change.* Romans 13:14 says, "Put on the Lord Jesus Christ, and make no provision for the

---

1. Cf. Joel 2:13; James 4:8; Ps. 139:13; 51:17; Ezek. 14:1–9; Jer. 3:10; 4:4; 29:13; Matt. 5:8; 15:8, 9; Acts 8:21; Rom. 2:5, 29; 2 Tim. 1:5; Heb. 4:12.

flesh in regard to its lusts." If a counselee has a problem with lust, that person must commit to destroy seductive materials, to stop watching television programs or movies with sexual content, and to avoid places that encourage temptation. A counselee must be willing to remove any obstruction to biblical change.

E—*Exert energy toward the goal.* Change is not an automatic overnight occurrence; it is hard work. The counselee will not make progress if there is no willingness to put effort into changing.

P—*Persevere in obedience.* Some people are ready to quit after two or three weeks if they do not see substantial progress. Therefore, counselees need to be reminded of the truth of Hebrews 10:36: "You have need of endurance, so that when you have done the will of God, you may receive what was promised." Change takes time, so counselees need to know that the counselor will meet with them for at least six or seven weeks before evaluating their progress.

T—*Trust God for the strength and resources to change.* Paul says in Philippians 2:12–13, "Work out your salvation with fear and trembling; for it is God who is at work in you, both to will and to work for His good pleasure." It is true, people who want to make biblical changes in their lives must work, but they must work trusting in Christ to provide the strength and resources necessary to make those changes. Without Him, living the Christian life and making godly changes is not only difficult, it is impossible. But when we look away from ourselves and trust Him, He enables us to do the impossible. He enables us to put off the old self, which is corrupt through deceitful desires, and to put on the new self, which is being renewed in true righteousness and holiness. As counselees commit themselves to obey Christ completely, they can be confident that the mighty power of God will accomplish His work of change in their lives.[2]

Sometimes a mere explanation of the essence of biblical commitment is not enough in counseling. If a counselor has reason to doubt a person's understanding of commitment and dedication to it, it can be helpful to ask that person to write out his or her commitment. Then, if necessary, help the person to modify that commitment according to biblical criteria. The counselor can also use the written commitment as a tool for account-

---

2. Phil. 4:13; John 15:1–16; 2 Cor. 9:8; Jude 24, 25; Heb. 12:1–4; Eph. 4:22–24; Col. 3:1–14; Matt. 19:26; 2 Cor. 7:1; 3:18.

ability if the counselee begins to waver. It can serve as a reminder of what was promised to the Lord.

HOW TO MOTIVATE COUNSELEES TOWARD COMMITMENT

Biblical counselors should make use of every legitimate means to motivate counselees to make a decisive commitment to obey the Lord. The Scripture provides much insight into how we can do this in a manner that pleases God.

Two Approaches to Motivation

A man-centered approach. People can be motivated through their control points—the things that are most important to them. They can be manipulated to act a certain way when they believe their satisfaction in strategic areas is guaranteed by those actions. That is why advertisers spend enormous amounts of time and money studying the control points—they want to find out what compels people to buy products. Not surprisingly, commercials are designed to promise the consumer that the product will fulfill his or her desires. Why are scantily clad women used to advertise everything from beer to automobiles? Because sexual fulfillment is a control point for many people. The products and the seductive women basically have no relation to one another, but the latter appeals to a control point and thus increases sales.

The desire for money is another control point for many people. So advertisements for Toyota appealed to that desire by asking the question, "What will you do with all the money you save?" The company sold thousands of cars on the basis of saving money instead of focusing on the virtue of the car itself.

Other people desire acceptance or approval. So businesses make promises like, "If you brush with this toothpaste, girls will come knocking at your door!" or "WARNING—This perfume causes boys to flock around you."

What is the effect of this type of man-centered motivation? Although it often induces the action desired, the emphasis is on personal satisfaction. Therefore, it encourages people to be concerned primarily with their own desires and with the visible, tangible, earthly things they think will satisfy them. Biblical counselors should never motivate people in a way that encourages this kind of idolatry (cf. 1 John 2:15–17). Man-centered motivation may induce a particular behavior, but the motives behind that action will be sinful and thus will make even the behavior unacceptable to God.

A God-centered approach. Biblical counselors want to take a God-centered approach in motivating people. Romans 11:36 says, "For from Him and through Him and to Him are all things. To Him be the glory forever." True change takes place when people make choices primarily for the purpose of bringing glory to God rather than seeking to meet their own needs. The focus of God-centered motivation is primarily on the immaterial not the material, the invisible rather than the visible, the eternal rather than the temporal (Matt. 6:33; 2 Cor. 4:18; Col. 3:1).

Paul's Method of Motivation

Many Scriptures teach us how to apply biblical principles of inducement, but none more clearly and thoroughly than Romans 6:1–14.[3] The apostle Paul's goal in that passage is to bring about a commitment to change in his readers (vv. 1–2). It will be helpful for us to see just how he pursues that goal.

1. **Paul motivated his readers through indicative statements about their position in Christ.**[4] In verses 3–10 he teaches that believers are free to change through identification with the Lord Jesus Christ. He says that we have been united with Christ in His death, burial, and resurrection—therefore we have "died to sin" and risen to "live with Him." Being dead to sin means that sin no longer reigns in our lives; the dominating power of sin has been shattered. Verse 7 says, "He who has died has been *freed* from sin." And living with Christ refers to the new power that is available in a new life in Christ. Through this power the believer is able to conquer any temptation or sin of the flesh (cf. Rom. 8:37).[5]

Paul understood that in order to change Christians need to be aware of their position in Christ and the resources available through Him. The

---

3. Cf. 2 Chron. 20:13; Ps. 57:7; Matt. 25:24–28; Luke 15:11–18; 1 Cor. 6:19–20; Gal. 5:1; Eph. 4:1–3; 1 Pet. 4:1–2.

4. *Indicative* refers to statements of fact, as opposed to *imperative* (commands), or *interrogative* (questions).

5. John Murray writes, "The future tense, 'we shall live' does not refer exclusively to the future resurrection state but, as found above (cf. v. 5), points to the certainty of participation in the resurrection life of Christ here and now; it is the life of Spiritual, mystical union." *The New International Commentary on the New Testament—Romans*, ed. G. D. Fee (Grand Rapids: Eerdmans, 1990), 223.

tendency is to see oneself as a helpless victim under the powerful control of sin. But as biblical counselors, we can say to Christians (on the authority of God's Word) that they have the ability to overcome any sinful pattern of thought or behavior. This ability comes only from the Holy Spirit (Gal. 5:16) as a result of our union with Christ. It is on that basis alone that we can call for commitment from people to obey God in their thoughts and actions, as Paul does in verses 11–14.

2. **Paul motivated his readers through imperative commands to live out their position in Christ.** Verse 11 says, "Even so consider yourselves to be dead to sin, but alive to God in Christ Jesus." Though we may not feel dead to sin, God said that we are dead to sin, and we must accept that by faith. The Greek word translated "consider" is an accounting term that means "to record something as fact." Paul commands his readers to think rightly about themselves and their actions in light of the truth he has taught them about their union with Christ. Then he goes beyond thoughts and calls for a commitment regarding actions: "Therefore do not let sin reign in your mortal body that you should obey its lusts, and do not go on presenting the members of your body to sin as instruments of unrighteousness; but present yourselves to God as those alive from the dead, and your members as instruments of righteousness to God" (vv. 12–13).

As John MacArthur, Jr. says,

> The key word is *yield*, or present (v. 13), which obviously has to do with the will. Because of the incomprehensible truths about his relationship to God that the believer knows with his mind and feels deeply committed to in his heart, he is therefore able to exercise his will successfully against sin and, by God's power, prevent its reign in his mortal body.
>
> In this present life, sin will always be a powerful force for the Christian to reckon with. But it is no longer master, no longer lord, and it can and must be resisted. Sin is personified by Paul as a dethroned but still powerful monarch who is determined to reign in the believer's life just as he did before salvation. The apostle's admonition to believers, therefore, is for them to not let sin reign, because it now has no right to reign. It now has no power to control a believer unless a believer chooses to obey its lusts.[6]

Paul concludes his call to commitment in verse 14 by reiterating the believer's position in Christ: "For sin shall not be master over you, for you

---

6. John MacArthur, Jr., *The MacArthur New Testament Commentary: Romans 1–8* (Chicago: Moody, 1991), 336–337.

are not under law, but under grace." He never wants to let his readers forget that only by the grace of God can they keep their commitments to Him.

Divine Motivation for Moses

Chapters 3 and 4 of Exodus contain another helpful example of biblical, God-centered inducement. In this passage, God convinces Moses to commit to something that Moses does not want to do—lead the people of Israel out of Egypt. How did God motivate Moses? Notice that God did not focus on Moses' control points—fleshly desires or sinful pride—but, rather, on Himself and His own glory.

One way God motivated Moses was through His *promises* (cf. 3:8, 12, 17–18). When people understand the character of God—His faithfulness, honesty, and absolute holiness—they discover that His promises are towers of strength in which they can take refuge. I have seen God use His promises in people's lives as an encouragement when all other counseling efforts seemed futile. We need to explain God's promises to people and apply those promises in a practical and relevant way.

God also motivated Moses by giving him *concrete and attainable goals* (cf. 4:15–17). He told Moses exactly what He wanted him to accomplish; He did not overload Moses with unattainable goals. Often, counselees are not motivated simply because the goals presented to them are unclear or are intimidating. They are not sure what they are being asked to do, and they are not sure whether they can accomplish it.

God also gave Moses *specific instructions* about how to accomplish those goals (cf. 3:14–22). Counseling falls short if people do not know how to achieve the things we challenge them to do.

Moses was motivated when God showed him *evidences of divine power* (cf. 4:1–8). When Moses threw his staff to the ground, God turned it into a snake. When Moses picked it up by the tail, it became a staff again. Then God told Moses to put his hand in his bosom, and it became leprous like snow. Sometimes, counselors must remind people of the mighty power of God. A vision of God's great power from the Scriptures or personal experience is sometimes all that is needed to motivate a counselee to action.

God also motivated Moses by *redirecting his focus* (cf. 4:10–12). Moses used his own inadequacy as an excuse for not doing what he had been called to do, but God redirected his outlook from human inadequacy to divine sufficiency. God affirmed to Moses the divine ability to overcome any human deficiency. When Moses said he could not speak very well, God responded that He was the One who made mouths and He was able to empower them.

Moses was also motivated by a *description of God's character and plan* (cf. 3:15–18). God not only reminded Moses of who He was but also assured Moses of His Divine presence and help. In addition, God provided *someone to help* Moses in his task; He sent Aaron to speak for Moses (4:14–16). After God's repeated motivational efforts, Moses responded in obedience and committed himself to leading the Exodus from Egypt. Biblical counselors can also make use of effective principles of motivation, emulating (as necessary) God's persistence in applying them.[7]

Other Biblical Principles of Motivation

Outlined below are numerous principles of motivation that are found throughout Scripture. Biblical counselors are encouraged to use these principles to help their counselees make scriptural commitments.

a. Share your perception of what is happening in the situation (Gal. 2:11–14; Col. 2:9; 1 John 1:7).

b. Provide biblical information designed to eliminate specific reasons for resistance (Matt. 28:18–20).

c. Remind the counselee who God is (Prov. 8:13; Isa. 6:1–8; Heb. 11:24–26).

d. Help counselees reflect on who they are in Christ (Ps. 90:3–6; 100:3; Isa. 2:22; 40:12–17; Jer. 10:23).

e. Talk about the love and grace of Christ (2 Cor. 5:14; 8:7–9; 1 John 3:1–4; 4:9–11).

f. Expound the greatness of our resources in Christ (Rom. 8:34; 2 Cor. 9:8; 10:4–5; Eph. 1:3; Phil. 2:1).

g. Share the promises of God (Isa. 41:10; Matt. 6:33; 28:20; Heb. 13:5, 6; 2 Pet. 1:3, 4).

---

7. Another helpful illustration of biblical motivation is found in the book of Hebrews. The audience of that book includes people who are thinking of entering the Christian life and those who are about ready to give up on it, so the author is trying to motivate them to commit themselves to Christ or to persevere in that commitment. Throughout the book the author exhorts the reader by saying, "Let us . . ." (4:1, 11, 14, 16; 6:1; 10:22, 23, 24; 12:1, 28; 13:13, 15). Each of those verses yields additional insights about biblical principles of motivation.

h. Confirm the consequences of obedience (Ps. 1:1–3; 37:5–6; Prov. 3:5–6; Luke 11:28; John 13:17; Gal. 6:7–8; Eph. 6:1–3; 1 Tim. 4:7; James 1:25).

i. Give specific instructions about what the counselee should do and how he or she should do it (Matt. 5:21–26; Phil. 4:6–9).

j. Show the reasonableness of obedience (Isa. 1:18; Rom. 12:1).

k. Challenge and exhort counselees to choose to obey (Rom. 6:11–13, 19, 20; 1 Tim. 5:21, 6:13, 14, 17).

l. Teach counselees about God's benevolent desires and concerns for them (Ps. 100:4–5, 136; Jer. 29:11; Rom. 8:28; Eph 2:4).

m. Point out the consequences of disobedience (Prov. 5:22–23; 6:32–33; 7:22–23; 13:15; 16:5, 18; 29:1; Gal. 6:7–8).

n. Express astonishment at resistance (Isa. 1:2–9; Gal. 1:6; 3:1).

o. Recall the counselee's previous interest in obedience (2 Cor. 9:1–2; Gal. 3:1ff; Phil. 1:4–7; 2:12).

p. Show how God is affected by disobedience (Ps. 66:18; Eph. 4:30).

q. Express personal concern and love for the counselee (Phil. 1:3–8; 2:17; 4:1; 1 Thess. 2:8, 19; 3:1).

r. Liken inappropriate actions to those of unsaved people (Luke 6:27ff; 1 Cor. 5:1; Eph. 4:17).

s. Give information about proper values and priorities (Prov. 15:16–17).

t. Demonstrate how resistance may affect others (Prov. 15:25, 27; 19:13; 27:11; 1 Cor. 5:6, 7).

u. Warn about the Father's discipline (Heb. 12:4–14; 1 Cor. 11:27, 28).

v. Explain the Bible's teaching about church discipline (Matt. 18:15–17; 2 Thess. 3:10ff.; Titus 3:9–11; 1 Cor. 5:1–13).

w. Call attention to that day when the counselee will stand in the presence of God (Rom. 13:11–14; 14:10, 12; Heb. 9:26; 1 John 2:18; Matt. 16:26).

DEALING WITH RESISTANCE TO COMMITMENT

The amount of change a counselee experiences is directly proportional to his or her level of commitment. If the counselor identifies the problem accurately and gives proper biblical instruction, yet sees little or no progress, this often indicates a resistance to commitment. In such cases, biblical counselors must be equipped to recognize and overcome the resistance.

Recognizing Resistance

Two kinds of resistance are encountered in the counseling process: overt and covert. The rich young ruler serves as an example of overt resistance. In Mark 10:17–26, Jesus told him to do something and he simply was unwilling to do it. Sometimes I have asked people to commit themselves to their marriage, and they have refused. Others have been openly unwilling to forgive someone. This type of overt resistance is painfully obvious.

The most frequent kind of resistance, however, is covert resistance in which the counselee gives outward assent to commitment but is not willing to follow through with it. The story told by Jesus in Matthew 21:28–30 illustrates this kind of resistance:

> "But what do you think? A man had two sons, and he came to the first and said, 'Son, go work today in the vineyard.' And he answered and said, 'I will, sir'; and he did not go. And he came to the second and said the same thing. But he answered and said, 'I will not'; yet he afterward regretted it and went. Which of the two did the will of his father?"

The disciples answered, "the latter," and Jesus told them they were right. The first son, unfortunately, typifies many counselees. Initially they seem excited about solving their problems biblically, but eventually they prove resistant to the commitment necessary to change. The following symptoms of covert resistance will help the counselor identify when a counselee is not willing to make a commitment.

Absenteeism. A person who frequently cancels appointments, particularly for questionable reasons, may be avoiding confrontation. If this is a repeated pattern, the counselee may be unwilling to change. Chronic tardiness can also be a sign that the counselee is avoiding pertinent issues.

Failure to do homework. A second symptom of covert resistance is failure to complete homework assignments. A pattern of incomplete or sloppy homework may indicate that the counselee prefers talking to working.

Distancing. In instances of distancing, the counselee keeps the counselor at arm's length. When asked about his or her life, the counselee is unwilling to reveal detailed information. This reticence may indicate a lack of desire to change. Unfortunately, counselors cannot help people who shut them out of their lives.

Threats. Some counselees make threats. In subtle ways they communicate, "If you are not careful, I will not come back." They may even make physical threats. For instance, a man once told me, "There is no telling what I might do if I get angry." When he proceeded to tell me some of the things anyway, it was obvious he was warning me to be careful in dealing with him.

Intimidation. Some counselees may become antagonistic, others withdrawn, or even tearful when the counselor addresses a particular issue. In these instances it can be tempting to avoid discussing those areas, since it can be difficult to confront the emotions or behavior of the counselee.[8] However, the reason for the counselee's sensitivity needs to be discovered so the counselor will not be intimidated and drawn off track by emotional reactions.

Manipulation. There are various ways counselees may attempt to manipulate a counselor. They may cry, or they may flatter the counselor. Whatever the tactic used, these are attempts to sidetrack the discussion. If the counselor's pride is susceptible to this type of manipulation, the sessions can turn into a buddy-buddy time where no profitable counseling takes place.

Stories designed only to elicit sympathy, irrelevant arguments, and repeated descriptions of trivial occurrences are other ways that counselees may try to manipulate the counselor and avoid sensitive issues. This is extremely harmful, because by maneuvering the sessions away from the biblical answers to their problems, they actually multiply their pain. It is important for the biblical counselor to identify and eliminate manipulation, because as long as it dominates the counseling session the counselor will never be able to address the issues that are foundational to change.

When we recognize any of these symptoms of resistance to commitment, we can point them out to our counselees and ask them to explain their resistance in light of the verbal commitments they have made or the desires for change they have expressed. Hopefully, they will realize how they are hindering the Holy Spirit's work and their resistance to commitment will cease.

---

8. Those who exhibit such behavior have probably used this technique many times in the past and have found that it kept them safe from having to be honest and admit their sin.

Recognizing the Reasons for Resistance

In order to overcome resistance it is necessary to understand why the resistance is taking place and to address the foundational issues of the problem. Following are some possible causes of resistance.

An unregenerate heart. In Acts 7:51, Stephen told his accusers, "You men who are stiff-necked and uncircumcised in heart and ears are always resisting the Holy Spirit." The people he addressed were unsaved and therefore could not be motivated to change biblically. As 1 Corinthians 2:14 says, "A natural man does not accept the things of the Spirit of God; for they are foolishness to him, and he cannot understand them, because they are spiritually appraised." In order to induce commitment from people who are unregenerate, the counselor must become an evangelist, because those persons first need to commit themselves to the Lordship of Christ.

Repeated failure. If a counselee has tried to solve a problem repeatedly, the counselor may have to deal with severe discouragement. The key to overcoming discouragement is providing biblical hope.[9] The counselor needs to encourage the person that biblical counseling has something better to offer than the advice they received elsewhere.

Fear. Many times counselees are resistant to commitment because they are afraid. I once worked with a lady whose husband had recently committed adultery. He had also had an affair eleven years earlier. Since he had acknowledged sin and asked for forgiveness after the first affair, the woman had difficulty believing the sincerity of this present acknowledgement of sin and recommitment to faithfulness. Now she wanted a guarantee that he would not do it again. She was afraid to put herself back in the same situation she had experienced earlier. Her real problem was fear, and she needed help from the Scriptures to overcome it.

Pride. Counselees may find it difficult to ask forgiveness from those they have sinned against—an act that requires great humility. This difficulty is heightened if those others have sinned against them as well. Also, those who need to make a public confession may find pride holding them back from this commitment.

Ignorance. Unbiblical ideas about the Christian life can be another reason for resistance. For example, some people believe in complete passivity in the Christian life. They believe they are supposed to "let go and let God." I once read a pamphlet telling of a woman who claimed that when Satan knocked at her door, she would send Jesus to answer it. Such

---

9. For further details see Chapter 11.

a concept removes all personal responsibility, and, in essence, makes Jesus responsible for human failures. Paul writes in Philippians 4:13, "I can do all things through Him who strengthens me." In that verse the balance of Christian living is evident. Believers cannot have victory apart from Christ's power; yet victory does not come without effort. In fact, Paul teaches that victory comes as a result of diligent effort, but effort exerted only through the strength Christ provides through the Holy Spirit.[10]

Other people go astray because they misunderstand the relationship between obedience and feelings. They argue that obedience apart from feelings is legalism. Of course, seeking to earn or maintain salvation through human works is legalism, but obedience motivated by Jesus' love, His sacrificial death, and His gracious forgiveness is simply evangelical obedience. By obeying the Lord in spite of how we feel, we acknowledge that the Lord is more important than our feelings. We need to remember that feelings are the caboose that follows the engine of obedience. If we desire, think, and do what is right regardless of how we feel, our emotions will eventually come into line as a result of our decision to obey.

Though some might object that such obedience is hypocritical, it is not, because hypocrisy is feigned obedience—not obedience without feelings. Jesus condemned the hypocrisy of the Pharisees because they sought the praise of people instead of God (cf. Matt. 6:1–6; 16–18). Hypocrites have wrong motives behind their actions. In contrast, obeying God in spite of how one feels displays virtuous motives.[11]

Unbelief. People who doubt the sufficiency and power of the Word of God to effect change in their lives are, in reality, doubting God. They may be unwilling to make a commitment because they are not convinced that God is able to do what He says He will do. That unbelief, if not confronted and dealt with, will cause them to turn their backs on their only hope for change.

Bitterness. Bitterness and resentment may also trigger resistance. Some see bitterness as a means of getting even with others. So they refuse to talk with them, ask their forgiveness, or take other steps toward reconciliation. However, until these individuals are willing to accept God's providential purpose for what happened (Rom. 8:28) and are ready to forgive those who offended them (Ps. 86:5), the process of biblical change will be hampered.

---

10. For a helpful discussion of this issue, see the chapter entitled "A Balance of Faith and Effort" in John MacArthur, Jr. *Our Sufficiency in Christ* (Dallas: Word, 1991).

11. Consider Christ in the Garden of Gethsemane, for example (Matt. 26:36–44). At that time He certainly did not *feel like* obeying God and facing the agonies of the cross (vv. 37–38), but despite His feelings He prayed, "Not as I will, but as Thou wilt."

Improper commitments. Counselees may resist committing themselves to obey God's Word because they have already committed themselves to sinful patterns or fleshly pursuits and are unwilling to break with them. As Jesus said, "No one can serve two masters; for either he will hate the one and love the other, or he will hold to one and despise the other" (Matt. 6:24). Charles Spurgeon said about that verse: "This is often misunderstood. Some read it, 'No man can serve *two* masters.' Yes he can; he can serve three or four. The way to read it is this: 'No man can serve two *masters.*' He can serve two, but they cannot both be his master." [12]

Other reasons for resisting commitment can include shifting the blame, making excuses, or failing to take sin seriously. As biblical counselors, we need to identify the causes of resistance and deal with them before we can expect to secure a biblical commitment from our counselees.

MOTIVATION THROUGH CHURCH DISCIPLINE

What if we apply all of the principles discussed above and still are not able to induce a counselee to change? One more biblical method of motivation remains for people who continue to resist change over an extended period of time and who prove unwilling to make the commitments required of them by Scripture. Matthew 18:15–18 teaches that method by providing guidelines for formal church discipline:

> "If your brother sins, go and reprove him in private; if he listens to you, you have won your brother. But if he does not listen to you, take one or two more with you, so that by the mouth of two or three witnesses every fact may be confirmed. And if he refuses to listen to them, tell it to the church; and if he refuses to listen even to the church, let him be to you as a Gentile and a tax-gatherer. Truly I say to you, whatever you shall bind on earth shall be bound in heaven; and whatever you loose on earth shall be loosed in heaven."

The biblical counselor may initially become involved at either the first or second step of that process. [13] If those steps are carried out and yet

---

12. Tom Carter, *Spurgeon At His Best* (Grand Rapids: Baker, 1988), 263.

13. This is the reason for most marriage counseling. Many couples try without success to solve their problems by themselves and then need to find help outside their relationship. They should not be hesitant or feel ashamed to share their problems with a godly counselor, because in doing so they will be following the command Jesus gave in Matthew 18:16.

they fail to effect change, then the counselor must see that the remainder of Jesus' commands are obeyed as well.

When a counselee continues to sin after repeated confrontation, Jesus admonishes us to "tell it to the church."[14] At this point the individual is to be publicly rebuked, as 2 Thessalonians 3:14 and 1 Timothy 5:20 affirm. The local church body should be exhorted to withhold fellowship from that person and to call him or her to repentance. In speaking about the sinning person Paul says, "Do not regard him as an enemy, but admonish [or warn] him as a brother" (2 Thess. 3:15). The goal of discipline is not to punish but to promote restoration and reconciliation. And in some cases, church discipline is absolutely necessary in order for this to happen. The Puritan pastor Richard Baxter wrote,

> In the case of public offenses, and even of those of a more private nature, when the offender remains impenitent, he must be reproved before all, and again invited to repentance. This is not the less of our duty, because we have made so little conscience of the practice of it. It is not only Christ's command to tell the church, but Paul's to 'rebuke before all;' and the Church did constantly practice it, till selfishness and formality caused them to be remiss in this and other duties. There is no room, to doubt whether this be our duty, and as little is there any ground to doubt whether we have been unfaithful as to the performance of it. Many of us, who would be ashamed to omit preaching or praying half so much, have little considered what we are doing, while living in the willful neglect of this duty, and other parts of discipline, so long as we have done. We little think how we have drawn the guilt of swearing, and drunkenness, and fornication, and other crimes upon our own heads, by neglecting to use the means which God has appointed for the cure of them.[15]

The final step of the process of church discipline is to treat individuals who continue to resist as unbelievers, since they evidence a lack of submission to the Lordship of Christ. Although we cannot judge their hearts, we can judge their fruit. And the church must act on that judg-

---

14. This is an important reason why biblical counseling is best done in the context of the local church (or at least in cooperation with it). Counseling outside of that context lacks a certain measure of authority that resides only in the leadership of the church (Matt. 18:18; Heb. 13:17). See Chapter 17 of this book for a discussion of the role of the church in counseling.

15. Richard Baxter, *The Reformed Pastor* (Carlisle, Penn.: Banner of Truth, 1989), 105.

ment to preserve the purity of the body of Christ (see 1 Cor. 5 and 6). This final step does not happen overnight; the process may take months to be carried out fully and correctly. But if repeated attempts to secure a godly commitment fail, there remains no option but to put the sinning person out of the church. Yet even at this point in the process, the goal should still be repentance and restoration (1 Cor. 5:5; 1 Tim. 1:20). This "delivering to Satan" (i.e. removing the sinner from the fellowship and protection of the church and placing that person in Satan's realm) is simply the best way to help people who continue to reject counsel and resist biblical commitment. Richard Baxter also wrote,

> Much prudence, I confess, is to be exercised in such proceedings, lest we do more hurt than good; but it must be such Christian prudence as ordereth duties, and suiteth them to their ends, not such carnal prudence as shall enervate or exclude them. In performing this duty, we should deal humbly, even when we deal most sharply, and make it appear that it is not from any ill will, nor any lordly disposition, nor from revenge for any injury, but a necessary duty which we cannot conscientiously neglect.[16]

Some might see the process Jesus taught in Matthew 18 as cruel and unloving, but in reality it is an act of kindness. God blesses those who obey His Word (James 1:25), so we need to use whatever means God has provided to help people experience that blessing. And church discipline is one of God's methods for motivating people to change.

The goal of biblical counseling is to help counselees become more like Jesus Christ—a process that necessarily involves commitment. Each counselee must *decide* to take definitive steps to "walk as He walked" (1 John 2:6). Some of them will say that they want to change and grow, but may not be sure they want to make the necessary commitment. These individuals are at an important crossroads, and through the grace of God and the biblical principles discussed in this chapter we must try to induce them to follow the Lord.

---

16. Baxter, *The Reformed Pastor*, 106.

16

Implementing Biblical Instruction

Wayne A. Mack

A final key element of the counseling procedure is implementation: the process of actualizing biblical instruction and making it permanent in the lives of counselees. Biblical counseling seeks to promote holiness or *biblical change* as a life-style. It endeavors to foster the implementation and integration of biblical principles into people's lives so they will become *consistently Christ centered and Christ-like in every area of life including their desires, thoughts, attitudes, feelings and behavior.*

This implementation process involves three major components: (1) The counselor plans specific strategies to help the counselee act on pertinent biblical directives (the counselor must not only clarify what to do but how to do it); (2) the counselee practices those strategies in the nitty gritty of life; and (3) the counselee perseveres in applying biblical principles until godly patterns of thinking, feeling, and living have been integrated in that person's life and he or she has become integrated into the life of the Church.

PLANNING STRATEGIES OF IMPLEMENTATION

Romans 12:17 says that we should "respect what is right in the sight of all men." The Greek word translated "respect" literally means "to plan ahead of time." So the verse speaks of advance planning for right behavior. This is necessary to make biblical instruction relevant and applicable.

Off With the Old

The first aspect of planning is to identify factors that hinder biblical change and to take steps to eliminate them. Romans 13:14 tells us to "make no provision for the flesh in regard to its lusts." The things that stir up the lusts of the flesh must be identified and eliminated. This may require that counselees break off undesirable associations with other people. The apostle Paul warns us, "Do not be deceived: 'Bad company corrupts good morals'" (1 Cor. 15:33).

The book of Proverbs also repeatedly warns of the dangers of wrong associations:

- "He who walks with wise men will be wise, but the companion of fools will suffer harm" (Prov. 13:20).
- "He who goes about as a slanderer reveals secrets, therefore do not associate with a gossip" (Prov. 20:19).
- "Do not associate with a man given to anger; or go with a hot-tempered man, lest you learn his ways, and find a snare for yourself" (Prov. 22:24-25).
- "Do not be with heavy drinkers of wine, or with gluttonous eaters of meat; for the heavy drinker and the glutton will come to poverty, and drowsiness will clothe a man with rags" (Prov. 23:20-21).

According to those verses, individuals who associate with wicked people often end up just like them. Biblical counselors, therefore, need to advise their counselees to break off any relationships with people who encourage them to do evil, if it is biblically legitimate to do so. This does not mean someone should file for divorce if his or her spouse is ungodly. But it may apply to roommates, friends, or co-workers who are bad influences. In some cases it may be necessary to move or change jobs in order to "make no provision for the flesh."

Counselees also need to avoid places that create unique sources of temptation for them. For example, one young lady who struggled with lesbianism discovered that she had difficulty with temptation when she was in dressing rooms in department stores. I asked her to keep a journal of where she was most tempted, and then encouraged her to avoid those places until she became strong enough to overcome the temptation. Similarly, a man struggling with homosexuality may be tempted if he goes to a gym or health club. He may need to avoid those places until he is strong enough to withstand the temptation.

Not only should our counselees avoid people and places that may lead to temptation but they must also deal with any practices that contribute to their problems. Whatever triggers the counselee's sin—whether daydreaming, fantasizing, watching certain movies or television programs, or listening to certain kinds of music—must be eliminated. Those who balk at doing this may not sincerely want to change, because God makes clear to us in His Word that it is often necessary to take drastic measures to eliminate sin in our lives. Jesus' admonition graphically illustrates that God expects believers to treat temptation seriously:

> "If your right eye makes you stumble, tear it out, and throw it from you; for it is better for you that one of the parts of your body perish, than for your whole body to be thrown into hell. And if your right hand makes you stumble, cut it off, and throw it from you; for it is better for you that one of the parts of your body perish, than for your whole body to go into hell" (Matt. 5:29–30).

The great preacher Martyn Lloyd-Jones explains that passage clearly and echoes the necessity of removing hindrances to biblical change:

> Our Lord was anxious to teach at one and the same time the real and horrible nature of sin, the terrible danger in which sin involves us, and the importance of dealing with sin and getting rid of it. So He deliberately puts it in this way. He talks about the precious things, the eye and the hand, and He singles out in particular the right eye and the right hand. Why? At that time people held the view that the right eye and hand were more important than the left. It is not difficult to see why they believed that. We all know the importance of the right hand and the similar relative importance of the right eye. Now our Lord takes up that common, popular belief, and what He says in effect is this: 'If the most precious thing you have, in a sense, is the cause of sin, get rid of it.' Sin is as important as that in life; and its importance can be put in that way.... He is saying that, however valuable a thing may be to you in and of itself, if it is going to trap you and cause you to stumble, get rid of it, throw it away. Such is His way of emphasizing the importance of holiness, and the terrible danger which confronts us as the result of sin.
> *We must never "feed the flesh."* "Make no provision for the flesh," says Paul, "to fulfill the lusts thereof." There is a fire within you; never bring any oil anywhere near it, because if you do there will be a flame,

and there will be trouble. . . . We must avoid everything that tends to tarnish and hinder our holiness. "Abstain from all appearance of evil," which means, "avoid every form of evil." It does not matter what form it takes. Anything that I know does me harm, anything that arouses, and disturbs, and shakes my composure, no matter what it is, I must avoid it. I must "keep under my body," I must "mortify my members." That is what it means; and we must be strictly honest with ourselves.[1]

To avoid temptation, counselees must shun whatever stimulates evil thoughts. One young lady who came to me for help with depression had previously been involved in an affair with a married man. I discovered that she still had letters, photos, and gifts that he had given her. She also listened to the kinds of music that they had enjoyed together. In order to eliminate all reminders of her sin, she destroyed the letters and threw away the photos and gifts. She also stopped listening to that music. These steps were crucial in helping her put off ungodly desires for an illegitimate relationship (a major factor in her depression dynamic) and put on a godly life-style.[2]

Similarly, after being confronted with the truth of Romans 13:14 the young lady who had been involved in lesbianism wrote a letter to her former lover. In that letter she confessed her part in their sinful relationship. Admitting she had failed to love the other woman as God expected her to, she asked for forgiveness. Since her life was now committed to obeying Jesus Christ, she made it clear that their relationship was over. To reinforce that point to her former lover (who continued to harass her), she threatened legal action if the woman continued to pursue the relationship.[3] Finally, she pleaded with the other woman to consider her ways and turn in repentance to God. By writing that letter, the counselee burned the bridges to her past sin and eliminated that source of temptation from her life.[4]

---

1. D. Martyn Lloyd-Jones, *Studies in the Sermon on the Mount*, vol. 1 (Grand Rapids: Eerdmans, 1959), 243 and 249–250.

2. Many times people struggle with feelings of guilt for sins they committed long ago because they recognize that the inner change God wants to accomplish has not occurred. They have ceased the sinful action, but their heart still longs for it from time to time. They have not yet learned to view it, as God does, with a holy aversion.

3. Romans 13:1–4.

4. Acts 19:17–19.

On With the New

The planning process involves not only eliminating sin but also cultivating godly thinking and behavior. Romans 13:14 not only says "make no provision for the flesh" but also commands us to "put on the Lord Jesus Christ." Indeed, the latter is the prerequisite for the former. Thus biblical counselors must help their counselees to develop a specific plan to put on the Lord Jesus Christ. That plan should involve at least the following elements.

Involvement in a local church. Since the Church is described as Christ's body, putting on the Lord Jesus Christ means getting involved in a local church (Col. 1:18, 24). We need to exhort our counselees to become vitally, not just casually, involved in a church where Christ can meet their needs in a special way.[6]

Godly associations. While the wrong kind of associations lead to sin, the right ones stimulate godliness. Paul told Timothy to "pursue righteousness, faith, love and peace, with those who call on the Lord from a pure heart" (2 Tim. 2:22). The godly virtues Paul mentioned are stimulated by associating with others who seek after them. Christians are to "stimulate one another to love and good deeds" (Heb. 10:24). The way to become wise, according to Proverbs 13:20, is to walk with wise men. Counselees need to develop relationships with other Christians who are mature in the faith, because we become like those with whom we associate.

Meaningful devotions. Since Jesus is revealed in the Scriptures, it is impossible to put on the Lord Jesus Christ without studying the Word of God.[6] This requires more than a mechanical or academic reading of the Bible. We may need to teach counselees how to study the Bible profitably and how to pray effectively. This might include guidance for Bible memorization and meditation. As someone aptly remarked, "Either sin will keep you from God's Word, or God's Word will keep you from sin."

Accountability. Sometimes during counseling, and many times after the counseling is over, it is helpful for counselees to establish a relationship of accountability with someone who will inquire how they are doing from week to week. This can be an important aspect of the implementa-

---

5. Acts 2:41–47; Heb. 13:17. For more information on the role of the church in counseling, see chapter 17.

6. John 5:39; Luke 24:44–48; Heb. 10:7. See Wayne A. Mack, *A Homework Manual for Biblical Living*, vol. 1 (Phillipsburg: Presbyterian and Reformed, 1979), 63–71 for helpful suggestions and plans for making devotions meaningful.

tion and integration process.[7] Just the assurance that someone else knows what they are struggling with and will ask questions about those struggles can provide the impetus to resist temptation and do the right thing. From my counseling experience, I have found that counselees who resist accountability usually do not successfully implement and integrate biblical change, whereas those who welcome it do.

Proper diet, rest, sleep, and exercise. Even seemingly mundane matters such as diet and sleep are important in our counselees' planning. It is much easier to resist evil when a person is not tired or sick. As 1 Timothy 4:8 implies, bodily discipline is important. We are to eat and drink to the glory of God, which implies that inappropriate eating (including neglect) and drinking dishonors God.[8] Adequate rest and sleep are also God's will for us: "The sleep of a working man is pleasant"; "He gives to His beloved sleep"; "My son, let them (godly teachings and commandments) not depart from your sight . . . then . . . when you lie down, your sleep will be sweet."[9] On occasion, Jesus denied himself sleep and food for special purposes, but there is no indication that He did this as a general rule. Rather, there is every indication that He recognized the importance of attending to the God-given physical needs of proper sleep and food. When we encourage people to put on the Lord Jesus Christ we need to help them be responsible in diet, exercise, rest, and sleep. People who are careless about these physical needs are not only disobeying God, they are also putting themselves in an unnecessary place of temptation.

Service for others. Jesus taught that when we serve other Christians we serve Him (cf. Matt. 25:40), and that unselfish service is a key to personal relationships (Matt. 20:28–28). Our Lord Jesus Christ, who came not to be served but to serve, exhorts us to follow His example.[10] Furthermore, His Word tells us that He has given spiritual gifts (divinely bestowed abilities for ministry in the Church) to His people, and that these spiritual gifts are to be used for the benefit of other believers.[11] Putting on the Lord

---

7. Heb. 3:13, 14; Rom. 12:10, 16; 15:14; 1 Cor. 12:25; Gal. 5:13; 6:2; 1 Thess. 4:18; 5:11; 5:14.

8. 1 Cor. 10:31.

9. Eccles. 5:12; Ps. 127:3; Prov. 3:21–24; Ps. 4:8; Luke 6:12; Matt. 4:1–4; 11:19; Mark 4:38.

10. Mark 10:45; John 13:13–17.

11. Eph. 4:10–16; Rom. 12:3–8; 1 Pet. 4:10, 11; 1 Cor. 12:1–7. For more information about spiritual gifts and the way they should be used, see chapter 18 of this book; see also Mack, *A Homework Manual*, 161–163, 93–99, 183–199.

Jesus Christ, therefore, includes following Christ's example in becoming a servant to other people. It involves accepting the teaching of the Bible about spiritual gifts, and discovering, developing, and deploying those gifts in service to others. Thus the implementation/integration aspect of our counseling should include some discussion of each counselee's spiritual gifts and a practical plan for using them in the Body.

A wise use of time. Ephesians 5:16 commands us to make the most of our time because the days are evil. In other words, our time is valuable and can be wasted or used wisely; it can be used for constructive purposes or destructive purposes, in godly ways or ungodly ways. It can be invested in ways that will honor God or dishonor God, in ways that will build lives up or tear lives down. Many people have careless attitudes about the use of time, but this was never true of the Lord Jesus Christ. He could say of the way He used time, as well as of everything else in His life, "I always do the things that are pleasing to Him [the Father]."[12] Putting on the Lord Jesus Christ means we will follow His example in the constructive use of time. We need to help counselees develop a time schedule, not only so they will have time for the important things, but also so they will not have time for sinful pursuits.[13]

All of these suggestions can be adapted to particular situations and applied effectively in counseling. For example, a counselor might ask a wife to write down specific ways she can show respect and love for her husband. To follow up on the plan she would report to the counselor each week about what she did and what the results were. Without a plan she might not do those things, or she would not be aware of their effects on the relationship and the blessing they can bring.

Prepare for Temptation

Planning also involves deciding how to handle temptation before it comes. Proverbs 22:3 says, "The prudent sees the evil and hides himself. . . ." Temptation is easier to face if we have decided in advance how to respond to it.

A woman whose husband was abusive and had a violent temper came to see me for counseling. In our planning session I asked her to think through those situations of temptation she was likely to face and to plan a

---

12. John 2:4; 7:6, 8, 30; 8:20, 29; 12:23; 17:3, 4.

13. See Mack, *Homework Manual*, vol. 1, 132–43, for a helpful study on planning the godly use of time.

biblical response to each. She listed over a dozen situations that could be troublesome. Among them, when her husband yelled at her for doing something he did not like (for example, when she spent money that was not in the budget); when he criticized how she handled their children; when he became angry when she put something away where he could not find it; and when he made derogatory remarks about her cooking. I then asked her to develop and record a biblical plan describing how God wanted her to respond when she encountered each of those situations. This type of detailed, advance planning can help counselees resist temptation successfully.

A plan for biblical response to temptation might include the following items: (1) recognize and acknowledge in the earliest stages of temptation that you are being tempted; (2) quickly ask God for His help to resist;[14] (3) if possible, remove yourself immediately from the source of temptation; (4) identify the unbiblical desire that would be served by yielding to the temptation;[15] (5) quote and meditate on appropriate Scripture; (6) remind yourself of God's presence, power, and promises;[16] (7) reflect on the purpose of Christ's death;[17] (8) mentally and verbally make a commitment to do the godly thing; (9) get busy with a mind-engaging, godly activity; (10) call a godly friend and ask for help; (11) repeat key aspects of this temptation plan until the power of the temptation is reduced.

The planning phase of the implementation process should also include strategies for dealing with failure. Since change is usually a process rather than an event, people often experience setbacks in their efforts to become more godly. Yet this frequently takes people by surprise, and because they have come to counseling with unrealistic expectations (that progress will be swift, easy, and continuous), they become discouraged by the struggles and failures. When this happens, they tend to think that no progress has been made, that counseling is useless, and that they have not, cannot, and will not ever change.

At this point it is critical for the success of the counseling to develop a recovery plan (a what-to-do-with-failure plan). Counselees must know

---

14. Ps. 50:15; 34:4–6; Is. 40:31.

15. First John 2:15–17. Is the person tempted by the lust of the flesh—a desire for pleasure; the lust of the eyes—a desire for possessions; or the pride of life—a desire for power and/or prestige? Identify the particular idolatrous desire the person is tempted to worship and serve. See also chaptre 13 of this book for more details on this issue.

16. Gen. 39:8, 9; Deut. 31:6; Ps. 55:21; Isa. 41:10; 43:1–3; 2 Cor. 9:8; Eph. 3:20, 21; 1 Cor. 10:13; Jude 24, 25; 2 Pet. 1:3, 4.

17. Gal. 1:4; 1 Pet. 2:24; Titus 2:11–13; 2 Cor. 5:14, 15.

that while failure is serious and was not unavoidable, it does not mean all
that they have judged it to mean. Lapses there may be, but the lapse (a
failure, a temporary defeat or setback) does not have to turn into a relapse
(a total defeat, a complete return to former ungodliness, a thorough domi-
nation by and yielding to sinful patterns). God's people may fall, but by
His grace and power they can and will get up, learn from the experience,
go on, and triumph over their sinful patterns of life.[18] Recovery from failure and transformation out of the control of indwelling sin(s) is possible if
people develop and follow biblical strategies for handling lapses.

A recovery plan could include the following steps: (1) call unbiblical
desires, thoughts, feelings, and actions what God does—sin; (2) take full
responsibility for the sin; (3) confess the sin, both to God and to any
others who were hurt;[19] (4) ask God for help in not doing it again; (5)
remind yourself what Christ has done and is doing for you; (6) reflect on
the resources available to believers in Christ; (7) meditate on God's promises of forgiveness and deliverance from the power of sin; (8) accurately
evaluate the changes that have already occurred and the progress that
has been made; (9) learn from failure by briefly examining what you did
that you should not have done and what you did not do that you should
have done; (10) make restitution where necessary; (11) purpose to put the
past behind you in a biblical way and to resume your efforts to change in
a godly manner.[20]

Planning is the necessary first step to implementation. By determining how they will handle both success and failure, our counselees will greatly
increase their chances for biblical change.

PUTTING BIBLICAL CHANGE INTO PRACTICE

Planning is an important first step in effecting biblical change, but
planning alone will accomplish nothing. For a plan to be effective, it must
be put into practice. A key to doing that is to understand the importance
of habits.

---

18. Prov. 24:16; 15:15, 16.

19. For a helpful discussion of what it means to confess, see Ken Sande, *The Peacemaker* (Grand Rapids: Baker, 1991), chapter 6. In this chapter Sande refers to what he calls
"The Seven A's of Confession": (1) address everyone involved; (2) avoid *if, but,* or *maybe;*
(3) admit specifically; (4) apologize for offending or hurting the other person(s); (5) accept
the consequences; (6) alter your behavior; and (7) ask for forgiveness.

20. Phil. 3:10-14; Ps. 32; 103:12; Isa. 43:25; 44:22; Mic. 7:19; 1 John 1:9; Prov. 28:13;
Eph. 1:7.

Habits are learned ways of living. A habit is created when something is done repeatedly until it becomes a pattern. Habits may be actions, attitudes, or patterns of thinking that have become so ingrained they are second nature. Hebrews 5:14, for example, speaks of people who "because of practice have their senses trained to discern good and evil," and 2 Peter 2:14 says that false teachers have "a heart trained in greed."

As that first verse indicates, habits are not necessarily evil. In fact, they are a gift from God, because if it were not for habits, we would have to continually relearn everything. For example, we go through a long process to learn how to walk, but once learned, walking is so habitual that we rarely think about it. Likewise, we seldom have to think about what to do when we get up in the morning. We just go through our morning ritual of getting out of bed, getting dressed, and getting ready for the day. These things have become habits that scarcely require a thought. If we had to think through these steps each morning, it would be noon before we got out of the bedroom!

We must remember, too, that habits can be unlearned as well as learned. First Corinthians 6:9–11 describes people whose lives had been characterized by adultery, immorality, homosexuality, thievery, greed, drunkenness, and slander. Paul says to these Corinthians, "Such were some of you; but you were washed, but you were sanctified, but you were justified in the name of the Lord Jesus Christ, and in the Spirit of our God" (v. 11). Those sinful habits had characterized their lives as unbelievers, but they had changed. Our counselees, too, can change patterns of thinking, attitudes, practices, or responses if they are willing. Through consistent practice unbiblical habits can be unlearned, and biblical habits can be learned or strengthened.

Paul wrote, "I have learned to be content in whatever circumstances I am" (Phil. 4:11). Contentment did not come naturally to Paul. He wrote earlier that the Law had convicted him of coveting (Rom. 7:7–8), which is an expression of discontent. But this discontented man was later able to proclaim, "I have learned to be content." Contentment does not come naturally to us either—it must be learned. We either train ourselves to be content, as did Paul, or we train ourselves to be discontent.

We can help our counselees to avoid frustration and discouragement by helping them to understand that change is a gradual process requiring practice. And we can help them through the change process by assigning homework that facilitates practice—not just homework that teaches principles but homework that requires application of those principles.

In the Word of God, learning is never a mere academic exercise but is always dependent upon practical responses in a person's life. The psalmist said, "It is good for me that I was afflicted, that I may learn Thy statutes" (Ps. 119:71). While he understood God's statutes intellectually, he learned them practically by experiencing affliction. True biblical learning always comes through obedience. Therefore, biblical counselors must help people to practice principles for living from the Word of God.

The following assignment, which I gave to the woman with the abusive husband, is an example of homework that facilitates practice. I asked her to go over her plans the first thing each morning. This reminded her how she planned to handle specific situations. She also prayed for about fifteen minutes, asking God to help her put her plans into action. Each day at noon she went over her plans and her journal to see where she had succeeded and failed. She then thanked God for her successes, and asked Him for His help throughout the afternoon. When she failed, she asked God to forgive her and then asked Him for help in changing in that area. In the evening, she reviewed the events of the afternoon, and then did the same for the evening before she went to bed. Each day she repeated this pattern and recorded everything in a journal for discussion in the counseling session at the end of the week.

Specific homework assignments like this help counselees to practice the biblical truths they are learning. We should never let our counselees merely make a mental or verbal commitment to change; instead, we should give them the opportunity to live out their commitment and make concrete changes in their lives. As they do this over time, new habit patterns will form, and the old sinful ones will begin to disappear.[21]

PERSEVERING IN BIBLICAL CHANGE

The third aspect of implementation is perseverance. As the writer of Hebrews said, our counselees "have need of endurance" (10:36), because

---

21. See Mack, *Homework Manual* vol. 1, for other examples of homework assignments that facilitate the practice of biblical principles. Many of these assignments were developed to fulfill the seven key elements of the counseling process presented in Part Three of this book. For example, different parts of the anger study on pages 1 through 11 will be useful in accomplishing all seven phases or elements of the counseling process. Pages 1 through 6 will focus mainly on elements 1 through 5, and pages 7 through 11 will be most helpful in the inducement and implementation phases. Pages 7 through 9 relate mainly to the planning aspect of implementation, whereas pages 10 and 11 highlight the practice phase. Other homework assignments that encourage the practice aspect of the implementation phase of counseling are found in Mack, *Homework Manual* vol. 2; Mack, *Strengthening Your Marriage*; Mack *Preparing for Marriage*; and Mack, *Your Family God's Way*.

biblical change following salvation is a process—it is seldom an instanta-neous event. "We all," says Paul in 2 Corinthians 3:18, ". . . are being transformed into the same image from glory to glory. . . ." In another place, Paul writes that we are "being renewed to a true knowledge according to the image of the One who created [us] . . ." (Col. 3:10). Some people learn and change more quickly than others, but it takes time for everyone to learn new habit patterns. Counselors should be aware of this and encourage counselees to persevere while they are involved in the change process.

Biblical change also requires daily practice. According to Jesus, we must deny ourselves, take up our cross, and follow Him on a daily basis.[22] Yesterday's practice will not do for today. Every day is, in a sense, a new day in our relationship with Christ and in the process of changing into His image. Coasting or relying on the past successes and victories is not a luxury believers can afford.

The Puritan Thomas Boston wrote, "Sin is fastened in our souls by nature, as with bands of iron and brass. Converting grace looses it at the root, but it must be loosed more and more, by the daily practice of morti-fication. 'For if ye live after the flesh, ye shall die; but if ye, through the Spirit, do mortify the deeds of the body, ye shall live'" (Rom. 8:13, KJV).[23]

Athletes can be in the best physical shape possible, but if they stop working out they will quickly lose the benefits of all their exercise. The same is true spiritually. If counselees do not persevere in practicing godli-ness on a daily basis, they will soon be back to where they started. Second Peter 2:20–22 warns that those who turn back to sin will be worse off than they were at the beginning. Some people begin well, and their movement toward godly living provides them with some freedom from their pain. But so often that pain served as a primary motivator, so when the pain is relieved, they quit practicing what is right. Before long they end up in the same mess they were in before. This time, however, they may feel hope-less, and decide that the counsel they received and the commitment they made did not work.

The problem in many such cases is caused not by the counsel or the commitment but by a lack of perseverance. That is why biblical counselors need to emphasize that change requires daily practice. The apostle Paul echoed this truth when he wrote to the Corinthians, "I die *daily*" (1 Cor. 15:31). In explaining the meaning of this verse, Thomas Boston wrote,

---

22. Luke 9:23.

23. S. MacMillan, ed., *Complete Works of the Late Rev. Thomas Boston*, 12 vols. (Wheaton: Richard Owen Roberts, 1980), 285.

We should as it were habituate ourselves to dying, and be frequently
making an essay of dying. . . . Ask yourselves what you would do, if
you were just to expire; and do the same. A Christian should be frequently making his testament. When you go to a duty, do it as if it
were the last you were ever to do on earth. When you awake in the
morning, do as if you were to have the grave for your next bed; and
when you lie down at night, so compose yourselves as if you were
never to awaken again.[24]

When significant change has occurred in a counselee's life I usually
lengthen the period of time between counseling sessions. This allows me
to monitor the progress of counselees and at the same time decreases counselor dependency. It also develops counselee initiative and responsibility,
and encourages the continuance of implementation. Instead of seeing
counselees every week, I may see them every two weeks, and then when
they have done well with a two-week arrangement, I may schedule them
for what I think will be a final check-up session in four to six weeks. At
that session we review what has happened in their lives, particularly in
reference to their original problems. I will ask them to list the specific ways
they have made progress since counseling began.[25] Then we use that list as
an opportunity to emphasize the importance of perseverance and the need
to continue developing godly patterns in specific areas of their lives. I warn
them that if they cease to implement the biblical principles we have discussed, they will revert to what they were previously or even worse.[26] If it is
evident that they have continued to implement the biblical principles and
strategies presented during the previous counseling, we terminate formal
counseling with praise to God for the changes that have occurred and encouragement to persevere.

---

24. MacMillan, *Complete Works.*, 287.

25. To me, the purposes of counseling are fulfilled and implemented when I observe
the following things happen: (1) the counselee understands what caused his/her problems
and the biblical way of handling them; (2) the counselee becomes comfortable with the
new response pattern; (3) the counselee begins to practice the new pattern automatically;
(4) the counselee has failed and can diagnose the reason for the failure and make plans for
correcting the problem; (5) the counselee can state specifically how he/she has changed; (6)
the counselee has been tested and has been victorious in the test; (7) others have verified
the changes in the counselee; (8) the counselee starts to share with others what he or she is
learning in counseling; the counselee becomes an informal and spontaneous counselor to
others.

26. Matt. 12:38–45; 2 Pet. 2:20–22.

Conclusion

Establishing involvement with counselees; inspiring them to have biblical hope; taking a thorough inventory; making a reliable, biblical interpretation of counselees and their problems; instructing them in an accurate and appropriately biblical way; inducing them to decisive commitment to biblical obedience—each is a vital dimension of biblical counseling. However, biblical counselors know that skillfully and faithfully fulfilling these elements is not all there is to biblical counseling. They know that each of these functions is a means to an end.

And what is that end? It is the ultimate goal stated at the beginning of this chapter. Biblical counselors want to promote *biblical change as a life-style*; they want to foster the implementation and integration of biblical principles into the lives of people so that they will become *consistently Christ centered and Christ-like in every area of life including desires, thoughts, attitudes, feelings, and behavior.*

That is what biblical counseling is all about. Biblical counseling is not primarily about making people happy or successful or fulfilled; it is not mainly about eliminating the emotional distress, the pain and hurts that people experience. Of course biblical counselors are concerned about these things, and, in fact, all of these desirable things and many more will happen in the fullest sense through biblical counseling. They are not, however, the main concern of biblical counselors; rather they are the byproducts of accomplishing the real purpose of biblical counseling, which is to promote holiness and biblical living as a life-style and thereby to help people be transformed into the image of Christ in every aspect of life.

Part IV

The Practice of
Biblical Counseling

17

Biblical Counseling and the Local Church

William W. Goode

Almost every week someone asks me how to start a counseling ministry in a local church—a question that, to me, illustrates a widespread misunderstanding of the true nature of counseling. For too long biblical counseling has been seen as an optional ministry in the church. Along with radio programs and homes for unwed mothers, it has been relegated to a growing heap of "frivolous" ministries, the ones we hope to get around to some day.

However, biblical counseling is not an option—a point on which Scripture never equivocates. Our Lord commanded believers to love one another, and to consider counseling an optional ministry is to withhold biblical love at the time it is needed most in the believer's life—when he or she is in trouble. As the apostle Paul commanded the Galatian believers, we must be about the business of restoring rather than ignoring such Christians.

The greatest threat to the process of discipleship is the believer who is overtaken by sin. The man or woman with a continual pattern of sin needs help to change and to reestablish a pattern of growth. Thus Paul addressed all church members—not just the pastors and elders—when he said, "We urge you brethren, admonish the unruly, encourage the fainthearted, help the weak, be patient with all men" (1 Thess. 5:14). On another occasion, Paul reminded the believers in Rome of their responsibility to counsel and encourage each other, assuring them that they were "able also to admonish one another" (Rom. 15:14).

Believers will never become like Christ if they are not winning the battle against sin in their lives and investing themselves in the lives of others. And there can be no discipling if there is no plan to help the disciple who gets into trouble. Restoring and encouraging cannot be separated from loving, as we see in the life of our Savior.

COUNSELING: AN INTEGRAL PART OF THE CHURCH

Counseling must never be thought of as a weekly hour of magic, or an independent ministry conducted aside from the church. Preaching, teaching, evangelism, discipleship, and counseling are all integral parts that make up effective, biblical ministry. The local church is the instrument Christ ordained to help believers grow into His likeness. It is the only organization—or better, organism—He promised to build, sustain, and use. Counseling is an essential part of the local church's ministry as it disciples and helps believers mature in Christ's image. Paul had this goal in mind when he wrote: "We proclaim Him, admonishing every man and teaching every man with all wisdom that we may present every man complete in Christ" (Col. 1:28).

The Pastor's Involvement and Leadership in Counseling

Counseling is the responsibility of each believer and its only rightful arena is the church. These truths carry a strong implication: the pastor's involvement and leadership is crucial.

In Ephesians 4, the purpose of the pastor-teacher and the church is described as "the equipping of the saints for the work of service to the building up of the body of Christ . . . to the measure of the stature which belongs to the fullness of Christ" (4:12–13). This includes a plan for believers who are tossed about by bad doctrine and deceitful philosophies. And so many of the problems we encounter in counseling are doctrinal problems based on an inadequate view of God, sin, or self. God wants these problems solved, and He has raised up pastor-teachers to equip the saints to do just that.

In the next few verses, it is as if Paul anticipated that some would doubt believers could be trusted with this job. So he describes the wonder of the spiritual gifts God has provided, assuring us that "the whole body, being fitted and held together by that which every joint supplies, according to the proper working of each individual part, causes the growth of the body for the building up of itself in love" (Eph. 4:16). In other words, all believers should be using their gifts, talents, and abilities to meet the needs of others. As Colossians 1:28 reiterates, the saints are equipped to use their gifts through preaching, counseling, and teaching.

It goes without saying that the pastor's involvement must be more than a token once-a-week venture. Paul reminded the Ephesian elders of his ministry to them, of his selfless sacrifice, and his bold, nouthetic confrontation (counsel) night and day as he ministered with tears. Paul dared not abandon his God-ordained duty. When he saw fellow believers in trouble, he did not hide—he counseled them day and night. Jesus said the hireling flees when the wolf comes, but the shepherd cares for the sheep when they are in trouble. This is the picture we see of Paul in Acts 20:31— a true shepherd actively involved in ministry whenever he is needed.

Yet a word of caution is necessary. Yes, the pastor needs to be involved in counseling, but it must be a balanced involvement. If the pastor pursues counseling to the neglect of his sermon preparation and study, his preaching will no doubt suffer, causing more counseling problems rather than strengthening the saints and furthering the maturation process.

In addition, if a pastor allows counseling to take the place of caring for his family, his health, or his own spiritual needs, he will not only be unprepared to counsel when the time comes, but his overall ministry will suffer dire consequences. Counseling is important, but it can only be effective when counselors understand correct spiritual priorities.

THE CHURCH—INCOMPLETE WITHOUT COUNSELING

Counseling and the Pastor's Effectiveness

When a pastor neglects the ministry of counseling others, crucial areas of his ministry suffer. For example, his preaching is dramatically affected. Paul said the weapons of our warfare are not carnal but spiritual, empowered by God to tear down the mental strongholds and arguments that have been raised against God. But when a pastor is not involved in the lives of his people, he loses touch with their difficulties and the thought processes and habits that lead to problems. Thus he is not prepared to provide the spiritual weapons they need to overcome those problems.

To illustrate, let's imagine a noncounseling pastor who preaches about drunkenness. Yet the people listening in the pews get drunk regularly for any number of reasons. They may succumb to peer pressure because they want to please people rather than God, or perhaps they are not able to communicate with their spouse, so they hide from their problems by drinking. It is possible that they worship possessions and material success, so they will do anything—including drinking with clients—to get what they want. They may drink to drown their guilt, or for the sheer pleasure of the drinker's high. The reason they drink may even be something as simple as gross irresponsibility. These are all reasons for drinking—reasons a pastor who does not counsel is likely to miss, but reasons he will readily realize if he is involved in counseling those in his congregation. Unless the issues of sin are seriously and properly dealt with, the preaching from the pulpit is merely a band-aid solution. Jesus said that what defiles a person is not what goes into the body, but what comes out of the heart—that is what drives the person to sin and that is what he or she must deal with (Matt. 15:17).

The apostle Paul spent a great deal of time counseling people. As he wrote to believers he would pause and state, "You will say to me. . . ." He cut to the heart of the matter because he knew the people he counseled intimately and was able to anticipate their response. He also knew God's Word and always appealed to it for the answers to their problems. Paul understood the fuzzy, confused thinking caused by sin, so he taught clear and specific principles for Christian living. Neither Christ nor Paul coddled those they were helping. They said, "Do this" and "Do not do that," because both knew well those they counseled and saw clearly the walls of excuses they hid behind. They preached with a mind to tear down those barriers.

The pastor who counsels, preaches not merely to inform but to bring about change, which is precisely what growth and progressive sanctification is all about. A pastor who is true to the Word must come to grips with the Church's one mission to believers: to facilitate growth in Christ. The pastor's job is not to thrill his congregation, nor should his goal be to stimulate emotions or intellect—his job is to preach God's Word for the purpose of change.

The pastor who counsels will long to be used of God, to preach and teach the Word, to show forth the worthiness of His holy Son, and to lead His people in growth. Why? Because he sees the results of a hard heart that refuses to deal with problems biblically—the shattered lives, the ruined marriages, the soured relationships, and the stunted spiritual growth. He understands the inextricable link between the failure to understand and apply God's Word and failure in the Christian life. With burning conviction, growth and change become the goal of his preaching.

One of the most tragic reasons pastors do not counsel people and help them understand progressive sanctification is because the pastors themselves do not understand the doctrine. These pastors easily get caught up in the fuzzy, meaningless jargon of pop Christianity. They encourage people to read the Bible for the sake of reading it, to pray for God to pour out a mystical zap to cure all their ills, or to pray for revival, all without a clear understanding of how God works in lives and how He changes hearts. Unfortunately, they are likely to be more a part of the problem than the solution.

That is why the pastor who desires to counsel biblically must become saturated with the truths of progressive sanctification and must come to terms with the sufficiency of Scripture. He must realize that when used correctly, God's Word can identify sinful thought processes and habits and replace them with biblical ones. If he is not counseling from the Word of God alone, he will often fail to differentiate between special revelation and human opinion, theory, or general advice.

Counseling and Evangelism

Biblical counseling can also benefit the local church in evangelism. While many evangelistic tools are effective and worthy of attention, it is important to notice that the scriptural model always began by addressing the challenges, sins, or trials that a person was facing. Thus the biblical counselor who follows Scripture will not simply dispense the Word but will endeavor to listen and ask questions, and then will present the gospel of Jesus Christ.

Over the years, this method of counseling has been a highly effective tool for evangelism in our church. There are many fine couples in our church today whose marriages were once broken, or who were living together before marriage. Yet through counseling they trusted Christ, resolved their problems, and are now effective, productive disciples. Others, who initially came to our church with deep depression and difficulties, not only found the answers they needed through biblical counseling but have become effective evangelists and counselors themselves to both believers and nonbelievers.

THE CHURCH—ESSENTIAL TO COUNSELING

While counseling is a necessary part of the local church, we must remember that it is only one part. An hour of counseling once a week for the hurting people in the church is not God's complete plan for their spiritual growth; it is only part of the plan. In God's blueprint for ministry, counseling is meant to be a synchronized part of the whole.

Indeed, the most effective use of counseling is when it is part of the local church. Counselees need the help of all church ministries: they need the pulpit ministry to teach and motivate growth and change, the love of the collective membership to assist and encourage, the fellowship of the church body for interaction and relationships, the authority of the Body for church discipline, and the example of leaders who are growing and changing. Above all, counselees need the decisiveness of a church committed to following biblical principles in practical areas such as communication, finances, and dealing with problems. There is nothing quite as compelling to a counselee as a church committed to leading by example.

DEVELOPING A BIBLICAL COUNSELING MINISTRY IN THE LOCAL CHURCH

Before we discuss the nuts and bolts of developing a counseling ministry in the church, let me make a rather bold statement: I believe there are only two ways to begin a counseling ministry. One way, unfortunately the pattern that is most often followed, is superficial and ultimately leads only to greater problems. It involves a counseling ministry that is developed hastily where the counselee is given direction from the Scriptures in the counseling center, but the same principles are not modeled in the church that is sponsoring the center. In these counseling situations, where progressive sanctification is not the biblical method of growth and church leaders are not committed to the Bible as the only sufficient standard of authority for daily decision, the counselee will be confused.

The other way, a biblical alternative, is actually rather uncomplicated. It begins through careful efforts that mold church leaders—pastors, elders, deacons, teachers, staff, and lay leaders—into a pattern of growth that people who seek counsel can follow, and it requires a church ministry that is built upon the biblical concept of progressive sanctification, which produces a God-centered model for growth and change.

Now the obvious question is: "How does one develop a biblical counseling program that is a *natural* part of the church's ministry—a program that moves beyond the superficial remedies adopted by the world and so many churches?" There are several steps to consider in developing a counseling ministry.

Leaders Must Be Dedicated

If a church is going to strive for spiritual growth and make earnest, spiritual change a priority, the pastor's life must exemplify that same kind of growth and change. If the Word is not effecting change in the pastor's life, he will have trouble teaching it with conviction and inspiring confidence in its sufficiency—and rightly so!

The pastor must also develop a relationship of mutual concern and loving encouragement with other leaders in the church. He must be willing to receive admonition as quickly and with as much grace as he administers it. His conviction that iron does indeed sharpen iron must be far more than mere lip service; he must believe it and rigorously and openly practice it. His relationship with those who serve with him must be marked by sincere encouragement and, if necessary, firm confrontation.

If a church is to grow spiritually, the pastor and leaders must be growing spiritually. The leadership team is the model the counselee will invariably look to as an example of Christian living. That is why a pastor does well to follow God's qualifications for a counselor when he selects teachers and leaders for the church (see Rom. 15:24). He must look for believers who are growing in their knowledge of the Scripture and who are applying it consistently to their lives.

The choices and decisions the pastor and church leaders make are also critical to the development of a biblical counseling ministry. For example, if the pastor admonishes counselees in the congregation to follow biblical principles, he and his leadership team must demonstrate obedience to those same principles. If he counsels a couple on the wise use of their finances, his decisions with regard to church finances must model wise stewardship. If he teaches a counselee about biblical principles of communication, his own communication within the church must be a positive example for that person.

Leaders Must Understand and Observe Progressive Sanctification

All biblical counseling and change must be accomplished through progressive sanctification: God's sole plan for spiritual growth. This truth must be clarified in the church through an articulate, written doctrinal statement. In addition, it must be taught clearly, because it is a truth that so often is poorly understood by counselees. In fact, it is often a major part of their problem. Many people are confused about how a believer grows and realizes positive change. They want spiritual growth and development on their own terms, easily and quickly. Some come for counseling expecting an instant solution from heaven, even though the apostle Paul, when teaching about spiritual growth, spoke not of mysterious, emotional experiences but of hard work. The growth process requires action. That is why Paul spoke of racing, wrestling, and fighting. In 1 Corinthians 9:27, he wrote, "I buffet my body and make it my slave . . ."—hardly the words of a man who expected spiritual growth to come through a heavenly zap!

Still others, confused about progressive sanctification, turn to morbid introspection and unwittingly take their eyes off of Christ. This is not to say that people who are confused about sanctification have wandered from that path on their own. Countless books, seminars, and lectures have passed along quasibiblical (sometimes antibiblical) advice that has only served to create more problems. Advice like, "feel good about yourself," "turn it all over to Jesus," "read the Bible seven minutes a day," and "talk to the dead to heal your memories" has created an environment hostile to biblical solutions. That is why a church's counseling ministry will only be biblical and successful if the church is committed to the Scripture's patterns for growth, and if it instills that same commitment in those who come for counseling.

Leaders Must Have a Clear Sense of Direction

Before a church begins a counseling ministry, it must establish a clear purpose for its program. Lloyd Jonas, of the National Association of Nouthetic Counselors, emphasizes that "in starting a counseling ministry there must not be anyone either higher up or close by in the chain of command who is not completely sold on nouthetic counseling" (presidential address, NANC conference, 1987).

All staff members must be equipped theologically to counsel others; they must demonstrate both the desire and the ability to counsel; and, ultimately, they must be willing to exert the time needed to train other lay counselors. When training counselors initially it can be helpful to use a counseling program that is approved by the National Association of Nouthetic Counselors. This will ensure that the church's trainees are taught counseling properly, both by observing counseling firsthand and by examining case-study situations.

Leaders Must Be Learners

All biblical counselors must be learners. Without a thirst for God, an appreciation for His Word, and a hunger to know it more deeply, counselors are not likely to have an interest in continuing their counseling education. They must constantly remind themselves that God said, "My thoughts are not your thoughts, neither are your ways My ways" (Isa. 55:8).

A firm grasp of that concept compels the counselor to further study and development. The counselor who feels adequate for the job and satisfied in his or her understanding of God's truth is likely to be, of all people, the most ill suited for the task.

Counselors must never forget the noetic effect of sin that demands continual nourishment from God's Word. The apostle Paul, a talented and industrious church planter, never boasted of reaching a great spiritual plateau but was ever pressing on. With an attitude of awe and a sound hermeneutical approach, the biblical counselor must regularly study the Word and desire to learn from others who study it.

Leaders Should Be Trained Within a Biblical Church Ministry

Just as church members need to be trained in evangelism, so they need to be trained in counseling. In what context should that training take place? This question is the watershed for the whole issue of counseling. For the biblical counselor, the training ground must be the local church. While some training takes place in counseling classes, most of the training of the biblical counselor comes through normal, active involvement in the church. If we believe the Word of God can bring genuine change, solutions, healing, and growth, then counselor preparation must focus more on the biblical responsibilities of pastoring and less on counseling as a separate, para-church skill.

In our church, although we offer several classes on biblical counseling, our lay people receive most of their training by simply becoming active participants in worship, ministry, and fellowship—all natural parts of every believer's life in the Body. The believer who clearly understands the spiritual-growth process of progressive sanctification and understands the heavenly resources that are at the believer's disposal is a long way down the path of not only realizing that growth but also of helping others along the way. The heart of biblical counseling is not the form but the substance: God's Word.

The mainstay of our training program for deacons, their wives, and church laymen consists of an eleven-week course. Trainees meet for eight hours each Monday, and in the process of the three-month period, receive forty hours of lecture and twenty-two hours of counseling observation. We also require that trainees complete extensive reading assignments, often between one- and two-thousand pages. We also occasionally offer short courses, consisting of two one-hour evening sessions combined with a pared-down schedule of counseling observation.

SOME HELPFUL DO'S AND DON'TS

- The church should clarify that its counseling ministry is based on biblical counseling principles.

- For legal protection, we feel it is wise to have nonmembers sign the following statement: "I understand that the counsel I receive will be according to the counselor's interpretation of the Bible." As a word of caution, this statement has not been tested in court. We are simply committed to being honest with our counselees about what they can expect from our counselors. In addition, we insist that each staff member who counsels nonmembers must successfully complete NANC certification.

- The church should not sacrifice the needs of its members to meet the counseling needs of those outside the church. God's plan for change is not based on one isolated hour each week. It is most effective when carried out within the context of a church's full range of biblical ministries. When counselors must choose between counseling someone from within the church—a church that teaches, encourages, and cares for its members biblically—and someone who does not benefit from that setting, they must make the choice that demonstrates the best stewardship of their time and love. Inevitably, there will be a need to make exceptions, but a basic principle to remember is that counselees need the ministry of the entire church.

CONCLUSION

A counseling ministry in a church can have profound, far-reaching effects in the lives of its congregation. In our church, each pastor counsels. As they interact with Scripture in the counseling setting, their understanding of the Word and its practical value deepens, and that, in turn, enters into their teaching from the pulpit. As a result, the members of our church have learned many of the biblical principles that are applied in counseling. Thus a ministry of counseling provides practical, relevant help based on sound principles from God's Word that enables believers to be adequately equipped unto every good work (2 Tim. 3:17).

18

Spirit-Giftedness and Biblical Counseling

John MacArthur, Jr.

We live in the age of the expert. The spirit of self-sufficiency that enabled our pioneer ancestors to settle the frontier has all but disappeared from our culture. People look increasingly to experts and professionals to help them do, or do for them, what they once did for themselves. The effect is not always positive.

Parenting, for example, was once based on common-sense wisdom handed down from generation to generation. In our day, however, various gurus specializing in child rearing have flooded the market with new, often contradictory, theories that debunk most of the old wisdom handed down to us from previous generations. The results have been disastrous for both the family and society.

Unfortunately, the Church has not escaped this onslaught of expert mentality. Ministries such as visiting the sick and evangelizing the lost are often handed over to paid professionals. Specialists are now deemed necessary to advise church leaders on everything from demographics, to church growth strategies, to administrative policies, to how to stage an entertaining Sunday service.

Nowhere has the veneration of "experts" had a more insidious impact than in the area of counseling. More and more voices from within the Church are touting the notion that counseling is an activity best left to skilled professionals—specifically trained psychotherapists. Psychologist O. Hobart Mowrer, although not an evangelical, noted the trend and asked pointedly, "Has Evangelical religion sold its birthright for a mess of psychological pottage?"[1] To our shame, the answer in many cases is yes. Incredibly, many churches that affirm the inerrancy and sufficiency of Scripture are nonetheless quick to shuffle their hurting members off to the psychological and psychiatric "experts"—often even non-Christian counselors utterly blind to the things of God (1 Cor. 2:14).

The psalmist who penned Psalm 1 would never have understood that practice. He noted the folly of seeking counsel from ungodly sources. He wrote, "How blessed is the man who does not walk in the counsel of the wicked, nor stand in the path of sinners, nor sit in the seat of scoffers" (Ps. 1:1)! He understood clearly what the Church seems to have forgotten—that true happiness comes not from following the futile speculations of humanistic psychology but from living out biblical principles. Listen to his description of the individual blessed by God:

> His delight is in the law of the LORD, and in His law he meditates day and night. And he will be like a tree firmly planted by streams of water, which yields its fruit in its season, and its leaf does not wither; and in whatever he does, he prospers (Ps.1:2–3).

COUNSELING: A FUNCTION OF FELLOWSHIP

Ephesians 4:15–16 gives a prescription for the spiritual health of Christ's body:

> Speaking the truth in love, we are to grow up in all aspects into Him, who is the head, even Christ, from whom the whole body, being fitted and held together by that which every joint supplies, according to the proper working of each individual part, causes the growth of the body for the building up of itself in love.

As the members of the Body minister to each other, speaking the truth in love, the Church is built up. The strengthening of each member results in a collective growing up to the fullness of the stature of Christ. Thus the entire Body is matured as the members minister to each other according to their giftedness.

Counseling is an important means through which the members of the Body are supposed to minister to each other. When the Body is functioning

---

1. Cited in Jay Adams, *Competent to Counsel* (Grand Rapids: Baker, 1980), xvi.

correctly, the unruly are admonished, the fainthearted encouraged, and the weak helped (1 Thess. 5:14). The notion that counseling is the exclusive domain of those who have been initiated into the esoteric secrets of modern psychological theory is utterly at odds with the scriptural concept of life in the Body. The Bible presents counseling, like all other aspects of ministry, as a function of fellowship that takes place naturally when the Body is healthy. Study the biblical passages pertaining to church life and fellowship, and this clear truth will emerge: all believers are *expected* to counsel one another. Every Christian is commanded to share in the ministry of exhorting, admonishing, and encouraging others in the flock. Our duty to counsel is even heightened—not diminished—when we see a brother or sister struggling with serious difficulties and sin. We cited some of the key passages on this matter at the beginning of chapter 1. Let's examine one of them a little more closely:

> Brethren, even if a man is caught in any trespass, you who are spiritual, restore such a one in a spirit of gentleness; each one looking to yourself, lest you too be tempted. Bear one another's burdens, and thus fulfill the law of Christ. For if anyone thinks he is something when he is nothing, he deceives himself. But let each one examine his own work, and then he will have reason for boasting in regard to himself alone, and not in regard to another. For each one shall bear his own load. And let the one who is taught the word share all good things with him who teaches (Gal. 6:1–6).

In that passage, Paul outlined a three-step process for restoring sinning members of the Body to spiritual health: pick them up, hold them up, and build them up.

Before someone who has fallen into sin can get back in the Christian race, that person must first be picked up. Those caught in sin's vicious grasp need help as much as they need rebuke. Counseling, therefore, involves helping people get back on their feet spiritually through confession of sin and repentance. That responsibility clearly lies with members of the congregation, not hired professionals—and certainly not with secular counselors. Only fellow believers, through the use of their spiritual gifts, are truly able to help those who stumble. The spiritually strong, writes Paul, "ought to bear the weaknesses of those without strength and not just please [themselves]" (Rom. 15:1).

Not only are those who are spiritually strong supposed to pick up those who fall; they must also help hold them up after the weaker brethren are back on their feet. Those who have just confessed and turned from their sin are extremely vulnerable to further temptation. Satan launches his most savage attacks after a spiritual victory. "Burdens" in this passage refers to the temptations to fall back into the very sins from which a believer has just been delivered. There is no more crushing burden than a persistent, oppressive temptation. Those delivered from the grasp of a stubborn sin often need further encouragement, counsel, and, above all, prayer.

Finally, after picking up and holding up sinning believers, the spiritually strong must build them up. "The one who is taught the word" and "him who teaches" are to "share all" the "good things" of the Word with each other. Note that the same command applies to the teacher and the taught one. Thus all believers—leaders, disciples, weak, and strong—are responsible for sharing the good things of the Word. This is the essence of biblical counseling.

If, as this passage affirms, all believers are responsible to counsel one another, then all must be gifted to some extent to do that. The apostle Paul confirms that truth in Romans 15:14: "Concerning you, my brethren, I myself also am convinced that you yourselves are full of goodness, filled with all knowledge, and *able also to admonish one another*" (emphasis added).

EQUIPPED WITH SPIRITUAL GIFTS

In what way are believers equipped to admonish and counsel one another? Through the spiritual gifts that are imparted to each member of the Body. The primary purpose of spiritual gifts is ministry in the Church itself: "There are varieties of ministries, and the same Lord. And there are varieties of effects, but the same God who works all things in all persons. But to each one is given the manifestation of the Spirit *for the common good*" (1 Cor. 12:5–7, emphasis added). Nearly all the spiritual gifts delineated in the New Testament have usefulness in the counseling ministry.

It is important that we understand that the spiritual gifts described in Scripture are not detached entities given in identical measure or stamped according to a singular pattern. Every believer has a distinctive spiritual gift: "To *each one* is given the manifestation of the Spirit for the common good" (1 Cor. 12:7). Each gift is thoroughly unique, designed by God's grace for each individual in particular: "There are varieties of gifts, but the same Spirit" (1 Cor. 12:4). "We have gifts that differ according to the grace given to us" (Rom. 12:6). Spiritual gifts are offered in infinite variety, each with a different design, like snowflakes. The gifts listed in the New Testament (e.g. Rom. 12, 1 Cor. 12) are simply categories. An individual's spiritual gift should comprise several features of the various abilities named as gifts in these passages. In other words, someone whose primary gift is teaching will probably also be gifted to some degree in wisdom, discernment, or mercy. That person's gift is a singular blend of abilities and characteristics that enable him or her to minister according to God's calling.

Let's examine some of the main kinds of gifts enumerated in Scripture.

Prophecy

Prophecy is commonly associated with foretelling the future. The Greek word *prophēteuō*, however, simply means "to speak forth," or "proclaim." It refers to the public proclamation of Scripture. In biblical times, of course, the work of a prophet often involved the reception and proclamation of new revelation. But the title *prophet* actually refers to anyone whose gift is declaring truth with authority, or preaching. Thus a prophet, particularly in this present age, is simply a proclaimer of biblical truth— not someone who receives revelation directly from God. The great Reformer John Calvin understood the gift of prophecy in that light. He wrote, "I prefer, however, to follow those who understand the word in a wider sense to mean the peculiar gift of revelation by which a man performs the office of interpreter with skill and dexterity in expounding the will of God."[2]

The apostle Peter said much the same thing when he exhorted those with the gift of prophecy in these words: "Whoever speaks, let him speak, as it were, the utterances of God" (1 Pet. 4:11).

Perhaps the clearest statement of how the gift of prophecy functions comes in 1 Corinthians 14:3-4: "One who prophesies speaks to men for edification and exhortation and consolation . . . one who prophesies edifies the church." The gift of prophecy can be employed to edify believers, call them to obey God's Word, and encourage them in time of need—edify, exhort, and console. What are those but aspects of biblical counseling? Thus the prophet is equipped to counsel simply by virtue of this gifting.

The importance of the gift of prophecy can be seen in Paul's emphasis on it in 1 Corinthians 14. There the apostle contrasts it with the gift of languages, demonstrating the superiority of prophecy. He exhorts the Corinthians to "pursue love, yet desire earnestly spiritual gifts, but especially that you may prophesy" (1 Cor. 14:1).

---

2. John Calvin, *The Epistles of Paul the Apostle to the Romans and to the Thessalonians* (Grand Rapids: Eerdmans, 1960), 269.

And in a sense, the preacher fulfills an important element of the counselor's task with every sermon. Acts 15:32 gives an example of the gift of prophecy in action. After delivering the letter from the Jerusalem Council to the church at Antioch, "Judas and Silas, also being prophets themselves, encouraged and strengthened the brethren with a lengthy message." They spent time strengthening the believers there by proclaiming to them the truths of the Word of God. Their prophetic preaching ministry itself had the same effect as good counsel.

One of Paul's final exhortations to his protégé Timothy stresses the importance of proclaiming the Word:

> I solemnly charge you in the presence of God and of Christ Jesus, who is to judge the living and the dead, and by His appearing and His kingdom: preach the word; be ready in season and out of season; *reprove, rebuke, exhort, with great patience and instruction.* For the time will come when they will not endure sound doctrine; but wanting to have their ears tickled, they will accumulate for themselves teachers in accordance to their own desires; and will turn away their ears from the truth, and will turn aside to myths. But you, be sober in all things, endure hardship, do the work of an evangelist, fulfill your ministry (2 Tim. 4:1–5, emphasis added).

In other words, preachers of the Word ought to exercise their gifts exactly like wise counselors—reproving, rebuking, and exhorting with all patience and careful instruction.

Preaching and counseling that is truly biblical will be applied to the heart by the Holy Spirit and will produce spiritual growth. After all, God's word is "profitable for teaching, for reproof, for correction, for training in righteousness" (2 Tim. 3:16). A pastor who faithfully exercises his prophetic office is acting as counselor for the whole congregation. By equipping them and instructing them, the pastor facilitates their giftedness and furnishes them with what they need to counsel one another effectively. Strong biblical preaching is thus inextricably linked to effective biblical counseling in the church. The counseling ministry begins with the pulpit and extends from there to every level of ministry in the church.

Teaching

Closely associated with prophecy is the gift of teaching. Indeed, biblical preaching must include a strong element of teaching as well. Unlike preaching, teaching is carried out on all levels of the church, not just from the pulpit. Those who teach Sunday School classes, lead Bible studies, or disciple others all exercise the gift of teaching.

The Greek word *didaskō* ("to teach") includes the idea of systematic training or instruction. The gift of teaching is the ability to lead others to a deeper understanding of Scripture.

An emphasis on teaching marked our Lord's ministry. At the conclusion of the Sermon on the Mount, "the multitudes were amazed at His teaching; for He was teaching them as one having authority, and not as their scribes" (Matt. 7:28–29). Matthew 4:23; 9:35; Mark 2:13; 6:6; Luke 13:22; 20:1, along with many other passages, describe the centrality of teaching in Jesus' ministry.

A strong emphasis on teaching also characterized the apostles' ministry. Acts 2:42 describes the early church as "continually devoting themselves to the apostles' teaching" (cf. 5:42). Acts 15:35 records that "Paul and Barnabas stayed in Antioch, teaching and preaching, with many others also, the word of the Lord." From Acts 18:11 we learn that Paul "settled [in Corinth] a year and six months, teaching the word of God among them." "I did not shrink," Paul testified to the Ephesian elders, "from declaring to you anything that was profitable, and teaching you publicly and from house to house" (Acts 20:20). In his letter to the Colossians, the great apostle summed up his ministry in these words: "We proclaim Him, admonishing every man and teaching every man with all wisdom, that we may present every man complete in Christ" (Col. 1:28).

The gift of teaching is a prerequisite for being an elder (1 Tim. 3:2; Titus 1:9). Not all elders are called to proclaim the Word publicly; however, all must be able to teach the Word systematically to those over whom they have oversight. It is that qualification that sets elders apart from deacons. Teaching the Word is a primary way elders exercise oversight of their flock (cf. 1 Tim. 4:6, 11, 13, 16; 5:17; 2 Tim. 2:15, 24; Titus 2:1). Through the teaching of the Word, elders guard the congregation from doctrinal and practical errors. They also teach principles for godly living.

What marks an effective teacher? First, the teacher must live consistently with biblical teaching. Paul admonished Timothy, "In speech, conduct, love, faith and purity, show yourself an example of those who believe" (1 Tim. 4:12). The godly Puritan Richard Baxter wrote, "He that means as he speaks will surely do as he speaks."[3]

Second, the teacher must be "constantly nourished on the words of the faith and of . . . sound doctrine" (1 Tim. 4:6). The greater the depths

---

3. Richard Baxter, *The Reformed Pastor* (Edinburgh: Banner of Truth, 1979), 68.

of doctrinal knowledge, the more effective will be the teaching. "He must not be himself a babe in knowledge," wrote Richard Baxter, "that will teach men all those mysterious things which must be known in order to salvation."[4] Like Timothy, the teacher must "be diligent to present [himself] approved to God as a workman who does not need to be ashamed, handling accurately the word of truth" (2 Tim. 2:15).

Third, such knowledge should produce humility, not pride. Those whose teaching is marked by an arrogant attitude contradict with their lives the very truths they teach. Paul described to Timothy the proper attitude for those who teach:

> And the Lord's bond-servant must not be quarrelsome, but be kind to all, able to teach, patient when wronged, with gentleness correcting those who are in opposition, if perhaps God may grant them repentance leading to the knowledge of the truth (2 Tim. 2:24–25).

Finally, a skilled teacher will be characterized by purity of heart and holiness of life. Paul's exhortations to Timothy to "discipline yourself for the purpose of godliness" (1 Tim. 4:7), and "pursue righteousness, godliness, faith, love, perseverance and gentleness" (1 Tim. 6:11) should be taken to heart by all who would teach God's Word.

The importance of teaching in counseling cannot be overstated. Counseling is essentially a process of teaching. The wise counselor must be able to listen carefully, then apply the Word of God accurately to whatever problems arise in the counseling session. Counselees will never live out principles they do not know. Teaching biblical principles, therefore, is at the heart of the biblical counseling process. Adams writes, "Nouthetic confrontation must be scriptural confrontation. Nouthetic confrontation is, in short, confrontation with the principles and practices of the Scriptures."[5] In contrast to the Rogerian "client-centered" nondirective methodology embraced by many today, the goal of biblical counseling is to change sinful patterns of thinking and living. This is done through the power of Scripture.

> The Bible is the only unchanging touchstone to measure thinking, feeling, and behaving. The Word of God abounds with guidance and direction for living. Therefore, the methodology of

---

4. Baxter, *The Reformed Pastor*, 68.

5. Adams, *Competent to Counsel*, 51.

biblical counseling relies on the Word of God rather than the wisdom of men. . . . Therefore, biblical counselors will seek to help their counselees live in submission to God's love, His Word, and His enabling.[6]

Those who are gifted to teach, then, are specially gifted for this aspect of counseling.

Exhortation

While prophecy proclaims biblical truth, and teaching systematizes it, exhortation demands a proper response to it. Romans 12:8 lists exhortation as one of the gifts of the Spirit. The Greek word is *paraklēsis*, also used in such passages as Acts 20:2; 1 Corinthians 14:3; 1 Timothy 4:13; and Hebrews 13:22. It means "to exhort," "to encourage," "to advise," or "to confront." Its relationship to the counseling ministry should be obvious.

To exhort is to challenge fellow believers to act consistently with God's will. As already noted, biblical counseling involves admonishing the unruly, encouraging the fainthearted, and helping the weak (1 Thess. 5:14). Through the gift of exhortation, counselors encourage sinning Christians to forsake their sin and practice righteousness, they comfort those devastated by trouble or sorrow, and they strengthen the faith of those who are discouraged and weak. Those particularly gifted in exhortation are invaluable counselors, often the backbone of a local church's counseling ministry.

Wisdom

The gift of wisdom, referred to in 1 Corinthians 12:8, is the ability to understand how the truths of Scripture apply to the practical issues of daily living. *Sophia* ("wisdom") is used frequently in the New Testament to describe the ability to discern and conform to God's will (cf. Matt. 11:19; 13:54; James 1:5; 3:13, 17). As such, some degree of wisdom is essential for all biblical counselors. Obviously, it would do little good to teach counselees biblical principles and exhort them to follow those principles without showing them specifically how to do that. Wise counsel is what the counselee needs (cf. Prov. 1:5; 12:15; 19:20), and the gift of wisdom enables the counselor to provide it.

---

6. Martin and Deidre Bobgan, *How to Counsel from Scripture* (Chicago: Moody, 1985), 54–55.

Knowledge

Foundational to preaching, teaching, and counseling is knowledge. The gift of knowledge is the God-given ability to understand the mysteries of God's revealed Word—those truths unknowable apart from God's revelation (cf. Rom. 16:25; Eph. 3:3; Col. 1:26; 2:2; 4:3). It also entails skill in presenting that knowledge so others can understand it. The gift of knowledge is not merely the ability to accumulate and collate facts but a spiritual ability to see biblical and doctrinal truth in a coherent and meaningful way.

Without some degree of spiritual knowledge, counselors have little to offer except the foolish and futile speculations of worldly wisdom. God's view of such counsel may be seen in His condemnation of Job's counselors. The gift of knowledge enables counselors to give the wise counsel from God's Word that alone offers hope to their counselees.

Administration

Mentioned in Romans 12:8 ("he who leads") and 1 Corinthians 12:28 ("administrations"), this is the gift of leadership. *Proistēmi*, the term used in Romans 12:8, means "to lead," "to manage," "to be in charge," or "to oversee," while *kubernēsis* (1 Cor. 12:28) means "to steer or pilot a ship." The gift of leadership, or administration, is the Spirit-given ability to organize, oversee, and motivate others to accomplish a task.

Since many counselees, especially those suffering from depression, lead unstructured lives, the gift of administration is a useful one for a counselor. To help counselees order their lives to glorify God is an important aspect of biblical counseling.

Mercy

Those with this gift have a special love for and sensitivity to those in misery—whether from poverty, physical illness, or the ravages of sin. The Lord Jesus Christ is the supreme example of One who showed mercy. In Luke 4:18, Jesus said,

> The Spirit of the Lord is upon Me, because He anointed Me to preach the gospel to the poor. He has sent Me to proclaim release to the captives, and recovery of sight to the blind, to set free those who are downtrodden.

Without the spiritual gift of mercy, counseling is often cold and clinical. Many people struggling with emotional upset, reeling from some disaster of life, or seeking relief from depression need to be able to share the burden with someone whose gift is mercy. Such people are often actually set back by psychoanalysis, which only prompts them to be introspective, self-focused, or obsessed with their feelings. What they really need is relief from the burden and a lightening of the load (cf. Matt. 11:28–29). Fellow believers with the gift of mercy are best equipped to help with such burden bearing.

Ministry in the Body

Healthy churches breed relationships that are conducive to spiritual growth and emotional health, because as Christians minister with their gifts to one another, much of the work of counseling takes place in the natural interaction of fellowship. As is evident in this brief list of key spiritual gifts, the express purpose of our giftedness is to help meet the needs that drive most people to seek counseling.

All ministry in the body of Christ thus incorporates features of counseling. Both formal and informal counseling should always be taking place in the local church at every level of ministry and fellowship. Gifted members naturally minister to one another by admonishing, encouraging, strengthening, and teaching—all forms of counseling. When these functions are moved out of the fellowship and into remote clinics, the whole life of the Body is disrupted.

Unfortunately, in the stampede to integrate psychology into the Church, gifted believers have often been discouraged from counseling fellow Christians according to Scripture. As a result, spiritual gifts have fallen into a severe state of neglect. People who should be admonishing, correcting, encouraging, and showing mercy are instead referring people to professional therapists. Many Christians have accepted the notion that tolerance and deference are the only acceptable attitudes we ought to communicate to struggling people. The unavoidable consequence is that many believers have unnecessarily stunted their own spiritual gifts.

I am convinced that a healthy emphasis on the ministry of spiritual gifts would alleviate much of the need for formal counseling. People would minister to one another more effectively as a natural result of everyday fellowship. And as gifted believers gained skill in employing their gifts, a whole new generation of spiritually capable counselors would arise from within the Church.

If that does not happen, the Church is doomed. The boom in counseling clinics is not producing healthier Christians. On the contrary, it is producing a generation of believers who are utterly dependent on therapy and unable to enjoy life in the body of Christ as it was meant to be. Professional psychologists are no substitute for spiritually gifted people. Moreover, the counsel psychology offers cannot replace biblical wisdom and divine power.

Each Christian is gifted uniquely by God to help meet the needs of fellow believers in the Body. If we can recover that simple truth and live it out with new enthusiasm in our fellowships, we can restore health to the Body and at the same time fill even the deepest needs of the most troubled lives.

19

Preaching and Biblical Counseling

John MacArthur, Jr.

The rise in psychotherapy and the decline of biblical counseling in the Church has paralleled a decline in biblical preaching. The psychology epidemic began infecting evangelical pulpits several years ago, and its effect on preaching has been disastrous.

Sermons in many evangelical churches contain no exposition of Scripture whatsoever. Biblical content has been replaced by illustrations, stories, allegories, and psychological discourses. Issues such as human relationships, depression, and behavior are dealt with from a psychological, rather than biblical, perspective. Psychological notions such as self-love and self-esteem have even driven the concepts of repentance and the sinfulness of humanity right out of the pulpit.

Some preachers seem to view psychotherapy with an awe that approaches reverence. The authorities they cite are not Scripture but eminent psychologists and behavioral experts. Psychology has laid siege to the pulpit, and biblical preaching is in serious decline.

This has set up a chain of events that only perpetuates the problems that drive people to therapy. By failing to offer biblical answers to people's problems, many preachers have actually given people the idea that Scripture offers no answers to the issues that trouble them. Then by offering psychology as a substitute, they have fed the widespread misconception that psychology's answers are more reliable, more helpful, and more sophisticated than "mere" biblical counsel.

The answer to such thinking is a renewed emphasis on the sufficiency of Scripture, starting in the pulpit. Scripture offers sufficient help for all the deepest needs of the human heart. When the preacher is confident of that truth, the counseling ministry will inevitably reflect the same faith in Scripture's sufficiency. And when the Word of God is preached with conviction, it begins to address the very problems that people often seek counseling for. The Word of God *always* accomplishes its intended purposes: "So shall My word be which goes forth from My mouth; it shall not return to Me empty, without accomplishing what I desire, and without succeeding in the matter for which I sent it" (Isa. 55:11). "The word of God is living and active and sharper than any two-edged sword, and piercing as far as the division of soul and spirit, of both joints and marrow, and able to judge the thoughts and intentions of the heart" (Heb. 4:12).

Our Sufficiency Is of God

Since Scripture itself claims to be a sufficient resource for meeting emotional and spiritual needs, I suggest that those who are saying it is not are in serious error. Since the Word of God teaches that all Christians possess ample spiritual means for genuine victory, shouldn't it be patently clear that modern psychology offers no spiritual benefit that the Church lacks?

Second Corinthians 3:5 sums up the matter of our spiritual sufficiency: "Not that we are adequate in ourselves to consider anything as coming from ourselves, but *our adequacy is from God*" (emphasis added). The King James Version states, "Our sufficiency is of God."

Expanding on that great truth later in the same epistle, Paul writes, "God is able to make all grace abound to you, that always having all sufficiency in everything, you may have an abundance for every good deed" (2 Cor. 9:8). The "alls" and "everys" of that verse underscore its utter comprehensiveness. In other words, there is nothing for which we are not sufficient through the provision of God's grace. If God is to glorify Himself through us, He must provide the necessary resources.

And He does. Peter wrote, "His divine power has granted to us *everything pertaining to life and godliness*, through the true knowledge of Him who called us by His own glory and excellence" (2 Pet. 1:3, emphasis added).

Scripture clearly warns us not to look beyond the resources God has so abundantly provided. Paul cautioned the Colossians, "See to it that no one takes you captive through philosophy and empty deception, according to the tradition of men, according to the elementary principles of the world, rather than according to Christ. For in Him all the fullness of Deity dwells in bodily form, and in Him you have been made complete . . ." (Col. 2:8–10). In another epistle he added, "He who did not spare His own Son, but delivered Him up for us all, how will He not also with Him freely give us all things?" (Rom. 8:32). What more does the Christian need? Certainly not the philosophizing and empty deception of a spiritually destitute system of behaviorism.

The resources that belong to every believer include many rich spiritual benefits—the fruit of the Spirit; the fellowship of other believers; the assurance of hope; and the eternal, abundant life Jesus promised (John 10:10). But all those realities are described for us and supplied to us through God's Word. So the sufficiency of the Bible itself is the overriding issue every preacher must come to grips with.

THE WORD OF GOD IS LIVING AND POWERFUL

Jesus prayed for His disciples, "Sanctify them in the truth; Thy word is truth" (John 17:17). That is as clear and comprehensive a statement as any in all Scripture that sanctification in its fullest sense is accomplished by God's Word.

Paul wrote that the Spirit of God revealed God's truth to us not in the words that human wisdom teaches but in words the Holy Spirit teaches (1 Cor. 2:13). And because we have the Word of God through the Holy Spirit, we can judge, appraise, evaluate *all things* (v. 15). Why? Because through the Scriptures and the Spirit we have been given the mind of Christ (v. 16).

In Mark 12:24 Jesus affirmed that to know the Scriptures is to experience the power of God. As we noted above, God's Word is living and powerful. It reveals the deepest part of a person's inner soul, "piercing as far as the division of soul and spirit, of both joints and marrow, and able to judge the thoughts and intentions of the heart" (Heb. 4:12). Scripture cuts to the very depth of the deepest part of a person's being so that "all things are open and laid bare" (v. 13). In other words, the Word can do what no psychotherapy can do: it opens the soul.

John adds, "The anointing which you received from Him abides in you, and you have no need for anyone to teach you; but as His anointing teaches you about all things, and is true and is not a lie, and just as it has taught you, you abide in Him" (1 John 2:27). That does not mean we have no need for pastors or Bible teachers; God has graciously supplied them for the edification of the Church (Eph. 4:11–12). The apostle John was talking about teachers of human wisdom. We who have the Holy Spirit living in us have the ability to comprehend eternal truth (1 Cor. 2:15–16). When it comes to spiritual truth, we have no need of human instruction.

The Law of the Lord Is Perfect

No passage in all the Old Testament deals with biblical sufficiency as succinctly as Psalm 19. (Psalm 119 covers the subject in more depth, but to cover it thoroughly would require more space than the limits of this brief chapter allow.) In Psalm 19:7–14 we have a brief, potent statement of the utter sufficiency of God's Word. In my view, this passage is definitive in showing why psychology is incompatible with biblical counseling.

The theme of the psalm is the revelation of God. The first six verses deal with *natural revelation*; that is, God's revelation of Himself as seen in creation (also described in Romans chapter 1). Verses 7 to 9 describe *special revelation*, or God's revelation of Himself in His Word. It is these verses we want to consider most carefully:

> The law of the LORD is perfect, restoring the soul;
>
> The testimony of the LORD is sure, making wise the simple.
>
> The precepts of the LORD are right, rejoicing the heart;
>
> The commandment of the LORD is pure, enlightening the eyes.
>
> The fear of the LORD is clean, enduring forever;
>
> The judgments of the LORD are true; they are righteous altogether.

First of all, the structure of the passage needs to be noted.

- There are six statements. Each contains three elements.
- There are six titles for Scripture. It is called *law* and *testimony* in verse 7. It is called *precepts* and *commandment* in verse 8. It is called *fear* and *judgments* in verse 9. Those are all titles for Scripture.
- There are six characteristics of Scripture, again two in each verse. It is *perfect*, it is *sure*, it is *right*, it is *clear*, it is *clean*, it is *true*.
- There are six benefits of Scripture. It *restores the soul*, it *makes wise the simple*, it *rejoices the heart*, it *enlightens the eyes*, it *endures forever*, and it is *righteous altogether*.

- There are six occurrences of the covenant name of YHWH translated in the phrase "of the LORD." And thus six times we are reminded that the source of special revelation is from God, in six statements about the Word of God.

These verses show the utter comprehensiveness of biblical sufficiency; they are God's own witness and testimony to the total adequacy of His Word for all spiritual needs. As we look at each of these six statements, note how sweeping is the claim God makes about the utter sufficiency of His Word to meet every spiritual need.

The law of the LORD is perfect, restoring the soul. The first title for Scripture in these verses is "law," or *torah*, a favorite biblical word for Scripture. This word identifies the Scriptures as divine instruction. It refers to the fact that Scripture is God teaching truth to humanity. It has in view divine instruction relative to creed and character and conduct. It pictures Scripture as a complete manual laying out God's law for our lives. In other words, the Bible is the law of the LORD for human living. As such, it is perfect. Here the psalmist is setting Scripture in contrast to the imperfect, flawed reasonings and instructions of mankind.

I once spent an afternoon looking up the Hebrew word translated "perfect" in my lexicons and following it through all the Old Testament to try to get a feel for what it meant. After several hours, I came to the conclusion that what this word really means is "perfect." It speaks of perfection in every sense of the word—not merely something that is perfect as opposed to imperfect, but also something that is perfect as opposed to incomplete. The word could also be translated accurately as "comprehensive." It speaks of something so complete as to cover comprehensively all aspects of a matter. In other words, the Word of God lacks nothing. It is flawless, comprehensive, completely sufficient.

The law of the LORD—this divine instruction that is utterly comprehensive—has the effect of restoring the soul, converting the soul, reviving the soul, and refreshing the soul. All of those could be apt translations of that Hebrew verb. "Soul" here is the Hebrew word *nephesh*, a Hebrew noun familiar to any Old Testament student. *Nephesh* is translated with at least twenty-one English words throughout the Old Testament: "life," "person," "self," and "heart" are some samples. It speaks of the inner person.

Here, then, is the sense of this first statement: Scripture, which is divine instruction, is so comprehensive that it can totally transform the inner person. That is a monumental claim. It means Scripture is utterly sufficient for conversion, transformation, restoration, and spiritual birth and growth to perfection. The statement is made without any equivocation, without any caveats.

The testimony of the LORD is sure, making wise the simple. The word "testimony" in this phrase speaks of Scripture as divine witness. It is God's own witness to Himself. It is His personal testimony about who He is. And it is "sure"; meaning it is unmistakable, trustworthy, unwavering, reliable. Scripture is more certain than anything else. It provides a foundation that will not move and on which a person may build a life and an eternal destiny without hesitation. And this sure Word, this sure testimony from God about Himself, makes simple people wise.

The Hebrew word translated "simple" in this verse comes from a root that describes an open door. The Old Testament saints viewed a simple-minded person as having an open door in the intellect. Did you ever hear somebody say, "I'm open-minded"? An Old Testament Jew would say, "Close it." In their way of thinking, a simpleton was someone who was literally open-minded—unable to keep anything in or out. The same Hebrew term is used often in the Proverbs to identify the naive person, the undiscerning, nondiscriminating, inexperienced, and uninformed fool. According to the psalmist, then, Scripture—the sure, reliable, trustworthy, unwavering testimony from God about Himself—comes to the one who is simple and makes that one wise.

Note carefully, the wisdom spoken of here is not intellectual data to be stored in the brain. The Hebrew concept of wisdom has more to do with the way one lives. In the Old Testament, wisdom is defined as the ability to make right choices in daily conduct; to live on earth with a heavenly understanding. The word *wise* really means "skilled in all aspects of holy living." The biggest fool of all is the one who knows the truth but does not live according to it.

Thus this couplet means that Scripture is so sure and reliable and trustworthy and unwavering that it takes the simple-minded, undiscerning, uninformed, ignorant person and makes that person skilled in all aspects of holy living. Therein is the sanctifying power of the Word.

The precepts of the LORD are right, rejoicing the heart. This third statement about Scripture speaks of God's Word as divine principles. In other words, the Word of God is a divine set of guidelines for living. And these principles are *right*. The intent of the Hebrew word here is that God's precepts lay out a right path. We are not left to wander around in a fog of human opinion. We have a true Word that lays out a true path that can be followed. And what is the product of that? "Rejoicing the heart." The life of true joy comes from walking according to divine principles. People who go the way of the world, away from the Word, find no joy. Those who live according to the path outlined in Scripture find complete and full joy.

And so this phrase is saying that God's Word lays down right principles that make a sure path on which all who walk will find fullness of joy. You can begin to see how these descriptions of Scripture dovetail, answering every need of the human heart.

The commandment of the LORD is pure, enlightening the eyes. The word "commandment" in this phrase pictures Scripture as the divine mandate. That is to say, the Word of God is authoritative, binding, and nonoptional. The Bible is not a book of suggestions from God. It contains divine commands, nonnegotiables. These demands, the psalmist says, are "pure," meaning, simply, "clear." The divine commandments are lucid, easy to see, and they give clear direction. The point is that Scripture enlightens our eyes to the dark things in life.

New Christians who have lived many years in darkness will understand the import of this phrase. You have probably noticed that whenever relatively new Christians speak of the change wrought in their lives, they frequently underscore this truth. When a person is born again, many dark things become clear. That is because the Word of God enlightens the eyes. So much becomes clear. The confusing things of life become understandable.

And so the Word of God is sufficient for salvation, total transformation of the inner person, the source of skill in all matters of holy living, the path to joy, and the source of a clear understanding of things.

The fear of the LORD is clean, enduring forever. The noun used here is *fear*, but because of the parallelism, we know it refers to Scripture. Why is Scripture spoken of as fear? Because the Bible is the manual on worship. It teaches us how to fear God, how to reverence Him. Since the habit of the human soul is to worship, we need instruction about Whom to worship and how to worship Him properly.

As a manual on worship, the Bible is "clean"—without evil, without corruption, and without error. The Hebrew word is *tahor*, meaning "without impurity, defilement, filthiness, or imperfection." The psalmist is saying that Scripture is unsullied by sin. A parallel verse is Psalm 12:6: "The words of the LORD are pure words; as silver tried in a furnace on the earth, refined seven times." There is no impurity in it. It is hallowed; it is holy. It is separated from sin.

The point is that the Word of God will lead us into purity. You will never find in Scripture any misrepresentation of God, man, Satan, angels, or demons. You will never find any misstatement of what is right or wrong.

Everything here is absolutely clean and unsullied. Here is a perfect resource for us.

And note that this "fear of the LORD" endures forever. It is permanently and eternally relevant. It does not need updating. It does not need editing. It does not need to be polished or refined. Any person living at any time in human history, in any culture, in any climate, will find the Bible completely applicable. The same basic principles of the Word of God apply equally to a myriad of different peoples and situations with the same powerful effect.

The judgments of the LORD are true; they are righteous altogether. The word *judgments* looks at Scripture as divine verdicts. This phrase views God as the judge of all the earth and the Scriptures as His pronouncement from the divine bench. These judgments, according to the psalmist, are true. There is a wealth of import in that simple adjective.

Where do we go to find salvation? Where do we go to find the skill of living in daily life? Where do we go to find an overcoming joy through all the trials of life? Where do we go to get light on the dark things of life? Where do we go for a permanent resource that never changes? Where do we go for truth?

There is only one answer: God's Word, the Bible. Nowhere else can we find that which can totally transform the whole person, make wise, bring joy, enlighten the eyes, be permanently relevant, and produce comprehensive righteousness.

Is it any wonder verse 10 says what it says? "They are more desirable than gold, yes, than much fine gold; sweeter also than honey and the drippings of the honeycomb." Is there anything as sweet? Is there anything as precious? "Moreover, by them Thy servant is warned; in keeping them there is great reward. Who can discern his errors? Acquit me of hidden faults. Also keep back Thy servant from presumptuous sins; let them not rule over me; then I shall be blameless, and I shall be acquitted of great transgression" (vv. 11–13).

Here the psalmist sums up what God is saying to us about His Word: Scripture is our greatest possession, more precious than gold. It is the greatest pleasure, sweeter than honey. It is the greatest protection, warning us from error. It offers the greatest promise: an eternal reward. It is the greatest purifier, keeping us from sin. And so in verse 14 the psalmist's response is predictable: "Let the words of my mouth and the meditation of my heart be acceptable in Thy sight, O LORD, my rock and my Redeemer."

The psalmist seems to have in mind Joshua 1:8: "This book of the law shall not depart from your mouth, but you shall meditate on it day and night, so that you may be careful to do according to all that is written in it; for then you will make your way prosperous, and then you will have success." What kind of meditation and what kind of words are acceptable? Scripture, according to Joshua 1:8. It is the only resource that is all sufficient, guaranteeing success to the one whose mind is fixed and meditating on its immense richness. Psalm 1:1–3 echoes the same thought: "How blessed is the man who does not walk in the counsel of the wicked, nor stand in the path of sinners, nor sit in the seat of scoffers But his delight is in the law of the LORD, and in His law he meditates day and night. And he will be like a tree firmly planted by streams of water, which yields its fruit in its season, and its leaf does not wither; and in whatever he does, he prospers."

PREACH THE WORD

Those passages preclude the possibility that the people of God can find essential spiritual truth in any other resource besides God's Word.

Second Timothy 3:16 settles the question of biblical sufficiency for the Christian. These verses are often thought of as an affirmation of inspiration, and they certainly are that. But notice how clearly and definitively they affirm the sufficiency of Scripture as well: "All Scripture is inspired by God and profitable for teaching, for reproof, for correction, for training in righteousness; *that the man of God may be adequate, equipped for every good work*" (emphasis added).

The preacher's task is to proclaim the all-sufficient Word of God, and nothing else. Paul wrote this to Timothy:

> I solemnly charge you in the presence of God and of Christ Jesus, who is to judge the living and the dead, and by His appearing and His kingdom: *preach the word*; be ready in season and out of season; reprove, rebuke, exhort, with great patience and instruction. For the time will come when they will not endure sound doctrine; but wanting to have their ears tickled, they will accumulate for themselves teachers in accordance to their own desires; and will turn away their ears from the truth, and will turn aside to myths" (2 Tim. 4:1–4, emphasis added).

Notice, Paul recognized that Scripture would not always be popular. He readily conceded that the time would come when people would turn away, seeking to have their ears tickled (or "needs met") by preachers who were willing to cater to selfish desires, offering an alternative message besides biblical truth. Yet Paul reminded Timothy that preaching the Word of God is the only reliable guide for teaching, reproving, rebuking, or exhorting people according to the will of God. Moreover, it is the only legitimate message for any preacher called by God. And so Paul solemnly charged Timothy to keep preaching the Word.

The preaching of the Word is, I am convinced, the necessary foundation on which an effective ministry of counseling must be built. Even the strongest biblical counseling is undermined if it is accompanied by weak or ambiguous preaching. On the other hand, clear and powerful preaching often succeeds in touching hearts resistant to wise counsel.

In contrast, preaching that is devoid of a clear biblical message can have little or no positive effect. Preachers who fill their sermons with psychology while minimizing biblical content will find more of their people struggling with chronic emotional and spiritual disabilities, and desperately seeking answers in all the wrong places. That is precisely the state of affairs in much of the contemporary evangelical church.

It is my conviction that the crisis and the controversy in church counseling today would soon fade away if preachers obeyed this simple directive from the apostle Paul: "Preach the Word." Preachers would be pointing their people to the only source of real help for their spiritual problems. People's confidence in the sufficiency of Scripture would be restored. The Word of God would be unleashed to accomplish its intended purpose. And the whole Church would be revolutionized.

20

Resources for Biblical Counseling

Dennis M. Swanson and Wayne A. Mack

The effective counselor must have a core library of materials at his or her disposal both for personal enrichment and to provide tools to help counselees. In this chapter we present a sampling of materials that are indispensable for biblical counseling. The materials are divided into seven categories: (1) basic resources for biblical counselors, (2) theological resources for biblical counselors, (3) suggested reading for biblical counselors, (4) resources for counselees, (5) audio and video resources, (6) periodicals, and (7) training opportunities. A brief annotation has been included with each listing. Works that are set in **bold-faced** type are recommended as the basic library for biblical counselors.

We gratefully acknowledge the work of David Powlison of the Christian Counseling and Education Foundation in Laverock, Pennsylvania, who developed much of this bibliography and the annotations. A large portion of this chapter has been taken from his work, supplemented by the input of the other contributors to this work and those involved in biblical counseling across the United States.

BASIC RESOURCES FOR BIBLICAL COUNSELORS

Adams, Jay *Competent to Counsel.* Grand Rapids: Zondervan, 1970.
This book launched nouthetic counseling with a polemic against psychotherapy and a call to view counseling as an aspect of ministry that aims at

sanctification and, hence, is dependent on the Holy Spirit and the Word of God. Psychiatry has usurped the pastor's work of the cure of souls and defined the problems of living in secular terms. The Church must regain its calling: "Qualified Christian counselors properly trained in the Scriptures are competent to counsel—more competent than psychiatrists or anyone else."

————. *Godliness Through Discipline.* Phillipsburg, N. J.: Presbyterian and Reformed, 1972.

With practical help from 1 Timothy 4:7, Luke 9:23, and Hebrews 5:13, this book encourages believers to live a life that is oriented toward godliness, to practice righteousness through the power of the Holy Spirit until it too becomes habitual.

————. *The Christian Counselor's Manual.* Grand Rapids: Zondervan, 1973.

This sequel and companion volume to *Competent to Counsel* is an instruction manual providing information not only on the philosophy of counseling but ample instruction on counseling methods. This book is a treasure trove that informs the would-be counselor and debunks the stereotyped criticisms of nouthetic counseling.

————. *The Christian Counselor's Casebook.* Grand Rapids: Zondervan, 1974.

This is "a workbook designed for individual or class use in conjunction with *Competent to Counsel* and *The Christian Counselor's Manual.*" There are three major purposes for the book: (1) to learn how to identify various problems according to biblical norms; (2) to lay out biblical plans of action for dealing with problems; and (3) to provide familiarity with types of problems that counselors encounter.

————. *Ready to Restore: The Layman's Guide to Christian Counseling.* Phillipsburg, N. J.: Presbyterian and Reformed, 1981.

This is an introductory textbook in nouthetic counseling. Accessible and compact, it covers both conceptual and methodological matters. It is written for individual study or for a class or Bible study group.

————. *Solving Marriage Problems: Biblical Solutions for Christian Counselors.* Phillipsburg, N. J.: Presbyterian and Reformed, 1983.

Here Adams provides practical training for counselors in how to understand and solve marriage problems. He answers questions such as, What are the basics of the biblical view of marriage? What sorts of problems destroy marriages: unbiblical concepts ("problems of error"); sinful living patterns ("problems of practice"); relationships with others (e.g., companions, in-laws, children, former spouse); and general influences in society? The book includes methods for discovering and solving marital problems.

————. *The Biblical View of Self-Esteem, Self-Love, and Self-Image.* Eugene, Ore.: Harvest House, 1986.

The self-esteem fad has spread as people combat what is seen as the great modern enemy: low self-esteem rooted in childhood neglect and criticism. Adams traces the roots of these ideas in Adler and Maslow. He challenges the notion of psychological needs and provides a clear exegesis of the two great commandments (love yourself?) and Romans 6 and Colossians 3 (man of infinite worth?). Most of the book refutes popular errors; the last seven pages give positive ideas for helping depressed counselees.

————. *A Call to Discernment: Distinguishing Truth from Error in Today's Church.* Eugene, Ore.: Harvest House, 1987.

The contemporary church lacks discernment. Christians attempt to sort out life from a conglomerate of "misinformation, disinformation, distortion, and truth." The Bible calls us to develop discernment, as opposed to the mentality that views discernment as synonymous with self-righteous heresy hunting. This book presents a plan for readers to grow in discernment.

————. *A Thirst for Wholeness.* Wheaton: Victor Books, 1988.

A study of the inner dynamics of human life from the book of James. Meant to be used personally or in a study group or class, the book covers themes such as anger, desires, doubt, prayer, peacemaking, and sickness, among others. The section on the "inner/outer aspects of sin" (chapter 3) refutes a host of misconceptions about nouthetic counseling as externalistic.

————. *The Grand Demonstration: A Biblical Study of the So-Called Problem of Evil.* Santa Barbara, Calif.: EastGate Publishers, 1991.

This book answers the large and primary question of why human beings have become objects of divine wrath. Why does a good God allow for evil, and, having allowed it, why does He complain when people sin, and why does He consign those who fail to repent to an eternity in hell?

Bobgan, Martin, and Deidre Bobgan. *Hypnosis and the Christian.* Minneapolis: Bethany, 1984.

"Hypnosis has been used as a method of mental, emotional, behavioral, and physical healing for hundreds and even thousands of years. . . . From witch doctors to medical doctors and from past to present, the rituals and results have been reproduced, revised, and repeated." Hypnotists use "techniques such as repetition, deception, stimulation of the imagination, and emotionally overtoned suggestions to effectively influence the will and condition the behavior of the subject." Discusses hypnotic regression and the links between hypnosis, occult activities, and Eastern meditative trances. "Hypnotism is demonic at worst and potentially dangerous at best."

————. *How to Counsel From Scripture.* Chicago: Moody, 1985.

God's love is the predominant factor in change: "God's love enables one to overcome sin and its consequences, to live in relationship to Him, and to be transformed into the image of Christ. His love engenders trust, which leads to obedience to His Word. . . . Biblical counseling is not a new idea. We are merely promoting a restoration of one of the oldest ministries. . . . The cure-of-souls ministry emphasizes the person's relationship with God from which comes renewal and change in the mental-emotional-behavioral areas of life."

————. *Psychoheresy: The Psychological Seduction of Christianity.* Santa Barbara, Calif.: EastGate Publishing, 1987.

Psychology is an antibiblical religious system, not a science. The Church has bought the system, rather than building counseling from the Bible. Labels and categories matter, because they either describe things truly or falsely (e.g., the myth of mental illness). Psychotherapy is quackery, with very little documentable success. "Although some disciplines in the broad field of psychological study have contributed some information about people, much of the information that has filtered down into popular literature and into the psychological office is spurious. The most seductively dangerous area of psychology is that part which seeks to explain why people are the way they are and how they change." Includes critiques of evangelicals who amalgamate psychology and Christianity: Richard Dobbins, H. Norman Wright, Larry Crabb, Paul Tournier, M. Scott Peck, H. Newton Maloney, Charles Solomon, and others.

————. *The Psychological Way—The Spiritual Way*. Minneapolis, Minn.: Bethany, 1989.

The cure of minds through psychotherapy (psychological way) has almost totally displaced the cure of souls through biblical counseling (spiritual way). "Psychotherapy is questionable at best, detrimental at worst, and a spiritual counterfeit at least."

————. *Prophets of Psychoheresy*. vol. 1. Santa Barbara, Calif.: EastGate Publishing, 1989.

Critiques the teachings of leading Christian psychologists and psychotherapists. "The largest of the four branches of psychotherapy is the humanistic one. The Association for Humanistic Psychology is the professional association of humanistic psychologists. Its president, Dr. Lawrence LeShan, says, 'Psychotherapy may be known in the future as the greatest hoax of the twentieth century.' It may also be known as the greatest heresy of twentieth-century Christianity."

————. *Prophets of Psychoheresy*. vol. 2. Santa Barbara, Calif.: EastGate Publishing, 1989.

Critique of James Dobson, primarily his use of the self-esteem concept as fundamental to his teachings. Dobson is a leader in "promoting the psychologizing of Christianity. . . . We use the word prophet to mean a spokesman for a cause or movement. The heresy is the departure from absolute confidence in the Word of God for all matters of life and conduct and a movement toward faith in the unproven, unscientific psychological opinions of men. Thus we call it 'psychoheresy.'"

————. *12 Steps to Destruction: Co-dependency/Recovery Heresies*. Santa Barbara, Calif.: EastGate Publishing, 1991.

The people labeled codependent have serious problems and need help. "However, we question the diagnoses, answers, formulas and systems that are being offered in the name of help, in the name of love, and even in the name of Christ. Beneath many programs that purport to be Christian lurk ideas, philosophies, psychologies, and religious notions that are antithetical to biblical Christianity." Extensive criticism of Twelve-Step programs.

————. *The Four Temperaments, Astrology, and Personality Testing*. Santa Barbara, Calif.: EastGate Publishing, 1992.

"From the beginning, typologies have been designed to help people both understand themselves and improve their condition." But, "The Bible does not categorize people according to temperament and personality. Instead, the richness of variety permeates the pages of God's Word." The four temperaments, the twelve signs of the zodiac, and psychological typologies describe universal traits that can apply to all human beings to a greater or lesser extent. They give the illusion of significant self-knowledge. Their net effect is to excuse sin, to feed pride, and to distract attention from the issues the Bible considers significant. Temperament theory and astrology have numerous links conceptually; modern psychological typologies are heir to many of the same faulty assumptions. Describes and assesses Meyers-Briggs, Personal Profile System, Taylor-Johnson, Spiritual Gifts Inventory, et al.

Bobick, Michael W. *From Slavery to Sonship: A Biblical Psychology for Pastoral Counseling.* Michael W. Bobick, 1989. (Presently available solely through Grace Book Shack, Sun Valley, California, see page 357.)

The author attempts to break fresh theoretical ground for understanding people biblically: "We need not choose between solving problems and understanding people; this is a false dilemma. . . . But in the absence of a published Biblical psychology that helps counselors . . . our present need is to emphasize the dynamics of motivation." Instead of a how-to format for specific problems, this book tries "to span the gap between theological anthropology and actual ministry." Part One develops a model of the sinful human heart as a maze of lies and "covenants with idols." The renewed human heart is increasingly ruled by God's truth and power in Christ. Part Two shows how the model can be used in the counseling process.

Broger, John C. *Self-Confrontation: A Manual for In-Depth Discipleship.* Rancho Mirage, Calif.: Biblical Counseling Foundation, [1978] 1991.

These twenty-four weekly lessons are intended to move a person through the change process personally as a foundation for becoming a counselor (Matt. 7:1–5). The book can be used for Sunday school and other classes or personal study.

———. *Instructor's Guide for the Self-Confrontation Course.* Rancho Mirage, Calif.: Biblical Counseling Foundation, [1978] 1992.

This guide provides lesson plans and instructions for teachers/leaders of the Self-Confrontation course.

Bulkley, Ed. *Why Christian's Can't Trust Psychology*. Eugene, Ore.: Harvest House, 1994.

This book is written to demonstrate the fallacies of an integrationist approach to counseling. Bulkley addresses some of the major myths of psychology and presents a positive biblical approach to counseling people.

Kruis, John G. *Quick Scripture Reference for Counseling*. Grand Rapids: Baker, 1988.

"The Scriptures are ideally suited for any and every counseling occasion. . . . As you do the Lord's work, the Holy Spirit is always the primary counselor, and he works powerfully, sovereignly through his own Word." Bible passages—some brief, some lengthy—that treat over fifty topics are assembled and arranged systematically. The purpose is to give counselors a ready reference and a source of homework assignments.

Lloyd-Jones, D. Martyn. *Spiritual Depression: Its Causes and Cure*. Grand Rapids: Eeerdmans, 1965.

"Christian people too often seem to be perpetually in the doldrums and too often give the appearance of unhappiness and of lack of freedom and absence of joy." Lloyd-Jones has compiled the answer to this pressing problem in a series of twenty-one sermons placed here in book form. He clearly proclaims that the loss of spiritual vitality is to be found in the loss of focus on the person and work of Christ and the nature of God. The final chapter on "Learning to be Content" is worth the price of the entire book.

MacArthur, John Jr. *Our Sufficiency in Christ*. Dallas: Word, 1991.

This is an excellent presentation of the believer's sufficiency in Jesus Christ and the resources of the Holy Spirit and the Word of God. It demonstrates the seductive, yet insufficient offerings of psychology, pragmatism, and mysticism as a basis for Christian living.

Mack, Wayne A. *The Biblical Concept of Church Discipline*. Cherry Hill, N. J.: Mack Publishing Company, 1974. (Although not currently in print, this book will be reissued soon by Grace Book Shack, Sun Valley, California, see page 357.)

Christ intended the organized Church to reflect His purity in the behavior of all members. The concept of church discipline has been neglected and even repudiated. This book introduces three types of discipline:

(1) preventative, which tests the credibility of a person's profession of faith; (2) formative, which disciples and edifies; and (3) exceptional, which corrects and punishes. The author also describes the authority (servant of the Lord) and the grounds (impenitent sins) of corrective church discipline, gives advice on the Matthew 18 process, and warns of the dangers in the two extremes of either excessive church discipline or no church discipline at all.

————. *Homework Manual for Biblical Living, Volume 1: Personal and Interpersonal Problems.* Cherry Hill, N. J.: Presbyterian and Reformed, 1979.

The counseling session is not the magic hour. This manual gives homework assignments that can help with a wide range of problems from anger and anxiety through communication and changing sinful thought patterns, to vocation and work. Typical assignments contain Bible studies, self-analysis questions, brief teachings, and plans to solve problems with a biblical course of action.

————. *Homework Manual for Biblical Living, Volume 2: Family and Marital Problems.* Phillipsburg, Penn.: Presbyterian and Reformed, 1980.

Homework assignments in this volume cover a wide range of marital and child-rearing issues: communication, finances, data gathering (e.g., "Rate Your Marriage" and "Log Lists"), ways to show love, how parents provoke children to wrath, and principles for bringing up children God's way. It includes teaching outlines, self-evaluation forms and questions, plans for biblical change, and Bible studies.

————. *Preparing for Marriage God's Way, Counselor/Teacher's Guide.* Tulsa, Ok.: Virgil W. Hensley, 1986 ; Sun Valley, Calif.: Grace Book Shack, 1993.

This counselor/teacher's guide is designed to be used in conjunction with the premarital manual *Preparing for Marriage God's Way.* It gives directions to the counselor or teacher for counseling or teaching couples who are preparing for marriage. Specific guidelines and suggestions for making classes or counseling sessions of maximum usefulness are included.

Payne, Franklin E. *What Every Christian Should Know About the AIDS Epidemic.* Augusta, Ga.: Covenant Books, 1991.

————. *Biblical Healing for Modern Medicine.* Augusta, Ga.: Covenant Books, 1993.

Franklin E. Payne is a medical doctor and Director of Covenant Enterprises. Specializing in medical ethics from a biblical perspective, he has written invaluable books for the biblical counselor that present various aspects of medical considerations most counselors will face.

Playfair, William L. *The Useful Lie.* Wheaton: Crossway Books, 1991.

Dr. Playfair, a medical doctor, demonstrates how the recovery industry has proliferated in America and how the so-called disease model has been used to entrap people in a nonending cycle of therapy groups and counseling. The disease model eliminates personal responsibility for the sins of drug and alcohol abuse and shifts blame elsewhere. At the same time, this model offers no real hope for those who are trapped in this sinful lifestyle. Playfair does an excellent job of documenting the origination, background, and goals of the recovery industry and its "Useful Lie."

Welch, Edward T. *Counselor's Guide to the Brain and its Disorders: Knowing the Difference Between Disease and Sin.* Grand Rapids: Zondervan, 1991.

"Biological psychiatry is claiming more and more of the human experience as part of its domain, and it is quickly usurping moral and ethical territory that was once seen as belonging to the church. . . . It states we are ultimately molecular, not spiritual." In this work Edward Welch attempts to reclaim territory—and break fresh theoretical ground—by defining the contribution of somatic components to problems. He establishes a biblical view of the person and the extent of personal moral responsibility during brain injuries and disorders and gives medical information relevant to counselors, discussing common diseases that alter intellect, emotions, or behavioral capabilities (Alzheimer's, MS, seizure, stroke, tumors, head injury, diabetes, female hormonal changes). Such things affect our spirits but do not break or control them. The author reinterprets the so-called psychiatric diseases from a biblical perspective, discusses the possibilities of misdiagnosis, and gives diagnostic clues. Throughout, the goal is to enable counselors to develop sensitivity to the interplay of organic and spiritual issues.

BASIC THEOLOGICAL RESOURCES FOR BIBLICAL COUNSELORS

The following list presents some of the works that explain the theological foundations of biblical counseling. Most of these are well known and there are many others that could be cited. Some works, while not exclusively related to counseling, touch on important issues the biblical counselor will deal with. These works are invaluable study tools not only for pastors but for all who are involved in biblical counseling.

Biblical counselors must be biblical, systematic, and practical theologians. It is impossible to do biblical counseling without a solid theological foundation, because the practice of counseling must be based on an understanding of biblical principles and convictions.

Adams, Jay E. *A Theology of Christian Counseling*. Grand Rapids: Zondervan, 1979.

Four major sections seek to articulate a biblical theology of counseling. The first seven chapters deal with the relevance of God and His Word to counseling (e.g., "God is man's environment"). The next four chapters deal with the nature of man in creation and in sin, and the final seven deal with the change process (salvation and sanctification), including a lengthy section on forgiveness. The book closes with a miscellany of other topics.

Berkhof, Louis. *Systematic Theology*. Grand Rapids: Eerdmans, 1959.

An excellent one volume systematic theology. The original *Bibliotheca Sacra* review stated, "Professor Berkhof is to be commended upon his able restatement of Reformed theology, keen analysis, impersonal treatment of opposing views, and an honest attempt to meet the theological problems current in our day."

Bloom, Allan. *The Closing of the American Mind*. New York: Simon and Shuster, 1987.

Although a non-Christian author, Bloom correctly chronicles and presents "[h]ow higher education has failed democracy and impoverished the souls of today's students."

Charnock, Stephen. *The Existence and Attributes of God*. Minneapolis, Minn.: Klock and Klock, 1977 (reprinted from the original 1797 edition).

Charnock presents a profound subject—the existence and attributes of God—in clear and simple terms. This book is written with depth of scholarship, yet, with simple language that anyone can read and understand.

Frame, John M. *The Doctrine of the Knowledge of God*. Phillipsburg, Penn.: Presbyterian and Reformed, 1987.

Frame writes, "We tend to forget how often in Scripture God performs mighty acts so that men will 'know' that He is Lord." This book focuses on knowing God. It emphasizes the idea that knowing God must be a priority above all things.

Hodge, A. A. *Outlines of Theology*. Grand Rapids: Eerdmans, 1949.

Something of an abridgment of his father's *Systematic Theology*, here A. A. Hodge provides an excellent one volume presentation of biblical doctrine in a clear systematic manner. An excellent reference tool.

Hodge, Charles. *Systematic Theology* 3 vols. Grand Rapids: Eerdmans, 1946.

These three volumes are available in different formats, but the full unabridged volumes are by far the best to have. Hodge has been called "the theologian" of the great Princeton tradition. His presentation of the doctrines of sin, salvation, God, the Scriptures, and sanctification are must reading.

Hoekema, Anthony A. *Created in God's Image*. Grand Rapids: Eerdmans, 1986.

In this important work, Hoekema presents a clear, biblical explanation of man as created in God's image. He discusses sin, the fall, total depravity, and common grace. One chapter discusses the issue of sovereignty versus free will and the ability to choose.

Lloyd-Jones, D. Martyn. *Authority*. Carlisle, Penn.: Banner of Truth Trust, 1985.

This small booklet is a reproduction of addresses given by Lloyd-Jones. "Things are as they are in the world today because the church has abandoned its authority. The authority of the Bible has been called into question and commonly today the church is left without any sense of divine authority." The choice for the Christian is, "The authority of truth in the Word of God, or the blackness of darkness forever."

MacArthur, John Jr. *The Gospel According to Jesus*. Grand Rapids: Zondervan, 1988.

This is the seminal book on the "Lordship Salvation" controversy. MacArthur presents the issues and the biblical teaching regarding repentance, saving faith, and sanctification. (Zondervan reissued this book with the addition of three new chapters in early 1994.)

————. *Faith Works: The Gospel According to the Apostles*. Dallas: Word, 1993.

This volume continues the discussion of *The Gospel According to Jesus*. In this book MacArthur clearly explains saving faith. The appendices are extremely helpful in dealing with dispensationalism and noted dispensationalists. Here MacArthur also demonstrates that the so-called Lordship position in not inconsistent with dispensational hermeneutics/theology and stands in the tradition of the history of orthodox Christian doctrine.

————. *Ashamed of the Gospel: When the Church Becomes Like the World*. Wheaton: Crossway, 1993.

In this work MacArthur effectively develops a comparison between the modern church in America and the "Downgrade" controversy that Charles H. Spurgeon fought in the late nineteenth century. Although the book does not deal specifically with counseling, it provides valuable insights on integration and compromise in the church today.

Owen, John. *Temptation and Sin*. Grand Rapids: Zondervan, 1958.

This classic work by the great Puritan divine is one of the best statements on this subject ever presented. Particularly helpful is information on how the Christian is to "mortify the flesh." This material will help counselors assist those who deal daily with sin and self.

Pink, A. W. *The Sovereignty of God*. Carlisle, Penn.: Banner of Truth Trust, 1968.

Pink presents a sound and cogent explanation of God and His sovereignty. His work is a classic in the field and should be read by counselor and counselee alike.

Piper, John and Wayne Grudem, eds. *Recovering Biblical Manhood and Womanhood: A Response to Evangelical Feminism*. Wheaton: Crossway Books, 1990.

This is a comprehensive work on the entire subject of the biblical roles of men and women, in the church, in the family, and in life. The writers present a thorough exegetical discussion of the biblical teaching on men and women including: headship, submission, motherhood, ministry, and men and women in the image of God. As the world seeks to eliminate the male-female distinctions, this book is a vital resource for the counselor.

Smith, F. Lagard. *Sodom's Second Coming: What You Need to Know about the Deadly Homosexual Assault.* Eugene, Ore.: Harvest House, 1993.

A pointed and well-documented presentation on the homosexual agenda in America. The author is a law professor at Pepperdine University and a graduate of Yale.

Wells, David F. *No Place for Truth or Whatever Happened to Evangelical Theology?* Grand Rapids: Eerdmans, 1993.

Perhaps one of the most important books to be released in recent times. Wells chronicles not only the de-emphasis in evangelical theology but the intolerance of it in much of modern evangelicalism. One review stated, *"No Place for Truth* is mandatory reading for anyone interested in evangelicalism's future. Every Christian could profit from the superlative diagnosis of an anemic Christianity that is more American than Christian and which has seemingly lost its biblical/theological reference point in God and the Scriptures."

SUGGESTED READING FOR BIBLICAL COUNSELORS

Adams, Jay *The Big Umbrella and Other Essays and Addresses on Christian Counseling,* Phillipsburg, Penn.: Presbyterian and Reformed, 1972.

This is a compilation of a dozen lectures meant to orient people to the basic ideas of Christian counseling. The "Big Umbrella" is the notion that mental illness explains any and every difficulty in life. The book treats evangelism in counseling, grief counseling, demon possession, marital and familial communication, abuses of small groups, drugs, masturbation, and homosexuality.

————. *Lectures on Counseling.* Grand Rapids: Zondervan, 1975.

Reprint of two books (*Coping with Counseling Crises* and *The Use of the Scriptures in Counseling*) and two pamphlets (*Your Place in the Counseling Revolution* and *Counseling and the Sovereignty of God*). Opens with a challenge to seminary students to consider their calling as pastor-counselors. One of Adam's "four fundamental books" on counseling.

————. *What About Nouthetic Counseling?* Grand Rapids: Baker, 1976.

A question and answer book with history, help, and hope for the Christian counselor, this work discusses the first ten years of the movement including the gains that have occurred and the opposition and misunderstandings that have arisen. Twenty-five questions and answers engage common mis-understandings and criticisms.

————. *Change Them? . . . Into What?: Counseling in America Today.* Laverock, Penn.: Christian Counseling and Educational Foundation, 1977.

Reprint of an address at the University Psychiatric Clinic in Vienna, Austria. It discusses the "general failure of the psychotherapeutic community to succeed in doing anything significant for people and their problems." Pastors in the 1950s either referred people to psychotherapists or sought to incorporate psychotherapy into their practice. Since the mid-60s, however, distinctively biblical counseling has developed. This is what such counseling looks like: speak the truth in love to responsible people who need to change in order to measure up to the image of Christ.

————. *The Christian Counselor's New Testament: A New Translation in Everyday English with Notations, Marginal References, and Supplemental Helps.* Phillipsburg, Penn.: Presbyterian and Reformed, 1977.

Adam's purpose for creating his translation of the New Testament was to put the Bible in the everyday speech of the American public, avoiding extremes of woodenness, archaic language, lofty literary tone, and loose paraphrase; he also wanted to capture the counseling nuances and pastoral concern inherent in the original writings—matters that are often lost in translation. Marginal notations and footnotes address dozens of topics of practical use to counselors. The Supplemental Helps contain a sixty-page summary of nouthetic counseling—both methodological and conceptual—and a ready reference.

————. *Matters of Concern to Christian Counselors: A Potpourri of Principles and Practices.* Phillipsburg, N. J.: Presbyterian and Reformed, 1977.

The first of a series (see *Update on Christian Counseling,* volumes 1 and 2) of books containing short essays on miscellaneous topics. This volume has forty-one short takes on everything from whether you should forgive yourself, to sleep, to halo data, to the use of the word "need," to teaching counselors, to dealing with foul language from counselees, to self-love.

————. *The Power of Error: Demonstrated in an Actual Counseling Case.* Phillipsburg, Penn.: Presbyterian and Reformed, 1978.

A summary of a pastoral counseling case that went on for many months, meandering and fruitless. Critiques both the pastor's handling of the case and the psychiatrist's supervision in the light of nouthetic principles.

————. *Update on Christian Counseling*. vol. 1. Phillipsburg, N. J.: Presbyterian and Reformed, 1979.

This is actually the second of a series that began with *Matters of Concern to Christian Counselors*. It includes thirteen essays on a range of topics: how counseling affects the counselor, counseling failure, a biblical approach to stress, prescription medications, the problem with apologies, twenty-five key presuppositions of biblical counseling, structuring counseling, and using a Personal Data Inventory, among others.

————. *The Church and Her Rights*. Laverock, Penn.: Christian Counseling and Educational Foundation, 1980.

Treats church-state relations, on the occasion of a lawsuit by an avowed homosexual who insisted on being reinstated as church organist without repenting of his lifestyle. The state's authority is given by God and limited by God's authority.

————. *Marriage, Divorce, and Remarriage in the Bible*. Grand Rapids: Zondervan, 1980.

A practical guide to both the exegetical and practical questions regarding marriage, divorce, and remarriage.

————. *Counseling and the Five Points of Calvinism*. Phillipsburg, N. J.: Presbyterian and Reformed, 1981.

Conservative churches virtually abandoned the ministry of counseling. A "double divorce" occurred: between counseling and Scripture (as secular authority reigned in counseling), and between counseling and preaching (with only the latter based on the Bible). Adams seeks to redress these problems.

————. *The Language of Counseling*. Grand Rapids: Zondervan, 1981.

"One of the major unifying themes in my rather zigzag career has been the central place language holds in all the activities in which I have been involved." Language and labels matter, because in the battle for men's minds language and ideas are the principal weapons. This book challenges the reader to take stock of the words one says and hears. Counselors must "deliberately adopt new words and constructions that more aptly express the biblical facts in each counseling situation."

————. *Update on Christian Counseling.* vol. 2. Phillipsburg, N. J.: Presbyterian and Reformed, 1981.

A continuation of the Update series, this book includes ten miscellaneous essays: "Do People Really Get Their Idea of God from Their Own Fathers?"; "Christian Liberty and Questionable Practices"; "Counseling Disabled People," among others.

————. *Insight and Creativity in Christian Counseling: An Antidote to Rigid and Mechanical Approaches.* Grand Rapids: Zondervan, 1982.

Counselors must do justice both to the fundamental commonalities and to the diverse particulars of counseling and life situations. "Insight into the inner workings of sinful human beings, into their outer circumstances and problems, and into the correct meaning and applicability of appropriate Bible passages is absolutely essential to counseling."

————. *Handbook of Church Discipline.* Grand Rapids: Zondervan, 1986.

Presents a clear description of church discipline, embedding the formal and remedial aspects in a context of informal, preventive, positive discipline. The five steps of discipline include three informal aspects (practice self-discipline; go one-on-one; take one or two others) and two formal aspects (take it to the church; hand over to the world). Lots of how-to and what-if to guide individuals and churches in church discipline.

————. *How to Help People Change: The Four-Step Biblical Process.* Grand Rapids: Zondervan, 1986.

Unfolds the counseling process through an exposition of 2 Timothy 3:14–17. Bases all on the centrality of God and the vertical dimension for counseling: The Holy Spirit and the Word work in concert. Change unfolds through teaching, conviction, correction and training. Contains a reprint of Adams' 1982 article on "Integration."

————. *Sibling Rivalry in the Household of God.* Denver, Colo.: Accent Books, 1988.

Adams writes about "the causes and effects of rivalry among brothers and sisters in Christ and what can be done about it. . . . Sibling rivalry in the

household of faith—just like at home—is due entirely to sin." Other supposed causes are not causes but occasions for self-centered human nature
to act. The Holy Spirit gives practical guidance in His Word for solving
rivalry and conflict through repentance, faith, and obedience.

————. *From Forgiven to Forgiving: Discover the Path to Biblical Forgiveness.* Wheaton: Victor Books, 1989.

Adam's work sheds light on all aspects of seeking and granting forgiveness and counters erroneous views. It defines, illustrates, motivates and
challenges people to deal with forgiveness issues biblically and tackles
unbiblical concepts such as forgiving self, forgiving God, apologizing,
"forgive and forget."

Bobgan, Deidre. *Lord of the Dance.* Eugene, Ore.: Harvest House, 1987.

The author employs the disciplines and techniques of ballet as an extended
metaphor for the Christian life. Although intended for women, most of
the teaching is applicable to all Christians: honoring God, putting off and
putting on, prayer, the Word, discipline, the tongue, submission to God
and to husband, bearing fruit.

DeBardeleben, Martha Graves. *Fear's Answer: A Case History in
Nouthetic Counseling.* Phillipsburg, Penn.: Presbyterian and Reformed, 1980.
(Foreword by Jay Adams.)

The author relates her personal experiences with an elderly woman crippled
with pain, fear, depression, manipulation, and hallucinations who came to live
with her in 1978. Together they seek for biblical solutions to the elder woman's
needs. This is an encouraging and uplifting example of nouthetic counseling.

Eyrich, Howard A. *Three to Get Ready: A Christian Premarital
Counselor's Manual.* Phillipsburg, Penn.: Presbyterian and Reformed, 1978.

A detailed program for seven sessions of premarital counseling, this book
covers the basics of biblical marriage, self-awareness of personal traits, communication, money, sex, and wedding details. It contains numerous
questionnaires and personal inventories to copy for use in counseling.

Payne, Franklin E. *Biblical and Medical Ethics.* Milford, Mo.: Mott
Media, 1985.

————. *Making Biblical Decisions: Birth Control, Artificial Reproduction and Genetic Engineering.* Escondido, Calif.: Hosanna Book House, 1989.

Resources for Counselees

Adams, Jay *Christ and Your Problems*. Nutley, N. J.: Presbyterian and Reformed, 1971 (pamphlet).

An exposition of 1 Corinthians 10:13 for the benefit of counselees. This pamphlet will help counselees understand that God is faithful, therefore they can have hope. However difficult the pressures seem, people can make godly choices through Jesus Christ.

————. *Christian Living in the Home*. Phillipsburg, N. J.: Presbyterian and Reformed, 1972.

The purposes and promises of God bring hope to families. This book gives practical help and how-to for communication and problem solving, singleness, husband and wife roles and relationship, child discipline, and living with an unbelieving spouse.

————. *How to Overcome Evil*. Nutley, N. J.: Presbyterian and Reformed, 1977.

Adams uses Romans 12:14–21 to give practical details for overcoming evil. He emphasizes learning to assess self and the situation accurately in the light of who God is. He encourages counselees to make plans how they will obey Christ in tough situations.

————. *What Do You Do When Anger Gets the Upper Hand?* Phillipsburg, N. J.: Presbyterian and Reformed, 1975 (pamphlet).

"Anger, like a good horse, must be bridled." Uncontrolled temper is a sin. Counselees can learn to release the energies of anger productively and under control to solve problems.

————. *What Do You Do When Fear Overcomes You?* Phillipsburg, N. J.: Presbyterian and Reformed, 1975 (pamphlet).

Counselees need to learn to commit themselves prayerfully to doing what God requires of them whether or not this will be a fearful experience.

————. *What Do You Do When You Become Depressed?* Phillipsburg, N. J.: Presbyterian and Reformed, 1975 (pamphlet).

Counselees must know God personally before they can expect Him to give them the help that they need. The goal must not be alleviation of depression but, rather, the desire to please God by doing what He says.

————. *What Do You Do When You Know that You're Hooked?* Phillipsburg, N. J.: Presbyterian and Reformed, 1975 (pamphlet).

Counselees who are hooked on alcohol or other drugs must learn to put off the old behavior and attitudes and put on the new. They need to repent of their sins and restructure their lives concretely.

————. *What Do You Do When You Worry All the Time?* Phillipsburg, N. J.: Presbyterian and Reformed, 1975 (pamphlet).

Worry is concern about something no one can do anything about. That is why it tears us apart. Counselees are encouraged to ask three questions: What is my problem? What does God want me to do about it? When, where and how should I begin?

————. *What Do You Do When Your Marriage Goes Sour?* Phillipsburg, N. J.: Presbyterian and Reformed, 1975 (pamphlet).

Love is not first a feeling, because God commands love: to wife, to neighbor, even to enemy. Counselees with problems in their marriages must learn how to give love. They must forgive. The husband is responsible to take the initiative in love.

————. *What to Do about Worry.* Phillipsburg, N. J.: Presbyterian and Reformed, 1980.

Worry is a sin that Christians can learn to overcome. Counselees are encouraged to pray with thanksgiving, find God's solutions, and work on the problem God's way. The author states that when people find themselves worrying rather than working, they need to sit down and answer the following three questions: (1) What is my problem? (2) What does God want me to do about it? (3) When, where and how should I begin?

————. *How to Handle Trouble: God's Way.* Phillipsburg, N. J.: Presbyterian and Reformed, 1982.

Based on Philippians 1, this book presents six steps for handling trouble: recognize God is in the problem; remember God is up to something; believe that He is up to something good; discover where and how God is at work; get involved in what He is doing; expect good results.

————. *The War Within: A Biblical Strategy for Spiritual Warfare.* Eugene, Ore.: Harvest House, 1989.

The Christian life is war. The holy war between God and Satan is played out in the inner self in the conflict between the Holy Spirit and the flesh. This book describes Satan's tactics and power, and provides strategies for victory: the Spirit's sword, prayer, faith, the help of believers. "The prime purpose of this book is to encourage faltering Christians."

Bertolini, Dewey M. *Sometimes I Really Hate You!* Wheaton: Victor Books, 1991 (pamphlet).

An excellent handout especially for teens, this pamphlet teaches them how to handle bitterness against parents or others who have abused them.

Blanchard, John. **Ultimate Questions**. Durham, England: Evangelical Press, 1987.

Perhaps the single best gospel tract available today. It is well-written, colorful, and forthright. This book is ideal for counselors who work with non-Christians. It presents God, the Scriptures, sin, and the plan of salvation.

Bridges, Jerry. **Trusting God**. Colorado Springs, Colo.: NavPress, 1989.

This book presents the biblical directive for trusting God, even in the troubles and turmoil of life. It is especially profitable for the counselee going through deep hurt and struggle.

Hodge, Charles. **The Way of Life: A Guide to Christian Belief and Experience**. Edinburgh: Banner of Truth Trust, 1978 (reprinted from the original 1841 edition).

Although he was one of the greatest theologians that America has ever produced, and the most famous of the "Princeton Theologians," Hodge knew how to write for the average Christian. In this work he opens the Scriptures in a systematic manner and answers the question of how the great doctrines of the Bible must be translated into the everyday life of the believer. This is a book every Christian should read annually.

Kinneer, Jack. *How to Grow in Christ*. Phillipsburg, Penn.: Presbyterian and Reformed, 1981.

This workbook on basic discipleship provides a dozen Bible studies covering salvation, prayer, the Holy Spirit's presence, the Bible, overcoming sin, loving others, suffering, negative emotions, marriage, stewardship of resources, and personal evangelism.

Klempel, Richard, and Lois Klempel. *Abused? How You Can Find God's Help*. Lima, Ohio: Fairway Press, 1991 (foreword by Jay Adams).

"Directs readers to biblical answers to questions and biblical solutions to problems" enabling people "to avoid the all-too-frequently-encountered trap of building a lifestyle around the tragedy." Workbook deals with re-actions to abuse, God as Father, and practical steps to work through in order to change one's reactions to abuse.

Mack, Wayne A. *The Bible's Answer to the Question: What is a Christian?* Cherry Hill, N. J.: Mack Publishing, 1972.

This book challenges six common answers to what makes a Christian: per-forming good works; having relatives who are active Christians; church activity; going forward to accept Christ; no one can really know; every-body is a Christian. The Bible says four things about people who are Christians: (1) they are radically changed by the power of God; (2) they are increasingly aware of their unworthiness in the sight of God; (3) they be-lieve that Jesus Christ is God in the flesh and the only Savior of sinners; (4) they have repented of their sins and believed on the Lord Jesus Christ.

————. *Where Are You in Relation to God?* Cherry Hill, N. J.: Mack Publishing, 1973.

This booklet shows the diverse ways people express their hostility and alien-ation from God and explains how God in Jesus Christ reconciles people to Himself.

————. *Strengthening Your Marriage*. Phillipsburg, Penn.: Presby-terian and Reformed, 1977.

Eight units cover the basics of marital unity: God's purpose for marriage, the wife's responsibilities, the husband's responsibilities, communication, finances, sex, raising children, and family religion. Each chapter provides outlined teaching followed by Bible study, self-analysis, and personalized response and application.

————. *A Homework Manual for Biblical Living*. Vol. 1 and 2. Phillipsburg, Penn.: Presbyterian and Reformed, 1979; 1980.

————. *Your Family God's Way: Developing and Sustaining Relation-ships in the Home*. Phillipsburg, Penn.: Presbyterian and Reformed, 1991.

The author unfolds the vision of godly family life in Psalm 128. He calls on a husband and father to be first and foremost a "God-fearing" man and calls on a wife and mother to become a "fruitful vine" because of the intimacy of her relationship with God. He also calls on parents to view their children as precious "olive plants." The book contains study and application assignments for each chapter and provides extensive and practical discussion of communication and problem-solving principles.

—————. and Nathan A. Mack. *Preparing for Marriage God's Way.* Tulsa, Ok.: Virgil W. Hensley, 1986.

This workbook discusses seven basic tools for a successful marriage. It enables counselees to: (1) assess their marital readiness; (2) know the other person for what he/she really is; (3) uncover any current problems and pinpoint future ones; (4) understand the solutions for both current and future difficulties; (5) develop skills for communication and conflict resolution; (6) prevent future heartache; and (7) prepare for a satisfying, fulfilling, and God-honoring marriage.

Matzat, Don. *Christ Esteem: Where the Search for Self-Esteem Ends.* Eugene, Ore.: Harvest House, 1990.

Matzat presents the biblical teaching that the answer to life's problems is not found by looking inward but by looking to Christ.

Mayhue, Richard. *Spiritual Intimacy: Developing a Closer Relationship with God.* Wheaton: Victor Books, 1990.

Although not a book on counseling per se, it is, rather, a book of preventative maintenance. This is an ideal book to put into the hands of new Christians or those who have not received good initial nurturing in the Christian faith. Dr. Mayhue, Dean of The Master's Seminary, writes in a clear style and presents a fine blend of truth and practical advice on both developing and maintaining a close relationship with God.

Owen, Jim. *Christian Psychology's War on God's Word: The Victimization of the Believer.* Santa Barbara, Calif.: EastGate Publishers, 1993.

Owen, an Associate Professor of History at The Master's College, clearly presents the ravaging effects that so-called Christian psychology is having in the lives of believers. Owen urges believers to trust fully in Christ's ever-present provisions, the power of His indwelling Holy Spirit, and the sure guidance of the inerrant Word of God.

Ray, Bruce A. *Withhold Not Correction.* Phillipsburg, Penn.: Presbyterian and Reformed, 1978 (forward by Jay Adams).

If children were animals, behavioral manipulation would be appropriate. If children were innocent, diverting them into other activities when they are angry or selfish would be appropriate. But children bear the image of God, distorted by sin and correctable by the Gospel. Therefore, child-rearing is a process of correction and reorientation, and it must be guided by Scripture. Ray presents eight principles for biblical correction of children and provides a Parents' Topical Reference to Bible passages on two dozen issues relevant to children.

Sande, Ken. *The Peacemaker: A Biblical Guide to Resolving Personal Conflict.* Grand Rapids: Baker, 1990.

The author describes four phases of the reconciliation process: (1) glorify God, (2) get the log out of your own eye, (3) go and show your brother his fault, (4) go and be reconciled. The motivation and foundation for peacemaking lies in who God is, not in pragmatic self-interest. Self-examination and repentance lay the foundation for dealing well with the sins of others. Constructive confrontation involves both speaking the truth in love and listening in order to pursue understanding of the situation. Reconciliation and forgiveness are the culminating phase of peace making.

Whitney, Donald S. *Spiritual Disciplines for the Christian Life.* Colorado Springs, Colo.: NavPress, 1991.

Whitney has put together an excellent and practical book on the well-maintained Christian life. The entire area of discipline has been forgotten in virtually every aspect of life and particularly in the Christian life. True Christian living is a matter of discipline—discipline for the lifetime, not simply a series of steps or completed workbooks. Whitney discusses Bible study, prayer, worship, evangelism, serving, stewardship, and fasting among other vital topics.

Wiersbe, Warren W. *Why Us? When Bad Things Happen to God's People.* Old Tappan, N. J.: Fleming H. Revell, 1985.

Wiersbe takes on the task of answering the book by Rabbi Harold S. Kushner, *When Bad Things Happen to Good People.* Kushner took the position that bad things were unfortunate, but that God was not able to prevent them. The problem of evil in the world and the suffering of God's children are age old, but Wiersbe presents biblical understanding and the compassion of a godly pastor. This book can be a great help to counselees going through any type of severe trial.

AUDIO AND VIDEO RESOURCES FOR BIBLICAL COUNSELING

A large number of audio and video tapes are available to help biblical counselors. Here are five reliable sources for the materials outlined below:

1. **Biblical Counseling and Living Supplies**
   2299 Broadhead Road
   Bethlehem, Pennsylvania 18017
   Telephone 215-758-8586

2. **Biblical Counseling and Living Supplies**
   C/o Mrs. Carol Mack
   18707 Nathan Hill Road
   Santa Clarita, California 91351
   Telephone 805-298-1668

3. **Sound Word Cassettes**
   430 Boyd Circle
   P. O. Box 2035, Mail Station
   Michigan City, Indiana 46360

4. **Grace to You**
   P. O. Box 4000
   Panorama City, California 91412
   Telephone 800-55-GRACE

5. **Grace Book Shack**
   13248 Roscoe Boulevard
   Sun Valley, California 91352
   Telephone 818-909-5555

Sessions at the annual NANC (National Association of Nouthetic Counselors) Conference are recorded and made available to those who request copies. Normally a single theme is emphasized each year. These tapes are available through Sound Word Cassettes. The materials listed below by Jay Adams and others involved in biblical counseling are also available through Sound Word Cassettes. Grace to You is the primary source for tapes and materials by John MacArthur. (While John MacArthur's ministry is one of biblical exposition, his material is invaluable for the counselor.) Grace Book Shack stocks a wide variety of books and materials by John MacArthur, Jay Adams, Wayne Mack, and other biblical counselors. Additional titles by various leaders in the biblical counseling movement are available through the sources listed above.

Adams, Jay. *Competent to Counsel Training Series*

The teaching sessions on these cassettes are designed to cover the basic training needed for Christians in biblical counseling. These tapes are also excellent for small study groups involving church officers and other leaders.

———. *Crisis Counseling Series*

This series is designed to train counselors for crisis situations that require immediate action.

———. *Biblical Forgiveness Series*

Adams focuses on what the Bible teaches about Man's need for forgiveness; The Meaning and Basis of God's Forgiveness; Jesus' Command to Forgive; Forgiveness: Promise or Feeling; Judging Your Brother; Church Discipline; Seeking Forgiveness; and Confession.

MacArthur, John Jr. *Guidelines for Singleness and Marriage*

These six tapes focus on decisions regarding marriage. They emphasize how to know when marriage is right and how to strengthen a marriage. Taken from 1 Corinthians 6–7, MacArthur presents a biblical exposition of all the issues of the Christian life in these areas.

———. *Breaking Sin's Grip*

MacArthur presents six solutions to the indwelling sins that so often paralyze believers. The series is designed to encourage Christians to grow in holiness and to maintain a close walk with God.

———. *Spiritual Bootcamp*

These tapes are designed to assist the new Christian to grow in the faith. Since Christians can expect to face many spiritual challenges, MacArthur presents the means to meet those challenges.

————. *The Fulfilled Family*

In this series the author presents the biblical model for a strong family life as taken from an exposition of Ephesians 5:21–6:4.

————. *Perfect Love*

MacArthur states, "Think how your relationship with your spouse, children, friends, family, and co-workers would change if you could dramatically increase your understanding of biblical love." This exposition of 1 Corinthians chapter 13 is designed to show what biblical love is all about.

Mack, Wayne. *Strengthening Your Marriage Series*

Twenty-Six tapes cover subjects such as: God's Blueprint for Marriage, Conflict Resolution in Marriage, Communication, Real Love or Reel Love, Getting Along with In-Laws, and Questions About Divorce.

————. *Strengthening Your Family Series*

Thirteen tapes deal with the entire spectrum of what God desires for the family.

————. *Solving Life's Problem Series*

Thirty-five tapes cover subjects such as anger, hope, anxiety, depression, loneliness, and getting along with people.

————. *Basic Biblical Counselor Training Course*

Twelve tapes and a syllabus are designed for the basic principles and practice of biblical counseling.

————. *Marriage and Family Counselor Training Course*

Eighteen tapes and a course syllabus are designed for those who are particularly interested in marriage and family counseling from a biblical viewpoint.

————. *Counseling Adolescents Seminar*

These four tapes specialize in counseling problems of adolescents.

————. *Counseling Incest Victims*

Two tapes deal with this traumatic issue from a biblical perspective.

————. *Be a People Helper*

A mini series of five tapes on how to be a biblical people helper.

————. *God's Plan for The Home*

Ten tapes covering many different aspects of family living.

————. *God's Plan for Rearing Children*

Five tapes discuss various aspects of biblical parenting.

————. *Preparing for Marriage Training Course Seminar*

A thirteen tape series that discusses important issues for people who are preparing for marriage. A syllabus containing outlines for each session is also available.

PERIODICALS

The Journal of Biblical Counseling (formerly *The Journal of Pastoral Practice*) is the triennial publication of the Christian Counseling and Education Foundation (CCEF). The address for subscription information is 1803 East Willow Grove Avenue, Laverock, Pennsylvania 19118. Telephone 215-884-7676. Currently subscription rates are eighteen dollars annually.

The Biblical Counselor is the regular newsletter of The National Association of Nouthetic Counselors (NANC). The address for subscription information is 5526 SR 26 East, Layfayette, Indiana 47905. Telephone 317-448-9100. The newsletter is offered free of charge, although contributions to offset costs are appreciated.

TRAINING OPPORTUNITIES

The Master's College
21726 Placerita Canyon Road
P. O. Box 221450
Santa Clarita, California 91322
Telephone 805-259-3540

Information about counseling studies and other majors is available on request. Under the direction of Dr. Wayne Mack, the Biblical Studies Department offers a degree in Biblical Studies with an emphasis in Biblical Counseling. The eight core courses in Biblical Counseling include:

(1) Introduction to Biblical Counseling, (2) The Theological Basis for Biblical Counseling, (3) Methods of Biblical Change, (4) Marriage and Family Counseling, (5) Problems and Procedures in Biblical Counseling, and (6) Counseling Practicum.

Biblical Counseling Foundation
P. O. Box 925
Rancho Mirage, California 92270

This foundation trains lay people and pastors in discipleship methods largely influenced by biblical counseling.

Faith Baptist Counseling Ministries
5526 State Road 26 East
Lafayette, Indiana 47905

This organization offers counseling in the local area and trains interested persons in the principles of biblical counseling. They also offer assistance to local churches in developing and refining a counseling ministry.

National Association of Nouthetic Counselors
5526 SR 26 East
Lafayette, Indiana 47905

NANC offers seminars throughout the United States featuring key leaders in biblical counseling. It also offers training at the headquarters in Indiana and serves as a resource center for local churches.

Christian Counseling and Educational Foundation
1803 East Willow Grove Avenue
Laverock, Pennsylvania 19118
Telephone 215-884-7676

CCEF presents extensive training in biblical counseling in several avenues: (1) instruction leading to a lay certificate in biblical counseling, (2) weekend training modules in local churches, (3) participation in M. A. programs at Biblical Theological Seminary and Westmininster Theological Seminary. Mr. John Bettler is the executive director.

The Masters' Seminary
13248 Roscoe Blvd.
Sun Valley, California 91352
Telephone 818-909-5627

The Masters' Seminary, as part of its regular Master of Divinity and Master of Theology programs, offers courses in biblical counseling as part of the required and elective course offering.

Biblical Theological Seminary
200 North Main Street
Hatfield, Pennsylvania 19440
Telephone 215-368-5000

Biblical Theological Seminary offers training in biblical counseling as part of its regular and elctive course offerings, as well as an M. A. track.

Westmininster Theological Seminary

(Philadelphia Campus)
Chestnut Hill
P. O. Box 27009
Philadelphia, Pennsylvania 19118
Telephone 215-887-5511

(Escondido Campus)
1725 Bear Valley Parkway
Escondido, California 92027
Telephone 619-480-8474

Both campuses of Westminister Theological Seminary (Philadelphia and Escondido) offer an M.A. program in biblical counseling, as well as biblical counseling courses and electives in other degree offerings.

21

Frequently Asked Questions About Biblical Counseling

Compiled and Edited by Dennis M. Swanson

The purpose of this book is to help both pastors and lay people become familiar with the principles of biblical counseling and to apply them in the life of the Church. Because the concept of integration has held sway for so many decades and the psychological model for counseling has been virtually unchallenged in the Church, Christians have raised many questions regarding the entire concept of biblical counseling. Jay Adams, in his book *What About Nouthetic Counseling* (Baker, 1976), dealt with many questions about this subject, but there have been additional and more pointed questions posed of biblical counseling since then. The questions presented here represent a sample of the questions that are most frequently asked. The answers to these questions have been prepared by various members of the staff and faculty of The Master's College, Grace Community Church, and others who contributed to this book.

Is there any difference between biblical counseling and Christian psychology or Christian counseling?

At a superficial glance, it would appear that a biblical counselor and a psychotherapist who is a Christian do many of the same things. Both converse with people; both care about people; both get to know people; both are interested in motivation, thoughts, emotions, and behavior; both explore the various pressures in a person's situation; both give feedback; perhaps both talk about Jesus or a passage of Scripture. So how do they differ?

To understand how Christianized psychotherapy differs from biblical counseling it is necessary to look closely at what each practices and teaches. Here are some of the distinctives of each.

Perspective of the Bible and its contribution to counseling. Most Christian psychologists view the Bible as an inspirational resource, but their basic system of counseling, both theory and methods, is transferred unaltered from secular psychology. Most are frankly and self-consciously eclectic, picking and choosing theories and techniques according to personal preference. In contrast, biblical counselors follow the Bible's view of itself as the source of a comprehensive and detailed approach to understanding and counseling people (2 Tim. 3:15–17; 2 Pet. 1:4).

Some Christian psychotherapists use few Scriptures; others use many. But frequency of citation is much less important than the way passages are used—or misused—and in the vast majority of cases the passages cited are completely misused. There is a dearth of contextualized exegesis (a critical interpretation of a text) and an abundance of eisegesis (interpreting a text by reading one's own ideas into it). Biblical counseling is committed to letting God speak for Himself through His Word, and to handling the Word of Truth rightly (2 Tim. 2:15).

Perspective of God. There are many aspects of God that Christian psychologists routinely ignore. In particular, His sovereignty, holiness, justice, kingly authority, and power are virtually unmentioned. The fatherly love of God is the great theme of these psychotherapists, but detached from the entirety of who God is, this love becomes the unconditional positive regard of a great therapist in the sky, indistinguishable from classic liberal theology. Biblical counseling follows the Bible and seeks to minister the love of the true and living God, whose love deals with sin and produces obedience (1 John).

Perspective of human nature and motivation. Almost every Christian psychologist espouses some variety of need theory. Needs for self-esteem, for love and acceptance, and for significance tend to dominate. If these needs are met, it is believed that people will be happy, kind and moral; if not met, people will be miserable, hateful, and immoral. Christian psychologists borrow their motivation theory directly from humanistic psychology. Scripture flatly opposes such need theories because it teaches that sinful human motivation roots in various cravings and lusts (Gal. 5:16–24, Eph. 2:3; James 1:14–16; 3:13–4:12). Scripture teaches that God changes our desires and that godly motivation is rooted in the desire for God and godliness. If people crave self-esteem, love, and significance, they will be happy if they get it and miserable if they don't, but they will remain self-centered in either case. On the other hand, if people desire God (Ps. 42:1f; 73:25), God's kingdom (Matt. 6:9–13; 6:33; 13:45f), godly wisdom (Prov. 3:15; 2 Tim. 2:22), and resurrection glory (Rom. 8:18–25), they will be satisfied, joyous, obedient, and profitable servants of God.

Perspective of the gospel. For most Christian psychologists, Jesus Christ is the meter of built-in psychic needs and the healer of psychic wounds. The love of God at the cross simply portrays how valuable one is to God in order to boost self-esteem and to meet the need to be loved. But in the Bible, Jesus Christ is the Lamb of God crucified in the place of sinners. The love of God actually demolishes self-esteem and the lust for self-esteem. It produces, instead, a great and grateful esteem for the Son of God, who loved us and gave His life for us—the Lamb of God who alone is worthy. The love of God does not meet our lust to be loved as we are. It demolishes that deluded craving in order to love us despite who we are and to teach us to love God and neighbor (1 John 4:7–5:3).

Perspective of counseling. Christian psychologists tend to view counseling the same way secular psychologists view it: as a professional activity without any necessary connection to the Church of Jesus Christ. A client with a felt-need engages a professional for help in attaining goals of personal adjustment, emotional happiness, stability, self-fulfillment, and the like. But biblical counselors follow the Bible and view counseling as a pastoral activity. Their counseling aims at progressive sanctification and must communicate the true contents of Scripture. Biblical counseling connects logically and structurally to worship, discipleship, preaching, pastoral oversight, use of gifts, church discipline, and other aspects of life in the body of Christ.

(David Powlison)

I have heard that those who practice biblical counseling are unsympathetic, mean-spirited, and callous. Is this true?

Biblical counselors are certainly none of these things. In truth, they are just the opposite. Biblical counselors want to come alongside counselees in concern and love as they address the problems. They want to help individuals find biblical solutions; they encourage change for God's glory primarily but also for the counselee's own benefit.

The apostle Paul serves as a good model for biblical counselors. He reminded the elders of the church at Ephesus (Acts 20:20) how he had not held back anything in his teaching that was profitable for them. He had even gone house to house in order to minister to them. Then in verse 31 he shows the spirit of humility in his heart as he says, "Night and day for a period of three years I did not cease to admonish (*nŏuthĕtĕō*) each one with tears." Even though Paul had to admonish these people and tell them the truth, he was not unsympathetic, mean-spirited, or callous with them.

Another passage illustrating Paul's compassion is 1 Thessalonians 2:7–9. There he makes the point with his readers that he was gentle with them (v. 7), and that he had imparted not only truth to them but his own life (v. 8). Paul was known for speaking the truth, but speaking it in love (Eph. 4:15, 29). And that is what a biblical counselor does. The counselor establishes involvement in the life of the counselee and gives hope that the person's problem can be overcome. Many counselees have never experienced this type of caring confrontation. They have never experienced true concern and compassion—traits that are essential prerequisites of a nouthetic counselor.

(*Carey Hardy*)

Do secular disciplines have absolutely nothing to offer to biblical counseling methodology?

Let us clarify first what we mean by counseling methodology. A counseling methodology is a *system* of theoretical commitments, principles, goals, and appropriate methods. It is a set of interconnected things; it is not a collection of random and eclectic bits of observation or technique. A counseling methodology is an organized, committed way of understanding and tackling people's problems.

Do secular disciplines have anything to offer to the methodology of biblical counseling? The answer is a flat no. Scriptures provide the system for biblical counseling. Other disciplines—history, anthropology, literature, sociology, psychology, biology, business, political science—may be useful in a variety of secondary ways to the pastor and the biblical counselor, but such disciplines can never provide a system of understanding and counseling people.

Secular disciplines may serve us well as they describe people; they may challenge us by how they seek to explain, guide, and change people; but they seriously mislead us when we take them at face value because they are secular. They explain people, define what people ought to be like, and try to solve people's problems without considering God and man's relationship to God. Secular disciplines have made a systematic commitment to being wrong.

This is not to deny that secular people are often brilliant observers of other human beings. They are often ingenious critics and theoreticians. But they also distort what they see and mislead by what they teach and do, because from God's point of view the wisdom of the world has fundamental folly written through it. They will not acknowledge that God has created human beings as God-related and God-accountable creatures. The mind-set of secularity is like a power saw with a set that deviates from the right angle. It may be a powerful saw, and it may cut a lot of wood, but every board comes out crooked.

Given this built-in distortion, how might secular observations, ideas, and practices be useful to Christians? They should play *no* role in our *model* of counseling. But, radically reinterpreted, they can play an illustrative role, providing examples and details that illustrate the biblical model and fill out our knowledge. They can also play a provocative role, challenging us to develop our model in areas we have not thought about or have neglected or misconstrued. Jay Adams stated this succinctly in *Competent to Counsel*, where he explains that psychology can be a "useful adjunct" to biblical counseling in two ways: (1) "for the purposes of illustrating, filling in generalizations with specifics"; and (2) "challenging wrong human interpretations of Scripture, thereby forcing the student to restudy the Scriptures".[1]

What do secular disciplines have to offer biblical counselors? God is the expert when it comes to people, and He has spoken and acted to change us and to equip us to help others change. Secularists have a twisted and blinkered perceptiveness that can only be useful to biblical counselors as it is radically reinterpreted according to the counseling methodology revealed in Scripture. (Chapters 11–17 of this book present a biblical methodology for helping people.)

(David Powlison)

Isn't biblical counseling overly simplistic?

If overly simplistic means that biblical counseling does not seem to be as sophisticated as say, psychology or psychiatry, with its intricate terms and methods, then yes, it is more simple. But note that it is not simplistic.

It has been well stated, "Simple language no more indicates simplistic thinking than complex language indicates profundity of thought." In its essence, biblical counseling is simple in that it seeks to find the answers

---

1. Jay Adams, *Competent to Counsel*, (Grand Rapids: Zondervan, 1970), xxi.

to the problems of sin from the pages of Scripture. It does not seek to find those answers anywhere else except in God's Word, for nowhere else is there a remedy for this desperately needed cure. Lest we be criticized unnecessarily at this point, let us clarify that the difficulties of this life are, admittedly, enormous—but they are not impossible to understand and they can provide impetus for growth. To simply assert that the problems of life and sin are simple and then to move on to something else is to miss the point entirely. God's Word has the simple yet profound truths that change people into the very image of Jesus Christ. Those whose commitment is to Scripture and its sufficiency will base their counseling efforts on the foundation of that standard.

Peter's commitment was spelled out in these terms: "His divine power has granted to us everything pertaining to life and godliness, through the true knowledge of Him [through Scripture] who called us by His own glory and excellence" (2 Pet. 1:3). Biblical counseling, then, provides the only sure and superior basis for helping people, and because this is so, it cannot inherently be called simplistic. If so, it would impugn the character of God Himself, as though He were simplistic. The truth is, in the final analysis, biblical counselors are actually the ones who go deep into the region of the soul—into all arenas of mankind's being—whereas others do not go deep enough! Only the man or woman who is equipped with God's tools (His Word and Spirit) can traverse the murky waters of the human heart. Proverbs 20:5 declares: "A plan in the heart of a man is like deep water, but a man of understanding draws it out." Biblical counselors, not those who pretend to deal with the deep issues, are the ones who can truly draw out the real issues of life.

Counselors who are committed to Scripture alone do not need to bend to the pressure of those who would want them to somehow see complex and intricate issues in every counseling situation. Of course, some situations are going to be more difficult than others, but it cannot be charged that biblical counseling is overly simplistic. Jay Adams deftly counters this charge by stating, "I consider both clarity and simplicity virtues, not vices. In my opinion, whatever darkens understanding is a detriment; whatever lightens it deserves praise. . . . I look on clarity as a sacred obligation of a Christian minister, whether he speaks from the pulpit or whether he writes with his pen. Obscurity is the father of heresy and ambiguity is the mother of all error. Clarity bears a close relationship to truth."[2]

(S. Lance Quinn)

---

2. Jay Adams, *What About Nouthetic Counseling?* (Grand Rapids: Baker, 1979), 3–4.

Since the Bible is not a textbook on psychology, don't we need to supplement it with other disciplines to understand and help people with deep psychological needs?

At first glance, this seems like a reasonable question. The scientific disciplines *have* shown us truth that goes beyond the truth of Scripture. All of us have benefited from medical knowledge that is, after all, extra-biblical. Appendectomies, for example, have saved countless lives in the past hundred years or so. Smallpox vaccinations have virtually wiped out the disease. If we limited ourselves in medicine to the remedies specifically revealed in Scripture, we would be at a tremendous disadvantage in the treatment of diseases.

Certainly, Scripture does *not* claim to be a thorough textbook on medicine, or physics, or any of the sciences.[3] But psychology differs from these in two important regards. First, psychology is not a true science (see discussion on pages 8–20). It does not deal with objective, measurable data that can be subjected to reliable tests and confirmed by the scientific method. It is a pseudo-science, and most of its cardinal doctrines are mere speculations, not reliable truth.

Second, and most significant, psychology, unlike medicine and physics, deals with matters that are fundamentally spiritual. In fact, the word *psychology* literally means, "study of the soul." What are deep psychological needs if they are not the spiritual issues the gospel is concerned with? And Scripture certainly does claim absolute sufficiency in addressing those needs: "All Scripture is inspired by God and profitable for teaching, for reproof, for correction, for training in righteousness; *that the man of God may be adequate, equipped for every good work*" (2 Tim. 3:16–17, emphasis added). "The law of the LORD is perfect, restoring the soul" (Ps. 19:7). Scripture itself promises believers the most comprehensive spiritual resources: "everything pertaining to life and godliness" (2 Pet. 1:3).

Is the problem depression? Scripture contains the only reliable remedy. Is the problem guilt? What can psychology offer that goes beyond the perfect solution Scripture suggests—"The blood of Christ . . . [that cleanses] your conscience from dead works to serve the living God" (Heb. 9:14)? Every so-called psychological need that is not traceable to physical causes is, in reality, a spiritual problem, and Scripture does indeed claim to be the only sufficient guide in handling spiritual problems. To attempt to

---

3. Wherever Scripture speaks on any of these matters, however, its revelation is true, reliable, and without error: "All Scripture is inspired by God and profitable for teaching . . ." (2 Tim. 3:16).

add psychological theory to the unfailing testimony of God's Word is to adulterate God's truth with human opinion.

(John MacArthur Jr.)

Is biblical counseling really necessary? Isn't discipleship sufficient?

Christian discipleship is the process of passing the truths of God's Word that one has learned and applied on to another believer (2 Tim. 2:2). It takes time. It may involve the investment of years of teaching, training, encouraging, and rebuking. The goal during this process is to help the disciplee grow to maturity in Christ, to walk consistently according to God's Word. The discipler equips the individual so that ultimately that person in turn begins to build biblical principles into the lives of others (again, 2 Tim. 2:2). The person who imparts truth about God to someone else will also sharpen and mature through the discipleship process.

From this perspective, it should be apparent that biblical counseling is actually a *part* of discipleship. It is not the distinct entity the world and many Christians make it. In fact, much of what one would say about discipleship could be said equally about counseling. In counseling, though, the discipleship process has progressed to more *specific* application of biblical principles, to more *specific* problems in the life of a believer. Perhaps the individual requires more structure and accountability than a normal discipling relationship might provide. This is especially true if the issues being dealt with are ingrained habits in the counselee's life.

Normally, in a counseling relationship specific problems are dealt with over a much shorter period of time than in a discipling relationship. It is not necessary to counsel an individual for years. In many cases, people who are saved need only a few weeks to understand the biblical principles involved to change their thinking concerning the issue and, thus, to change their behavior or responses to their circumstances.

There are instances in the discipling process when specific problems are identified, and in the course of addressing those issues the discipler counsels the individual. It is also true that in the process of biblical counseling a person may be able to resolve the issue that necessitated the counseling but will want to continue in a discipling relationship with a mature believer for help with further spiritual growth. Thus, discipling at times necessitates counseling, and counseling at times functions as a concentrated form of discipleship.

(Carey Hardy)

How do God's grace and the gospel fit into biblical counseling?

The Bible speaks of God's grace in the good news of Jesus Christ. When Jesus opened the minds of His disciples to understand the Scriptures, He explained to them the things concerning Himself. The Bible is *about* Jesus Christ the Savior and Lord; therefore, biblical counseling is *about* Jesus Christ the Savior and Lord. When Jesus opened the minds of His disciples to understand the Scriptures, He spoke of repentance, the forgiveness of sins, and making disciples. The Bible is *about* making sinners into children of the Father; therefore, biblical counseling is *about* making sinners into children of the Father. When Jesus opened the minds of His disciples to understand the Scriptures, He taught them to minister like their gracious Master; therefore, biblical counseling carries a gracious message. Biblical counselors embody a gracious method: loving candor, humility, prayerful dependency, wisdom, gentleness, boldness, kindness, persistence, courage, authority, flexibility, self-sacrifice, and patience. The Bible is *about* equipping counselors to minister the whole counsel of God. Therefore biblical counseling is *about* equipping counselors to minister the whole counsel of God.

What then is the place of God's grace and gospel in biblical counseling? That is rather like asking, "What is the place of water and oxygen in human physiology"? The gospel is the fundamental material of biblical counseling. Every part of biblical counseling is made of gospel and grace; from understanding people and their problems to solving those problems.

Why do people wonder whether grace is central to biblical counseling? There are three possible reasons. First, many people think that the purpose of the Bible is to get people saved and tell them what to do. From that perspective, all the counselor can say to people is, "Here is how to accept the gospel and God's forgiving grace so you will go to heaven. Now, until then, do this. Do not do that. Shape up. Just say, 'no.' Be a good person." Such moralizing, however, is antibiblical. The Bible does not tack willpower and self-effort onto grace. The gospel and grace of God are not only about forgiveness for the guilt of sin but about God's power to change believers progressively throughout their lives. The indwelling Spirit intends to change people in the practical details of life. God's self-revelation becomes the environment we live in; God's promises become the food we live on; God's commands become the life we live out. Can anyone doubt that biblical counseling worthy of the name is a ministry of God's own power in the gospel, changing people both inwardly and outwardly?

Here is a second reason people ask about the place of grace in biblical counseling. Biblical counselors aim for practical obedience. Many people think that emphasizing obedience to God's commands means ignoring or contradicting the free grace of the gospel. But free grace is effective grace. It is no treat to be forgiven adultery and yet remain adulterous. It is no glory to God to forgive anger and yet leave people given to angry outbursts. It is no honor to the gospel if anxiety can be forgiven yet people who are nervous wrecks continue to live in unbelief. It is no advance for God's kingdom to forgive self-centered people, if they do not learn in some measure how to consider the interests of others. It is no happiness for a grumbler to be forgiven, if that person remains utterly self-absorbed, demanding, and pessimistic. It does no good to either the world or the Church if forgiven war makers do not learn how to become practical peacemakers. God is in the business of making disciples through the grace of the gospel. The Spirit will produce His desires and His fruit, and biblical counseling is a servant of such practical and sweet-tasting changes.

The third reason people ask about the place of grace in biblical counseling is that would-be biblical counselors sometimes fall short of being biblical. What biblical counselor is not aware of failures in pastoral wisdom when seeking to minister the counsel of God? The solution to this dilemma is short and succinct: biblical counselors need to become more biblical. They need to ask God to reveal their shortcomings; they need to repent of folly; they need to seek the God who gives wisdom without reproaching; and they need to humbly learn from more skilled and mature biblical counselors. Biblical counseling is the ministry of God's grace to individuals, just as biblical preaching is the ministry of God's grace to the multitudes.

(David Powlison)

Why do biblical counselors refuse to use information from science and psychology?

First of all, biblical counselors are primarily concerned with the problem of sin and how people can change and grow (sanctification) for God's glory. Science (in general), as we now know it, does not concern itself with either the problem of sin or God, so there is no reason for biblical counselors to use science for the purpose of man's sanctification to the glory of God. The question of the use of psychology in counseling is a bit different. It must be said up front that psychology, as such, is not science per se. While psychologists would want people to assume that it is, psychology is the *study* of human behavior, not the *science* of human behavior. Human behavior cannot be scientifically studied, as though someone with a white coat could take a person's attitude and analyze it in a test tube. Even if, somehow, all of the issues of the human heart could be empirically quantified and verified, no psychologist or scientist could provide the proper interpretations or solutions of problems apart from the revealed Word of God and its direct application to the human heart.

It must be stated as clearly as possible that biblical counselors do not object to psychology or to psychologists as such. There are some in the general field of psychology who are performing important tasks, say, in the area of studying sleep patterns of individuals and what profit can be gained from such study. The objection biblical counselors have to psychologists (and even psychiatrists for that matter) is when they attempt to give nonbiblical (and in many cases, patently unbiblical) solutions to people's sin problems. As one of the leaders in the biblical counseling movement, Jay Adams has rightly observed, "When psychologists attempt to change men, although they have no warrant from God to do so, no standard by which to determine what are proper or deviant attitudes or behavior, no concept of what man *should* look like, and no power by which to achieve the inner change of heart and thought that are so necessary, I cannot help but be concerned"[4]

When it comes to true "soul work," only those ordained by God to do so can be used by God to change lives. The apparatus necessary is the Word of God—shared through illumination by the Spirit of God, given by and administered through those called by God in the local church. Psychology or psychiatry, though it may purport to be under the aegis of the local church, if it is not under the functioned control of Holy Scripture, is not useful or helpful to the biblical counselor and could even be (and certainly is!) destructive to the counseling process.

We cannot assume that when psychologists make judgments regarding human behavior, they are doing so in a purely unbiased and scientific way if they go on to suggest solutions for change in that behavior apart from the control of God's Word. All proposed solutions to the problem of sin come down to our view of God and His Word. Any attempt to provide solutions apart from biblical exegesis, theology, and the application of the fruit of that study to the heart will result in faulty counseling, whether from psychologists or pastors.

(S. Lance Quinn)

Is it true that biblical counseling de-emphasizes graduate studies and overly emphasizes training in biblical discipleship?

In most professions today a graduate education is either required or highly recommended. If one were to pursue state licensure in any of the helping professions, such as psychology or marriage and family counseling, a graduate education would be required. Normally, this would

---

4. Adams, *Nouthetic Counseling*, 31.

require at least one year beyond the B. A. plus numerous hours of supervised internship. This is the normal approach for most Christian psychology programs.

But biblical counseling does not follow this conventional educational track, and because of that is perceived by some as less academically rigorous and, therefore, lacking in substantive content. The question must be asked, however, "What does one study in a Christian psychology curriculum?" If we looked in the catalogue of any Christian college in America, we would readily see that the courses taught at both the undergraduate and graduate levels primarily consist of theory and applied classes in psychology. Typically, students who pursue this curriculum complete a core of lower-division Bible courses along with courses in their major of counseling or psychology, which are taught largely by instructors who have a minimum academic background in biblical studies. But how can instructors who lack theological education properly integrate psychology and the Bible? And how can they possible use the Bible as the infallible reference point for psychology?

Since biblical counselors believe the Bible is sufficient for dealing with all matters of faith and practice, students who desire to pursue a biblical counseling ministry are encouraged to continue their education at the graduate level in a graduate program that is theologically based and offers courses in biblical counseling ministry and technique. At the heart and soul of biblical counseling are the knowledge and application of God's Word. This must be the foundation of any biblical counseling education at both the undergraduate and graduate level.

All who are committed to the biblical counseling movement must strenuously pursue academic excellence in counselor training. This demands a high level of formal education, which should take place in colleges and seminaries that hold to a high view of Scripture. Faculty at these institutions should be highly skilled in understanding and applying theology, biblical content, and practical theology. Based on this foundation, practical courses in biblical counseling should be taught by faculty who have both biblical and theological skill coupled with practical experience in biblical counseling. The third part of this academic preparation should be an internship in a local church under the guidance of both faculty and pastors. We must produce men and women who, because of their understanding of Scripture and what it reveals about the human condition, are qualified by academic training and commitment to Christ and His Word to counsel others.

(John P. Stead)

Does biblical counseling deny the existence of mental or emotional illness and the healing that is necessary in these areas?

The concept of mental illness is a theory based upon a medical model of illness. In the medical model an organic illness is the cause of various symptoms in the body. The body is sick because something from without has affected it. Thus, a person has the flu because of a flu virus. It is not that person's fault that he or she has the flu. That person cannot be held responsible for the inability to work since the illness is the result of something that affected the body.

This same logic is used in dealing with behavior that is difficult to explain. When a person has bizarre behavior and no organic cause for the behavior is found by laboratory studies, nonbelievers have theorized that the person is mentally sick. Just as the body gets sick, they conclude the mind is sick. Since the mind is sick, the person cannot control the behavior and thus is not responsible for any actions. Any time a person functions in an abnormal (irresponsible) way, that person is considered mentally or emotionally ill—with a mind and emotions that are believed to be sick.

The difficulty with this theory is that it cannot be proved. There are tests that measure thinking, but these cannot prove that the mind is sick. Even though the mind uses the brain, the mind is not the brain. Tumors, severe injuries, strokes, etc. can damage part of the brain and may affect how the person thinks and acts, but these are not mental illnesses, they are organic illnesses that can be proved in the laboratory. They can cause the brain to be sick but not the mind. While parts of the brain that are damaged may not be available to the mind, the mind is not sick. There is brain damage, not mental illness. The concept of the mind being sick is a theory with no scientific proof.

Psychiatry uses disease labels to describe different groups of symptoms. When an organic illness is found, it is given a label that describes the problem in the body. For example, it may be found through a medical examination that a person with the diagnosis of depression has an underactive thyroid. In this case, the diagnosis is changed from depression to hypothyroidism. If mental illness had an organic basis the term *mental illness* would be substituted by the name of the physical disease in the body.

One argument for the existence of an organic basis for behavior problems is based on the improvement some people achieve through medications. Yet this logic is unscientific. Two concurrent events do not automatically mean one caused the other. For example, 100 percent of the people who ate carrots in 1825 are now dead. If we followed that argument's reasoning, we would conclude that carrots are a dangerous food—obviously an illogical conclusion. Yet it is also illogical to conclude that because medications improve a person's feelings, the person has an organic illness.

The biblical counselor is accused of denying reality. Yet who is to say this is reality? Even though the majority of people in our society accept the theory of mental illness as a fact, that still does not make it a fact. Such reasoning is not scientific but philosophical. This is the same logic that says believers deny the existence of Santa Claus or the Easter Bunny. Many people believe they exist, so does that make them real? Since mental illness is a theory and not a fact, biblical counselors do not deny the existence of something that has been proven to exist by empirical data gained in the laboratory. There is no need to deny the existence of something that does not exist.

The behavior and thinking characterized as mental illness totally ignores what the Bible teaches. When people's problems are not handled biblically, the results are confused thinking and bad feelings. These add to the problems that must be handled. When people live by their feelings, their behavior is affected. Attempts are made to improve the feelings and through this to improve the behavior. But when these attempts fail (as they will), further problems are created; the thinking becomes more and more confused attempting to deal with the difficult situations. As this spiral continues, the person ends up with bizarre thinking and behavior. The problem is not the feelings or emotions but the thinking and actions. When the Bible is not used to deal with problems, thoughts, and feelings, the result will be confused thoughts and actions. This continues until the thinking and behavior are bizarre. The emotions do not need to be healed since they are not sick; they are the natural result of unbiblical thinking.

The question also implies that the failure to accept mental illness as a reality is cruel since this means that healing is not available, thus the biblical position is cruel. In reality, however, the opposite is true. Those who label the behavior as illness are cruel since they remove the hope and victory available through the application of biblical principles. When the medical model argues that the person is sick, can it guarantee that a cure is even possible? How is healing to be defined? What happens if it does not occur? Since, in reality, there is no mental illness, to offer healing is to encourage a fraudulent and futile hope. In essence this removes true hope and that is the *truly* cruel action.

Biblical counselors can offer something superior to healing—they can offer victory in the midst of difficult circumstances, rather than improved feelings or attempts to change the circumstances. This is biblical and far superior to a healing that cannot be defined or measured. Biblical counseling is loving because it produces the victory God has promised.

(Robert Smith, M.D.)

Why does biblical counseling hold to a dichotomous rather than a trichotomous view of mankind?

Dichotomy teaches that people are composed of two distinct elements, body and soul. The body represents everything material, while the soul represents everything immaterial. In this case, the terms *soul* and *spirit* are understood as viewing the immaterial aspect of human nature from different vantage points. That is, the numerical essence of *soul* and *spirit* is one.

Evidence for dichotomy can be found in Scripture's interchangeable usage of the terms *soul* (*nephesh* in the OT and *psyche* in the NT) and *spirit* (*ruah* in the OT and *pneuma* in the NT). For instance, compare Genesis 35:18 and 31:5, as well as John 12:27 and 13:21. Another line of argument is the importance of the *soul* as it is used in various contexts to represent the totality of the immaterial aspect of mankind. For example, see Mark 12:30; Luke 1:46; Hebrews 1:18–19; and James 1:21. Finally, Scripture uses *body* and *soul* together as a representation for the whole person, such as in Matthew 10:28 and 16:26.

In evaluating dichotomy, the strongest defense is the argument from creation. Genesis 2:7 records that man became a living *soul*. The term is inclusive of everything that constitutes a living, breathing being. It would be more accurate then, to say that man *has* a *spirit*, but *is* a *soul*. Furthermore, the interchangeability of the terms argues for dichotomy. On the negative side are those passages (1 Thess. 5:23 and Heb. 4:12) that seem to distinguish between *soul* and *spirit* as advocated by trichotomists.

Trichotomy says that humans are composed of three distinct elements: body, soul, and spirit. The *soul* includes the principle of animation and the faculties of human nature, such as mind, heart, and will. The *spirit*, on the other hand, is the spiritual capacity to relate to God. This is what is reborn in salvation.

Evidence for the position is found in some Scripture passages that point to a distinctive function for each, *soul* and *spirit*, such as Matthew 16:26 (what will a man give for his *soul*, not his *spirit*) and Romans 8:16 (the Holy Spirit testifies to our *spirit*, not our *soul*). Furthermore, the terms are distinguished from one another in 1 Thessalonians 5:23. More importantly, Hebrews 4:12 indicates that *soul* and *spirit* are capable of being divided by the Word of God and, therefore, should be understood as comprising different entities.

By way of evaluation, a trichotomy view best explains how an individual can be physically alive and yet spiritually dead. Accordingly, many gospel presentations are built on a trichotomist view of mankind. But this advantage is offset by the lack of biblical support for the position. Concerning 1 Thessalonians 5:23, it must be observed, first of all, that Paul is engaged in prayer. He is not delivering a discourse on the human constitution. Secondly, the "and" connecting *soul* and *spirit* could be understood as an epexegetical *kai* rather than a simple connective, so that the terms in question would represent different ways of referring to the same immaterial aspect of man. Third, the verb "be preserved" and the modifying adjective "entire" are both singular. Even though a singular verb can modify plural neuter subjects in Greek grammar, the Rule of Concord suggests that "when a collective subject is taken in mass, the verb is singular."[5] Finally, the word "whole" is *holoteleis* rather than *holomereis*, meaning that it has no reference to parts. Thus, the lexical, contextual, and grammatical indicators significantly undercut the trichotomist interpretation of the verse.

The case made for Hebrews 4:12 is equally problematic. The passage is not teaching division of soul *from* spirit, because the preposition, either *ek*, *apo*, or *kata*, is absent. Also, there is no verb to indicate a division *between* two things. The objects of the participle are a series of genitives, such as "dividing *of* soul and *of* spirit." In other words, what is being affirmed is the ability of the Word of God to divide the soul *from itself* and the spirit *from itself*. Further support for this understanding of the verse is found in the reference, "of both joints and marrow." This does not mean a separation of the joints *from* the marrow, since they are unrelated. Rather, the division is of the bones in the joint from one another and the marrow of the bone from the surface of the bone. Consequently, Hebrews 4:12 cannot be used exegetically to defend trichotomy.

The dichotomist has a better way of relating *soul* and *spirit* to one another consistent with biblical interpretation. The *soul* animates the body and is the center of consciousness and personality, including the intellect, affections, and will. The *spirit* refers to the same immaterial faculties in relation to God. A spiritually dead person is one in whom the capacities of the soul are not rightly related to God. In regeneration, the Spirit reori-

---

5. Harvey E. Dana and Julius R. Mantey, *A Manual Grammar of the Greek New Testament* (New York: MacMillan, 1957), 164–65.

ents the faculties of the soul in a godward direction so that the soul is made spiritually alive.

(Ken L. Sarles)

Why are those involved in biblical counseling so critical and condemnatory of other believers who hold differing views?

It would be grossly unfair to characterize the entire biblical counseling movement as critical and condemnatory. Having read much of the literature of the movement, I have been impressed with the balanced, thoughtful, proactive, biblical reasoning employed by men such as Jay Adams, Richard Ganz, Wayne Mack, and others.

The error that the biblical counseling movement seeks to address, however, is extremely serious, dealing with the integrity and authority of the Scriptures. Much is at stake. Those who are committed to biblical counseling understand that to dilute Scripture with foolish worldly wisdom (cf. 1 Cor. 1:20; 3:19) is to forfeit the power and blessing of God in counseling ministries.

Is it inherently unkind or condemnatory to say someone else's view is errant? Not if one has biblical authority for saying so. In fact, to remain silent and allow error to go unexposed and uncorrected is an abdication of the elder's role (Titus 1:9). The apostle Paul publicly called Peter a hypocrite for compromising biblical principles (Gal. 2:11–15). Peter had been publicly hypocritical; it was right that he be rebuked publicly (cf. 1 Tim. 5:20).

To disagree with or critique someone's published views does not constitute a personal attack. If the Church cannot tolerate polemic dialogue between opposing views—especially if Christian leaders cannot be held accountable for whether their teaching is biblical—then error will have free reign.

(John MacArthur Jr.)

What can biblical counseling offer non-Christians who come for counseling?

First, biblical counseling recognizes that believers and nonbelievers cannot be counseled in the same way. We cannot use Scriptures to counsel a nonbeliever who has not been bound to its authority. Indeed, counselees cannot and will not respond to truth if their blinded spiritual eyes are not opened by God. As Paul says, "But a natural man does not accept the things of the Spirit of God; for they are foolishness to him, and he cannot understand them, because they are spiritually appraised.

But he who is spiritual appraises all things, yet he himself is appraised by no man" (1 Cor. 2:14-15). So, in order for people to change, they must have submitted their will to the will of God. The only change that can come to a nonbeliever is a superficial change that never changes the heart. And that is precisely what biblical counseling speaks to—changing the heart in order to respond to God.

Then what can biblical counseling offer to the unregenerate person? We can communicate the truth that no one can change to any significant degree without embracing Jesus Christ as Savior and Lord. That is where true change must begin. Biblical counseling can offer the gospel—the answer to the most profound human need. This is the goal and basis of any counseling with nonbelievers. If the person refuses to acknowledge a need for Christ's saving work, there is really no other way to help that person.

(S. Lance Quinn)

What theological commitments are basic to the nouthetic method of biblical counseling?

The question can be answered in two parts: first, what theological commitments are involved, and second, what theological issues are not involved.

Generally speaking, the biblical counselor seeks to affirm the fundamental doctrines of the faith in the tradition of the Protestant Reformation. Specifically, three doctrinal commitments are foundational to biblical counseling. The first commitment is to the authority and sufficiency of Scripture. This truth, more than any other, distinguishes biblical counseling from all other counseling approaches. The Word of God, used by the Spirit of God, is sufficient to solve all the spiritual, psychological, and relational problems of the child of God (2 Tim 3:16-17). No other branch of knowledge is to be integrated with the Bible—it stands alone and speaks with absolute and final authority.

The second commitment is to the person and will of God, who is both the author and the subject of Scripture. Every counseling problem can ultimately be traced to wrong thinking about the character and will of God (Isa. 55:8-9). Therefore, all heartaches, tragedies, trials, and sufferings are to be placed in proper relationship to His glorious, majestic person. Since He alone is God, and there is no one else besides Him, difficulties of whatever sort must be related to His sovereign plan (Rom. 8:28-30).

The third commitment involves the doctrine of sin, a distinctive of biblical counseling. Only the nouthetic method gives due regard to the radically defective nature of mankind. The most fundamental dilemma is not that people are in pain, or that they lack self-esteem, or that they come from a dysfunctional family; rather, the root problem is that they are fallen (Gen. 3) and are rebellious against God (Rom. 5:10). They worship and serve the creature instead of the creator (Rom. 1:25).

Though the nouthetic approach is nonintegrationist, that does not eliminate all theological or denominational diversity among those who use the approach. For instance, there are no ecclesiological or eschatological implications in biblical counseling. A biblical counselor could be dispensational, covenantal, or neither. The counselor could be an Episcopalian, Presbyterian, Baptist, or Congregationalist regarding form of church government and could be premillennial, postmillennial, or amillennial concerning the prophetic future. Biblical counseling is nonsectarian and interdenominational. It is not tied to any one individual, church, or organization. Aside from the theological principles that are foundational to nouthetic practice, this method of counseling does not align one with any particular theological camp. As a result, wherever the fundamentals of the faith are affirmed, biblical counseling can be utilized regardless of the church structure or eschatological position.

(Ken L. Sarles)

How can biblical counselors classify drug and alcohol addictions simply as sin when medical science has proven they are diseases?

The idea that addictions are diseases has become so pervasive it seems foolish to speak against it. However, the idea that medical science has proven addictions to be actual organic diseases is entirely without foundation. The medical and scientific communities remain greatly divided over the issue of the disease versus the nondisease models.[6] The California Supreme Court, in its famous Sundance Case (*Sundance versus The City of Los Angeles*, 43 Cal 3rd 1101), sided with the disease model and in so doing legally removed personal responsibility for drunkenness and set in motion governmental and private treatment programs. In fact, what Dr. William Playfair has called the "Recovery Industry" has been so effective in spreading the idea that addiction is a medical disease that a 1990 survey showed 87 percent of Americans holding this view.

On the other hand, the Bible declares that drunkenness—the non-medical, nonprescribed introduction of chemicals into the body for the purpose of gaining pleasure or altering perceptions of reality in order to

---

6. David G. Benner, ed. *Baker Encyclopedia of Psychology*, (Grand Rapids: Baker, 1985), 38.

cope with or escape from the trials and struggles of life—is sin (Gal. 5:17–21; Eph. 5:18; 1 Pet. 4:3–5). These chemicals are alcohol or drugs of various types. The ingestion of these substances is a personal choice completely within the control of the individual. To postulate otherwise is to suggest a genetic predisposition to addiction or to suggest that as the substance-abuse continues a person gradually loses the ability to choose not to continue in this pattern of life.

The genetic answer is currently the most popular idea, even in Christian circles. In this model a person is born an alcoholic or addict in the same manner as a person might be born with brown or blue eyes. The thing that triggers the pattern of alcoholism or drug addiction is the first drink or first pill. These individuals have no options, they are victims of their genetic makeup. This concept, besides being unbiblical, is also not even agreed upon in the medical community.[7] The other model, which says that a person gradually loses the ability to refrain from abusing these substances, is simply a modification of the disease model, and again, it has no unity of opinion among medical professionals.

When a person is brought under the control of a substance, breaking that bondage is not easy. That is why Paul warns so strongly about being mastered by anything apart from the Holy Spirit (1 Cor. 6:12). The only effective treatment with substance abuse is to recognize that it is sinful behavior, repent of it, and cease doing it. This may not be pleasant. It is well known that the physical withdrawal symptoms of longstanding habits are often uncomfortable. Some extreme cases, such as in the case of heroin addiction, may even require medical supervision. However, the biblical way to deal with these sins is clear: repent and cease the sinful activity. The problem of substance abuse and addiction is not—popular opinion notwithstanding—an undefined disease, genetics, environment, or any other exterior force; it is the willful and sinful choice of a fallen individual.

(Dennis M. Swanson)

Is it true that the foundation of biblical counseling is rooted in legalism?

Legalism is a term that is frequently tossed around without much thought to its meaning. Essentially, legalism means to attain spirituality by means of what one does or does not do. In legalism someone establishes an external standard of spirituality and then judges everyone by that standard. Since the individual has established the standard, normally that

---

7. William L. Playfair, and George Bryson, *The Useful Lie*, (Wheaton: Good News/Crossway, 1991), 45–47.

person always achieves it. The Apostle Paul denounced this activity in 2 Corinthians 10:12 where he railed against those "who measure themselves by themselves and compare themselves with themselves."

Biblical counseling has been caricatured by its critics as being legalistic, and it must be granted that occasionally, on the part of some, that charge has been true. But biblical counseling is not rooted in legalism. It is narrow in its accepted source of authority—God's revealed truth in His Word—and there is no tolerance for the integration of secular psychological concepts or practices in the area of counseling. But biblical counselors do not set themselves up as the standard for life and godliness. Rather, they point people to the Scriptures so that they may see God more clearly and realize that He has provided for them "every spiritual blessing in the heavenly places in Christ" (Eph. 1:3). The biblical counselor is like Paul, who admitted, "Brethren, I do not regard myself as having laid hold of it yet; but one thing I do: forgetting what lies behind and reaching forward to what lies ahead, I press on toward the goal . . ." (Phil. 3:13). The biblical counselor also points the counselee in the direction that Paul took when he said, "I can do all things through Him who strengthens me" (Phil. 4:13).

To call biblical counseling legalistic is to deny the truth. Biblical counseling seeks to honor God in all things, to come alongside brothers and sisters in Christ with admonition, counsel, and rebuke when necessary, to demonstrate to non-Christians that their problems are pale compared to their need for salvation in Christ, and to declare to all the omniscient, omnipotent, and omnipresent God who alone is able to save and then empower to serve Him in this world.

(Dennis M. Swanson)

Do you ever refer people to psychologists or psychiatrists for help?

I never make such referrals for counseling unless the person bearing the title is committed to biblical counseling—as such, the professional title is incidental. Many biblical counselors happen to have degrees in psychology, psychiatry, neurology, general medicine, nursing, education, or social work. They studied secular counseling theories and methods that they have rejected in favor of biblical theory and practice.

Would I ever refer to a psychiatrist or psychologist for other reasons? A psychiatrist's medical training could help in determining whether neurological or other organic problems contribute to a person's problems in living, and a psychologist might help by intelligence testing. But, unfortunately, psychiatrists and psychologists too often adopt the role of a psychotherapist. They trespass into the domain of the Spirit, the Word, and ministry because they counsel people in unbiblical ways. A letter from a leading Christian organization contained the following statement:

> Psychologists do far more than engage in the practice of psychotherapy. To whom would you take a six-year-old boy to determine whether he were emotionally and physically ready to enter the first grade? . . . To whom would you turn if your wife became schizophrenic and ran screaming down the street? Would your pastor be able to deal with that situation? What if you wished to make a career change in mid-life, and wanted an objective evaluation of your strengths and interests? Whom could you ask to help you? To whom would you go to seek help with an adolescent who was extremely rebellious and resentful of his father? In each of these instances, and in a hundred others, you would look for a psychologist whose first love and highest commitment is to Jesus Christ and to the Word of God. And how silly to say, "There is no such thing."[8]

Let me interact with this statement sentence by sentence.

"Psychologists do far more than engage in the practice of psychotherapy." Indeed they do. Of course, psychotherapy is the money-making staple for most Christian psychologists. But such counseling practice is legitimated by a great deal of popular writing and speaking. In fact, psychologists' biggest influence in the Christian church at this time is not through psychotherapy, but through scores of best-selling books, conferences, video tapes, and radio shows. The statement stresses the service roles that psychologists have assumed. But (at least in this quote) he does not mention their biggest role: teachers about human nature, about problems and solutions. In an ominous development for the Church, psychologists have gained three kinds of authority: (1) the right to interpret human beings and their problems; (2) the right to work with people experiencing problems in living; and (3) the right to endeavor to solve people's problems.

The dilemma is this: Christian psychologists' interpretations of people are systematically twisted by error. What do they teach? Diverse as they are in the details, popular Christian psychologists are united in teaching that mankind's fundamental problem stems from some lack, emptiness, unmet need, woundedness, or trauma (e.g. "low self-esteem," "deep yearnings for relationship," "love hunger," "search for significance").

---

8. The quotation is presented in a form letter sent out by Focus on the Family, 9 November 1989. The letter is signed by David Tompkins, a personal assistant to Dr. James Dobson.

In contrast, the Bible teaches that our fundamental problem stems from the active desires, thoughts, and intentions of the heart. Are we basically sinful, or do we simply react sinfully to the failings of primary care givers to meet our needs?

The excerpt cited appeals to the *de facto* institutionalization of psychology within contemporary secular and Christian culture, as if this establishes psychologists' legitimacy. The authority is made to appear self-evident—because people go to psychologists, psychologists are needed. However, each of the examples cited above proves dubious upon inspection.

"*To whom would you take a six-year-old boy to determine whether he were emotionally and physically ready to enter the first grade?*" Take him to a medical doctor for the physical questions. Take him to the principal and kindergarten and first-grade teachers for the other questions. They have dealt with hundreds of kids over the years. Other parents are also a resource. Experienced people can give you good advice to weigh into *your* determination of your child's readiness.

"*To whom would you turn if you wife became schizophrenic and ran screaming down the street? Would your pastor be able to deal with that situation?*" If your wife's behavior and thinking became bizarre, between a medical doctor, the police, and your pastor (or otherwise pastoral counselor) you should be able to do what can be done humanly. Psychologists' success with so-called schizophrenics is not noteworthy.

"*What if you wished to make a career change in mid-life and wanted an objective evaluation of your strengths and interests? Whom could you ask to help you?*" A career counselor could provide interest and aptitude testing, and a knowledge of the job market. Any pastoral counselor worthy of the name could help you think through your motives for considering a change, as well as help you with other aspects of the decision-making process. People who know you well and people in your current and contemplated careers could also offer practical advice.

"*To whom would you go to seek help with an adolescent who was extremely rebellious and resentful of his father?*" This is bread-and-butter biblical counseling. Bring both the adolescent and the parents into counseling. Find out why the young person is resentful and rebellious, and whether this is due to provocation from the father. Help them both to make necessary changes.

"*In each of these instances, and in a hundred others, you should look for a psychologist whose first love and highest commitment is to Jesus Christ and to the Word of God. And how silly to say, 'There is no such thing.'*" I honestly cannot think of any instances, except perhaps intelligence testing from a school psychologist, where the title *psychologist* would be significant. Biblically wise people from many walks of life might prove helpful in these instances. My biggest problem with the "psychologists whose first love and highest commitment is to Jesus Christ and to the Word of God" is that most of the ones I have met and read deviate markedly from that professed commitment in both their theory and practice. Verbal commitment to the Word of God coexists with deviant teachings from enemies of that Word.

Christians who are psychologists almost have to deviate in order to define themselves as legitimate professionals with some unique expertise. After all, the territory they are claiming is not theirs by some natural right. It is the territory of parents, pastors, teachers, doctors, friends, and a host of practical advisors who make no pretense to being psychologists. It is the territory of life's problems. And wisdom in that territory lies open on the pages of Scripture. Though hard won through experience in applying truth to life, such wisdom is available to all who seek it.

(David Powlison)

Appendix

IDENTIFICATION DATA:

Name _____ Phone _____

Address _____

Occupation _____ Business Phone _____

Sex _____ Height _____

Birth Date _____ Age _____

Marital Status: Single _____ Going Steady _____ Married _____

Separated _____ Divorced _____ Widowed _____

Education (last year completed): _____ (grade)

Other training (list type and years completed) _____

Referred here by _____

Address _____

HEALTH INFORMATION:

Rate your health (check): Very Good _____ Good _____ Average _____

Declining _____ Other _____

Your approximate weight (lbs.) _____

Weight changes recently: Lost _____ Gained _____

List all important present or past illnesses or injuries or handicaps:

_____

_____

Date of last medical examination _____ Report: _____

Your Physician _____ Address _____

---

1. This material is taken from Jay Adams, *The Christian Counselor's Manual: The Practice of Nouthetic Counseling* (Grand Rapids: Zondervan, 1986) and is used by permission.

Are you presently taking medication? Yes _____   No _____

What? _____

Have you used drugs for other than medical purposes? Yes _____   No _____

What? _____

Have you ever had a severe emotional upset? Yes _____   No _____

Explain _____

Have you ever been arrested? Yes _____   No _____

Are you willing to sign a release of information form so that your counselor may write for social, psychiatric, or medical reports? Yes _____   No _____

Have you recently suffered the loss of someone who was close to you?

Yes _____   No _____   Explain _____

Have you recently suffered loss from serious social, business, or other reversals?

Yes _____   No _____   Explain: _____

RELIGIOUS BACKGROUND

Denominational preference: _____   Member _____

Church attendance per month (circle): 1 2 3 4 5 6 7 8 9 10+

Church attended in childhood? _____

Baptized? Yes _____   No _____

Religious background of spouse (if married) _____

Do you consider yourself a religious person?

Yes _____   No _____   Uncertain _____

Do you believe in God? Yes _____   No _____   Uncertain _____

Do you pray to God? Never _____   Occasionally _____   Often _____

Are you saved? Yes _____   No _____   Not sure what you mean _____

How much do you read the Bible? Never _____   Occasionally _____   Often _____

Do you have regular family devotions? Yes _____   No _____

Explain recent changes in your religious life, if any _____

_____

PERSONALITY INFORMATION

Have you ever had any psychotherapy or counseling before? Yes _____

No _____   If yes, list counselor or therapist and dates: _____

What was the outcome? _____

Check any of the following words which best describe you now:

active _____ ambitious _____ self-confident _____ persistent _____

nervous _____ hardworking _____ impatient _____ impulsive _____

moody _____ often-blue _____ excitable _____ imaginative _____

calm _____ serious _____ easy-going _____ shy _____ good-natured _____

introvert _____ extrovert _____ likable _____ leader _____ quiet _____

hard-boiled _____ submissive _____ lonely _____ self-conscious _____

sensitive _____ other _____

Have you ever felt people were watching you? Yes _____ No _____

Do people's faces ever seem distorted? Yes _____ No _____

Do you ever have difficulty distinguishing faces? Yes _____ No _____

Do colors ever seem too bright? _____ Too dull? _____

Are you sometimes unable to judge distance? Yes _____ No _____

Have you ever had hallucinations? Yes _____ No _____

Are you afraid of being in a car? Yes _____ No _____

Is your hearing exceptionally good? Yes _____ No _____

Do you have problems sleeping? Yes _____ No _____

MARRIAGE AND FAMILY INFORMATION

Name of spouse _____ Phone _____

Address _____

Occupation _____ Business phone _____

Your spouse's age _____ Education (in years) _____

Religion _____

Is spouse willing to come for counseling? Yes _____ No _____ Uncertain _____

Have you ever been separated? Yes _____ No _____ When? _____

Date of marriage _____

Your ages when married: Husband _____ Wife _____

How long did you know your spouse before marriage? _____

_____

Length of steady dating with spouse _____ Length of engagement _____

Give brief information about any previous marriages: _____

_____

Information about children:

PM*	Name	Age	Sex	Living Y or N	Education in years	Marital status

*Check this column if child is by previous marriage.

If you were reared by anyone other than your own parents, briefly explain:

How many older brothers _____ sisters _____ do you have?

How many younger brothers _____ sisters _____ do you have?

BRIEFLY ANSWER THE FOLLOWING QUESTIONS:

1. What is your problem?

2. What have you done about it?

3. What can we do? (What are your expectations in coming here?)

4. As you see yourself, what kind of person are you? Describe yourself.

5. What, if anything, do you fear?

6. Is there any other information we should know?

Index of Authors

Index of Scriptures

Index of Subjects

Aaron, 275

ACCEPT, 269–70

Adam, 121, 129, 130; compared with Christ 122

Adams, Jay, 13, 44, 54, 143–44, 173, 183, 318, 362, 366–67, 372, 378; early life and background, 50; evalation of counseling books, 7; on nouthetic counseling, 52; rediscovering biblical counseling, 49; seminal writings of, 51–52,

Addiction, genetics and, 381

Admnistration: as a spiritual gift, 320

Alcohol addiction, 380

Ames, William, 24, 25, 31; definition of conscience, 30

Analogia scriptura, 258

Auschwitz, 113

Baldessarini, Ross, 14

Baxter, Richard, 282–83, 317–18

Beecher, Henry Ward, 251

Behavior modification, 11

Behavorial sciences, 95

Bettler, John, 53

Biblical counseling: academic standards for, 373; as an alien system, 46; basic assumptions, 117; the Church and, 303; as church-based, 59; definition, 56; and epistemology, 57; the future of, 56; gathering information, 211ff; as God-centered, 57; its godward focus, 154ff; and the Gospel, 58; inducement, 268ff; instilling hope, 189; interpreting data, 231ff; involvement, 175, 187; needs for association, 54; objectives, ix–xi; the pastor and, 302; as a pastoral

activity, 59; pastoral responsibility, 7; and progressive sanctification, 58; providing instruction, 250; rediscovery of, 46; as simplistic, 367–69; and sin, 58; and sovereignty of God, 58; training for, 309, 362; to the unbeliever, 14, 139, 379

Biblical Counseling Foundation (BCF), 54

Biblical counselors: commitment to glorify God, 160; as confronters, 165; as church members, 145; dealing with criticism, 149; as disciplers, 148; as evangelists, 147; physical well-being of, 152; testing interpretations, 247ff; as theologians, 146

Biblical Theological Seminary, 53

Biblical words, 255–56

Boston, Thomas, 295

Bridges, Jerry, 203

Broger, John, 54

Brooks, Thomas, 36, 44

Bunyan, John, 32, 44

Calvin, John, 315

Capitol Records, 110

Catholic causitry, 31

Charnock, Stephen, 34

Christ: compared with Adam, 122; union with, 119, 122, 125

Christian counseling, 362

Christian Counseling and Educational Foundation (CCEF), xi, 53, 266

Christian media, 17

Christian Psychologists, 4

Christian Psychology: 4, 362; curriculum for 373; an oxymoron,

List of Contributors

Douglas Bookman, M.Div, Th.M., Th.D (ABD)
Professor of Bible Exposition and Theology at The Master's College.

William Goode, D.D.
Senior Pastor of Faith Baptist Church, Lafayette, Indiana.

Carey Hardy, B.A.
Director of Counseling, Grace Community Church.

John G. Hotchkiss, M.A.
Chairman of the English Department; Professor of English at The Master's College.

John F. MacArthur, Jr., D. D. , Litt. D.
President of The Master's College and Seminary; Professor of Pastoral Ministries.

Wayne A. Mack, D.Min.
Chairman of the Biblical Counseling Department; Professor of Biblical Counseling at The Master's College.

David Maddox, M.Div.
Vice President of Student Affairs; Associate Professor of Bible at The Master's College.

David Powlison, M.Div.
Staff member at the Christian Counseling and Education Foundation in Laverock, Pennsylvania; Editor of *The Journal of Biblical Counseling*.

S. Lance Quinn, M.Div.
Senior Associate Pastor, Grace Community Church.

Ken L. Sarles, Th.M., Th.D. (ABD)
Professor of Theology at The Master's Seminary; Dean of Logos Bible Institute.

Robert D. Smith, M.D.
Staff member of Faith Baptist Counseling Ministries; Member and Fellow of the American Academy of Family Physicians.

John P. Stead, Ph.D.
Vice President for Academic Affairs at The Master's College.

Dennis M. Swanson, M.Div.
Director of Academic Assessment at The Master's College; New Testament Instructor at Logos Bible Institute.

David Swavely, B.A.
Staff Pastor, Grace Community Church; Director of Counseling for Grace to You Radio Ministries.